Dynamic Issues in Applied Commercial Policy Analysis edited by Professors Baldwin and Francois focuses on the *explicit* specification of dynamic mechanisms in the formal analytics of trade models. A wide range of modelling approaches is employed to investigate an even wider range of policy issues, with an overall objective of further extension of the basic conceptual framework of applied commercial policy analysis in the direction of dynamic issues and applications.

Emphasis is placed on methods for the analysis of interactions between commercial policy and leading policy issues, including investment performance, economic growth and innovation, the location of industry, migration, and the environment.

Dynamic Issues in Applied Commercial Policy Analysis is the latest book in the successful sequence of monographs from CEPR and will be a standard reference for anyone interested in the assessment of international trade and investment policy, and applied study of the dynamic implications of trade policy.

RICHARD EDWARD BALDWIN is Professor of International Economics at the Graduate Institute of International Studies, University of Geneva, and Co-director of CEPR's International Trade Research Programme. He was Senior Staff Economist for the President's Council of Economic Advisors in the Bush Administration (1990–1) and has advised the European Commission on several European Integration issues.

JOSEPH F. FRANCOIS is Professor of Economics and Chair of International Economic Development at the Erasmus University Rotterdam and a Senior Fellow of CEPR's International Trade Research Programme. He is also a Fellow of the Tinbergen Institute.

T0334612

Centre for Economic Policy Research

The Centre for Economic Policy Research is a network of over 400 Research Fellows, based primarily in European universities. The Centre coordinates its Fellows' research activities and communicates their results to the public and private sectors. CEPR is an entrepreneur, developing research initiatives with the producers, consumers, and sponsors of research. Established in 1983, CEPR is a European economics research organization with uniquely wide-ranging scope and activities.

CEPR is a registered educational charity. Institutional (core) finance for the Centre is provided by major grants from the Economic and Social Research Council, under which an ESRC Resource Centre operates within CEPR; the Esmée Fairbairn Charitable Trust; the Bank of England; the European Monetary Institute and the Bank for International Settlements; 21 national central banks; and 44 companies. None of these organizations gives prior review to the Centre's publications, nor do they necessarily endorse the views expressed therein.

The Centre is pluralist and non-partisan, bringing economic research to bear on the analysis of medium- and long-run policy questions. CEPR research may include views on policy, but the Executive Committee of the Centre does not give prior review to its publications, and the Centre takes no institutional policy positions. The opinions expressed in this volume are those of the authors and not those of the Centre for Economic Policy Research.

Dynamic Issues in Applied Commercial Policy Analysis

Edited by

RICHARD E. BALDWIN

and

JOSEPH F. FRANCOIS

CAMBRIDGE
UNIVERSITY PRESS

CAMBRIDGE UNIVERSITY PRESS
Cambridge, New York, Melbourne, Madrid, Cape Town, Singapore,
São Paulo, Delhi, Dubai, Tokyo, Mexico City

Cambridge University Press
The Edinburgh Building, Cambridge CB2 8RU, UK

Published in the United States of America by Cambridge University Press, New York

www.cambridge.org
Information on this title: www.cambridge.org/9780521159517

First published 1999
First paperback edition 2010

A catalogue record for this publication is available from the British Library

Library of Congress Cataloguing in Publication data

Dynamic issues in applied commercial policy analysis / edited by
Richard E. Baldwin and Joseph F. Francois.
    p.   cm.
Includes index.
ISBN 0 521 64171 3 (hardback)
1. Commerce-Mathematical models. 2. Commercial policy.
I. Baldwin, Richard E. II. Francois, Joseph F.
HF1008.D94 1998
382'.3-dc21 98-29540 CIP

ISBN 978-0-521-64171-5 Hardback
ISBN 978-0-521-15951-7 Paperback

Contents

Figures

Tables

xiv

Preface

This volume contains the proceedings of the conference 'Dynamic Issues in Applied Commercial Policy Analysis' held in Geneva, Switzerland (26–28 January 1996). The conference was organized jointly by the Centre for Economic Policy Research (CEPR) and the Graduate Institute of International Studies in Geneva. It was financed by the Ford Foundation's MIRAGE project and we wish to express our gratitude to the Foundation.

Economists have long argued that the dynamic effects of policy changes are much more important in the real world than the static effects, yet most policy analyses focus solely on the latter. A number of researchers throughout the world are in the process of developing and refining methods and models that allow quantification of dynamic effects. A wide range of modelling approaches has been employed to investigate an even wider range of policy issues. The aim of this conference was two-fold: (1) stock-taking of methods employed to date, including free-ranging discussion of the merits and drawbacks of each method, and (2) discussion of how to improve the methods. Both goals, we feel, were met and are reflected in the chapters and discussions in this volume.

The editors would like to thank CEPR's permanent staff for their support, especially Constanze Picking, Toni Orloff, and Kate Millward. Denise Ducroz assumed most of the local organizing tasks and we thank her for admirable Swiss efficiency. Finally, the volume has benefited enormously from the editorial efforts of Liz Paton and the final shepherding duties of Lorna Guthrie.

Richard E. Baldwin
Graduate Institute of International Studies, Geneva
Joseph F. Francois
Tinbergen Institute, Erasmus University Rotterdam
January 1998

Conference participants

Bernardin Akitoby *Université de Montréal*
Richard E. Baldwin *Graduate Institute of International Studies, Geneva, and CEPR*
Rikard Forslid *University of Lund and CEPR*
Joseph F. Francois *Erasmus Universiteit Rotterdam and CEPR*
Jan I. Haaland *Norwegian School of Economics and Business Administration, Bergen, and CEPR*
Timothy J. Kehoe *University of Minnesota*
Christian Keuschnigg *Institut für Höhere Studien, Wien, and CEPR*
Wilhelm K. Kohler *Universität Essen*
Ulrich Kohli *Université de Genève*
Bradley J. McDonald *World Trade Organization*
James Markusen *University of Colorado and CEPR*
J. Peter Neary *University College Dublin and CEPR*
Doug Nelson *Tulane University*
Håkan Nordström *World Trade Organization and CEPR*
David Roland-Holst *OECD Development Centre and Mills College, California*
Thomas F. Rutherford *University of Colorado*
André Sapir *ECARE, Université Libre de Bruxelles, and CEPR*
Elena Seghezza *Graduate Institute of International Studies, Geneva*
Clinton R. Shiells *International Monetary Fund*
Alasdair Smith *University of Sussex and CEPR*
Paul Tang *Netherlands Bureau of Economic Policy Analysis, The Hague*
David G. Tarr *World Bank*
Sweder van Wijnbergen *Universiteit van Amsterdam and CEPR*
Anthony J. Venables *London School of Economics and CEPR*
Ian Wooton *University of Glasgow and CEPR*

1 Introduction

RICHARD E. BALDWIN, JOSEPH F. FRANCOIS,
and JAN I. HAALAND

Economic processes are dynamic. Human, physical, and knowledge capital stocks change over time, as do natural resources stocks. People and capital migrate, populations grow, and investment rates change. Although these assertions are self-evident, most applied commercial policy analysis ignores them. For the simple reason that dynamic processes are difficult to capture formally, most applied analysts work with static models. This is an important shortcoming because commercial policies can have dynamic effects and the presence of time-varying factor stocks, technologies, etc. can affect the way in which we evaluate commercial policy. Moreover, trade theory now offers rigorous, formal treatment of many dynamic issues, including interactions between, on the one hand, commercial policy and, on the other hand, the endogeneity of factor endowments (location and size of stocks), natural resource depletion, and the evolution of the technology and skills base.

This volume brings together the work of research economists who are developing and refining methods and models that allow quantification of dynamic effects in applied computation models. The overall objective of the volume is to extend the basic conceptual underpinnings of applied commercial policy analysis in the direction of dynamic issues and applications. Our immediate objective in this introductory chapter is more modest. In this chapter, we offer our own brief tour of major issues related to the extension of applied trade models to address dynamics issues better. In the process of this tour, we provide an overview of the chapters in the volume, placing them within our own characterization of the broader thematic context.

1 Neoclassical growth and trade

From its roots in the seminal work of Solow and his contemporaries (see Stiglitz and Uzawa (1969)), neoclassical growth theory has emphasized

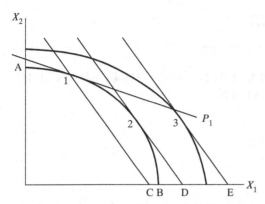

Figure 1.1 Steady-state impact of trade liberalization with endogenous capital stocks.

two important dynamic mechanisms: ongoing technical change (treated as an exogenous mechanism) and population growth. Population growth can contribute to an increase in per capita income, or to a simple expansion of the base of economic activity, with no consequent increase in per capita income. The latter is called extensive growth, while the former is called intensive growth (Reynolds 1983). At the extreme, population growth may actually depress long-run per capita income growth by taxing limited and non-renewable resources (Brander 1992). Physical capital accumulation is also an important factor in the dynamics of neoclassical growth models. A process of continuous capital accumulation is generally necessary to maintain income levels for a growing population, while transitional growth is intimately linked to accumulation. However, with a diminishing marginal product for capital, capital accumulation alone is not a source of sustained economic growth in the neoclassical framework.

Although capital accumulation may not have long-run growth effects in these models, it can still involve important shifts in steady-state national resource bases, as well as significant transitional effects. Figures 1.1 and 1.2 illustrate what we mean by both steady-state and transitional effects in the context of a simple trade model. The production possibility frontier for a small economy producing and trading two goods is represented by AB in Figure 1.1. An initial tariff-distorted equilibrium is represented by production point 1, at world price P_W and internal price P_1. In a static general equilibrium model, trade liberalization moves the economy from point 1 to point 2, with internal prices $P_2 = P_W$. The shift in GDP (at world prices) is then CD. In a general equilibrium model with capital accumulation, however, this is not the end of the story. From

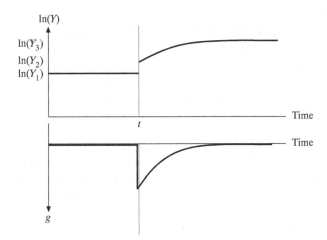

Figure 1.2 **Transitional output effects of trade liberalization with endogenous capital stocks.**

point 2, there may be induced changes in the capital stock, such that there is a shift in the production possibility frontier, leading to a new equilibrium at point 3. The shift in GDP is then from C to D to E. Furthermore, for large countries, there may also be induced changes in the terms of trade (not shown).

Figure 1.2 illustrates the transitional growth effects of such an experiment. The GDP level at point 1 in Figure 1.1 is represented in Figure 1.2 by GDP level Y_1. The static impact of the policy shock, where production moves from point 1 to point 2 in Figure 1.1, involves a shift in GDP from Y_1 to Y_2 in Figure 1.2. The accumulation of additional capital implies a new steady-state level of income, represented by point 3 in Figure 1.1 and by income Y_3 in Figure 1.2. Comparative steady states then involve incomes Y_1 and Y_3, while dynamic adjustment involves economic growth during the transition to the higher level of GDP. Underlying growth rates are represented in the bottom of Figure 1.2, where for convenience we have assumed that permanent (exogenous) growth rates are zero.

The theoretical literature, which has elaborated these basic effects in much greater detail, shows that adding neoclassical growth mechanisms yields substantially different results from those derived in a static framework (see Smith (1976, 1977), Srinivasan and Bhagwati (1980), Baldwin and Seghezza (1996)). Moreover, some empirical work, e.g. Levine and Renelt (1992), finds support for the theoretical prediction that trade openness can affect economic growth via its impact on investment.

In the applied context the impact of trade policy on national capital stocks was recognized in a number of early studies (see Baldwin (1989, 1992), de Melo and Tarr (1992: Ch. 6)). More recently, however, applied commercial policy analysts increasingly allow for endogenous physical capital stocks (see Francois and Shiells (1994), Harrison et al. (1994), Keuschnigg and Kohler (1996)). Although the importance of including induced capital formation effects is now widely recognized, analysts are still experimenting with a variety of approaches and methods.

Three chapters in this volume make significant contributions to this literature. First, Baldwin, Forslid, and Haaland (BFH), Chapter 8, examine the interaction of capital accumulation and preferential trade liberalization, taking the European Union's Single Market programme as an example. They demonstrate that discriminatory liberalization tends to increase the steady-state capital stock of the integrating region and to cause capital depletion elsewhere. Hence, in addition to the static diversionary impact of discriminatory liberalization, regional integration may also lead to shifts in steady-state capital stocks, i.e. 'investment diversion'. The economic channel highlighted in BFH is simple. Since traded goods tend to be more capital intensive than non-traded goods (think of industry versus government services), preferential liberalization within a region tends to raise the derived demand for capital in the integrating region and to lower the capital demand in excluded regions. In the first instance, this shock raises the return to capital in the integrating region and lowers it in the excluded region. Of course, in order to restore capital rates of return to their pre-liberalization levels, a higher capital stock is required in the integrating region and lower steady-state capital stocks are required in the excluded regions.

Whereas the BFH chapter is concerned with regional integration, Francois, McDonald, and Nordström (FMN), Chapter 7, consider more methodological issues. The existing applied general equilibrium models have adopted two distinct approaches to determining steady-state capital stocks: constant savings rates (as in the Solow model) and intertemporal optimization (as in the Ramsey model). According to the standard back-of-the-envelope method for assessing accumulation effects in steady state (based on Baldwin (1989)), the savings specification is not critical because both constant savings rates and Ramsey-type endogenous savings rates lead to the same reduced-form result. This equivalence, however, depends upon assumption of a stylized Cobb–Douglas GDP function. FMN show that this is actually a very special case. Theoretically, they show that with more general GDP functions – ones that allow for more sectors or for more general functional forms – assumptions on savings behaviour matter in the sense that one obtains fundamental differences in the qualitative results depending upon whether one assumes constant savings rates or optimal savings rates. To drive this point home, they use an applied general equilibrium model to evaluate the Uruguay Round of multilateral trade liberalizations under the two alternative savings rules. What they find is that differences in the representation of savings behaviour can lead to opposite conclusions regarding the direction and magnitude of the regional impact of trade liberalization under the Uruguay Round. The message is that our understanding of underlying savings behaviour is critical to our understanding of the long-run dynamic implications of commercial policy.

Both the BFH and FMN chapters are concerned with comparative steady-state analysis, namely the long-run effects and the characteristics of the steady state. In contrast, Francois, Nordström, and Shiells (FNS), Chapter 2, focus on the importance of transition dynamics for trade policy analysis, particularly for developing countries. In terms of Figure 1.2, this involves examination of the *path* from Y_1 to Y_3, rather than just comparing the values of Y_1 and Y_3. To make their point formally, the authors employ a simple growth model, for which they develop the transitional dynamics, contrasting policy reforms in countries near their steady-state income levels (developed countries) with countries far from steady-state income levels (developing countries). Their results show that policy reforms that appear identical based on applied analysis in a static or steady-state framework can have a substantially greater impact on developing countries once transitional accumulation effects have been accounted for. This in turn implies that steady-state analysis alone may miss important dynamic effects related to the welfare effect of transitional adjustment. These effects are going to be most important for countries undergoing relatively rapid transitional growth. They further support the relevance of this point by arguing that the empirical evidence from cross-country growth regressions points to important transitional growth effects related to trade policy reforms.

Applied trade policy analysis with dynamic considerations inevitably raises the issue of the appropriate reference scenario and time-frame used to evaluate policies. The standard static approach is to calibrate a simulation model to actual values in a base year and then to use the model to produce a counterfactual outcome. In essence, this approach asks what the world would have looked like in the base year if other policies than those actually pursued had been in effect. However, once one admits that dynamic considerations are important, this standard approach makes less sense. Two shortcomings are worth noting.

First, the interaction between the trade agreements being analysed and the underlying policy environment may be important. In the absence of forward progress in negotiations, the appropriate counterfactual may involve a worsening of trade restrictions, rather than maintenance of the status quo. Hence, to the extent that ongoing liberalization serves as insurance against protectionist backsliding, the true welfare effects of incremental trade liberalization are much greater than the results from comparative static exercises would normally suggest.

Secondly, because the underlying economy undergoes many changes – for example, growth – the actual effects may differ substantially from those predicted by the counterfactual base year approach (the 'counterfactual' approach for short). For instance, the efficiency loss of a particular quantitative restriction, say the Multi-Fibre Agreement quotes, grows along with domestic demand. Consequently, the timing of the liberalization matters greatly. If a quota is phased out immediately, the counterfactual base year will give a reasonable answer. However, if it is phased out over ten years and economies grow during this time, the counterfactual approach will significantly understate the gains from liberalization. An alternative, which might be called the 'prospective' approach, is to simulate what the economy would look like in ten years (assuming GDP growth rates, etc.) without liberalization. The evaluation would then consist of comparing this simulated no-liberalization case with a simulated liberalization case, with both cases representing what the economy would look like in ten years.

This point has important implications in the endogenous capital models discussed in BFH, FMN, and FNS. In many of these models, many of the gains from liberalization stem directly or indirectly from economy-wide scale effects. That is, the gains from freer trade follow from increased competition and fuller exploitation of scale economies. As economies grow, however, domestic markets may become larger relative to economies of scale in production, so, even without liberalization, domestic monopoly distortions are reduced. It follows, therefore, that the pro-competitive effects of trade will be correspondingly smaller. In other words, competition and scale are limited by the extent of the market. To extend the market, one can open trade or wait for the domestic economy to grow.

Of course, this need not happen in the real world; for instance, the minimum efficient scale of production may rise over time, or new sectors with ever-larger scale economies may emerge. However, given the standard function forms assumed in virtually all applied general equilibrium models, this sort of dilution of gains from trade will occur. For example, with constant elasticity of substitution (CES) preferences over differentiated products, the proportional increase in utility (i.e. dU/U) from a marginal increase in the number of varieties (i.e. dn) equals $1/(\sigma-1)n$ times dn, where $\sigma > 1$ is the elasticity of substitution.

Thus, a very common functional form for preferences implies diminishing gains from extra variety. Another example comes from models (e.g. Haaland and Norman 1992) with small-group monopolistic competition (i.e. models that assume that the perceived elasticity of firms depends upon market shares as well as σ). In such models, increasing market sizes without liberalization allows the equilibrium number of firms to rise, resulting in greater firm size and lower market-power distortions. There are two implications of this. First, it is important to realize that the use of counterfactual or prospective approaches will affect results. Secondly, it may be worth exploring function forms that avoid this dilution effect.[1]

2   Endogenous growth and trade

There is now a sizeable theoretical literature linking international trade with endogenous growth. This literature attempts to provide formal mechanisms for representing the interplay between trade policies and income growth, without recourse to exogenous assumptions regarding the sources of long-run growth. The empirical foundations for believing in such a linkage seem compelling, with numerous studies reporting a positive correlation between an 'open' trade regime and growth performance (see, for example, Henrekson et al. (1996) on regional integration and growth).

In neoclassical growth theory, technical change is taken to be exogenous. In contrast, recent research on endogenous growth has emphasized the mechanisms driving technical change. In particular, the new growth theories have focused attention on formal modelling of how market forces can give rise to technical change and in turn to economic growth. Such economic theories are said to model technical change 'endogenously' (i.e. as a result of the explainable, rational actions of individuals) rather than as the result of unexplained, 'exogenous' developments that are beyond the influence of the economic decisions made by individuals. In such models, the actions of individuals responding to market forces can lead to endogenous technical change and hence to permanent growth. Because trade liberalization can change the market conditions under which firms operate, including available technologies and the incentives for funding education and research, in these models trade liberalization can also lead to changes in the rate of long-run economic growth.

Models of endogenous technical change closely resemble, in terms of mathematical structure, static models of external scale effects. In both, there is a decline in production costs associated with increased industry-

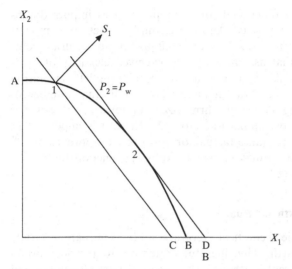

Figure 1.3   Endogenous growth in a small open economy.

level output. In particular, both endogenous growth models (see Grossman and Helpman (1991)) and static models of two-way trade (see Ethier (1982) and Helpman and Krugman (1985)) emphasize vertical or horizontal differentiation of intermediate or final goods. Changes in specialization, in turn, yield changes in the cost of producing utility, either directly in the case of consumer goods, or indirectly in the case of intermediate goods. The basic difference is that, in endogenous growth models, these changes are realized over time. Whether static or dynamic, such scale effects are called 'external' because the benefits that follow from increased specialization are not within the control of individual firms, because they depend on the activities of all of the firms in an industry.

We illustrate some of the differences between neoclassical and endogenous growth models with Figures 1.3 and 1.4, in conjunction with Figures 1.1 and 1.2. As in Figure 1.1, the production possibility frontier for a small economy is again represented by AB in Figure 1.3. However, with an endogenous growth model, we now assume that some feature of the underlying model generates a permanent underlying rate of growth, so that over time the production possibility frontier is shifting out. As drawn, this involves a path of steady-state equilibria as illustrated by the path S_1. In terms of Figure 1.4, this means that there is a steady-state growth path for income such as Y_1, and growth rate g_1. A trade policy shock at time t can, in an endogenous growth model, lead to a shift in the

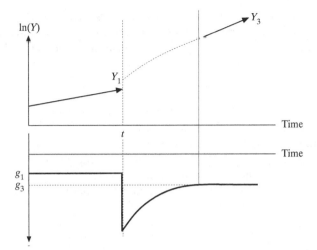

Figure 1.4   Transitional and permanent growth effects with endogenous growth.

steady-state path of income, illustrated in Figure 1.4 by the eventual shift to Y_3 and g_3. In comparing Figures 1.2 and 1.4, transitional effects will again lead to an acceleration of growth. The critical difference is that, because we have modelled permanent growth rates explicitly, the policy shock leads to a permanent rather than temporary surge in growth rates in Figure 1.4, whereas in Figure 1.2 the underlying long-run or perma-nent growth rate remained unchanged.

Three chapters in this volume, by Baldwin and Forslid (BF), Keusch-nigg and Kohler (KK), and Rutherford and Tarr (RT), are concerned with the adoption of endogenous growth theory to applied trade policy models. In Chapter 3, BF examine the analytical aspects of trade policy in endogenous growth models, including discussion of practical imple-mentation issues raised by the standard forms of these models. Their emphasis, like that of much of the theoretical literature on endogenous growth, is placed on long-run growth rates and steady-state growth paths. In contrast, the emphasis of both Chapters 4 and 9 is on the transition. They explicitly trace dynamic adjustment paths between steady states. Like the FNS chapter regarding neoclassical growth mechanisms, the RT chapter shows that, because of differences in dynamic adjustment paths, two policies with the same implications for the steady state can have dramatically different implications for welfare. A similar point is made in the KK chapter. In a model that includes accumulation of both physical and human capital, KK examine the implications of trade and education policy for countries in transition to the steady-state growth path. Taken as a group, the FNS, KK, and RT chapters all point to the importance of modelling adjustment paths and transition dynamics, especially for developing and transition economies.

3   Other dynamic issues

While roughly half of this volume is devoted to accumulation or innovation-based dynamic effects, the remaining papers address a more diverse set of dynamic issues. This set of issues includes the geographic location of factors and production, natural resource depletion and environmental degradation, and the implications of underlying macro-economic trends for the definition of appropriate analytical baselines.

3.1   Open economy demographics

The literature on old growth, new growth, and trade policy generally assumes away underlying population dynamics. This reflects the em-phasis placed on the dynamics of the capital stock. However, population dynamics also has interesting ramifications for trade and trade policy. Developing-country population growth has fuelled worries about trade-related wage erosion in the OECD countries (see Francois (1996)), while concern about the underlying demographics of the North African countries has prompted the European Union to promote economic stability in the region through regional trade agreements (WTO 1995).

Two of the chapters in this volume are concerned with the interaction of demographics with trade and trade policy. Chapter 12 by Roland-Holst examines internal migration and the possible effects these population movements may have on the production structure. An applied example is offered involving population movements within China, where internal migration rivals any contemporary cross-border movement of population.

Whereas Roland-Holst is concerned with internal migration, Francois and Nelson (FN), Chapter 10, are concerned with population growth and the incentives for cross-border migration. Their chapter develops stylized structural links between trade policy and the incentives for migration. This basic theoretical structure is then introduced to a stylized two-region computable model that includes population growth. The chapter highlights the importance of including migration mechanisms when examining the wage effects of trade policy. When viewed in a static model with regional capital and labour stocks, trade protection of labour-intensive industries can, under appropriate conditions, be an effective mechanism for raising wages. However, this depends critically on whether or not there is migration. With population dynamics (including the combination of population growth and migration), trade policy that raises wages in the short run may, over the longer term, induce migration through those same higher wages. This can undo the short-run wage gains. A related point involves the manipulation of terms of trade. Such manipulation can also induce migration, so that beggar-thy-neighbour policies prove to be, in a dynamic context with migration, invite-thy-neighbour policies.

3.2   Foreign investment and the location of industry

Another set of inherently dynamic issues relates to cross-border capital flows and the location of industry. The chapters by Venables and by Markusen and Venables emphasize the implications of modelling multi-national firms and firm location. Chapter 6 points to important questions related to dynamic stability. In a dynamic setting, imperfect competition and input–output linkages between firms may lead to hysteresis effects, with the potential for commercial policy to induce significant regime shifts, including the collapse of regional industry. In this context, therefore, industry-wide externalities have implications for modelling not only the dynamics of industrial growth (the subject of many of the chapters in this volume) but also industrial location.

In Chapter 5, Markusen and Venables focus on a different set of firm-related questions. These involve the effects on employment patterns of a firm's decision to act as a multinational (i.e. with different activities carried out in different locations). The formation of multinationals may have important effects on the evolution of employment, the evolution of skilled and unskilled wages, and the effect of protection on wages.

3.3   Environment

Chapter 11 addresses linkages between the environment and trade. This has been an active area of research, and includes work on global warming (Jorgenson and Wilcoxen 1990, 1993, Piggot et al. 1993) and on linkages between trade flows and environmental degradation (Roland-Holst 1997). The chapter by Beghin, Roland-Holst, and van der Mensbrugghe (BRV) is concerned with the long-run modelling of linkages between trade and the environment. The paper addresses the question of whether or not trade liberalization induces developing countries to engage in pollution-intensive activities, and the relationship between piecemeal tariff reform and environmental policy. BRV illustrate the issues they identify through the application of a dynamic model of the Indonesian economy.

Notes

1. Haaland and Norman (1996) provide a number of numerical examples that nicely illustrate these points. The paper also shows that counterfactual exercises underestimate the gains to liberalization in cases where, absent the liberalization, levels of protection would have risen. The Uruguay Round, for example, is often cited as having avoided an important increase in US and European protection.

References

Baldwin, R. E. (1989), 'The Growth Effects of 1992', *Economic Policy* 9(2): 247–81.
    (1992), 'Measurable Dynamic Gains from Trade', *Journal of Political Economy* 100(1): 162–74.
Baldwin, R. E. and E. Seghezza (1996), 'Testing for Trade-induced, Investment-led Growth', NBER Working Paper No. 5416.
Brander, J. (1992), 'Innis Lecture: Comparative Economic Growth: Evidence and Interpretation', *Canadian Journal of Economics* 25(4): 792–818.
Ethier, W. (1982), 'National and International Returns to Scale in the Modern Theory of International Trade', *American Economic Review* 72: 950–59.
Francois, J. F. (1996), 'Labour Force Growth, Trade, and Wages', *Economic Journal* 107(339): 1586–609.
Francois, J. F. and C. R. Shiells (1994), 'AGE Models of North American Free Trade: An Introduction'. In J. F. Francois and C. R. Shiells (eds.), *Modeling Trade Policy: Applied General Equilibrium Models of North American Free Trade*. New York: Cambridge University Press.
Grossman, G. and E. Helpman (1991), *Innovation and Growth in the Global Economy*. Cambridge, Mass.: MIT Press.
Haaland, J. I. and V. D. Norman (1992), 'Global Production Effects of European Integration'. In L. Alan Winters (ed.), *Trade Flows and Trade Policy after '1992'*. Cambridge: Cambridge University Press, Chapter 3.
    (1996), 'Scenarios as Tools to Assess the Effects of Trade Policy', SNF Working Paper No. 11/1996, Bergen.
Harrison, G., T. Rutherford, and D. Tarr (1994), 'Product Standards, Imperfect Competition and the Completion of the Market in the European Community', World Bank mimeo No. 6.
Helpman, E. and P. Krugman (1985), *Market Structure and Foreign Trade*. Cambridge, Mass.: MIT Press.
Henrekson, M., J. Tortensson, and R. Tortensson (1996), 'Growth Effects of European Integration', CEPR Discussion Paper No. 1465, September.
Jorgenson, D. W. and P. J. Wilcoxen (1990), 'Intertemporal General Equilibrium Modeling of US Environmental Regulation', *Journal of Policy Modeling* 12(6): 715–44.
    (1993), 'Reducing U.S. Carbon Dioxide Emissions: An Assessment of Different Instruments', *Journal of Policy Modeling* 15(5/6): 491–520.
Keuschnigg, C. and W. Kohler (1996), 'Commercial Policy and Dynamic Adjustment under Monopolistic Competition', *Journal of International Economics* 40: 373–411.

Levine, R. and D. Renelt (1992), 'A Sensitivity Analysis of Cross-Country Growth Regressions', *American Economic Review* 82(4): 942–63.

Melo, J. de and D. Tarr (1992), *A General Equilibrium Analysis of US Foreign Trade Policy*. Cambridge, Mass.: MIT Press.

Piggot, J., J. Whalley, and R. Wigle (1993), 'How Large Are the Incentives to Join Subglobal Carbon-Reduction Initiatives', *Journal of Policy Modeling* 15(5/6): 437–90.

Reynolds, L. G. (1983), 'The Spread of Economic Growth to the Third World', *Journal of Economic Literature* 21(3): 941–80.

Roland-Holst, D. (1997), 'Trade and the Environment'. In J. F. Francois and K. A. Reinert (eds.), *Applied Methods for Trade Policy Analysis: A Handbook*. New York: Cambridge University Press.

Smith, M. A. M. (1976), 'Trade. Growth and Consumption in Alternative Models of Capital Accumulation', *Journal of International Economics* 6: 385–88.

(1977), 'Capital Accumulation in the Open Two-Sector Economy', *Economic Journal* 87: 273–82.

Srinivasan, T. N. and J. N. Bhagwati (1980), 'Trade and Welfare in a Steady State'. In J. S. Chipman and C. P. Kindleberger (eds.), *Flexible Exchange Rates and the Balance of Payments*. Amsterdam: North-Holland.

Stiglitz, J. E. and H. Uzawa (1969), eds., *Readings in the Modern Theory of Economic Growth*. Cambridge, Mass.: MIT Press.

WTO (World Trade Organization) (1995), *Trade Policy Review – The European Union*. Geneva: WTO.

2 Transition dynamics and trade policy reform in developing countries

JOSEPH F. FRANCOIS, HÅKAN NORDSTRÖM, and CLINTON R. SHIELLS

1 Introduction

There is now a sizeable theoretical literature linking international trade with endogenous growth. This literature attempts to provide formal mechanisms for the interplay between trade policies and income growth, without recourse to exogenous assumptions regarding the sources of growth. The empirical foundations for believing in such a linkage seem compelling, with numerous studies reporting a positive correlation between an 'open' trade regime and growth. However, although there appears to be a positive linkage between openness and growth, and although this linkage seems to work indirectly through investment (see, e.g., Levine and Renelt (1992) and Baldwin and Seghezza (1996)), the results of the cross-country literature do not offer strong evidence of an endogenous growth mechanism at play. Endogenous growth models predict permanent growth effects following policy regime changes, the existence of which cannot be detected through standard cross-country correlation analysis. Moreover, the recent studies that test directly for the implications of endogenous growth models have so far failed to establish anything but a transitory impact from policy reforms on growth rates (see Jones (1995)).

In parallel with the development of the new endogenous growth theory, some authors have gone back to take a second look at classical growth theory, associated foremost with Solow (1956). They have found that an augmented version of the Solow growth model that includes accumulation of human capital as well as physical capital provides a surprisingly good description of the cross-country data. For example, Mankiw, Romer, and Weil (1992) have found evidence of 'conditional convergence', that is, convergence in income per capita across countries controlling for differences in savings rates, human capital, population growth, and other variables that predestine coun-

14

tries for different steady-state incomes. In their regressions, the (logarithm of) income per capita in the initial year of their data set (1960) enters with a negative sign, indicating that poorer economies, other things equal, tended to grow faster than their wealthier counterparts. This is consistent with the transitional dynamics of the Solow model, but somewhat at odds with the endogenous growth theory that (absent adjustment costs or imperfect knowledge transmission) downplays transitional dynamics.

At the same time, Mankiw et al. have found that the Solow model performs worse for a subsample of twenty-two OECD countries (the full data set covers ninety-eight countries). This suggests, perhaps, that the Solow model is useful for explaining growth based on capital deepening (human and physical) in transition to steady state, which intuitively is a dominant source of growth for developing countries, while being less useful in shedding light on the determinants of steady-state growth for developed countries at the technological frontier. Indeed, the Solow model treats steady-state growth as exogenous. Hence, the determinants of worldwide technological change, and the adoption and assimilation of technology to local conditions, lie outside the scope of the traditional model. This is an area where the endogenous growth literature has and will continue to play an important role, although the empirical literature has yet to establish which model specifications and assumptions are empirically relevant.

A common approach in numerical simulation models has been to treat countries at all levels of development as being in steady state,[1] although this is clearly an invalid assumption, as shown by the negative coefficient on initial income per capita in cross-country growth regressions. Arguably, if just a single country is out of steady state, the global system, and its regional subcomponents (including the OECD), must be out of steady state as well. If the focus of the analysis is on short-term issues, it may not matter much whether a country is (falsely) assumed to be in steady state or not. However, as far as the medium- and long-term impacts of trade policy are concerned, the steady-state assumption may overlook important transitory growth effects.

This paper shows theoretically that policy reforms can spur growth temporarily, and more so for countries that are far away from their steady-state income levels. Thus, policy reforms that appear identical in a static framework can have a qualitatively different impact on developing countries than on developed ones. This is because they may accelerate growth along the transition path, thereby allowing higher incomes to be realized at an earlier date.

The remainder of the paper is organized as follows. Section 2 briefly reviews the empirical literature on trade and growth, arguing that the positive linkages typically found do not, so far, firmly establish the existence of particular endogenous growth mechanisms. Our maintained hypothesis is instead that cross-country regressions highlight the transitory impact on growth of trade reforms. Section 3 provides an overview of the treatment of accumulation effects in numerical trade models. Essentially, starting from the assumption that all countries are initially in steady state, these models solve for the new, post-reform steady state using a macro closure of either a fixed savings rate or a fixed net real return to savings and investment. This assumption may prejudice the results quantitatively, as demonstrated in section 4. The paper concludes with observations on the implications of this differential impact for quantitative analysis of trade policy, particularly for multi-country models mixing countries at different stages of development.

2   Empirical studies of trade and growth

There is a large literature that has examined the importance of trade liberalization and international openness in fostering economic growth. These studies will be reviewed briefly in subsection 2.1.[2] They generally find a positive association between an 'open' trade regime and economic growth for both developed and developing countries, and over different time-periods. Although the evidence seems compelling, linking trade to growth through investment, one should keep in mind the conceptual and methodological problems facing this literature. One problem has been the construction of satisfactory measures of concepts such as 'openness' and 'trade orientation'. It is difficult to form comparable indexes across countries of the myriad of trade and commercial practices employed at a single point in time, much less to form a time-series of such measures.[3] Further, these studies have not always been based on rigorous theoretical models, so the channels through which trade influences economic growth remain unclear.[4]

Recently, some studies have explicitly examined the empirical validity of the theory of trade and endogenous growth. Coe and Helpman (1993) have examined the extent of international research and development (R&D) spillovers in relation to economic growth, while Irwin and Klenow (1994) have looked at learning-by-doing spillovers in the semiconductor industry. Jones (1995) has conducted time-series tests of R&D-based models of trade and economic growth. Subsection 2.2 briefly reviews endogenous growth theory to pinpoint testable hypotheses, and then discusses the associated empirical work.

2.1   Empirical linkages

A pioneering attempt to classify trade regimes was conducted in an NBER study directed by Bhagwati (1978) and Krueger (1978). They classified trade regimes according to five phases of liberalization, defining phase I as the most restrictive regime, with across-the-board quantitative trade restrictions, and phase V as the most liberal trade regime. On the basis of this classification, two hypotheses were tested. The first was that countries with more liberal trade regimes have higher rates of export growth. This hypothesis was confirmed for both traditional and non-traditional exports on a sample of ten countries for the period 1954–72. The second was that a more liberal trade regime is correlated with higher real GDP growth. This hypothesis was indirectly confirmed by data. The degree of openness of the trade regime was positively correlated with export growth, which was in turn positively correlated with real GDP growth.

A second large-scale attempt to classify countries by trade orientation was conducted by the World Bank (1987). Four groups of countries were distinguished: (1) strongly outward oriented; (2) moderately outward oriented; (3) moderately inward oriented; and (4) strongly inward oriented. Data on average growth rates per capita over the periods 1963–73, 1974–85, and 1986–92,[5] respectively, suggest that outward-oriented countries on average grow significantly faster than inward-oriented countries (Figure 2.1 on page 18). Formal statistical confirmation of this pattern has been provided by Alam (1991).

An attempt to classify the trade regimes of the 135 countries included in version 5.5 of the Summers and Heston (1991) data set has been undertaken by Sachs and Warner (1995). They judged a country to have a closed trade policy (during the sample period 1970–89) if it had at least one of the following characteristics: (1) non-tariff barriers (NTBs) covering 40 per cent or more of trade; (2) an average tariff rate of 40 per cent or more; (3) a black market exchange rate that had depreciated by 20 per cent or more relative to the official exchange rate, on average, during the 1970s or 1980s; (4) a socialist economic system (as defined by Kornai (1992)); or (5) a state monopoly on major exports.

Sachs and Warner ran a series of Barro (1991) type cross-country regressions, using their classification of trade regimes (open or closed) as an additional explanatory variable. They report positive effects for the standard variables – educational attainment and investment/GDP ratio. As expected, the openness variable entered with a significant positive sign. On average, open economies were estimated to grow by 2.5 percentage points more per annum than closed economies. They also found evidence

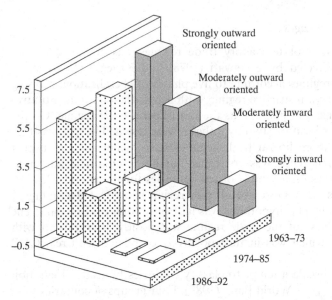

Figure 2.1   Real GDP growth (average annual rate): 1963–73, 1974–85, 1986–92.
Source: data from World Bank (1987) and IMF (1993). See these
publications for classification of economies by trade orientation.

of 'conditional convergence'. Countries tended to grow faster the greater
the gap between their initial income level and their own long-run (steady-
state) per capita income level, the latter being determined by policies
affecting savings rates, human capital formation, etc. (Note that this
finding is consistent with the transitional dynamics of the simple Solow
model.) The link between an open trade regime and growth seems at least
partially to be an indirect one, operating through investment. The open
economies in their data set had significantly higher investment/GDP
ratios, on average 5.4 percentage points, and, since a high investment ratio
tends to be positively associated with growth, this suggests an indirect link
between the trade regime and growth through investment.

Given the inherent problem of classifying multidimensional trade
regimes with a single index, some authors have used actual trade flows as
a proxy for trade orientation. The assumption is that more open
economies experience faster export growth than less open ones. In a
second stage, real GDP growth is correlated with export growth, and a
positive correlation indicates that open economies experience more rapid
average rates of economic growth than closed economies. Following this
approach, Michaely (1977) and Feder (1983), for instance, have found
positive correlations between exports and growth.

However, trade flows are at best imperfect proxies for trade policy orientation. Small countries, for instance, tend to trade more than large countries, given the level of trade barriers. To isolate the effect of the trade regime on trade flows it is necessary to control for other factors affecting trade: country size, resource endowments, natural trade barriers, etc. For instance, Syrquin and Chenery (1989) grouped 106 countries according to size and export specialization. Approximating outward orientation by the share of exports in GDP, they found real GDP growth to be higher on average for outward-oriented countries within each of the following groups: small primary goods exporters; large primary goods exporters; small manufacturing goods exporters; and large manufacturing goods exporters. The annual growth premium from outward orientation ranged from 0.2 percentage points for large manufacturing exporters to 1.4 percentage points for small primary exporters. (Note that large manufacturing exporters tend to be OECD countries closer to steady state.)

Balassa (1985) constructed an index of trade orientation based on the deviation of actual exports from that predicted by a structural model of trade. Specifically, exports were assumed to depend on per capita income, population, and natural resource endowments. After estimating a linear export equation for a sample of forty-three countries, Balassa used the difference between actual and predicted exports as a measure of trade orientation. A positive difference was interpreted as a sign of outward orientation, and a negative difference as a sign of inward orientation. Using this index as an explanatory variable for growth, he found a statistically significant positive correlation and concluded that countries with more outward-oriented trade policies grow faster on average.

Balassa's approach was refined by Leamer (1988), who used an empirical Heckscher–Ohlin model with nine productive factors to estimate net trade flows for 183 commodities and 53 countries (30 of which were less developed countries, LDCs). Based on the difference between predicted and actual trade flows, he constructed two sets of trade policy indexes: openness indexes measuring the way in which trade policy restricts imports, and intervention indexes capturing the way overall commercial policy distorts trade (imports and exports). Using the Leamer indexes, Edwards (1992) specified a theoretical endogenous growth model based on the Lewis (1955) 'learning-by-looking' idea that more internationally integrated economies have an advantage in absorbing new technologies. This link was confirmed empirically using a sample of thirty LDCs for the period 1970–82. Two other variables were included in the regressions: investment as a share of GDP, and initial per capita real GDP. The positive estimated coefficient corresponding to investment supports the view that investment in physical (and human) capital is conducive to growth. Moreover, the negative coefficient on initial GDP supports the 'catching-up' hypothesis – that countries starting at a lower level of income per capita tend, other things equal, to grow faster during the catch-up process of absorbing the knowledge and technology of the more advanced countries.

Price comparisons have also been used to measure trade orientation. Barro (1991), for instance, formed a price distortion index of investment goods for a sample of ninety-eight countries over the 1960–85 period. He found a significant negative relationship between price distortions and growth. The estimates imply that increasing the price distortion for investment goods by one standard deviation from the sample mean would have reduced per capita growth by 0.4 percentage points.

Dollar (1992) computed a real exchange rate index, measuring the extent to which the trade regime distorts relative prices away from world market prices. Defining outward orientation in terms of relatively low real exchange rate distortions and low variability of the index over time, he found a positive correlation between openness and growth in per capita GDP using a sample of ninety-five developing countries over the 1976–85 period. The average per capita growth rate in the least distortive quartile of mostly Asian countries was 2.9 per cent, falling to 0.9 per cent for the second quartile, -0.2 per cent for the third quartile, and -1.3 per cent for the most distortive quartile. The estimated coefficients imply that a reduction of the real exchange rate distortion to the Asian level would add 0.7 percentage points to Latin American growth and 1.8 percentage points to African growth.

Easterly (1993) has used a relative price distortion index similar to Dollar's. He first showed theoretically that distortions of relative input prices (caused by trade policy) have large effects on growth and welfare because they distort investment decisions. Testing the model on a sample of fifty-seven countries over the 1979–85 period, he found a significant negative relationship between price distortions and growth.

Lee (1993) has developed a model in which trade distortions induced by tariffs and exchange controls reduce growth in countries where foreign inputs are essential for production. He showed that small, resource-scarce countries are hurt more by import restrictions than are large, resource-abundant countries because of the larger dependence of the former countries on foreign inputs. Restricting or distorting the price of foreign inputs reduces the productivity of domestic industry, leading to slower per capita income growth. The empirical results confirm that tariff rates and exchange rate distortions (approximated by the black market premium) indeed had a significant negative effect on per capita income growth. The estimated coefficients suggest that a distortive policy, such as a 25 per cent import tariff and exchange controls leading to a 50 per cent black market premium, would reduce growth by 1.4 percentage points for a country whose size and resource endowment imply a trade share of 20 per cent of GDP under free trade.

Harrison (1993) has drawn together a variety of openness measures to test the robustness of the relationships between trade restrictions and economic growth obtained previously in the literature. The first two measures were annual indexes of trade liberalization for two samples of developing countries over the periods 1960–84 and 1978–88, respectively. The third measure was the black market premium, defined as the deviation of the black market rate from the official exchange rate. The fourth measure was the share of trade in GDP, defined as the ratio of exports plus imports to GDP. The fifth index measured movement of internal prices toward international prices in different countries. The sixth index was a modified version of the price distortion index used in Dollar (1992). The seventh index measured the relative bias against agricultural production. All indexes that were statistically significant showed a positive relationship between liberal trade regimes and economic growth. Harrison also found that causation between openness and economic growth runs in both directions. Periods of high growth seem to provide an impetus for more open markets, presumably because this alleviates adjustment problems and reduces resistance to change, while more open markets are in turn conducive to growth.

In a cross-sectional study using data for 1967–87, Matin (1992) tested whether the general finding that increased openness improves growth performance holds true for sub-Saharan Africa. This had been questioned by Helleiner (1986), among others, who argued that a certain level of development is required before the benefits of international trade can be fully realized. The evidence provided by Matin points to a positive link between openness and growth even for the poorest countries. The result was robust to different measures of openness (trade shares, black market premium, the Halevi–Thomas index of trade liberalization, and Dollar's index of outward orientation) and to the inclusion of other policy variables. Furthermore, the estimated coefficients did not differ significantly from those of a control sample of other North African countries. That is, the openness–growth performance link seemed to be as strong for sub-Saharan Africa as for other parts of the continent.[6]

Levine and Renelt (1992) tested the robustness of cross-country regressions. They made the following intriguing observation: 'Given that over 50 variables have been found to be significantly correlated with growth in at least one regression, readers may be uncertain as to the confidence they should place in the findings of any one study' (p. 942). Testing the robustness of coefficient estimates with respect to alteration in the set of explanatory variables, they were able to identify two 'robust' correlations: first, a positive correlation between growth and investment as a share of GDP; and, second, a positive correlation between investment as a share of GDP and trade as a share of GDP.[7]

The Levine and Renelt result of investment-induced growth stimulated by trade liberalization has recently been confirmed empirically by Baldwin and Seghezza (1996). First, they have shown that the theoretical impact of trade liberalization on growth is not always clear-cut. On the one hand, trade liberalization may reduce the return to capital if the import-competing sector is capital intensive (the Stolper–Samuelson effect). On the other hand, when imports and locally produced substitutes are inputs into capital formation, trade liberalization may encourage investment by lowering the cost of capital. Although theoretically ambiguous, their empirical investigation showed a negative impact of domestic (and foreign) trade barriers on investment and thereby growth. This confirms the Levine and Renelt finding of two-stage linkage between trade and growth, through investment. Indeed, in contrast to the specification adopted in many endogenous growth models, they found no evidence for 'direct' trade-induced technology-led growth. More precisely, system estimation found that trade barriers were not significant in the growth equation when they were also included in the investment equations. However, as they point out, the apparent absence of a direct linkage may be due to a close correlation between capital investment and technological progress that makes it problematic to isolate the impact of trade on endogenous growth.

In summary, this literature provides a striking set of stylized facts. Countries that are relatively open to trade tend to grow faster. This linkage seems to relate trade to investment, and investment to growth. Whatever the theoretical mechanisms, the pattern of post-war development provides very strong evidence that trade liberalization is, on net, an important aspect of successful growth policies.

However, it does not follow that trade reforms necessarily give rise to permanently higher growth rates, as suggested by the endogenous growth literature (see discussion below). The overall pattern might be consistent with a series of trade liberalizations undertaken in the post-war period, foremost the eight rounds of multilateral trade liberalizations under the auspices of the General Agreement on Tariffs and Trade, but also unilateral trade liberalizations and liberalizations in the context of various regional agreements. In a classical growth context, the post-war liberalization process might be compared with a series of 'level effects', shifting steady-state incomes upwards, inducing temporarily higher growth rates in the course of adjustments to the new, higher steady-state incomes for participating countries. Under this interpretation, it may be that no permanent trade-related growth effects are at work.

2.2 Endogenous growth: theory and evidence

This subsection provides a brief recapitulation of the new trade theory with endogenous growth. This is followed by a survey of the empirical evidence. What are the testable implications of the theory, and what limited empirical evidence is available at this stage?

Four main types of theoretical model are used to explain growth due to endogenous technical change. The first relies on the existence of specialized intermediate inputs. Growth occurs if the range or quality of such inputs increases over time. A second theory is based on learning-by-doing in production. If knowledge obtained in accumulated production of old goods is partially applicable to newly developed goods, then learning-by-doing may lead to growth. Human capital accumulation is the basis for a third theory of economic growth. This refers to the accumulation of increased productive capacity by workers by virtue of their education or labour market experience. A worker's education, for instance, can yield productivity improvements for a wide range of products. The fourth theory models the development and introduction of new or more sophisticated products through R&D activity.

In each theory, there is a dynamic spillover or externality of some type from the growth-generating activity to the rest of the economy (and possibly to the rest of the world), and this spillover allows economies to escape the straitjacket of diminishing returns that otherwise inevitably brings growth back to the exogenous rate in traditional growth models. Learning-by-doing in the production of existing goods, for example, must be at least partially applicable to the production of other products. That is, there must be a spillover from learning-by-doing to generate sustained economic growth. In theories based on R&D investment, skilled labour is used to create blueprints for new products. To generate continual new product introduction and growth, external benefits must result from R&D activity. That is, the amount of skilled labour needed to develop a new blueprint must fall as the level of general knowledge increases. Without spillover benefits, improved incentives for R&D yield an increase in the level of output per worker, but with no permanent effects on growth.

The new growth theory emphasizes how forward-looking investment by firms (and workers in the case of schooling) in response to market incentives could give rise to economic growth without the need to assume that technical change occurs exogenously. However, a significant additional step is needed to link trade and trade liberalization to models of endogenous innovation and growth. In particular, to affect growth, trade liberalization must change the conditions underlying growth.

The various linkages between trade and growth in endogenous growth models of knowledge accumulation via R&D have been thoroughly catalogued and analysed in Grossman and Helpman (1991b). International trade may affect the underlying conditions for growth by expanding the potential market size, allowing firms to spread the costs of R&D over greater volumes. This will stimulate innovative activities, but it will not lead to sustained growth unless the R&D sector generates spillovers or additions to the general stock of knowledge from which subsequent innovations can benefit. Essentially, the cost of each innovation must fall because of the larger stock of knowledge available to draw from. This is a testable hypothesis that seems to be partially refuted by data, which instead suggest that more resources need to be devoted to R&D over time to keep up the momentum in particular innovative activities.

One strand of the empirical literature tests for certain critical elements of the endogenous growth theory, such as learning externalities. Along these lines, Irwin and Klenow (1994) used data on the semiconductor industry to test for the existence of learning spillovers, both nationally and internationally. They employed quarterly data on the average industry selling price and on shipments by each of thirty-two firms from 1974 Q1 to 1992 Q4 for each of seven generations of dynamic random access memory (DRAM) chips. They have found that firms learned three times more from their own production experience than from that of other firms (domestic and foreign). Notwithstanding this, because world output was large in relation to a typical firm's output, international learning spillovers were still important sources of productivity growth for semiconductor firms.[8] However, Irwin and Klenow found little evidence of learning spillovers from one generation of DRAM chips to another, thereby providing little support for explaining the superior growth performance of countries such as Korea based on endogenous growth models with learning-by-doing, as in Lucas (1993).

Coe and Helpman (1993) examined the empirical relationship between domestic and foreign R&D stocks and total factor productivity (TFP) growth using a pooled data set consisting of twenty-one OECD countries (plus Israel) during 1970–90. In addition to confirming the strong link between domestic R&D stocks and TFP growth found in previous studies, they found evidence of sizeable international R&D spillovers. In a subsequent paper, Coe et al. (1995) showed that R&D undertaken in OECD countries spills over not just to other OECD trading partners but also to developing countries. In their preferred model specification, the foreign R&D capital stock affected productivity only when interacted with the import share. The more open the country, the larger the marginal benefit from foreign R&D.

Although these studies provide empirical evidence for national and international R&D spillovers in line with theoretical R&D-based endogenous growth models, they do not argue that these spillovers are sizeable enough to escape diminishing returns. In fact, the evidence presented by Jones (1995), discussed next, suggests the contrary.

Jones has formulated and implemented a time-series test of R&D models of endogenous growth. The basic idea behind this test is that endogenous growth models based on investment in R&D, formulated by Romer (1990), Grossman and Helpman (1991a), and Aghion and Howitt (1992), imply that constant or declining economic growth should not be associated with an increase in the number of scientists and engineers, or in the amount spent on R&D. Yet, over the 1950–87 period, there was a strong upward trend in the number of scientists and engineers engaged in R&D in France, Germany, Japan, and the United States, while trends in total factor productivity growth have been stable or declining over this period. These results underscore the need to modify and refine the basic R&D-based endogenous growth models for empirical work, in particular calling into question their relevance for advanced OECD economies for which growth rates have been rather stable.

Jones also investigated the time-series properties of the historical growth rate between 1880 and 1987 for the United States in an effort to detect evidence of persistent effects of policy changes. Such evidence, if found, would be an indication of endogenous growth mechanisms at work. He considered the following thought experiment: 'An economist living in the year 1929 (who has miraculous access to historical per capita GDP data) fits a simple linear trend to the natural logarithm of per capita income from 1880 to 1929 in an attempt to forecast per capita GDP today, as in 1987. How far off would that prediction be? We can use the prediction error as a rough indicator of the importance of the permanent movements in growth rates' (1995: 519).

The surprising result is that the prediction is off by only 5 per cent. A time-trend test (augmented Dickey–Fuller test) confirmed that the US growth rates are well described by a process of constant mean and very little persistence. He concluded: 'The implication for [endogenous growth] models is rather stark: either nothing in U.S. experience since

1880 has had a large, persistent effect on growth rates, or whatever persistent effects have occurred have miraculously been offsetting' (1995: 519).

Finally, he investigated whether the strong positive trend of investment/ GDP ratios for many OECD countries has had any persistent effect on growth rates, which would be the case if the simple AK model, associated with Romer (1987) and Rebelo (1987), held true. The AK model can be seen as a reduced form of the class of endogenous growth models with constant returns to scale in the factors of production that can be accumulated through investments. Investigating the time-series properties of individual OECD countries, he found no persistent upward shifts in GDP growth that would be associated with the documented upward drift in the investment/GDP ratio. He concluded: 'a permanent increase in the investment rate does not produce a permanent increase in the growth rates, but rather the effects on growth are transitory.'

To summarize, cross-country regressions provide strong evidence of a positive linkage between trade and growth. The linkages seem mainly to be indirect through investment, though trade may also directly affect growth by facilitating transmission of knowledge between countries. However, there is little evidence, so far, that trade reforms lead to permanent increases in growth rates. Rather, in spite of the continuous process of liberalization in the post-war era, time-series results fail to establish anything but a transitory impact. This is inconsistent with endogenous growth theory, but consistent with the traditional growth theory of temporarily higher growth rates during movement towards new, higher steady-state incomes made possible by each stage of the reform process.

3   Trade reforms and steady-state effects

This section provides an overview of the treatment of growth effects in applied trade models. Although some studies have started the process of incorporating endogenous growth mechanisms, large-scale models have so far been confined to steady-state comparisons.

One of the first efforts to quantify accumulation effects is due to Baldwin (1989, 1992), who computed estimates of potential dynamic gains from the EC92 programme to eliminate all barriers to trade and factor movements within the European Communities. He distinguishes between a 'medium-term growth bonus' due to induced capital formation and a 'long-term growth bonus' due to induced technical change. Using Solow's terminology, the medium-term growth bonus is a level effect whereas the long-term growth bonus is an endogenous growth effect. The medium-term growth bonus, derived from an initial steady-state assumption and being identical to the steady-state version of equation (10) below, is assumed to come about as EC92 increases the productivity of existing factor endowments, thereby leading to increased income, savings, and investment. Baldwin shows that the medium-term growth bonus can be quite substantial as compared with the usual static gains from economic integration, concluding that the Cecchini Report's estimates of the economic benefits of EC92 were at least 30 per cent too low.

Baldwin (1989) also calculates the long-run growth impact of EC92 using two simple endogenous growth models. In the AK model, the steady-state rate of output growth is equal to the savings rate times the steady-state output/capital ratio, minus the rate of depreciation. Estimated static gains of EC92 point to an increase in the output/capital ratio of 2.5 to 6.5 per cent and, based on a savings rate of 10 per cent, this leads to an increase in the growth rate of one-quarter to three-quarters of a percentage point. This represents a permanent growth effect rather than a level effect because there are, by assumption, dynamic increasing returns to capital accumulation. Baldwin also calibrates the R&D-based model of Krugman (1988). This model features investment in R&D to lower the cost of producing existing product designs (process innovation as opposed to product innovation). On this basis, 1992 would add about 0.3–0.8 percentage points to the permanent growth rate.

Kehoe (1994) constructed rough estimates of the effects of economic reform in Mexico, including trade reform, on the steady-state rate of economic growth, as a result of both learning-by-doing and specialization. Growth for the economy as a whole is a weighted average of growth rates for individual industries, with weights given by industry output shares. Levels of experience in production, and hence productivity, differ among industries. To the extent that trade leads to specialization in industries with high rates of productivity, this can lead to increased economic growth for the economy as a whole. Kehoe developed a specialization index to capture the relationship between trade, inter-industry specialization, and economic growth. This index was subsequently used in a regression to estimate the effects of free trade on Mexican economic growth.[9] The assumed policy changes, when combined with coefficient estimates from the regression, yielded an estimated increase in the growth rate of Mexican manufacturing output per worker of 1.6 per cent per year.

Calibration studies of multilateral trade liberalization under the Uruguay Round have also incorporated medium-term growth effects related to capital accumulation. The results of this literature are driven by classical capital accumulation mechanisms, and have not been extended to examination of endogenous growth effects. Essentially, starting from the assumption that all countries are initially in steady state, the post-reform steady state is solved using a macro closure of either fixed savings rates, or alternatively fixed net real returns to savings and investment that are based on an infinite horizon model. For example, Francois et al. (1995) report that the medium-term investment effect, conceptually identical to Baldwin's, multiplied the static gain by some 50 to 250 per cent, depending on model specification. Other Uruguay Round studies including accumulation mechanisms include Haaland and Tollefson (1994), Harrison et al. (1995), and Goldin et al. (1993).

4   Policy reform and transitional effects

As pointed out above, global trade models have so far been confined to steady-state comparisons. This approach, while convenient, may pre-judice the numerical estimates, especially for developing countries. This is shown next using a simple Solow (1956) model.

The key elements of the model are as follows. Production is aggregated across the entire economy. Physical capital and labour are combined to produce a single final output. The aggregate supply of labour is assumed to grow at a constant rate. Labour-augmenting technical change is assumed to occur at an exogenously specified rate. Final output can be either consumed directly or used as an investment good. We adopt the classical assumption of a fixed savings rate. This economy tends toward a steady state in which output per capita grows at a constant rate that is equal to the rate of technical progress. However, to reach the steady state takes time. Indeed, the economy never quite gets there (Deardorff 1971). The main point of the analysis is to show that policy reforms during the transition period may considerably speed up the process of reaching higher income levels.

A Cobb–Douglas production function is assumed. This facilitates explicit solution for the transitional growth path.

$$Y(t) = K(t)^{\alpha}[A(t)L(t)]^{1-\alpha}, \quad 0 < \alpha < 1, \tag{1}$$

The notation is standard: $Y(t)$ denotes the output at time t, $L(t)$ labour, $K(t)$ capital, and $A(t)$ efficiency. $L(t)$ and $A(t)$ are assumed to grow exogenously at rate n and g, respectively,

$$L(t) = L(0)e^{nt}, A(t) = A(0)e^{gt}. \tag{2}$$

The savings rate, s, is fixed and capital depreciates at rate δ. Define $k(t) = K(t)/A(t)L(t)$ as the stock of capital per effective unit of labour. The evolution of $k(t)$ is governed by the following differential equation:

$$\dot{k}(t) = sk(t)^\alpha - (n + g + \delta)k(t), \tag{3}$$

where a dot signifies a variable's time derivative. A simple solution procedure exists for this non-linear Bernoulli equation. Dividing (3) by $k(t)^\alpha$, using the variable transformation $z(t) = k(t)^{1-\alpha}$, and noting that $dz(t)/dt = (1-\alpha) k(t)^{-\alpha} dk(t)/dt$, results in a linear differential equation in $z(t)$ that can be solved using normal procedures. Substituting back into $k(t)$ we get the solution to the original non-linear differential equation:

$$k(t) = \left\{ \left[\frac{k(0)^{(1-\alpha)}}{k^*} - 1 \right] e^{-(1-\alpha)(n+g+\delta)t} + 1 \right\}^{\frac{1}{(1-\alpha)}} k^*,$$

$$k^* = \left(\frac{s}{n+g+\delta} \right)^{\frac{1}{(1-\alpha)}}, \tag{4}$$

where $k(0)$ and k^* are the initial and the steady-state capital stock per effective unit of labour, respectively. The output per capita, $y(t) = Y(t)/L(t)$, evolves according to

$$y(t) = \left\{ \left[\left(\frac{k(0)}{k^*} \right)^{(1-\alpha)} - 1 \right] e^{-(1-\alpha)(n+g+\delta)t} + 1 \right\}^{\frac{\alpha}{(1-\alpha)}} y^*(t),$$

$$y^*(t) = (k^*)^\alpha A(0)e^{gt}, \tag{5}$$

with a growth rate of

$$\frac{\dot{y}(t)}{y(t)} = g + \alpha \frac{\dot{k}(t)}{k(t)},$$

$$\frac{\dot{k}(t)}{k(t)} = -(n + g + \delta) \frac{\left[\left(\frac{k(0)}{k^*} \right)^{(1-\alpha)} - 1 \right] e^{-(1-\alpha)(n+g+\delta)t}}{\left[\left(\frac{k(0)}{k^*} \right)^{(1-\alpha)} - 1 \right] e^{-(1-\alpha)(n+g+\delta)t} + 1}. \tag{6}$$

The growth per capita is equal to the exogenous rate of labour-augmenting technical change plus the capital–output elasticity α times the

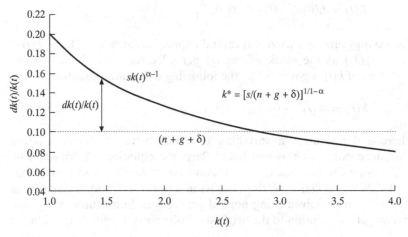

Figure 2.2   Growth in capital per unit of effective labour.

growth rate of the capital stock per effective unit of labour. The growth rate of capital per unit of effective labour has a simple diagrammatic representation (see Figure 2.2). For a given $k(t)$, capital growth per effective unit of labour is given by the vertical distance between $sk(t)^{\alpha-1}$ and $(n + g + \delta)$, and growth in output per capita by $g + \alpha[sk(t)^{\alpha-1} - (n + g + \delta)]$. Because of diminishing returns, the growth rate slows down the closer the capital stock gets to the steady state. An increase in the savings rate shifts the $sk(t)^{\alpha-1}$ schedule upward, leading to a temporary increase in growth during the transition to the new steady state. Whereas steady-state incomes are affected, the long-run growth rate is not.

The time needed to close a proportion ω of the gap between initial and steady-state output is given by:[10]

$$t_\omega = -\frac{\ln(Z)}{(1-\alpha)(n+g+\delta)}, \quad Z = \frac{\left(\frac{k(0)}{k^*}\right)^{(1-\alpha)(1-\omega)} - 1}{\left(\frac{k(0)}{k^*}\right)^{(1-\alpha)} - 1}. \tag{7}$$

The half-time of convergence increases slightly as the output per capita approaches the steady state. That is, the time that it takes to close half of the remaining gap becomes longer and longer, and the economy never quite gets there.[11] Figure 2.3 shows the convergence time for different values of the capital–output elasticity. The example assumes that the initial capital per unit of effective labour is 75 per cent of the steady-state value, and $(n + g + \delta)$ is 0.1. In this case, the first half of the distance $(\omega =$

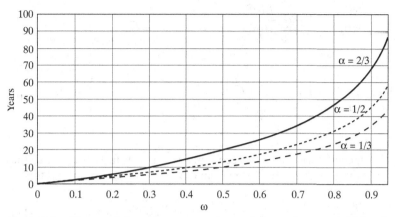

Figure 2.3 Time needed to close a proportion ω of the gap between initial and steady-state output.

0.5) is covered in 9.7 to 20.1 years, depending on the value of α. The next half (taking us to $\omega = 0.75$) takes somewhat longer: 10.0 to 20.4 years, depending on the value of α. The larger the α, the slower the convergence rate to steady state.

Let us now calculate the static impact and the medium-run accumulation effect of a policy change undertaken during the transition to steady state. In our simple framework, we can represent trade policy reform (or any other reform) as an enhancement to the efficiency of productive resources, captured in the model by an increase in $A(0)$. We assume that an appropriate policy reform makes it possible to produce a greater quantity of output using the same quantities of productive factors. The increased productivity will also affect the incentives to accumulate capital, reinforcing the initial impact over time. Differentiation of (5) yields the following equation:

$$\frac{dy(t)}{y(t)} = \left(1 - \alpha \frac{\left(\frac{k(0)}{k^*}\right)^{(1-\alpha)} e^{-(1-\alpha)(n+g+\delta)t}}{\left[\left(\frac{k(0)}{k^*}\right)^{(1-\alpha)} - 1 \right] e^{-(1-\alpha)(n+g+\delta)t} + 1} \right) \frac{dA(0)}{A(0)}. \quad (8)$$

Equation (8) gives the percentage change in output per capita at time t due to a policy change at time 0 that raises the efficiency by a proportion $dA(0)/A(0)$, accounting for the policy-induced capital accumulation between the time of the policy reform (0) and the time of evaluation (t). Equation (8) can be decomposed into a static and medium-run impact (super index B):

$$\frac{dy(0)}{y(0)} = (1 - \alpha)\frac{dA(0)}{A(0)}, \tag{9}$$

$$\frac{dy^{B}(t)}{y^{B}(t)} = \left(\frac{\alpha}{1 - \alpha}\right)\left(1 - \frac{\left(\frac{k(0)}{k^*}\right)^{(1-\alpha)}e^{-(1-\alpha)(n+g+\delta)t}}{\left[\left(\frac{k(0)}{k^*}\right)^{(1-\alpha)} - 1\right]e^{-(1-\alpha)(n+g+\delta)t} + 1}\right)\frac{dy(0)}{y(0)}. \tag{10}$$

For the special case when the economy is initially in steady state, the medium-run growth bonus (for marginal policy changes) simplifies to:

$$\frac{dy^{*B}(t)}{y^{*B}(t)} = \left(\frac{\alpha}{1 - \alpha}\right)\left[1 - e^{-(1-\alpha)(n+g+\delta)t}\right]\frac{dy(0)}{y(0)}. \tag{11}$$

In the limit, the medium-run impact collapses to the Baldwin multiplier: $dy^{B}(\infty)/y^{B}(\infty) = (\alpha/1 - \alpha)dy(0)/y(0)$. For example, an α of 1/3 implies an eventual 50 per cent growth bonus on top of the static impact gain. However, in finite time, the medium-run bonus is smaller. This observation may be of some importance since the process of convergence to the new steady state may be quite slow. Indeed, as shown above, it may take ten to twenty years to close half the distance. On an applied level, this suggests, for example, that the income gains attributed to the Uruguay Round over the medium run tend to be inflated. For example, Francois et al. (1995) implicitly assume that the world has fully adjusted to the new policy regime by 2005. Yet a rough estimate, using equation (7) and Figure 2.3, suggests that only some 50 per cent of the 'medium-run' accumulation effects will have materialized by then.

On another level, applied studies may be guilty of underestimating the value of the Round, especially for developing countries, by assuming that all countries (regions) are initially in steady state. As detailed above, cross-country regressions consistently find a significant negative impact of initial income on growth, suggesting that low-income economies, other things equal, tend to grow faster than their wealthier counterparts. Interpreted in the context of a Solow growth model, this evidence suggests that developing countries are (on average) further away from their steady-state incomes than are developed countries.

This raises the following question. Does a policy reform undertaken during transition to steady state have a different impact than if initially in steady state? In other words, is the medium-run growth bonus larger in percentage terms for developing countries than for developed countries?

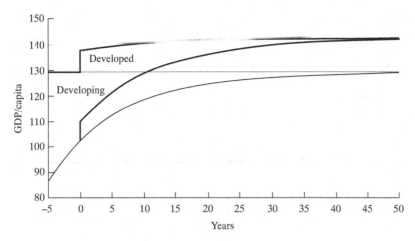

Figure 2.4   Transitional growth and trade reforms.

To study this issue, consider two economies with the same underlying parameters and policies, but where one economy is close to steady state (developed country) while the other is on the transition path far from the same steady state (developing country). It can be shown by comparing (10) and (11) that the medium-run growth bonus is larger for economies starting far *below* steady state for any finite time.[12] The transitional growth accelerates more for the economy out of steady state than for the economy near steady state. To see this, recall that, for a given $k(t)$, growth in k is given by the vertical distance between $sk(t)^{\alpha-1}$ and $(n + g + \delta)$, and growth in output per capita by $g + \alpha[sk(t)^{\alpha-1}-(n + g + \delta)]$. An increase in $A(t)$ shifts the $sk(t)^{\alpha-1}$ schedule in Figure 2.2 upward by $sk(t)^{\alpha-1}dA(t)/A(t)$. (Recall the definition of $k(t) = K(t)/A(t)L(t)$.) Because the schedule is non-linear, reflecting diminishing returns, the impact of the shift is larger the lower the initial $k(t)$. Hence, the transitional growth rate accelerates more for economies out of steady state, and more so the further away from steady state an economy is initially. (The asymmetric growth impact can also be shown directly by differentiating equation (6).)

The time-path of output per capita and the corresponding growth rates are illustrated in Figures 2.4 and 2.5. In the example, the underlying exogenous growth rate g has been set to zero for expositional reasons. However, the result holds irrespective of the underlying exogenous growth rate. At time 0, it is assumed that a policy change takes place that raises $A(0)$ by 10 per cent. This lowers the capital stock per unit of effective labour, inducing additional capital accumulation. Both

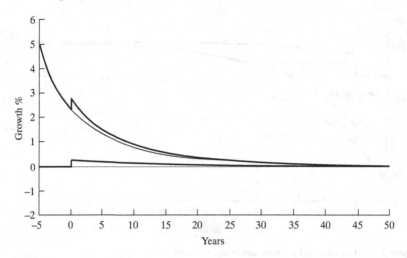

Figure 2.5   Trade reforms and transitional growth.

economies experience a transitional increase in growth rates above what they would otherwise have been, but more so for the developing economy, which embarks on a steeper transition path to the new steady state.

Note that after the policy reform the developing economy reaches the old steady-state income in just ten years (in this example), whereas absent the policy reform it would have taken far longer, indeed an infinite number of years. This suggests that an important aspect of a policy reform for developing countries is that it may allow economies to reach higher levels of income in a much shorter time than otherwise. In present-value terms, a policy change may hence be far more important than suggested by the static effects if it sets the economy on a higher transitional growth path.

To explore this issue further, let us consider the effect of a policy reform on the present value of GDP. Through numerical integration of equation (5), we provide an example to illustrate our point. Table 2.1 gives the change in present discounted value of per capita GDP, as a percentage of initial GDP, following a policy reform with a 1 per cent static impact on GDP ($dA(0)/A(0) = 0.01/(1 - \alpha)$). In terms of Figure 2.4, we calculate the discounted area between the bold (post-reform policy) and light (pre-reform policy) lines for the developed and developing country, respectively. The discount factor (real interest rate, r) is taken to be 5 per cent, 3 per cent above the assumed exogenous growth rate. The other underlying parameters of the example are given in the table. We distinguish between a developed country that is initially in steady state,

Table 2.1   Change in the present value of per capita GDP, as a percentage of initial GDP, following a policy reform with a 1 per cent static impact on GDP

	Developing 1 $k(0)/k^* = 1/4$	Developing 2 $k(0)/k^* = 1/2$	Developing 3 $k(0)/k^* = 3/4$	Developed $k(0)/k^* = 1/1$
Infinite horizon				
$\alpha = 1/3$	69	56	50	46
$\alpha = 1/2$	102	75	63	56
$\alpha = 2/3$	151	104	84	73
Ten-year horizon				
$\alpha = 1/3$	13.3	11.5	10.6	10.1
$\alpha = 1/2$	15.3	12.7	11.6	10.9
$\alpha = 2/3$	16.3	13.7	12.5	11.8

Note: $s = 0.2$.

and three developing countries with initial capital stocks below steady state, as given by $k(0)/k^* = 0.25$, 0.5, and 0.75, respectively. A graphic illustration of the relationship between the initial development level (in relation to steady state) and the impact of a trade policy reform in terms of changes in present-value GDP is provided in Figure 2.6.

The results of our analysis suggest that the implications of policy reforms for developing countries are qualitatively different from those for developed ones. This is because of the impact on transitional growth. By setting their economies on a higher transitional growth path, a policy

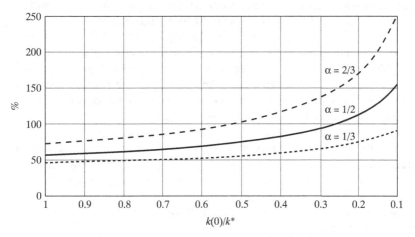

Figure 2.6   Change in present-value GDP, as a percentage of initial GDP, following a policy reform with 1 per cent static impact.

reform allows 'the fruits of development' to be realized at an earlier date. Even a 'modest' policy reform worth 1 per cent in static income is in present value 'worth' perhaps 50 to 150 per cent of initial GDP, depending on the initial state of development and the rate of convergence to steady state (which depends critically on the value of α), and, of course, the discount factor. The more underdeveloped the economy is initially (in relation to its own steady-state income), the greater the present-value income gain of being set on a higher transitional growth path. The impact of policy reforms depends crucially on the initial state of development.

A final word of caution is called for when interpreting these income effects. In the present framework, with a single composite good and a fixed marginal propensity to save or consume, movements in the present value of consumption (and hence of temporal welfare) must, by construction, follow that of GDP. However, in a more general framework, and particularly in one with explicit intertemporal optimization, changes in the present value of GDP are not necessarily indicative of changes in intertemporal welfare.[13]

5   Concluding observations

Dynamic effects have featured prominently in recent studies of trade liberalization and integration. Recent calibration studies of the North American Free Trade Agreement (NAFTA), the European Communities' economic integration (EC92) programme, and the Uruguay Round of multilateral trade negotiations have all attempted to quantify various dynamic effects of trade liberalization on economic growth, both due to standard transitional growth effects (i.e. level effects) and due to permanent endogenous growth effects. These effects have also featured in the policy debate during negotiation and ratification of these agreements and programmes. Although our understanding of the relevant mechanisms is incomplete, it is clear that dynamic effects are important, and can probably overwhelm the static efficiency gains.

The literature on calibrated numerical models of international trade with endogenous growth is still at an early stage. The theoretical literature on endogenous growth has concentrated on highly stylized models in order to identify the various channels through which optimizing behaviour may give rise to economic growth, and the empirical literature has yet to establish which mechanisms are most relevant empirically.

Meanwhile, the incorporation of dynamic effects into applied trade models has focused mainly on comparison of steady states, abstracting from transition paths. Considerable effort appears necessary to bridge the gap between these simple stylized steady-state models and large scale applications involving transitional dynamics well outside the region of steady-state equilibria. Given the current level of understanding of trade and growth linkages, specifying the transition process based on classical growth theory would appear to be a practical and relevant area for current research as a complement to endogenous growth theory. This paper has shown that focusing on the steady state involves suppressing crucial aspects of the dynamic story, particularly for developing countries. Trade policy reforms can spur growth, if not permanently then at least temporarily, and more so the further away a country is from its steady state. Thus, the impact of policy reforms depends importantly on the initial state of development, a point that has been largely overlooked in the applied modelling literature.

Notes

The views expressed in this paper are strictly those of the authors and are not meant to represent those of any institution with which they are or have been affiliated, including the International Monetary Fund and the World Trade Organization.

1. At a recent World Bank sponsored conference on the Uruguay Round and developing countries, documented in Martin and Winters (1995), several of the efforts to assess capital accumulation effects of the Round involved implicit steady-state assumptions, including Francois, McDonald, and Nordström (1995).
2. For a thorough review, see Edwards (1993).
3. Pritchett (1993) reviews some commonly used indexes and reaches the disconcerting conclusion that the correlation between them is low. Also, a country may choose to liberalize when general economic conditions are good, so that the direction of causation underlying the positive cross-country correlation between trade liberalization and economic growth is unclear.
4. Some studies, such as Edwards (1992) and Lee (1993), have attempted to use endogenous growth models as a guide to their empirical work.
5. The data for 1986–92 are from IMF (1993), Chapter VI.
6. However, there is some evidence, based on a broader set of countries, that suggests that the trade–growth link may be stronger for medium-income countries than for low-income countries (see, for instance, Michaely (1977) and Ram (1985)). Nevertheless, the stronger link found for medium-income countries might simply reflect a more consistent set of economic policies in medium-income countries, and not an inherently stronger trade–growth linkage.
7. Note that it does not matter whether trade is defined as exports, imports, or the sum. This leads Levine and Renelt to conclude that 'studies that use export indicators should not be interpreted as studying the relationship between growth and exports per se but rather as studying the relation between growth and trade defined more broadly' (1992: 959).

8. These results should be viewed with some caution because firm-level rather than plant-level data were used, and because significant spillover effects were detected only when the effects of production experience on a firm's costs were misspecified. Notwithstanding these caveats, these results suggest that it might be reasonable as a starting point for modellers to specify learning spillovers along the lines of Irwin and Klenow's specification, assuming that marginal cost is a semi-logarithmic function of production experience, with production experience equal to cumulative firm output plus world cumulative output (net of the firm's output) multiplied by a constant (in the neighbourhood of 0.2 to 0.3 in Irwin and Klenow's sample).

9. Regressions using a cross-country data set for a large number of countries over the 1970–85 period were reported in Backus et al. (1992).

10. t_ω is solved from the following expression: $\ln y^*(t) - \ln y(t) = (1 - \omega)[\ln y^*(0) - \ln y(0)]$.

11. In the limit, $k(0) \rightarrow k^*$, t_ω approaches $t_\omega = -\ln(1-\omega)/(1-\alpha)(n + g + \delta)$. As we rarely know how far the economy is from steady state, this formula can be used as a first approximation of convergence time. For example, the time it takes for half the initial gap to be closed, $t_\omega = \ln(0.5)/(1-\alpha)(n + g + \delta)$, is 10.4 years if α is equal to 1/3 and $(n + g + \delta)$ is equal to 0.1.

12. The undiscounted medium-run bonus of the policy reform is equal in the limit as time approaches infinity.

13. Indeed, the current model specification does not allow comparison of intertemporal welfare in the context of intertemporal maximization, because such a process has not been modelled. The present analysis, with classical savings behaviour, is similar in some ways to the reduced-form structure of simple variations of overlapping-generations macro models with relatively inflexible savings rates. The extension to the case of an infinite horizon framework with endogenous savings, while straightforward in principle, is beyond the scope of this paper.

References

Aghion, Philippe and Peter Howitt (1992), 'A Model of Growth through Creative Destruction', *Econometrica* 60(2): 323–51.

Alam, S. (1991), 'Trade Orientation and Macroeconomic Performance in LDCs: An Empirical Study', *Economic Development and Cultural Change* 39(4): 839–48.

Backus, David K., Patrick J. Kehoe, and Timothy J. Kehoe (1992), 'In Search of Scale Effects in Trade and Growth', *Journal of Economic Theory* 58: 377–409.

Balassa, Bela (1985), 'Exports, Policy Choices, and Economic Growth in Developing Countries after the 1973 Oil Shock', *Journal of Development Economics* 18(2): 23–35.

Baldwin, Richard E. (1989), 'The Growth Effects of 1992', *Economic Policy* 9(2): 247–81.

    (1992), 'Measurable Dynamic Gains from Trade', *Journal of Political Economy* 100(1): 162–74.

Baldwin, Richard E. and Elena Seghezza (1996), 'Testing for Trade-Induced Investment-Led Growth', CEPR Working Paper No. 1331, February.

Barro, Robert J. (1991), 'Economic Growth in a Cross Section of Countries', *Quarterly Journal of Economics* 106(2): 407–44.
Bhagwati, Jagdish (1978), *Anatomy and Consequences of Exchange Control Regimes*. Cambridge, Mass.: Ballinger Publishing Co. for the National Bureau of Economic Research.
Coe, David T. and Elhanan Helpman (1993), 'International R&D Spillovers', IMF Working Paper WP/93/84, Washington, D.C., November.
Coe, David T., Elhanan Helpman, and Alexander W. Hoffmaister (1995), 'North–South R&D Spillovers', CEPR Working Paper No. 1033, February.
Deardorff, Alan V. (1971), 'Growth Paths in the Solow Neoclassical Growth Model', *Quarterly Journal of Economics* 84: 134–39.
Dollar, David (1992), 'Outward-Oriented Developing Economies Really Do Grow More Rapidly: Evidence from 95 LDCs, 1976–1985', *Economic Development and Cultural Change* 40: 523–44.
Easterly, William (1993), 'How Much Do Distortions Affect Growth?' *Journal of Monetary Economics* 32: 1–26.
Edwards, Sebastian (1992), 'Trade Orientation, Distortions, and Growth in Developing Countries', *Journal of Development Economics* 39(1): 31–57.
(1993), 'Openness, Trade Liberalization, and Growth in Developing Countries', *Journal of Economic Literature* 31(3): 1358–93.
Feder, Gershon (1983), 'On Exports and Economic Growth', *Journal of Development Economics* 12(1/2): 59–73.
Francois, Joseph F., Bradley McDonald, and Håkan Nordström (1995), 'Assessing the Uruguay Round'. In W. Martin and L. Alan Winters (eds.), *The Uruguay Round and Developing Economies*. World Bank Discussion Paper No. 307. Washington D.C.: World Bank, pp. 215–84.
Goldin, I., O. Knudsen, and D. van der Mensbrugghe (1993), *Trade Liberalization: Global Economic Implications*. Paris: OECD Development Centre.
Grossman, Gene M. and Elhanan Helpman (1991a), 'Quality Ladders in the Theory of Growth', *Review of Economic Studies* 58: 43–61.
(1991b), *Innovation and Growth in the Global Economy*. Cambridge, Mass.: MIT Press.
Haaland, Jan and T. C. Tollefson (1994), 'The Uruguay Round and Trade in Manufactures and Services. General Equilibrium Simulations of Production, Trade and Welfare Effects of Liberalization', CEPR Discussion Paper No. 1008.
Harrison, Anne (1993), 'Openness and Growth: A Time-Series, Cross-Country Analysis for Developing Countries', manuscript, World Bank, October.
Harrison, Glenn, Thomas Rutherford, and David Tarr (1995), 'Quantifying the Uruguay Round'. In W. Martin and L. Alan Winters (eds.), *The Uruguay Round and Developing Economies*. World Bank Discussion Paper No. 307. Washington D.C.: World Bank, pp. 215–84.
Helleiner, Gerald K. (1986), 'Outward Orientation, Import Instability and African Economic Growth: An Empirical Investigation'. In Sanjaya Lall and Frances Stewart (eds.), *Theory and Reality in Development: Essays in Honour of Paul Streeten*. London: Macmillan.
Ho, M. S. and D. W. Jorgenson (1994), 'Trade Policy and U.S. Economic Growth', *Journal of Policy Modeling* 16(2): 119–46.
IMF (1993), *World Economic Outlook*. World Economic and Financial Surveys. Washington D.C.: International Monetary Fund, May.

Irwin, Douglas A. and Peter J. Klenow (1994), 'Learning-by-Doing Spillovers in the Semiconductor Industry', *Journal of Political Economy* 102(6): 1200–27.

Jones, Charles I. (1995), 'Time Series Tests of Endogenous Growth Models', *Quarterly Journal of Economics* 110(2): 495–525.

Kehoe, Timothy J. (1994), 'Toward a Dynamic General Equilibrium Model of North American Trade'. In Joseph F. Francois and Clinton R. Shiells (eds.), *Modeling Trade Policy: Applied General Equilibrium Models of North American Free Trade*. New York: Cambridge University Press.

Kornai, Janos (1992), *The Socialist System: The Political Economy of Communism*. Princeton, N.J.: Princeton University Press.

Krueger, Anne O. (1978), *Foreign Trade Regimes and Economic Development: Liberalization Attempts and Consequences*. Cambridge, Mass.: Ballinger Publishing Co. for the National Bureau of Economic Research.

Krugman, Paul R. (1988), 'Endogenous Innovations, International Trade and Growth', Working Paper presented at SUNY-Buffalo Conference on Development.

Leamer, Edward E. (1988), 'Measures of Openness'. In Robert E. Baldwin (ed.), *Trade Policy and Empirical Analysis*. Chicago: University of Chicago Press.

Lee, Jong-Wha (1993), 'International Trade, Distortions, and Long-Run Economic Growth', *IMF Staff Papers* 40(2): 299–328.

Levine, Ross and David Renelt (1992), 'A Sensitivity Analysis of Cross-Country Growth Regressions', *American Economic Review* 82(4): 942–63.

Lewis, W. Arthur (1955), *The Theory of Economic Growth*. London: Allen & Unwin.

Lucas, Robert E., Jr. (1993), 'Making a Miracle', *Econometrica* 61: 251–72.

Mankiw, N. G., D. Romer, and D. N. Weil (1992), 'A Contribution to the Empirics of Economic Growth', *Quarterly Journal of Economics* 2: 407–37.

Martin, W. and L. Alan Winters, eds. (1995), *The Uruguay Round and the Developing Economies*. World Bank Discussion Paper No. 307. Washington D.C.: World Bank.

Matin, K. (1992), 'Openness and Economic Performance in Sub-Saharan Africa: Evidence from Time-Series Cross-Country Analysis', WPS 1025, World Bank, November.

Michaely, Michael (1977), 'Exports and Growth: An Empirical Investigation', *Journal of Development Economics* 4(1): 49–53.

Pritchett, Lant (1993), 'Measuring Outward Orientation in LDCs: Can It Be Done?' Manuscript, World Bank, October.

Ram, Rati (1985), 'Exports and Economic Growth: Some Additional Evidence', *Economic Development and Cultural Change* 33(2): 415–25.

Rebelo, S. (1987), 'Long-Run Policy Analysis and Long-Run Growth', University of Rochester, manuscript.

Romer, Paul M. (1987), 'Growth Based on Increasing Returns Due to Specialization', *American Economic Review* 77(2): 56–62.

(1990), 'Endogenous Technological Change', *Journal of Political Economy* 98(5): S71–S103.

Sachs, Jeffrey D. and Andrew Warner (1995), 'Economic Reform and the Process of Global Integration', *Brookings Papers on Economic Activity* 1: 1–118.

Solow, Robert M. (1956), 'A Contribution to the Theory of Economic Growth', *Quarterly Journal of Economics* 70: 65–94.

Summers, L. and B. Heston (1991), 'The Penn World Table (Mark 5): An

Expanded Set of International Comparisons, 1950–1988', *Quarterly Journal of Economics* 2.

Syrquin, Moshe and Hollis Chenery (1989), 'Three Decades of Industrialization', *World Bank Economic Review* 3: 145–81.

World Bank (1987), *World Development Report 1987*. New York: Oxford University Press for the World Bank.

Discussion

RICHARD E. BALDWIN

Francois, Nordström, and Shiells have given us a very nice paper that reviews the empirical literature and growth (showing that there is a great deal of evidence supporting a positive correlation between openness and growth), reviews the treatment of accumulation (growth) effects in computable general equilibrium models, and then goes on to show theoretically that standard estimates of trade's impact on the present value of output suffer several shortcomings. In particular, they argue that a particular trade liberalization will have a much larger impact on an economy that is initially far from its steady state. Since developing countries are typically further from their long-run equilibriums than are developed nations, this important result suggests that the growth effects of trade liberalization are even more important for poor countries. I concentrate my comments on their last point.

Francois, Nordström, and Shiells provide a very neat and clever closed-form solution for the time-path of output in a Solow growth model (i.e. one-good economy, neoclassical production function, constant savings rate) in their expression (5). The authors' point about the differential impact of trade policy on rich and poor countries is a statement about the proportional increase in the level of output at any point in time (short of the long run). That is, the proportional impact on per capita output dy/y due to a proportional increase in allocation efficiency $dA(0)/A(0)$ is:

$$\frac{dy/y}{dA(0)/A(0)} = 1 - \frac{\alpha e^{n+g+\delta}}{1 - e^{n+g+\delta} \, GAP}; \quad GAP \equiv \frac{k^{*1-\alpha} - k(0)^{1-\alpha}}{k(0)^{1-\alpha}} \quad (1)$$

so clearly the proportional impact (left-hand side) is increasing in the initial gap between the starting level of k, $k(0)$, and its steady-state level, k^*.

As a short paragraph at the end of the paper, the authors provide a word of caution about interpreting these results. Basically they say that income effects may differ substantially from welfare effects when consumers optimize over time. Here I would like to amplify this comment by working out the welfare effects when consumers do optimize over time.

Consider an economy that is very much like that of Francois, Nordström, and Shiells (one good, neoclassical per capita production function $y = f(k,\tau) = A(t)k(t)^{\alpha}$, where $k(t)$ is defined as $K(t)^{\alpha}L^{\alpha}$). To focus on welfare issues I introduce one complication and two simplifications. The complication is to allow consumers to maximize utility over time, where their utility is $U = \sigma/(1 - \sigma)_0 \int^{\infty} e^{-\rho t}c(t)^{1-1/\sigma}dt$. The simplifications are to ignore exogenous growth so that $A(t) = A(0)$ (for all t), and to assume that the nation is initially in steady state.

Now suppose the trade liberalization $d\tau < 0$ improves allocation efficiency. This will, in turn, raise the steady-state output path owing to a direct effect on the production $dA(0)$ and indirectly by inducing capital formation, i.e. $dk/d\tau > 0$. The impact on utility is $dU/d\tau = (\bar{c})^{-1/\sigma}_0 \int^{\infty} e^{-\rho t}c_{\tau}(t)dt$ where $c_{\tau}(t)$ gives the change in the consumption time-path at any point in time. Thus we see that the welfare impact depends on the Laplace transform of the induced change in the consumption path. More generally, consider an arbitrary liberalization described by $\tau = \tau(0)[1 + \varepsilon h(t)]$, where $h(t)$ is an arbitrary function (usually a step function). The evolution of the dynamic system is described by two non-linear differential equations: the Euler equation $\dot{c}/c = \sigma(\tau - \rho)$ and k's law of motion, which is $\dot{k} = y - c$. In matrix form, this is:

$$\begin{pmatrix} \dot{c}_{\varepsilon} \\ \dot{k}_{\varepsilon} \end{pmatrix} = J \begin{pmatrix} c_{\varepsilon} \\ k_{\varepsilon} \end{pmatrix} + \begin{pmatrix} \tau \bar{c} h(t) r_{\tau} \\ \tau h(t) f_{\tau} \end{pmatrix} \tag{2}$$

Solving this system (see Baldwin (1992) for details), we get an algebraic system in Laplace transform. Evaluating this for the step function h (i.e. $h(t) = 1$ for all $t > 0$):

$$\frac{dU/\bar{U}}{d\tau/\tau} \bigg/ \frac{dU/\bar{U}}{dc/c} = \left[\frac{1}{\rho}\left(\frac{dy/y}{d\tau/\tau}\right)\right] + \left[\left(\frac{\rho - f_k}{\bar{c}\sigma r_k + \rho^2 - \rho f_k}\right)\sigma\left(\frac{1}{\rho} - \frac{1}{\mu}\right)\left(\frac{dr/\bar{r}}{d\tau/\bar{\tau}}\right)\right] \tag{3}$$

where μ is the positive eigenvalue of J, r is the rental rate on capital, and other terms follow standard notation. The first term is the present value of the static gain. The second term is the welfare impact of the induced capital formation effect. Note that if the social rate of return, f_k, equals the market rate of return ρ, then the induced capital formation has *no* impact on welfare. Intuition for this stark result is a straightforward application of the envelope theorem. If consumers are maximizing on their savings behaviour, there are no distortions, and the economy is in steady state, then it must be that consumers are just indifferent to having a little more capital at the cost of a little more forgone consumption (savings).

What this set-piece of maths shows is that it is quite likely that the present value on output (the focus of the authors' study) almost surely overestimates the welfare effects. After all, consumers must forgo consumption today in order to build up the capital stock. The present value of the extra income that this produces tends to be equal to the present value of the forgone consumption due to the investment decision. Unfortunately, in frameworks (such as the Solow model) where one ignores the intertemporal dimension of the investment/savings decision, this point cannot be made formally.

Reference

Baldwin, R. E. (1992), 'Measurable Dynamic Gains from Trade', *Journal of Political Economy* 100(1), 162–74.

3 Putting growth effects in computable equilibrium trade models

RICHARD E. BALDWIN
and RIKARD FORSLID

1 Introduction

Many applied commercial policy analyses measure only the static effects of trade liberalization, despite the fact that most economists believe that the greatest benefits lie in the growth effects. Putting growth effects into computable trade models is, therefore, an important subject. This paper considers some of the analytical and practical issues involved in doing so. Before turning to the analysis, however, we set the stage by (1) briefly reviewing the basic logic of trade and growth, and (2) briefly reviewing the evolution of computable general equilibrium (CGE) models in order to put accumulation effects into perspective.

1.1 The logic of growth

If a nation's labour force is to produce more year after year, the economy must provide the workforce with more 'tools' year after year. Here 'tools' is meant in the broadest possible sense, i.e. of any type of capital, and we must distinguish three categories: physical capital (machines, etc.), human capital (skills, training, education, etc.), and knowledge capital (technology). With capital thus defined, it is plain that capital accumulation is what drives growth. Now capital accumulation is – for the most part – driven by private profit-motivated investment by firms and individuals. Consequently, the key to determining an economy's rate of growth is to study the costs and benefits of investment in human, physical, and knowledge capital.

This sequence of rather obvious statements directs our attention to the only way that trade liberalization can affect growth, namely via its impact on investment in machines, skills and technology. Some policies directly alter the rate of investment but, for the most part, they act on growth by changing the incentives facing private agents. Although all this is quite clear, it is important to make these points given the confusion that the term 'export-led growth' has created. At best, the notion of export-led growth is a leftover from naive Keynesianism; at worst, it is used as a catch-all phase that removes the need for serious thought. More recently, the notion of growth due to 'outward orientation' has added to the confusion.

1.2   Evolution of CGE models

The sophistication of computable equilibrium models has greatly advanced over the past three decades. Yet because CGE models cannot rely on informal reasoning (computer code requires precise mathematical formulations), advancement of CGE models is constrained by theoretical developments. For instance, early trade theorists could not handle many real-world considerations such as imperfect competition, increasing returns, and endogenous factor supplies. First-generation theoretical trade models (Ricardian, Heckscher–Ohlin, etc.) therefore assumed away these facets of reality and first-generation CGE models (e.g. Deardorff and Stern 1986) followed suit. Yet because these models captured only a narrow range of the true economic effects of trade policy, they found that trade liberalization led to very small economic effects. Deardorff and Stern (1986: 230), for example, state: 'We have consistently found, as have other investigators, that tariff reductions such as those of the Tokyo Round will have effects on trade, employment, and welfare that are so small as to be negligible among all the other changes that continually occur in the world.' This deficiency of first-generation CGE models prompted researchers to search for ways to expand the range of economic effects captured by CGE models.

Following theoretical advances in the 1980s, researchers developed a second generation of CGE models that allowed for imperfect competition and scale economies. Harris and Cox (1982) was the seminal attempt, but it adopted a form of imperfect competition (Eastman–Stykolt pricing) that is not well founded theoretically. Smith and Venables' (1988) was perhaps the first second-generation computable simulation model to be based on a model that was game-theoretically sound. That model, however, was partial equilibrium. The inclusion of game-theoretically-sound imperfect competition into a CGE model came only with Haaland and Norman (1992) and Gasiorek et al. (1992). Second-generation CGE models have supplanted first-generation models because they permitted researchers to capture all of the first-generation effects plus a significant range of new effects (especially scale effects). Not surprisingly, second-generation models typically find that trade liberalization has a much larger economic effect than did first-generation models. Indeed, it is not uncommon for a second-generation model to produce numbers that are ten times larger than those of first-generation models.

The third generation of CGE models goes beyond investigation of the allocation (i.e. static) effects by allowing trade policy to affect factor supplies – the physical capital stock in particular. The link between trade liberalization and the capital stock was first demonstrated by Ricardo and explored more thoroughly by Smith (1984) and Findlay (1984). In the context of trade policy analysis, induced capital formation was popularized by Baldwin (1989, 1992a) and is now routinely included in CGE models. Third-generation models generally find trade liberalization to have larger economic effects than second-generation models. This is not surprising, because the most advanced third-generation models capture all of the second-generation effects plus induced capital-formation effects.

A fourth generation of CGE models, which allow for trade policy to affect long-run growth, is just beginning to emerge. The third- and fourth-generation models, however, focus on two very different growth channels. Third-generation models concentrate on induced capital formation, i.e. trade-induced investment-led growth. Fourth-generation models, however, focus on the accumulation of knowledge capital, i.e. trade-induced productivity-led growth.

The rest of the paper is organized in five sections. Sections 2 and 3 consider some analytical aspects of medium-run and long-run trade and growth models (i.e. investment-led and technology-led growth). Section 4 considers a number of practical considerations that must be addressed in fourth-generation models. Section 5 presents a simple fourth-generation CGE model that is calibrated to notional data. Section 6 contains our concluding comments.

2   Analytical considerations

The theoretical literature on trade and growth developed in two distinct phases. In the 1970s, trade economists explored the neoclassical growth theory in the context of the Heckscher–Ohlin trade model. In the late 1980s and early 1990s, trade economists explored endogenous growth theory in the context of imperfect competition trade models. This evolution missed an important phase as far as CGE modellers are concerned, namely old growth theory in new trade models.

This is an important omission for two main reasons. First, trade liberalization has been very much a win–win proposition as far as growth is concerned, but the old-growth/old-trade literature predicts that it should have been a win–lose growth proposition. Basically, a medium-run growth effect arises in the neoclassical growth theory for any policy change that boosts the return to investment (this raises the steady-state capital/labour ratio and stimulates above-normal capital accumulation and above-normal growth in the transition to the new steady state). According to the Heckscher–Ohlin model, global trade liberalization raises capital's rental rate and the return to investment in nations that export capital-intensive goods, but lowers it in countries that import capital-intensive goods. In short, the massive post-war liberalization of trade among industrialized nations should have stimulated investment in some and depressed it in others. This theoretical prediction contradicts the econometric evidence of, *inter alia*, Barro (1991), Levine and Renelt (1992), and Baldwin and Seghezza (1996).

Additionally, the old trade models are intrinsically inappropriate because they cannot explain intra-industry trade without resorting to the ad hoc Armington assumption. Not only is much of world trade among rich countries and consists of intra-industry trade, it is exactly this type of trade that has been the focus of post-war trade liberalization. Consequently, any reasonable applied trade model must work with the new trade theory. However, once one wishes to put medium-run growth effects into such a model, the modeller inevitably finds himself or herself in the theoretically uncharted world of old-growth/new-trade models.

The next subsection lays out the basic logic of old growth theory in a new trade model. It is, however, far from complete for the simple reason that almost no theoretical work has been done on this area. The presentation here draws heavily on Baldwin and Seghezza (1996).

2.1 A neoclassical model with imperfect competition

Consider a world with two identical countries (H and F) each with two factors (labour, L, and physical capital, K) and three sectors (X, Z, and I). The L supply is fixed, but K is the accumulated output of the I (investment goods) sector. The X sector (think of this as the manufactured goods sector) is modelled as the Flam–Helpman version of the Dixit–Stiglitz monopolistic competition model (see Flam and Helpman (1987) and Dixit and Stiglitz (1977)).[1] Namely, production of each X variety requires one unit of K (regardless of output) plus 'a' units of labour per unit of output (think of a unit of capital as a design for a unique variety of X embedded in the machines needed to manufacture it). Thus, $\pi + wax$ is the cost function where w and π are the factor rewards of L and K. Z (think of it as services) is a homogeneous good produced from labour according to the cost function wbZ. We chose units such that $a = b = 1$. For convenience we refer to this as the Flam–Helpman–Ramsey model.[2]

With ρ as the time preference parameter, representative consumer preferences are:

$$\int_{t=0}^{\infty} e^{\rho t}\ln C_t dt, \quad C_t = \left(C_X^{(1-\frac{1}{\theta})} + \Gamma C_Z^{(1-\frac{1}{\theta})}\right)^{\frac{1}{(1-1/\theta)}}, \quad C_X = \left(\Sigma_i \, c_i^{(1-\frac{1}{\sigma})}\right)^{\frac{1}{(1-1/\sigma)}} \quad (1)$$

where θ and σ are elasticities of substitution between (respectively) the X composite and Z, and among X varieties, and Γ is a binary (0 or 1) parameter that we use to 'turn off' the Z sector in simplified versions of the model. Full employment in both countries implies that $2K$ is the number of varieties. Total national income Y equals $wL + \pi K$. Note that the upper-tier utility function limits to Cobb–Douglas as θ approaches 1.

Utility optimization yields standard CES demand functions for X varieties and a demand function for Z, namely:

$$c_j = \frac{p_j^{-\sigma}\mu E}{\Sigma_{i=1}^{2K}p_i^{1-\sigma}}, \qquad Z = \frac{(1-\mu)E}{p_Z} \tag{2}$$

where μ equals $[1 + (P_X/p_Z)^{\theta-1}]^{-1}$ and E is consumer expenditure. Notice that the optimal expenditure share on X (denoted as μ) is a decreasing function of P_X/p_Z, where P_X and p_Z are the standard constant elasticity of substitution (CES) price index and the price of Z respectively. Optimization also yields the standard Euler equation $\dot{E}/E = r - \rho$, where r is the rate of return on savings.

Calculations are facilitated by three special features of Dixit–Stiglitz monopolistic competition. Each X-sector firm: (i) produces a unique variety, (ii) engages in 'mill pricing' where $w/(1 - 1/\sigma)$ is the local market price and τ is fully passed on to foreign consumers, and (iii) earns operating profit equal to $(\Sigma_i s^i \mu E^i)/\sigma$, where s^i is the firm's share of market-i expenditure.[3] Given capital's variety specificity, capital's reward is the Ricardian surplus, i.e. operating profit. Also if X-sector trade is balanced (obviously true with symmetrical nations and/or Z and K non-traded), each country's consumer expenditure on X equals the producer value of output, thus, from (iii):

$$\pi = \mu E \, / \, \sigma K \tag{3}$$

since symmetry means $\Sigma_i s^i = 1/K$.[4]

The perfectly competitive I sector employs L to produce new capital under constant returns and perfect competition. The I-sector marginal cost and production functions are:

$$F = \beta w, \quad Q_k = \frac{wL_I}{F}, \quad Q_K = \dot{K} + \delta K, \tag{4}$$

where F is marginal cost, β is the unit labour requirement, Q_K is the flow output of K (gross investment), L_I is the L employed, and $\dot{K} = Q_K - \delta K$ assuming a constant rate of depreciation δ. Owing to perfect competition, the price of capital (denoted as P_K) equals F.

2.1.1 Transforming the system into L_I and K space

At some level of abstraction, all growth models are two-sector models, with one sector producing final goods and the other sector producing capital. We denote the capital-producing sector the I sector – the I stands for investment goods (in neoclassical models) or innovations (in endogenous growth models). Now, as it turns out, it is very useful to think of the steady state in terms of the division of primary resources between the I sector and the final goods sectors. The reason is simple. If a particular policy is to have a positive medium-run growth effect, then it must raise the steady-state K. This, in turn, requires a rise in employment in the capital-formation sector (in steady state $L_I = \delta F \bar{K}$, where $\bar{K}$ is the steady-state K) and – because L is fixed – a drop in manufacturing employment. Thus, instead of asking: 'How will a particular policy change affect the transitional growth rate in a dynamic model?' we could ask: 'How will the policy change affect sectoral employment in a static model?' Because trade economists have very strong intuition about the answers to the latter question, it is probably simpler to analyse policy in terms of its long-run effects on resource allocation.

This trick is powerful but it is deceptively obvious, so we restate it in other terms.[5] In the above old-growth/new-trade model, one sector produces a flow of a composite final good with an increasing returns production function and the other sector produces a flow of new capital with a constant returns production function. Although the intertemporal dimension of the model is not trivial – the flow of new capital accumulates into the K stock that is employed in the final good sector – the steady state is identical to the static models of the 'new' trade theory, taking K as the number of firms. The impact of trade policy in this sort of two-sector economy is well-trodden ground for trade economists. Consequently, understanding the medium-run growth effects of trade policies should be a simple matter.

More carefully, if the system is stable, then a policy change will lead to a positive medium-run growth effect if and only if the policy raises the steady-state K. Moreover, a policy can raise K if and only if at least one of the following is true: the policy raises L_I, or the policy raises the primary productivity of labour in the capital goods sector, i.e. β. Because trade policies are not traditionally thought of as altering production functions, the latter case will not generally be relevant to medium-run growth analysis. Consequently, tracing out the employment effects of a trade policy is sufficient for tracing out its growth effects.

To follow up on this intuition, we take real investment, L_I, and K as the state variables, despite the fact that the traditional approach is to take E and K as the state variables (e.g. see Barro and Sala-i-Martin (1995: Ch. 2)). Fortunately, a simple change of state variables eliminates E from the Euler equation. With I as nominal investment, nominal factor income Y equals $E + I$, where I equals wL_I (owing to zero I-sector profits, the value of the sector's output equals the value of inputs and, in equilibrium, all of the sector's output is purchased for investment). We have, therefore, that $E = wL + K\pi - wL_I$, and, using $\pi = \mu E/K\sigma$:

$$E = \frac{w(L - L_I)}{1 - \mu/\sigma}. \tag{5}$$

Taking L as the numeraire and real investment (namely L_I) as a state variable, we see $\dot{E} = 0$ in steady state because $\dot{L}_I = 0$ by definition of steady state. From the Euler equation, $\dot{E} = 0$ implies $r = \rho$. This facilitates calculation of the present value of introducing a new variety.

2.1.2   Steady-state analysis with Tobin's q

Given that the rate of investment is the key to growth, it seems natural to appeal to Tobin's q-theory of investment in a general equilibrium setting (Tobin 1969). Tobin's q-theory of investment focuses on the ratio of a firm's stock market value to the replacement cost of its capital – the stock market value being the present value of the π income stream (net of maintenance costs) and its replacement cost being P_K. Tobin's famous $q = 1$ condition determines the steady-state capital stock or, equivalently given (4), the steady-state rate of real investment L_I. Labelling the stock market value of a unit of capital as J and noting that π is time invariant in steady state, we have $J = (\pi - \delta)/\rho$.[6] By definition, $q = J/P_K$, so, using the above expressions, we know that in steady state:

$$q = \frac{J}{F} = \left[\frac{\mu(L - L_I)}{L_I(\sigma - \mu)} - \frac{1}{F}\right]\frac{\sigma}{\rho} = \left[\frac{\mu(L - \delta FK)}{K(\sigma - \mu)} - \delta\right]\frac{1}{\rho F}. \qquad (6)$$

Clearly, in steady state, Tobin's q is a simple monotonically decreasing function of L_I or alternatively of K. The $q = 1$ condition therefore pins down the steady-state L_I (denoted as $\bar{L}_I$) and the steady-state K. Specifically:

$$\bar{L}_I = \frac{\mu \delta F L}{(\rho F + \delta)(\sigma - \mu) + \delta \mu F}, \quad \bar{K} = \frac{\mu L}{(\rho F + \delta)(\sigma - \mu) + \mu \delta F}. \qquad (7)$$

It is worth noting that it is I- and X-sector free entry that forces q to unity at all times. To see this, observe that, with free entry, X firms create new varieties up to the point where the present value of doing so (viz. J) equals the one-time cost (viz. P_K). Consequently, an I firm producing a flow of Q_{Ki} machines earns instantaneous pure profits:

$$(J - F)Q_i = (q - 1)L_{Ii}, \qquad (8)$$

where L_{Ii} is the firm's employment and the second expression follows from (4) and the definition of q. With perfect competition, I-sector employment jumps to the point where $\Sigma_i L_{Ii}$ is always such that $q = 1$. This shows that $q - 1$ is the shadow value of moving resources into the I sector. Tobin's q is an insightful approach exactly because $q - 1$ is the shadow value of moving more resources into capital accumulation. Trade liberalizations that create an incipient rise in a country's q will draw more resources to the accumulation sector until q is restored to unity. This results in investment-led growth during transition to the new steady state.

2.1.3   The focus on steady-state analysis

Characterizing the transitional dynamics of this model involves well-known techniques (see the appendix at the end of the paper). The only germane result from such a characterization, however, is that the transition between steady states takes a long time (because consumers smooth consumption). For this reason, the paper focuses on comparative steady-state analysis, using the fact that an increase in the steady-state K will generate decades of above-normal growth (in this model the steady-state growth rate is zero).

2.2   Trade and endogenous growth

The early new-growth/new-trade literature (e.g. the seminal work by Grossman and Helpman (1991)) made important contributions to the study of trade and growth. It has, none the less, two big shortcomings as far as CGE modellers are concerned.

First, because CGE models and their results cannot be tested with standard statistical procedures, modellers must be quite confident that the economic structures they assume do in fact reflect reality. In this light, it is quite disturbing that there is a growing body of econometric evidence contradicting the assumptions and predictions of the early trade and endogenous growth models. Consider the econometric evidence on the simple new growth models employed in the early literature. Jones (1995) establishes that US growth (and that of many other advanced industrial economies) has been stationary since the industrial revolution. He then establishes that measures of R&D inputs – such as the number of scientists and engineers engaged in R&D, or real R&D expenditure – are stochastically trending upwards. Consequently, he rejects the simple linear production function for knowledge that is at the very heart of the early new-growth/new-trade literature. As concerns trade and growth, the fundamental contradiction is that productivity in rich nations has proceeded at a steady (or even falling) rate in the post-war period, whereas global openness has trended upwards. Consequently, openness and productivity-led growth cannot be monotonically linked as in the new-growth/new-trade literature. Another way to put this is to focus on the calibration of CGE growth models. If modellers wish to fit actual time-series data in OECD countries, they must find a way to account for continual trade liberalization in the face of approximately constant growth.

Next consider the econometric evidence on the theoretical predictions of new-growth/new-trade literature. Many cross-country econometric studies – e.g. Levine and Renelt (1992) and Baldwin and Seghezza (1996) – show that trade liberalization seems to promote growth only by promoting investment. That is, when investment rates are controlled for, openness has no additional impact on growth. This questions the main prediction of the new-growth/new-trade literature – that trade affects growth by influencing the rate of productivity growth. It seems, therefore, that trade-induced productivity-led growth is not empirically important enough to show up in cross-country data.

The second major drawback is that the early new-growth/new-trade literature did not focus on marginal trade policy analysis. That is, most of this literature considered either autarky-to-free-trade liberalizations, or marginal protection in the neighbourhood of free trade. Of course, this theoretical approach is quite convenient analytically because autarky and free trade both involve closed economies. Applied policy analysts, however, are unable to adopt such tactics because their aim is to understand the impact of actual liberalizations.

Despite these shortcomings, it is important to begin work on CGE models that allow for endogenous growth. If nothing else, these efforts should point out the directions in which theoretical models need to be developed in order to explain reality better. However, given the lack of econometric evidence on the link between trade liberalization and productivity-led growth, the numerical results of these models may not be credible for quite a while.

The next subsection presents the fundamental logic of trade and endogenous growth models. In doing so, it points out that the new growth models produce steady-state growth only for certain fairly restrictive functional forms. This aspect has important ramifications for CGE modellers. In short, if one wants to have a model that produces a constant steady-state growth rate that is endogenously determined, then one must accept some fairly draconian restrictions on functional forms. The section draws heavily on Baldwin and Forslid (1996).

2.2.1 A simplified Romer model of production innovation

As it turns out, it is extremely simple to turn the section 2.1 model into an endogenous growth model. Growth in the section 2.1 model ceased because the return to capital was diminishing in K, yet the cost of new capital was not. The trick that drives Romer's famous 1990 model is to assume that the capital goods sector is subject to knife-edge external economies of scale.[7] As a result of these assumed externalities, the cost of capital falls at exactly the same rate as the return to capital. In other words, K drops out of Tobin's q. Although K drops out of q, the level of real investment (or alternatively of the growth rate of K, as we shall see below) affects q in two ways. First the higher is L_I, the lower is E and so the lower is π. Also, higher L_I corresponds to faster growth and, since this implies that marginal utility declines faster, savers/consumers discount future π at a higher rate.

More specifically, the I sector employs L to produce new capital under constant private returns and perfect competition. Following Lucas (1988) and Romer (1990), external scale economies stemming from national capital stocks of a very specific type are assumed. Namely, the I-sector production and marginal cost functions are:

$$\dot{K} = L_I(K + \lambda K^*), \quad F = w/(K + \lambda K^*), \tag{9}$$

where L_I is sectoral employment, F is the average (and marginal) cost of $K, 0 \leq \lambda \leq 1$ and K^* is the non-local capital stock. We have also assumed $\delta = 0$ to simplify the algebra.

Notice that, even though no K is employed in the I sector, the national

K stocks enter the production and marginal cost functions. A variety of well-known stories are used to justify these externalities; the most convincing ones take K to be knowledge capital (Romer) or human capital (Lucas). The extent to which externalities occur internationally is regulated by the parameter λ ($\lambda = 1$ or 0 indicates perfect or zero international spillovers). From the previous expression:

$$g \equiv \dot{K}/K = L_I(1 + \lambda), \tag{10}$$

where g is the growth rate of K. Note that a constant L_I yields constant capital stock growth. The dual of this is that F falls at the rate of capital stock growth. By perfect competition, F is the supply price (replacement cost) of capital.

Dynamic analysis with Tobin's q
All endogenous growth models, including the simple one presented above, make assumptions such that constant real investment (i.e. constant application of resources to capital-formation L_I in the model) yields constant capital stock growth and therefore constant output growth. It seems natural, therefore, to take real investment as the main state variable. We eliminated E from the Euler equation as before, again take L as numeraire, and the home and foreign L_I's as the state variables. Thus $\dot{E} = 0$ in steady state, so $r = \rho$ in both countries. Observe that in this model all state variables are 'jumpers', so the model is always in steady state.

Baldwin and Forslid (1996) investigate the dynamic system equations in more detail. Here we focus on the steady-state growth rate. The stock market value of a unit of capital, which we call J, is the present value of the π stream, and in steady state:[8]

$$J(t) = \int_{s=t}^{\infty} e^{-r(s-t)} \, \pi(s) \, ds = \frac{\pi(t)}{\rho + g}. \tag{11}$$

To streamline the algebra, we assume that $\Gamma = 0$, so $\mu = 1$. In steady state, q equals unity, so, using $\pi = (L - L_I)/K(\sigma - 1)$ and (9), the home steady-state condition is:

$$q[g] = \frac{\pi/(g + \rho)}{F} = \frac{L(1 + \lambda) - g}{(\sigma - 1)(\rho + g)} = 1. \tag{12}$$

Clearly Tobin's q is a very simple monotonically decreasing function of g. Solving, we have $g = [L(1 + \lambda) + (1 - \sigma)\rho]/\sigma$. Since $g = L_I(1 + \lambda)$, q can alternatively be expressed as a simple function of real investment L_I.

With country asymmetries, the analysis becomes much more complicated (see the appendix in Baldwin and Forslid (1996)) Using an obvious notation, the system has four state variables: the relative wage rate, the relative number of firms, K_F/K_H, and the two real investment variables, L_{IH} and L_{IF}. The evolution of these is described by the two transformed Euler equations, the differential equation for the proportional change in K_F/K_H, and the trade balance condition.

Common steady-state growth rates
As long as $\lambda \neq 0$, this model forces $g_H = g_F$ in steady state. This commonality of steady-state g's is an important feature of all endogenous growth and trade models. (It rules out, for instance, the possibility of beggar-thy-neighbour growth policy.) The commonality of growth rates can be seen intuitively from (9). That expression shows that if K_F/K_H limits to zero – which would happen if $g_H > g_F$ forever – the productivity of foreign L_I grows without bound while that of home L_I falls to unity. These shifts attract labour to the foreign I sector, repel labour from the home I sector, and thereby narrow growth rate differences. Similarly, $g_F \not> g_H$ in steady state.

Note that again it is the absence of pure profits in the I sector that forces q to unity. To see this, note that an I-sector firm producing $\dot{K}_i$ designs per period earns pure profits of:

$$(J - F)\dot{K}_i = (q - 1)L_{Ii} \tag{13}$$

where L_{Ii} is the firm's employment and the second expression follows from (9). Free entry ensures that L_I always jumps to the point where pure profits are eliminated. This also formally shows why $q - 1$ is the shadow value of moving resources into the I sector.

Calculating output growth is simple. Nominal income is constant at $L + \pi K$, because π falls at the rate K rises. Real income rises because the aggregate price index (the standard CES price index) falls with K accumulation. Specifically, P_X equals $K^{-1/(\sigma-1)}$ times $h[\tau]$, where h is increasing in τ, but is time invariant in steady state.[9] Thus real consumption and output grow at $g/(\sigma - 1)$.

3   Illustration of key trade and growth links

This section studies the trade and growth links in the basic old-growth/new-trade model and new-growth/new-trade model introduced above; again it draws heavily on Baldwin and Forslid (1996) and Baldwin and

Seghezza (1996). It is not necessary to address the neoclassical and endogenous growth models separately because the fundamental logic of the links is identical. The only difference is that, in the old-growth/new-trade model, international liberalization can affect growth only by changing the steady-state capital stock. In the endogenous growth model, it changes only the growth rate of capital.

It may be helpful to push this similarity even further. In both models, the steady-state L_I is time invariant, so we could focus entirely on the amount of resources devoted to capital accumulation. In the old growth model, a constant L_I corresponds to a constant K, whereas in the new growth model it corresponds to a constant growth rate of K. Consequently, if the modeller is content to focus on long-run equilibria, the entire model can be programmed as a static model in which the long-run conditions are treated as equilibrium conditions.

In what follows, we trace out the growth effects in a sequence of models. The assumptions of the various models, like controls in an experiment, allow us to focus on the various channels through which trade can affect growth.

3.1   The absence of trade and growth links in simple models

One feature of the early new-growth/new-trade models that has not been widely appreciated is the fact that marginal trade liberalization has no growth effect in the simplest models, even though growth effects do occur when we consider autarky-to-free-trade experiments. Here we go over three simple models in which marginal trade liberalization has the usual level effects but no growth effects. These help us pinpoint the mechanisms that do lead to growth effects.

3.1.1   One primary factor, one final good sector

Inspection of the expression for steady-state q's in the exogenous and endogenous growth models – (6) and (12) – reveals no dependence on τ. Consequently, reciprocal trade liberalization has no growth effect. In fact, since balanced trade in X implies that $\pi = E/\sigma K$, regardless of home and foreign τ, we see that no trade liberalization has a growth effect. For example, a reciprocal trade liberalization has no impact on growth or production, even though it does increase consumption and lower the X-sector price index in each country. A unilateral liberalization by, say, the home country leads to a drop in π_H and a drop in w_H (taking foreign labour as the numeraire makes w_H the relative wage). Although this affects the level of home welfare, it does not affect L_{IH}. The point is that the drop in w_H reduces F_H by the same amount as the drop in π_H.

Intuition

This lack of growth effects can intuitively be understood by focusing on the derived demand for home L and K. We start by considering why a unilateral trade liberalization creates no growth effect. A unilateral reduction of τ^H shifts expenditure from home varieties to foreign varieties. *Ceteris paribus*, this lowers demand for home X-sector output. This, in turn, has two effects. It lowers the derived demand for home L and K employed in the X sector. Indeed, owing to the invariancy of the markup in the monopolistic competition model, π_H (the rental rate on home K) is proportional to home X sales. Thus, the derived demand for home K drops exactly as much as the derived demand for home L. Consequently, full employment of L and K requires w_H (home wages relative to foreign wages) and π_H to fall in proportion.[10] Since L is the only input into K production, the ratio of the rental rate to marginal cost of K (i.e. π/F) does not change, so no growth effect occurs.

A second way of thinking about this is to focus on the ratio of the two producer prices in the H country: P_{KH} (the I-sector producer price) and the X-sector producer price, which equals $w_H/(1 - 1/\sigma)$. A lack of a link between trade policy and growth means that trade policy creates no pressures to reallocate L from the X sector to the I sector. Clearly, a sufficient condition for this is that the ratio of producer prices remains unchanged by trade policy. A unilateral home liberalization would, via that trade balance condition, put downward pressure on $w_H/(1 - 1/\sigma)$. However, $P_{KH} = F = w_H/K(1 + \lambda\phi)$, so there is no change in relative producer prices.

The lack of a growth effect from a reciprocal liberalization is even easier to understand. Starting from symmetrical protection levels, liberalization of both τ^H and τ^F leads to no expenditure shifting and therefore no change in π_H, π_F, or w_H.

3.1.2 Adding non-traded sectors

Since about two-thirds of economic activity is in non-traded goods, applied trade models cannot ignore these sectors. Unfortunately, adding in more final goods sectors does not allow a trade and growth link – as long as the new sectors are non-traded and upper-tier preferences are Cobb–Douglas. To see this more carefully, we turn on the Z sector by assuming $\Gamma = 1$ and impose constant expenditure share by assuming $\theta = 1$ (with $\theta = 1$, expenditure is equally divided between X and Z). Finally, we must expand our definition of *ceteris paribus* to included a fixed allocation of L between X, I, and Z.

The new expressions for K_H's rental rate and E^H are:[11]

$$\pi_H = \frac{E^H}{2\sigma K_H}, \qquad E^H = \frac{w_H(L_H - L_{IH})}{1 - 1/2\sigma}; \tag{14}$$

so, again, both τ's drop out of home's steady-state condition. They also drop out of the foreign steady-state condition. Consequently, trade policy changes have no growth effects.

This result required three key facts: trade is balanced in X, the markup is invariant to trade policy, so operating profit is proportional to expenditure, and expenditure shares are constant.

3.1.3   Adding primary factors

To show that the lack of growth effects does not fundamentally depend upon the presence of a single primary factor, we add another factor (skilled labour, denoted as H) whose supply is fixed. Furthermore, we allow for general factor intensities in the X, Z, and I sectors. Adding an extra factor to the final goods sectors is simple given constant returns. We assume $g[L_{IH},H_{IH}](1 + \lambda\phi)K_H$ is the new I-sector production function, where the function g is linear homogeneous, where $\phi = K_F/K_H$. Plainly, F_H equals $(a_{IL}L_{IH} + a_{IH}H_{IH})/(1 + \lambda\phi)K_H$.

These changes do nothing to alter the expression for π_H, but:

$$E^H = \frac{w_H(L_H - L_{IH}) + v_H(H_H - H_{IH})}{1 - 1/2\sigma}, \tag{15}$$

where v_H is the wage of home's skilled labour and H_H is its supply.[12] The steady-state condition now becomes:

$$\frac{\pi_H}{F_H(\rho + g)} = 1 \quad <=>$$

$$\frac{w_H(L_H - L_{IH}) + v_H(H_H - H_{IH})}{2\sigma - 1} = \frac{w_H a_{IL} + v_H a_{IH}}{(1 + \lambda\phi)}(\rho + g), \tag{16}$$

where the a_{Ij} are the I-sector unit input coefficients for L and H.

Although neither τ enters this expression, it is still possible that trade policy influences growth via a general equilibrium effect on factor prices. For instance, we know that a unilateral liberalization will change home factor prices relative to foreign factor prices. This, in turn, will lead to an incipient change in q unless (i) factor intensities are equal in all sectors (in which case we really have a single composite factor), or (ii) w_H and v_H change by the same proportion.[13] As we shall see, the latter is always true when the single traded-good sector is marked by monopolistic competition.

Any change in the τ's will trigger a change in relative marginal costs (denoted as $\Psi = m_F/m_H$, where m_i is marginal cost) such that the trade balance condition:

$$\frac{E_X^F}{1 + \phi(\Psi/\tau^F)^{1-\sigma}} = \frac{\phi E_X^H}{(\Psi\tau^H)^{\sigma-1} + \phi} \tag{17}$$

continues to be satisfied.[14] Trade balance also implies that E_X^i equals the value of country i's X production evaluated at producer prices. Thus, E_X^H/E_X^F equals $(X_H/X_F)/\Psi$, where X_i is total X-sector output in country i. Since the allocation of primary factors is fixed by our *ceteris paribus* assumption, the X's are fixed and we see that Ψ is determined by the τ's.

By perfect competition in the I sector and constant returns in X production, the equilibrium factor prices must satisfy:

$$\begin{pmatrix} J_H \\ m_H \end{pmatrix} = A \begin{pmatrix} w_H \\ v_H \end{pmatrix}, \quad A \equiv \begin{pmatrix} a_{IL} & a_{IH} \\ a_{XL} & a_{XH} \end{pmatrix}, \tag{18}$$

where A is the matrix of unit input coefficients. Since Z is non-traded, its price-equals-marginal-cost condition provides no independent constraint on the factor prices.

The value of m_H is pinned down by the trade balance and J_H is determined by the present value of the Ricardian rents it would produce. By our *ceteris paribus* assumption, J_H must equal $\pi_H/(\rho+g)$. From trade balance, E_X^H must equal the value of home X-sector output evaluated at producer prices, namely $X_H m_H/(1-1/\sigma)$, where X_H is the total output of the home X sector.[15] Using this fact, π_H equals $m_H X_H/(\sigma-1)K_H$, so:

$$\begin{pmatrix} w_H \\ v_H \end{pmatrix} = A^{-1} \begin{pmatrix} J_H \\ m_H \end{pmatrix} = A^{-1} \begin{pmatrix} \frac{X_H}{(\sigma-1)K_H(\rho+g)} \\ 1 \end{pmatrix} m_H \tag{19}$$

Given the assumed constancy of the division of primary factors, the only thing that trade policy can change on the right-hand side is m_H. Consequently, even if a trade liberalization does induce a general equilibrium shift in factor prices, this expression shows us that both factor prices will move by the same proportion. This indicates that condition (ii) from above is satisfied for all trade policy changes. In others, because all factor prices move by the same percentage, the producer prices of all three sectors' goods (X, Z, and I) move together.

With no change in the relative producer prices, there is no tendency to reallocate primary factors. Our presumption that the initial steady state is undisturbed is therefore confirmed. In other words, trade policy changes have no growth effect.

Intuition
Several key modelling assumptions are responsible for this result. The constancy of the X-sector markup is crucial. It implies that the X-sector producer price is proportional to marginal cost and it makes π_H proportional to worldwide consumer expenditure on home's X-sector output. Trade balance in X implies that this worldwide expenditure is proportional to home expenditure on X, and also implies that home consumers' expenditure on X equals home output of X evaluated at producer prices. Lastly, since $\rho = r$ in steady state, the contemporaneous J is proportional to the contemporaneous π_H. Using all the above-mentioned facts, we see that the expenditure-shifting aspect of trade policy has no effect on relative producer prices. It is therefore not surprising that trade policy has no impact on the sectoral allocation of resources and therefore no impact on growth.

3.2   Traded intermediate inputs in the I sector and the price of capital

The first trade-and-growth link works on the denominator of Tobin's q. When the production of K involves traded intermediate inputs, the price of traded goods enters the I sector's cost function. Since the level of trade barriers can lower these prices, F becomes a function of trade barriers. Consequently, global liberalization can lower P_K in both countries, thereby creating an incipient increase in q. In our old growth model this raises the steady-state capital stock and triggers medium-run growth. In the new growth model it raises the steady-state growth rate. In the context of the old growth literature, this openness and growth link is related to the literature on imported capital goods, which have long played an important role in the trade and development literature (see, for instance, Lee (1993, 1994)). Baldwin and Forslid (1996) demonstrate it for an endogenous growth model.

3.2.1   The old-growth/new-trade model
To illustrate this link as simply as possible, we modify the basic model by assuming that the I sector employs L and trades intermediate inputs (specifically, a CES composite of all X varieties with an elasticity of substitution σ) to produce new capital under constant returns. The assumed marginal cost and net investment functions are:

$$F = w^\alpha P_X^{1-\alpha} = \left(\frac{[K(1+\tau^{1-\sigma})]^{\frac{1}{1-\sigma}}}{1-1/\sigma}\right)^{1-\alpha}, \quad \dot{K} = \frac{wL_I + P_X X_I}{F} - \delta K, \quad (20)$$

where P_X is the standard CES price index, and X_I and L_I are the X-sector composite and L employed. The second expression for F follows from the first, using the definition of the standard CES price index and $w = 1$.

By inspection of (6), q is diminishing in both $\bar{K}$ and F. Therefore anything that lowers F triggers investment-led growth. From (20), a drop in τ tends to lower F and thereby tends to increase the steady-state capital stock. However, F is also decreasing in $\bar{K}$ (in particular, dF/F equals $-(1-\alpha)/(\sigma-1)$ times $d\bar{K}/\bar{K}$), so there exists the aberrant possibility that the liberalization lowers K enough to more than offset the F-reducing impact of the τ cut. We refer to this as aberrant because it implies that global liberalization would raise the CES price index of traded goods in all countries.[16] Formally to characterize the openness and growth link, we must find sufficient conditions that rule out this aberrant case. Because the impact of $\bar{K}$ on F depends upon $1/(\sigma - 1)$, it is intuitively obvious that the aberrant case disappears if σ is sufficiently large. Specifically, it can be shown that $\sigma > 2$ is sufficient to ensure that $d\bar{K}/d\tau$ is negative.[17]

3.2.2 The new-growth/new-trade model

In the new growth model, the economic mechanism underlying this trade and growth link is exactly the same. However, as we saw before, a constant steady-state growth rate occurs only when K drops out of the q. With traded intermediates in the I sector, F depends upon P_X, which in turn depends upon K. Thus, we must assume a different form of externalities in order to ensure that F falls at the same rate as π. The new I-sector marginal cost function – which is actually more general than equation (9) – must be:

$$F = \frac{P_X}{K^\Omega(1+\lambda)}, \quad (21)$$

where P_X is the CES price index, where Ω equals exactly $(\sigma-2)/(\sigma-1)$. Of course, the assumption of unitary elasticity in the basic model – see (9) – has a certain elegance that $(\sigma-2)/(\sigma-1)$ lacks and elegance matters in theory. But, in any case, both assumptions are equally arbitrary, equally unfounded empirically, and equally necessary for constant steady-state growth.

Evaluating P_X, we see that K's replacement cost rises with τ. Specifically, we have that F equals $(1 + \tau^{1-\sigma})^{1/1-\sigma}/2K(1 - 1/\sigma)$.[18] Given markup pricing, imported X varieties cost τ times more than local varieties, so I-sector firms will employ τ^{σ} times more of local varieties, thus the I-sector production function simplifies to:[19]

$$g = \frac{L_I}{(1 + \tau^{1-\sigma})^{1/(1-\sigma)}}. \tag{22}$$

Of course, all labour is employed in the X sector, but we reinterpret L_I as the X-sector labour whose output is earmarked for sale to the I sector. Notice that protection lowers I-sector labour productivity.

Calculating J requires consideration of the sales to both nations' X and I sectors. Since the X and I demand functions have the same elasticity, X firms earn $\sigma(E + I)/K$. Using the usual manipulation, this means that π equals $L/(1 - 1/\sigma)K$.[20] Thus J is $\pi(\rho + g)$ and q is:[21]

$$q = \frac{2L}{\rho\sigma(1 + \tau^{1-\sigma})^{1/(1-\sigma)} + \sigma L_I}. \tag{23}$$

Plainly, reciprocal trade liberalization (i.e. $d\tau < 0$) leads to an incipient rise in q, thereby forcing a positive growth effect. Growth rises because L_I rises to restore $q = 1$ and because liberalization boosts I-sector labour productivity directly. This link between trade policy and growth is easy to understand intuitively. On impact, reciprocal liberalization lowers the replacement cost of capital without affecting π. This creates incipient I-sector profits that draw resources to capital formation.

3.3　Imperfect competition in the I sector

Both the basic new growth and basic old growth models described above assume perfect competition in the I sector. Real-world production of investment goods is usually subject to scale economies. The assumption of constant returns and perfect competition is, therefore, rather objectionable when K is viewed as physical capital. The assumption is even more objectionable in the new-growth/new-trade model. A popular interpretation of these models views K as knowledge capital (i.e. designs or blueprints) and the I-sector firms as R&D labs. Under this interpretation the assumption of constant private returns requires more than the usual suspension of disbelief. After all, developing a new product or process is not like driving a taxi. Developers must invest a good deal of time in learning about the state of the art before being able to come up with their own advancements. In addition to its lack of contact points with reality, the assumption of I-sector perfect competition rules out the possibility that trade liberalization has a pro-competitive effect on the price of capital. To allow for this, we enrich the basic model by introducing scale economies and imperfect competition into the I sector. As we shall see, this enrichment of the model generates an openness and growth link that is novel, although it is related to Baldwin (1992b).

To illustrate the link, consider a symmetrical-country version of the basic model with the I-sector cost function generalized to include an overhead cost (i.e. a flow of fixed costs) of G units of labour in addition to the variable cost F. I-sector firms sell K in the home and foreign markets. We assume, however, that trade in K is hindered by a range of cost-raising barriers. The cost is intended to capture a wide range of common real-world barriers, but standards provides a concrete example. Most new products need to be certified as meeting industrial, health, safety, and/or environmental standards. The certifying boards are typically influenced by local industries (directly, when the board has industry representatives, or indirectly via political pressure on the national government) for whom the new product constitutes a threat. It is quite common, therefore, for standards to provide *de facto* discrimination against foreign varieties. In keeping with the standards-certification example, we model these barriers as posing a one-time cost.

K can be thought of as a homogeneous good. That is to say, when sold by an I firm, they are perfect substitutes (given the symmetry of varieties) even though they produce a unique variety after they are sold. In other words, they are putty-clay capital. With this homogeneity, the most natural market structure assumption for the I sector is a Cournot oligopoly with segmented markets. The resulting trade in K is analogous to the reciprocal dumping trade of Brander and Krugman (1983).

Once this analogy has been established, the outcome of reciprocal liberalization is obvious given the analysis of the pro-competitive effect by Smith and Venables (1988). Heuristically, reciprocal liberalization defragments the markets, thereby raising the degree of competition. This reduces the average markup of J over F, thereby lowering prices and creating incipient I-sector losses. The incipient losses force exit, partially offsetting the competition increase. With a lower number of innovating firms, however, the remaining firms are better able to exploit scale economies, making a lower equilibrium price of K possible. Since this price is the replacement cost of capital as far as the X sector is concerned, the pro-competitive effect in the I sector leads to an incipient rise in Tobin's q in both economies. In the old-growth/new-trade model, a higher steady-state capital stock is the result. In transition to the new steady state, the economy would experience above-normal investment-led growth. In the new-growth/new-trade model, higher output growth is the result. See Baldwin and Forslid (1996) for details.

3.4   Imperfect competition in financial intermediation

One of the many simplifications adopted in the trade and growth literature is to assume costless intermediation between savers and investors. Although convenient, this assumption is not particularly realistic. Furthermore, given the rapid expansion of international trade in financial services, it seems appropriate to investigate a model in which financial services trade is allowed to play a role in capital formation. As we shall see, enrichment of the basic model in this direction establishes an interesting openness and growth link. Here we rely on the section 2 model because it can generate two-way trade in financial services.

The basic logic of our model is quite simple. Imperfectly competitive home and foreign banks lend in the local and non-local markets, but frictional barriers (e.g. spurious regulation) hinder non-local lending. Reciprocal financial services liberalization has a pro-competitive effect on banks' markups. Since these markups put a wedge between what savers earn and what investors pay, reciprocal liberalization lowers the cost of borrowing. This boosts the stock market value of a typical unit of capital and thereby creates an incipient rise in q; the rise is avoided by a rise in r and L_I. As usual, this leads to a medium-run growth effect.

To illustrate this link simply, we use the section 2 model modified in three ways. First we assume the existence of a banking sector. Investors (i.e. firms that wish to introduce a new X variety) must borrow from banks because individuals deposit their savings in banks. To keep the model as streamlined as possible, we rely on a simple motive for banking. Namely, we assume that, if loans are to be paid off, they must be monitored. Monitoring is costless on the margin but requires a flow of overhead costs of B units of labour. Since B is finite yet consumers/savers are atomistic, savers never lend money directly to X-sector firms. Also, because banking involves an overhead cost B (not related to the volume of loans), the sector is marked by increasing returns and imperfect competition.

The second modification is to assume the existence of riskless government bonds (in fixed supply) that provide a return without monitoring. Since consumers/savers can always invest in bonds, banks are price-takers in the market for savings. The natural market structure for the banking sector is a Cournot oligopoly because banks 'sell' a homogeneous product that they 'produce' at a variable cost (the interest rate that they must pay to savers). In short, the cost function for a typical bank is $B + rFK_i$, where r is the return on savings and FK_i is its volume of loans.

The third modification is to allow trade in financial services, to assume that the markets for loans are segmented, and to assume that this trade is impeded by frictional barriers. This cost is meant to reflect real and regulatory barriers to trade in financial services. (We suppose that the cost is per loan. An interesting extension would be to consider a per bank market-entry cost.) We measure it with the parameter $\Psi \geq 1$ ($\Psi = 1$ indicates free trade in financial services).

Given this setup, it should be obvious that reciprocal dumping of financial services will occur. In equilibrium, the rate paid by investors will be a markup of what is paid to savers. The stock market value of a unit of capital, which is a stream of income discounted at the rate paid by investors, will be decreasing in this markup. Moreover, a reciprocal liberalization of Ψ will – via the pro-competitive effect – lower the banking markup in both countries. An incipient increase is q is the end result, and in the old growth model this creates transitional investment-led growth. In the new growth model, a higher growth rate is the result.

3.5   Specific and ad valorem *tariffs*

Since tariffs on most OECD trade are low, remaining trade barriers are frequently modelled as frictional barriers. None the less, tariffs still exist, so we study the growth effects of tariff liberalization. Interestingly, tariff liberalization can have a growth effect even when the liberalization of frictional barriers does not. Moreover, the exact nature of the tariff matters. For instance, in a well-known article, Rivera-Batiz and Romer (1991a) demonstrated a U-shaped relationship between tariffs and endogenous growth. That is, reciprocal tariff liberalization between identical nations raises growth for low initial tariff levels, but lowers it for high initial levels. Baldwin and Forslid (1996) show that this U-shape depends entirely on the nature of the barriers.

3.5.1   The forms of protection
In the basic section 2.1 and 2.2 models, we saw that trade policy had no long-run growth effects when the τ's represented frictional barriers. Here we modify the basic models by supposing that the countries impose three types of import barriers: an *ad valorem* tariff (which we write as $\tau = 1 + t$, where t is the tariff rate), a specific (i.e. per unit) tariff Υ, and frictional (i.e. iceberg) barriers such that $\phi \geq 1$ units must ship to sell one unit in the foreign market. A typical X firm's objective function is therefore $(p - w)x$ plus $(p^*/\tau - w\phi - \Upsilon)x^*$. K's reward is π and:[22]

$$\pi = (S + \frac{S^*}{\tau})(\frac{E}{\sigma K}), \quad S = [1 + (1+\tau)^{1-\sigma}]^{-1}, \quad S^* = 1 - S, \quad (24)$$

where S^* and S are the X-market value shares of local and non-local firms in a typical market; for short, we write this as $\pi = \Psi E / K\sigma$, noting that $\Psi \leq 1$. Tariff revenue is either returned lump-sum to consumers or destroyed, depending upon the scenario studied.

Three aspects of this profit function are important: (i) profits are unaffected by specific tariffs or frictional barriers, (ii) profits are identical in autarky and in free trade, (iii) there is a U-shaped relationship between π and that *ad valorem* τ.[23] To investigate the U-shape, differentiate (24) to get:

$$\frac{d\pi}{d\tau} = (\frac{dS}{d\tau})(\frac{E}{\sigma K}) + (\frac{S^*}{\tau})(\frac{dS^*/d\tau}{S^*} - \frac{1}{\tau})(\frac{E}{\sigma K}). \quad (25)$$

The first right-hand term is the positive impact of domestic protection on the π earned in the local market. The second is the negative impact of foreign protection on the π earned in the export market. The sum may be positive or negative. When τ is initially low, the export market matters a lot, so the negative second term outweighs the positive first term. Basically τ lowers S^* as much as it raises S, but $d\tau$ also lowers revenue per export sale while leaving revenue per local sale unaffected. For high enough τ, S^* is small enough to ensure dominance of the positive first term. As we shall see, this is the fundamental source of the Rivera-Batiz–Romer U-shaped relationship. The inflection-point τ falls as σ rises. Specifically, it is the τ that solves $(\sigma - 1) = (1 + \tau^{1-\sigma})/(\tau - 1)$.[24]

The two conflicting effects (home protection boosts π while foreign protection lowers it) also operate for ϕ and Υ, yet ϕ and Υ have no impact on revenue per sale, so the conflicting effects cancel, the fundamental reasons being that $S + S^* = 1$.

3.5.2   *Tariffs and growth*

To keep ideas clear, we isolate effects in simplifying assumptions. In particular, we look at only one type of barrier at a time, starting with frictional barriers. By inspection of (24), frictional barriers have no impact on q and therefore have no growth effect. The fundamental reason is that the pro- and anti-profit effects of reciprocal protection cancel out, so $\partial\pi/\partial\phi = \partial q/\partial\phi = 0$.

A specific tariff, however, does affect growth via a tariff-revenue effect for a simple reason. With monopolistic competition's constant markup, the specific tariff Υ has no effect on operating profit, yet the returned revenue changes income and expenditure measured in units of L. Changing E affects π, so $\partial\pi/\partial\Upsilon \neq 0$ and $\partial q/\partial\Upsilon \neq 0$, and growth effects occur. Moreover, R is a bell-shaped function of the tariff – similar to the Laffer curve – so we have a bell-shaped relationship between growth and a specific tariff. More formally, $R = \Upsilon$ (S^*E/p^*) simplifies to Υ times $(1 - 1/\sigma)\beta^{-\sigma}/(1 + \beta^{1-\sigma})$, where $\beta = 1 + \Upsilon$. It is easy to show that $d\Upsilon > 0$ lowers R, E, and therefore π for low Υ, increasing them for high Υ.[25] The inflection point decreases as σ increases.[26] Note, however, that tariff revenue must alter consumer expenditure for the link to work. The classic assumption is to return R to consumers, but the link might fail were R spent on public goods.

Finally we turn to an *ad valorem* tariff and to isolate effects we assume tariff revenue is destroyed (or wasted) by the government. Given our discussion of the profit function's U-shaped relationship with τ, it is clear that the link between growth and τ is also U-shaped. This line of reasoning explains the Rivera-Batiz–Romer U-shaped growth and tariffs link.

3.6 Increased international spillovers

The literature on international technology transmission (e.g. Segerstrom (1991)) suggests that international knowledge transmission is fostered by a wide range of international commercial activities. One popular channel is trade in goods (see Coe and Helpman (1995)). However, many other channels are not collinear with trade in commodities – multinational corporations, trade in technical and engineering services, mobility of skilled labour, trade in intellectual property rights, etc. Moreover, recent trade liberalization initiatives – such as the Uruguay Round and the European Union's (EU's) Single Market Programme – have emphasized liberalization of non-commodity trade. In the EU, examples of such deeper-than-tariff-cutting integration include capital market integration, labour mobility, mutual recognition of professional credentials, rights of establishment, common standards on competition and state aid policies. What all this goes to say is that deep integration efforts may alter the extent to which I-sector productivity in one country is related to the K's in other countries. In terms of our model, this suggests that λ is altered by deep integration initiatives, although a complete analysis would require specification of the microfoundations of the link between liberalization and λ.

Suppose, however, that liberalization does raise λ, inspection of (12) shows that lowering λ leads to an incipient rise in q and thereby in the long-run growth rate. A direct and an indirect effect are at work. Raising

λ directly boosts I-sector labour productivity and draws more L into the I sector via an indirect general equilibrium effect.

3.7   Intersectoral expenditure switching

In the basic model, the return to capital, π, increases with the share of total expenditure on the X sector, namely μ. Moreover, for CES preferences over X and Z, μ increases as the price of traded goods falls relative to non-traded goods. This suggests a simple openness and growth link. Starting from positive levels of protection, reciprocal liberalization lowers the price index of the X-composite, P_X, relative to that of non-traded goods, p_Z. The relative price change shifts expenditure patterns, thereby boosting π and creating an incipient increase in Tobin's q. This in turn causes r to jump, thereby triggering faster capital accumulation and investment-led growth in the medium run.

This link should, in principle, work in the new growth model as well. However, unless the upper-tier preferences are Cobb–Douglas, the model does not have a constant steady-state growth rate. The point is that P_X falls as K rises but p_Z does not, so μ limits to unity. Note that the model would still display positive endogenous growth, but it would not be constant. One could think of several ways of redressing this imbalance. The most obvious would be to assume that the Z also had a Dixit–Stiglitz market structure.

4   Practical considerations

The simple models used above served admirably for illustration purposes. Unfortunately, the assumptions that are necessary for tractability are unrealistic and prevented us from analysing many important policy changes. For instance, for simplicity's sake we limited the number of factors, but there is a good deal of empirical evidence that growth depends upon the accumulation of three types of capital: physical, human, and knowledge. Thus, if we include unskilled labour, we should work with a model with a minimum of four productive factors (L and three types of capital). Because there is strong empirical evidence that the rate of accumulation of physical and knowledge capital depends upon trade policy variables, we should allow both knowledge and physical capital to be endogenous. It seems likely, *a priori*, that the accumulation of human capital is also endogenous; however, there is little evidence to suggest that trade policy is an important determinant of human capital formation. Likewise, the simple models assume away most input–output relationships even though these are very important in the real world.

Analytical reasoning also places restrictions on the range of policy experiments that could be considered. Three sets of policy changes that could not be handled analytically strike us as particularly important:

1. What are the growth effects in the case of liberalization (either reciprocal or unilateral) between a large and small country?

    As the recent economic geography literature has demonstrated, analysis of equilibrium conditions with asymmetrical countries (even only two) quickly exceeds the capacity of our analytical tools. Simulation, therefore, is necessary. This is true *a fortiori* for a growth model.

2. What are the growth effects of discriminatory liberalization (e.g. formation or expansion of a free trade area)?

    Almost every member of the World Trade Organization participates in a preferential trade arrangement (Japan is the notable exception). This implies that each country faces a matrix of trade barriers, with one element corresponding to every bilateral import and export flow. Again, analysis of a change in a subset of these barriers would be far too complicated to derive analytically. One question of this type concerns the link, if any, between the initial size of a trade bloc and the growth effects of expanding the bloc.

3. What are the growth effects of sector-specific liberalization?

    Given that sectors vary in factor intensity, growth effects should depend very much upon which sectors are liberalized. Analytical answers can be derived in simple models. With many sectors and factors, however, the analytical link between capital rental rate and trade policy is too complex to analyse in the abstract. This is especially true when one considers intersectoral linkages that arise from intermediate inputs. The import of all this is clear. In order to analyse the growth effects of interesting trade policy changes in a minimally realistic model, we must turn to simulation analysis.

    Putting growth effects into a CGE model brings up a number of practical considerations. We now turn to a brief discussion of some of these issues.

4.1 Modelling the I sectors

When translating the simple theoretical model of endogenous growth into a multi-country, multi-sector CGE model, the modeller is immediately confronted with the issue of how to model the I sector (i.e. the sector that produces the continuous stream of physical, knowledge, or human capital).

Suppose, for instance, that the CGE model has ten final goods sectors and we assume that nine of them are innovative, in the sense that they are like the X sector in section 2. The modeller must decide whether to have one I sector that supplies new K to all nine sectors, or an I sector for each final good sector. Given the way in which I sectors are modelled in the endogenous growth literature (perfect competition, constant returns with externalities), the real issue here is that of intersectoral spillovers. That is, does the level of one sector's K affect the marginal cost of producing K for another sector. This is analogous to the question of international spillovers. The easiest, if not the most realistic, way of dealing with this is to assume that there is only one I sector per country. This allows us to avoid the difficulty of having to obtain the intersectoral spillover parameters.

Calibrating the international spillover parameter (λ in section 2) poses another problem. There have been a number of empirical studies of this issue. Coe and Helpman (1995), for instance, estimate the relationship between the level of national Solow residuals and the cumulated stock of national and foreign R&D spending (the foreign cumulate is trade weighted). They find that the point estimate on cumulated foreign R&D inputs is about three-fourths of that of the domestic cumulate. Roughly speaking, this suggests a value for λ equal to 0.75. This is the parameter value used in our simulation model.

4.2   Other considerations

4.2.1   The homogeneity property

Given the usual specification of I-sector externalities, any model with a continuously growing number of firms must have a very special property. Equiproportionate changes in the firms in all sectors and all countries can have no impact on the employment pattern of primary resources. We call this the homogeneity property with respect to the number of firms. In particular, this requires that innovating and non-innovating sectors are nested in a Cobb–Douglas upper-tier utility function. Also, if the CES aggregate is used as an input into the I sector, the sector must have a Cobb–Douglas cost function.

The reason for this is obvious upon reflection. The model is solved for a typical moment in time. If the model is to have a time-invariant growth rate (driven by rising K), then the endogenously determined g must be completely independent of the number of firms. A practical way of checking this is to re-run the base-case model holding all parameters constant but doubling the number of firms in every sector in every country. If the model has the necessary homogeneity property, the resulting g should be unaffected.

This property has the unfortunate side-effect of ruling out market integration effects of the type discussed by Smith and Venables (1988) and Haaland and Norman (1992). Those models allow the equilibrium price–cost margins to be a function of market shares. Because market shares would continually fall when the number of firms continually rose, this feature is inconsistent with a constant π/F.

4.2.2   Welfare and transitional dynamics

In principle, modellers are interested in the welfare impact of a trade policy change as well as its impact on the growth rate. Unfortunately, this is not easy to do in a model with transitional dynamics. The reason is that growth requires forgone consumption, so the time-path of growth affects the present value of utility in a complex manner. Baldwin (1992a) shows how Laplace transforms can be employed to deal with this in a simple growth model. Applying this method to CGE results would require calculation of the transition path as well as the steady state. This latter task would be very difficult because it is essentially requiring the solution of non-linear differential equations.

4.2.3   Real-world differences in growth rates

One of the great drawbacks of endogenous growth and trade models is that they require countries to grow at the same rate in steady state. Even the most casual glance at data shows us that growth rates differ widely, so this requirement will make it difficult to calibrate a multi-country model to actual data. One solution is to take the average long-run growth rate of the countries in the model. In our simulation model, we calibrate to 3 per cent long-run growth.

5   The simulation model

To simulate long-run growth effects, we construct a multi-sector, multi-good, and multi-factor version of the endogenous growth model described in section 2.[27] The model consists of four regions (which may be interpreted as subregions within a country, individual countries, or groups of fully integrated countries), three standard factors of production (skilled labour, unskilled labour, and capital), and two types of goods (differentiated products and perfect competition goods). Each region produces a non-traded perfect competition good and several varieties of differentiated products. Additionally, each region has an I sector (i.e. an R&D sector), which uses the three factors of production and other varieties as intermediates to produce knowledge capital.

Preferences for the representative consumer in a typical country are given by (1) with Cobb–Douglas preferences over the two final goods (i.e. $\theta = 1$). The variable cost function for a typical region-R firm in sector j (j = X, Z, and I) is:

$$MC_{j,R} = B_{j,R} \left(\sum_{f=1}^{3} a_{f,j} w_{f,R}^{1-s} \right)^{\frac{1}{1-s}} Q_{j,R}, \tag{26}$$

where B is a multiplicative productivity parameter, the $a_{f,j}$'s determine factor intensities, $w_{f,R}$ is the wage of factor f in region R, and $Q_{Kj,R}$ is the output of a typical j-sector firm located in region R (for the perfect competition sector, Q_K is sectoral output). To arrive at total cost for region-R firms in the monopolistic competition sector, we add the rental rate on knowledge capital, namely π_R. Variable cost is total cost in the perfect competition sector.

The cost of developing a new unit of knowledge capital is:

$$F_R = \frac{(FIX) \cdot MC_{I,R}^{1-\alpha} \cdot P_{X,R}^{\alpha}}{\left(n_R + \sum_{M \neq R} \lambda_{M,R} \cdot n_M \right)^{1+\frac{\alpha}{1-\sigma}}}, \tag{27}$$

where FIX is a constant, the n_i equals region i's stock of knowledge capital, and $\lambda_{M,R}$ is the parameter governing spillovers that are realized in region R from knowledge created in region M. The model is simulated with α equal to 1 and 0. In the latter case, no intermediates are used in the sector developing new blueprints, while in the former case only intermediates are used.

Normalizing the wage rate of unskilled labour in one region, dE/dt is zero in steady state, so $r = \rho$. The growth rate of the number of varieties developed by each region is therefore given by the standard $r_R = \rho$ condition. The steady-state constraint of a common g for all regions is achieved by holding constant the n in one region (at an arbitrary level) and letting relative n's change.

Since our intention is to explore the long-run growth effects in a CE model rather than to evaluate a particular policy change, we calibrate the model to a notional data set. Initial production values are set so that we have symmetrical regions, each with two equally sized final goods sectors. In addition, factor shares are identical across regions. Initial nominal factor prices are 1.0 for unskilled labour, 1.1 for capital, and 1.2 for skilled labour. The elasticity of substitution among X-sector varieties is $\sigma = 2$, and the elasticity of substitution in production is $s = 1.2$.

After setting the values of σ and s, we run a calibration procedure where the fixed cost in R&D is used to determine the growth rate in one region from (12), and relative n to make the growth rates in the other regions equal. The 'anchor' n is set arbitrarily. Because the steady-state conditions should be valid at any point in time, changing the 'anchor' n must not affect the growth rate. Furthermore, factor shares determine the parameter a in the cost function, while the productivity parameter B is used to calibrate the expenditures to data. The rest of the calibration is straightforward. Given wages and all the parameters in the cost function, we get prices and thereafter demands. Factor stocks are given from the cost functions by Shepard's lemma. Finally, the top-level Cobb–Douglas shares are calibrated.

Unskilled labour in region 4 is used as the numeraire. Factor supplies are chosen such that each region's income minus its spending on the I sector (i.e. savings) is equal to its consumption expenditure. This implies balanced trade for each region, so the condition that world trade must sum to zero is superfluous.

5.1 Results

All experiments are compared with the base case, which assumes that frictional trade costs are initially 20 per cent and that the technology spillover coefficient, λ, is 0.75 between regions. The basic model assumes away intermediates inputs in the I sector and takes the supplies of labour and physical capital as fixed. Two variants on the basic model are used. The first allows national stocks of physical capital to be endogenously determined. In particular, we find the set of national capital stocks that returns physical capital's wage to its steady-state level. The second variant keeps physical capital supplies fixed, but considers intermediates in the I sector.

The following policy experiments are performed using each of the three models:

- a reduction in frictional trade costs by 2.5 per cent on an MFN basis;
- a reduction in frictional trade costs by 2.5 per cent on a preferential basis (between region 1 and region 2 only);
- increasing technological spillovers, λ, by 2.5 per cent on an MFN basis;
- increasing technological spillovers, λ, by 2.5 per cent on a preferential basis (between region 1 and region 2 only).

Table 3.1   Change in growth rate of knowledge capital: no intermediates inputs in I sector and fixed physical capital stock (%)

	Trade cost reduction		Increased spillovers	
	MFN	Preferential	MFN	Preferential
Region 1	0.0	0.0	2.0	0.3
Region 2	0.0	0.0	2.0	0.3
Region 3	0.0	0.0	2.0	0.3
Region 4	0.0	0.0	2.0	0.3
Region 1's % change in:				
π	0.00	0.36	−0.55	−0.50
F	0.00	0.36	−2.26	−0.79
Region 4's % change in:				
π	0.00	0.00	−0.55	−0.09
F	0.00	0.00	−2.26	−0.38

Note: Preferential liberalizations are between regions 1 and 2. Base-case growth rate is 3%. Trade cost is reduced by 2.5%. Spillover parameters are increased from 0.75 to 0.775.
π = operating surplus; F = the price of knowledge capital.

5.1.1   Basic model: fixed K stocks and no intermediates in I sector

The top panel of Table 3.1 shows growth results for the four policy experiments with the basic model. As predicted by analytical reasoning in section 2, neither MFN nor preferential trade liberalization have growth effects. As can be seen in the first two columns in the bottom panel of the table, π and F are unchanged in all regions in the MFN case. In the preferential case, the integrating countries experience an equipropor-tional rise in both π and F.

In the top panel, we see that the growth effects of increasing knowledge spillovers are unrealistically large in the basic model. Although we certainly do not believe that increasing knowledge flows by 10 per cent would raise long-run growth by two percentage points, it is hard to know which aspects of our notational data set and arbitrary parameter choices are responsible for this large effect. The fact that the MFN change in λ increases g by six times more than a preferential increase is also quite interesting. Although the magnitude of this difference is difficult to understand, its direction is not. The point is that lowering λ on three foreign knowledge stocks is bound to lower F more than lowering it on only one. Notice that any change that raises g also raises savings at the expense of expenditure. Because operating profits are proportional to

Table 3.2   Change in growth rate of knowledge capital: no intermediates inputs in I sector and endogenous physical capital stock (%)

	Trade cost reduction		Increased spillovers	
	MFN	Preferential	MFN	Preferential
Region 1	0.0	0.1	2.0	0.4
Region 2	0.0	0.1	2.0	0.4
Region 3	0.0	0.1	2.0	0.4
Region 4	0.0	0.1	2.0	0.4
Region 1's % change in:				
π	0.00	0.33	-0.55	-0.53
F	0.00	0.24	-2.26	-0.93
Region 4's % change in:				
π	0.00	-0.03	-0.55	-0.13
F	0.00	-0.11	-2.26	-0.52

Note: Preferential liberalizations are between regions 1 and 2. Base-case growth rate is 3%. Trade cost is reduced by 2.5%. Spillover parameters are increased from 0.75 to 0.775.
π = operating surplus; F = the price of knowledge capital.

expenditure in the monopolistic competition model, a drop in π typically accompanies a rise in g.

5.1.2   Endogenous K stocks and no intermediates in I sector

Table 3.2 shows the interaction between medium-run and long-run growth effects. MFN trade liberalization has no impact on the demand for physical capital and so it leads to no medium-run growth effect. However, a preferential liberalization leads to investment creation in the integrating regions. This makes these economies – call them the EU for brevity's sake – economically larger, thereby boosting the EU's π. It also raises these countries' labour wages relative to the non-integrating countries and this tends to raise the integrating countries' F. On net, however, π/F rises in the integrating country. Growth in all regions is equalized by a shift in the relative number of firms. In particular, the EU's n rises relative to that of the other countries. Although this lowers non-EU firms' operating profits, it also lowers the non-EU F.

5.1.3   Fixed K stocks with intermediates in I sector

The last set of results is displayed in Table 3.3. Here we find that reciprocal trade liberalization has an enormous impact on growth. Namely, a 2.5 per cent drop in trade costs raises steady-state growth by

Table 3.3   Change in growth rate of knowledge capital: With intermediate inputs in I sector and fixed physical capital stock (%)

	Trade cost reduction		Increased spillovers	
	MFN	Preferential	MFN	Preferential
Region 1	3.7	0.6	3.9	0.6
Region 2	3.7	0.6	3.9	0.6
Region 3	3.7	0.6	3.9	0.6
Region 4	3.7	0.6	3.9	0.6
Region 1's % change in:				
π	1.05	-0.42	1.10	-0.53
F	-2.16	-1.72	-2.26	-1.50
Region 4's % change in:				
π	1.05	0.43	1.10	0.32
F	-2.16	-0.88	-2.26	-0.66

Note: Preferential liberalizations are between regions 1 and 2. Base-case growth rate is 3%. Trade cost is reduced by 2.5%. Spillover parameters are increased from 0.75 to 0.775.
π = operating surplus; F = the price of knowledge capital.

3.7 per cent, thus more than doubling the base-case growth rate. Again this figure is unrealistically high, but the result is qualitatively plausible. Intuition for the result is presented in section 2 above.

6   Summary and concluding remarks

This paper considered some of the analytical and practical issues involved in capturing accumulation (i.e. growth) effects in computable general equilibrium models. It first presented a simple old-growth/new-trade model and a simple new-growth/new-trade model, using the q-theory approach to characterize the steady-state capital stock in the former and steady-state growth rate in the latter. The next section illustrated a number of economic mechanisms linking integration to medium-run and long-run growth effects. The paper then addressed a number of practical considerations. The most important among these – as far as endogenous growth models is concerned – are the fairly strict limitations on functional forms. In particular, the economies must be homogeneous with respect to the number of firms. That is, doubling the number of firms in all innovative sectors in all countries should have no impact on the sectoral employment of primary resources in equilibrium.

It appears to us that a great deal of work can and should be done on putting growth effects into CGE models. One area that we did not touch on was transitional dynamics. This is, however, very important when it comes to welfare calculations. In an intertemporal model, today's policy changes will have long-lasting effects. Evaluating the welfare impact requires us to discount the costs and benefits back to the initial period. To do this, we must have detailed knowledge about the timing of the costs and benefits. Although this is manifestly important, we have no easy solutions to offer. This and much more we leave for future research.

Appendix: Transitional dynamics with Tobin's q

Owing to I-sector perfect competition and X-sector free entry, we have that $q = 1$ at all moments, so $J = F$ at all moments. The stock market value is, by definition:

$$J(t) = \int_{s=t}^{\infty} e^{-\bar{r}[s](s-t)} (\pi[s] - \delta)ds; \qquad \bar{r}[s] = (1/s) \int_{v=0}^{s} r[v]dv. \qquad (A1)$$

Differentiating J with respect to time and recalling that F is time invariant ($F = \beta$), we have that $r_t J_t = \pi_t - \delta + \dot{J}_t = \pi_t - \delta$ or equivalently $r_t = (\pi_t - \delta)/F$, using time subscripts instead of the usual $x(t)$ notation. We see from this that changes in π are instantaneously transmitted to changes in r. The two state variables are real investment, L_I (a jumper), and K (a non-jumper). Taking $\Upsilon = 0$ so $\mu = 1$ to simplify the algebra, the two system equations are the Euler equations (with a change of variables to eliminate E):[28]

$$\dot{L}_I = (L - L_I)(\rho - r_t) = \frac{L - L_I}{F}\left(\rho F + \delta - \frac{L - L_I}{(\sigma - 1)K_t}\right) \qquad (A2)$$

and K's law of motion:

$$\dot{K} = \frac{L_I}{F} - \delta K. \qquad (A3)$$

Clearly the isokines $\dot{L}_I = 0$ and $\dot{K} = 0$ are respectively negatively and positively sloped, as shown by the solid lines in Figure 3A.1. The stable arm is negatively sloped as drawn.

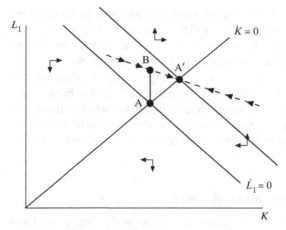

Figure 3A.1 Transitional dynamics.
   Note: Direction of motion refers to original isokines.

Supposing that the system starts in steady state, a policy shock – such as an I-sector production subsidy (paid for with lump-sum taxation) – that lowers F will shift the isokine for L_I up as shown in Figure 3A.1. The system jumps from A to B and proceeds to approach A′ along the saddle-path.

Notes

The authors acknowledge financial support from the Swiss National Science Foundation (Subsidy #1214-043580.95/1). Rikard Forslid also acknowledges the Humanistisk–Samhallsvetenskapliga Forskningsradet (HFSR) (#F 59/95). We thank Elena Seghezza and Phillippe Martin for helpful comments and suggestions.
1. Flam and Helpman (1987) were the first thoroughly to explore the Dixit–Stiglitz framework with K used only in the fixed costs.
2. The basic structure is similar to that of Grossman and Helpman (1991: Ch. 3.1).
3. Fact (i) comes from the fact that it is always more profitable to be a monopolist in a new product than to be a duopolist in an existing product. Facts (ii) and (iii) follow from the first-order conditions $p(1-1/\sigma) = w$ and $p^*(1-1/\sigma) = w\tau^*$, where the asterisk indicates export market variables. Rearranging the local first-order condition, $(p-w)c = pc/\sigma = s\mu E/\sigma$, where s is the local market share and c is local consumption of local varieties. Fact (iii) follows from this and a similar rearrangement of the export market first-order condition. For more details see Helpman and Krugman (1985). The mill pricing term reflects the fact that firms charge the same price 'at the mill' regardless of a good's destination.
4. By symmetry of nations, operating profit is:

$$\pi = \frac{s\mu E}{\sigma} + \frac{s^* \mu E^*}{\sigma} = (s + s^*) \frac{\mu E}{\sigma}.$$

By symmetry of firms and nations, $Ks + Ks^*$ must equal unity, so $s + s^* = 1/K$.

5. This interpretation comes through in many other studies. But none of the early trade and growth models fully exploits this trick by taking L_I as a state variable.

6. Here we use the facts that, in steady state, $r = \rho$, and K and E are time invariant in steady state.

7. This trick also is crucial in the trade and growth models developed by Rivera-Batiz and Romer (1991a,b) and Grossman and Helpman (1991).

8. Here we use the facts that, in steady state, $r = \rho$, E is time invariant, and K grows at g.

9. Specifically, $h[\tau]$ equals $(1 + \tau^{1-\sigma})^{1/(1-\sigma)}/(1 - 1/\sigma)$.

10. Recall that $\pi_H = w_H(L_H - L_{IH})/(\sigma - 1)K_H$, so π_H move proportionally with w_H.

11. To see this more carefully, note that:

$$\pi_H = s_H^H \frac{E^H}{2\sigma} + s_H^F \frac{E^F}{2\sigma} = \frac{E^H}{2\sigma}(s_H^H + \phi s_F^H) = \frac{E^H}{2\sigma K_H}$$

$$E^H = Y^H - I^H = w_H L + K_H \pi_H - w_H L_{IH} = \frac{w_H(L_H - L_{IH})}{1 - 1/2\sigma}.$$

12. Dropping national subscripts for convenience, $E = Y - I = wL + vH - wL_I - vH_I + K\pi$. Trade balance in X implies $K\pi = E/2\sigma$, so $E = [w(L - L_I) + v(H - H_I)]/(1 - 1/2\sigma)$.

13. These two possibilities follow from the fact the w and v coefficients on the left-hand side are proportional to the unit input coefficients in the X sector.

14. Defining s_H^F as the share of a typical H-based firm in the F market, the intermediate steps are:

$$\frac{p_H^F c_H^F}{E^F} = s_H^F = \frac{(q_H \tau^F)^{1-\sigma}}{K_H(q_H \tau^F)^{1-\sigma} + K_F(q_F)^{1-\sigma}} = \frac{1}{K_H + K_F[q_F/(q_H \tau^F)]^{1-\sigma}}$$

$$= \frac{1}{K_H + K_F[m_F/(m_H \tau^F)]^{1-\sigma}} = \frac{1/K_H}{1 + \phi(\Psi/\tau^F)^{1-\sigma}}$$

$$s_F^H = \frac{(q_F \tau^H)^{1-\sigma}}{K_H(q_H)^{1-\sigma} + K_F(q_F \tau^H)^{1-\sigma}} = \frac{1}{K_H[q_H/(q_F \tau^H)]^{1-\sigma} + K_F}$$

$$= \frac{1/K_F}{(1/\phi)[m_H/(m_F \tau^H)]^{1-\sigma} + 1} = \frac{1/K_F}{(1/\phi)(1/\Psi \tau^H)^{1-\sigma} + 1}$$

so we have:

$$K_H s_H^F E_X^F = K_F s_F^H E_X^H \iff \frac{E_X^F}{1 + \phi(\Psi/\tau^F)^{1-\sigma}} = \frac{\phi E_X^H}{(\Psi \tau^H)^{\sigma-1} + \phi}.$$

15. Because trade barriers are frictional, export earnings are evaluated at producer prices equals import expenditure evaluated at consumer prices.

16. This outcome has long been recognized in the context of a unilateral liberalization – Helpman and Krugman (1989) refer to it as the home market

effect. Here home liberalization forces a decrease in the number of home firms and an increase in the number of foreign firms, so, even though τ is reduced, more varieties must be imported. Depending upon parameter values, P_X may actually rise.

17. Log total differentiating the expression:

$$\hat{q} = 0 = q_K \hat{K} + q_F \hat{F} \iff \frac{\hat{K}}{\hat{F}} = \frac{-q_F}{q_K} < 0,$$

where the two partial elasticities q_F and q_K are:

$$q_F \equiv \left(\frac{\partial q}{\partial F}\right)\left(\frac{F}{q}\right) = \frac{-\delta \mu F}{\mu L/K - \delta \mu F - \delta(\sigma - \mu)} - 1 < 0$$

$$q_K \equiv \left(\frac{\partial q}{\partial K}\right)\left(\frac{K}{q}\right) = \frac{-\mu L/K}{\mu L/K - \delta[\mu(F - 1) + \sigma]} < 0$$

(the signs are established by noting that both the numerator and the denominator of q are positive). Log total differentiating (20), we have:

$$\hat{F} = (1 - \alpha)\left(\frac{\hat{K}}{1 - \sigma} + \frac{\tau^{1-\sigma}}{1 + \tau^{1-\sigma}}\hat{\tau}\right) \iff \frac{\hat{F}}{\hat{\tau}} = (1 - \alpha)\left(\frac{\hat{K}}{(1 - \sigma)\hat{\tau}} + \frac{\tau^{1-\sigma}}{1 + \tau^{1-\sigma}}\right).$$

Thus:

$$\frac{\hat{K}}{\hat{\tau}} = \left(\frac{\hat{K}}{\hat{F}}\right)\left(\frac{\hat{F}}{\hat{\tau}}\right) = \frac{-q_F}{q_K}(1 - \alpha)\left(\frac{\hat{K}/\hat{\tau}}{(1 - \sigma)} + \frac{\tau^{1-\sigma}}{1 + \tau^{1-\sigma}}\right)$$

$$\iff \frac{\hat{K}}{\hat{\tau}} = \frac{q_F(1 - \alpha)\tau^{1-\sigma}(\sigma - 1)/(1 + \tau^{1-\sigma})}{q_F(1 - \alpha) - q_K(\sigma - 1)}.$$

The numerator of $\hat{K}/\hat{\tau}$ is negative because q_F is negative. Thus $\hat{K}/\hat{\tau}$ is negative (this is sufficient to establish the openness and growth link) when its denominator is positive. Investigating the denominator more closely, we see that:

$$q_F(1 - \alpha) - q_K(\sigma - 1) > 0 \iff \frac{(1 - \alpha)}{(\sigma - 1)} < \frac{q_K}{q_F}.$$

From expressions for the two partial elasticities q_F and q_K:

$$\frac{(1 - \alpha)}{(\sigma - 1)} < \frac{q_K}{q_F} = \frac{-\mu L/K}{-\delta \mu F - \mu L/K + \delta \mu F + \delta(\sigma - \mu)}$$

$$\iff \delta(1 - \alpha)(\sigma/\mu - 1) + (\alpha + \sigma - 2)\frac{L}{K} > 0.$$

Because L/K must be positive and the first term is positive, a sufficient condition for $\hat{K}/\hat{\tau}$ to be negative is $\sigma + \alpha > 2$. Lastly, because $0 \le \alpha \le 1$, we know that $\sigma > 2$ will always be sufficient to ensure that $\hat{K}/\hat{\tau}$ is negative.

18. The intermediate steps are:

$$F = \frac{P_X}{K^{\Omega}(1 + \lambda)} = P_X(2K^{1-\frac{1}{\sigma - 1}})^{-1},$$

since $\lambda = 1$ by assumption. Noting that local varieties cost $1/(1-1/\sigma)$ and imported varieties cost $\tau/(1-1/\sigma)$, and expanding the CES price index, we have:

$$F = \frac{P_X}{2K^{1+\frac{1}{1-\sigma}}} = \frac{[K(1+\tau^{1-\sigma})]^{\frac{1}{1-\sigma}}/(1-1/\sigma)}{2K^{1+\frac{1}{1-\sigma}}} = \frac{1+\tau^{1-\sigma})^{\frac{1}{1-\sigma}}}{2K(1-1/\sigma)}.$$

19. Defining x_I and x_I^* as the amounts of typical local and non-local X varieties used in K production, Q_I as the total amount a typical X-sector firm ships to the I sectors, and Ψ as the fraction of this shipped to the non-local I sector, we have:

$$X_I = [K(x_I^{1-1/\sigma} + (x_I^*)^{1-1/\sigma}]^{\frac{1}{1-1/\sigma}}$$
$$= K^{\frac{\sigma}{\sigma-1}}\left([(1-\Psi)Q_I]^{\frac{\sigma-1}{\sigma}} + \left(\frac{Q_I^*}{\tau}\right)^{\frac{\sigma-1}{\sigma}}\right)^{\frac{\sigma}{\sigma-1}}.$$

Since $Q_I = L_I/K$, where L_I is defined as the amount of X-sector L whose output is earmarked for sale to the I sector, we have:

$$X_I = L_I K^{\frac{\sigma}{\sigma-1}}\left[\left(\frac{1-\Psi}{K}\right)^{\frac{\sigma-1}{\sigma}} + \left(\frac{\Psi}{K\tau}\right)^{\frac{\sigma-1}{\sigma}}\right]^{\frac{\sigma}{\sigma-1}}$$
$$= L_I K^{\frac{1}{\sigma-1}}\left[(1-\Psi)^{\frac{\sigma-1}{\sigma}} + \left(\frac{\Psi}{\tau}\right)^{\frac{\sigma-1}{\sigma}}\right]^{\frac{\sigma}{\sigma-1}}.$$

Now, manipulating the X-sector first-order conditions:

$$\frac{p^*}{p} = \tau = \left(\frac{x^*}{x}\right)^{-1/\sigma} \iff x^* = x\tau^{-\sigma} \iff$$
$$Q_I = x + \tau x^* = x(1+\tau^{1-\sigma}) \iff 1 - \Psi = \frac{1}{1+\tau^{1-\sigma}}$$

we see $\Psi = \tau^{1-\sigma}/(1+\tau^{1-\sigma})$, so:

$$X_I = \frac{L_I K^{\frac{1}{\sigma-1}}}{1+\tau^{1-\sigma}}\left[1 + (\tau^{-\sigma})^{\frac{\sigma-1}{\sigma}}\right]^{\frac{\sigma}{\sigma-1}} = \frac{L_I K^{\frac{1}{\sigma-1}}}{1+\tau^{1-\sigma}}(1+\tau^{1-\sigma})^{\frac{\sigma}{\sigma-1}}$$
$$= L_I K^{\frac{1}{\sigma-1}}(1+\tau^{1-\sigma})^{\frac{1}{1-\sigma}}$$

The formula in the text is found by plugging this into the I-sector production function.

20. Because $Y = E + I = L + \pi K$, and $\pi = Y/\sigma K$, $Y = L/(1 - 1/\sigma)$.
21. Recalling that:

$$F = \frac{(1+\tau^{1-\sigma})^{\frac{1}{1-\sigma}}}{2K(1-1/\sigma)}, \quad J = \frac{\pi}{\rho+g} = \frac{L}{(\sigma-1)K(\rho+g)},$$

we have:

$$q = \frac{L}{(\sigma - 1)K(\rho + g)} \left(\frac{2K(1 - 1/\sigma)}{(1 + \tau^{1-\sigma})^{1/(1-\sigma)}} \right)$$

$$= \frac{2L}{(\rho + g)\sigma(1 + \tau^{1-\sigma})^{1/(1-\sigma)}}$$

and, since

$$g = \frac{L_1}{(1 + \tau^{1-\sigma})^{1/(1-\sigma)}},$$

$$q = \frac{2L}{\rho\sigma(1 + \tau^{1-\sigma})^{1/(1-\sigma)} + \left(\frac{L_1}{(1+\tau^{1-\sigma})^{1/(1-\sigma)}} \right)\sigma(1 + \tau^{1-\sigma})^{1/(1-\sigma)}}$$

$$= \frac{2L}{\rho\sigma(1 + \tau^{1-\sigma})^{1/(1-\sigma)} + \sigma L_1}.$$

22. The first-order conditions are $p(1 - 1/\sigma) = w$ and $p^*(1 - 1/\sigma)/\tau = w + \phi w + \Upsilon$. Rearranging and multiplying by profit-maximizing sales, we have $(p - w)x = px/\sigma$ and $(p^*/\tau - w + \phi w + \Upsilon)x^* = p^*x^*/\sigma\tau$. These are the operating profits earned on local and export sales. Adding them gives the result in the text.
23. Special features (i) and (ii) of the Dixit–Stiglitz setup are well known and widely exploited in the economic geography literature. See, for instance, Krugman (1991).
24. The inflection point is where expression (2) equals zero. This implies:

$$\left(\frac{-dS}{d\tau} \right) = \left(\frac{S^*}{\tau} \right) \left[\frac{dS^*/d\tau}{S^*} - \frac{1}{\tau} \right].$$

Using the facts that $S + S^* = 1$ and $S_\tau = -S_\tau^*$, we have:

$$\frac{dS}{d\tau} = \frac{-dS^*/d\tau}{\tau} + \frac{S^*}{\tau^2} \Longleftrightarrow \frac{dS}{d\tau}\left(1 - \frac{1}{\tau}\right) = \frac{S^*}{\tau^2} \Longleftrightarrow \frac{dS}{d\tau}(\tau^2 - \tau) = S^*.$$

The expression for $S = (1 + \tau^{1-\sigma})^{-1}$ and $S^* = 1 - S$, so $S_\tau = -(1 + \tau^{1-\sigma})^{-2}$ $(1 - \sigma)\tau^{-\sigma}$. With this:

$$\frac{dS}{d\tau}(\tau^2 - \tau) = S^*$$

$$\frac{(\sigma - 1)\tau^{-\sigma}}{(1 + \tau^{1-\sigma})^2}(\tau^2 - \tau) = \frac{\tau^{1-\sigma}}{1 + \tau^{1-\sigma}} \Longleftrightarrow \frac{(\sigma - 1)(\tau - 1)}{(1 + \tau^{1-\sigma})} = 1.$$

Rearranging, we have $(\sigma - 1) = (1 + \tau^{1-\sigma})/(\tau - 1)$. Note that the left-hand side is decreasing in τ, so increases in σ move the inflection point to the left. Intuitively, this is due to the fact that S^* (and thus export earnings) falls more rapidly with τ when σ is large.
25. Given that:

$$Y = L + \pi A + R = E + I, \quad R = E\left(\frac{\Upsilon\beta^{-\sigma}(1 - 1/\sigma)}{1 + \beta^{1-\sigma}}\right), \quad \pi A = \frac{E}{\sigma},$$

we have

$$E = \frac{L - L_I}{1 - 1/\sigma - \Delta}, \quad \Delta = \left(\frac{\Upsilon \beta^{-\sigma}(1 - 1/\sigma)}{1 + \beta^{1-\sigma}}\right).$$

Now, because $\pi = E/\sigma A$ for specific tariffs:

$$\pi = \frac{(L - L_I)/A}{\sigma(1 - \Delta) - 1}.$$

Since Δ is the tariff revenue per unit of expenditure, it is obviously less than unity.

26. The inflection point is a very involved algebraic expression that must be evaluated numerically.
27. The GAMS code for the model is available from the authors upon request (send a 3.5 inch diskette with request).
28. The intermediate steps are:

$$\dot{L}_I = (L - L_I)(\rho - r_t)$$

$$r_t = \frac{\pi_t - \delta}{F} = \frac{E_t/(\sigma K_t) - \delta}{F} = \frac{E_t}{\sigma F K_t} - \frac{\delta}{F} = \frac{L - L_I}{F(\sigma - 1)K_t} - \frac{\delta}{F}.$$

References

Baldwin, R. (1989), 'The Growth Effects of 1992', *Economic Policy* 9(2): 247–81.

(1992a), 'Measurable Dynamic Gains from Trade', *Journal of Political Economy* 100(1): 162–74.

(1992b), 'On the Growth Effects of Import Competition', NBER Working Paper No. 4045.

Baldwin, R. and R. Forslid (1996), 'Trade Liberalization and Endogenous Growth: A q-theory Approach,' NBER Working Paper No. 5549.

Baldwin, R. and E. Seghezza (1996), 'Testing for Trade-induced, Investment-led Growth', NBER Working Paper No. 5416.

Barro, R. (1991), 'Economic Growth in a Cross-section of Countries', *Quarterly Journal of Economics* 106(2): 407–43.

Barro, R. and X. Sala-i-Martin (1995), *Economic Growth*. New York: McGraw-Hill.

Brander, J. and P. Krugman (1983), 'A "Reciprocal Dumping" Model of International Trade', *Journal of International Economics* 15: 313–23.

Coe, D. T. and E. Helpman (1995), 'International R&D Spillovers', *European Economic Review* 39(5): 859–87.

Deardorff, A. and R. Stern (1986), *The Michigan Model of World Production and Trade*. Cambridge, Mass.: MIT Press.

Dixit, A. and J. Stiglitz (1977), 'Monopolistic Competition and Optimum Product Diversity', *American Economic Review* 67: 297–308.

Findlay, R. (1984), 'Growth and Development in Trade Models'. In R. Jones and P. Kenen (eds.), *Handbook of International Economics*, vol. I. Amsterdam: North-Holland.

Flam, H. and E. Helpman (1987), 'Industrial Policy under Monopolistic Competition', *Journal of International Economics* 22: 79–102.

Gasiorek, M., A. Smith, and A. Venables (1992), '"1992": Trade and Welfare – A General Equilibrium Model'. In L. Alan Winters (ed.), *Trade Flows and Trade Policy after '1992'*. Cambridge: Cambridge University Press, Chapter 2.

Grossman, G. and E. Helpman (1991), *Innovation and Growth in the World Economy*. Cambridge, Mass.: MIT Press.

Haaland, J. and V. Norman (1992), 'Global Production Effects of European Integration'. In L. Alan Winters (ed.), *Trade Flows and Trade Policy after '1992'*. Cambridge: Cambridge University Press, Chapter 3.

Harris, R. and D. Cox (1982), *Trade, Industrial Policy and Canadian Manufacturing*. Ontario: Ontario Economic Council.

Helpman, E. and P. Krugman (1985), *Market Structure and Foreign Trade*. Cambridge, Mass.: MIT Press.

(1989), *Trade Policy and Market Structure*. Cambridge, Mass.: MIT Press.

Jones, C. (1995), 'Time Series Tests of Endogenous Growth Models', *Quarterly Journal of Economics* 110: 495–525.

Krugman, P. (1991), *Geography and Trade*. Cambridge, Mass.: MIT Press.

Lee, J.-W. (1993), 'International Trade, Distortions and Long Run Growth', *IMF Staff Papers* 40(2): 299–328.

(1994), 'Capital Goods Imports and Long Run Growth', NBER Working Paper No. 4725.

Levine, R. and D. Renelt (1992), 'A Sensitivity Analysis of Cross-country Growth Regressions', *American Economic Review* 82(4): 942–63.

Lucas, R. (1988), 'On the Mechanics of Economic Development', *Journal of Monetary Economics* 22: 3–42.

Rivera-Batiz, L. and P. Romer (1991a), 'International Trade with Endogenous Technological Change', *European Economic Review* 35: 715–21.

(1991b), 'International Integration and Growth', *Quarterly Journal of Economics* 106: 531–55.

Romer, P. (1990), 'Endogenous Technological Change', *Journal of Political Economy* 98: S71–102.

Segerstrom, P. S. (1991), 'Innovation, Imitation and Economic Growth', *Journal of Political Economy* 99: 807–27.

Smith, A. (1984), 'Capital Theory and Trade Theory'. In R. Jones and P. Kenen (eds.), *Handbook of International Economics*, vol. I. Amsterdam: North-Holland.

Smith, M. A. M. and A. Venables (1988), 'Completing the Internal Market in the European Community: Some Industry Simulations', *European Economic Review* 32: 1501–25.

Tobin, J. (1969), 'A General Equilibrium Approach to Monetary Theory', *Journal of Money, Credit and Banking* 12: 15–29.

Discussion

CHRISTIAN KEUSCHNIGG

This is a very stimulating paper that will prove important in the further development of the applied CGE trade literature. It discusses seven important channels through which trade liberalization may induce growth effects in levels and possibly in long-run growth rates as well: (1) pro-competitive effects in output markets, (2) intersectoral expenditure shifting, (3) international expenditure shifting, (4) international knowledge spillovers, (5) use of traded goods in the capital goods or research (R&D) sector, (6) imperfect competition in the capital goods sector introducing pro-competitive effects on the price of capital, and (7) imperfect competition in financial intermediation introducing pro-competitive effects of integration on the markups between lending and borrowing rates. Some of these channels are well known by now (e.g. 2, 3, and 4). The implications of pro-competitive effects for capital accumulation (1) and the use of traded goods in R&D technology (5) are less well known and may introduce potentially powerful growth effects from integration. The latter is discussed in great detail in Keuschnigg and Kohler (1996) as well, and its potential is also demonstrated by the authors' illustrative calculations of growth rate effects from integration in Table 3.3. Unfortunately, the most novel extensions to the established literature, (6) and (7), are not particularly elaborated in this paper. It would have been interesting to see their quantitative importance. Apart from elaborating various modelling alternatives, the paper contains a separate methodological contribution that may help considerably in the interpretation of numerical results in more complex models. It shows how a growth model may be transformed to obtain a stationary, time-invariant representation of the long-run equilibrium. This representation may be treated much like a static two-sector trade model for which trade economists have developed good intuition. For example, one may show how integration affects the rates of return for fixed stocks of the accumulating factors. If the rates of return improve, then they have a knock-on effect on investment in the accumulating factors and give rise to medium- or even long-run growth. At least for simplified models with a small number of state variables this seems to be a powerful trick.

The paper reveals an aspect of endogenous growth models that may prove somewhat disappointing and frustrating for CGE modellers. While all of the above-mentioned channels can be introduced in a model of medium-run growth with long-run level effects only, the same is not possible any more with endogenous growth models. One is forced to make rather restrictive assumptions on preferences and technology in order to support a balanced growth equilibrium. The very same assumptions may actually shut off some of the pro-growth channels that one wanted to include in order to capture growth-creating effects from integration. For example, trade liberalization tends to shift expenditure from non-traded towards traded goods sectors if the elasticity of substitution in demand exceeds unity. If the traded sector is capital intensive, this intersectoral expenditure shifting boosts demand for capital and its rate of return, which, in turn, attracts more investment and gives rise to medium-run growth. Because the prices of the two goods may grow at different rates in an endogenous growth model, one is forced to use a Cobb–Douglas (CD) aggregator to support a steady-state equilibrium with constant expenditure shares. However, the CD aggregator also keeps fixed the expenditure shares in the comparative statics exercise and, thus, prevents the growth-creating effects of intersectoral expenditure shifting.

The paper holds another frustration for CGE trade modellers: in turning to an endogenous growth model, one may have to give up the growth-creating pro-competitive effects from trade liberalization. In Chapter 8 in this volume, Baldwin, Forslid, and Haaland use a model with oligopolistic competition and show that trade liberalization may reduce the market share of firms and, thereby, squeeze markups and prices. If the definition of the capital stock makes intensive use of these goods, the pro-competitive effect reduces the relative price of capital goods and, thus, triggers an investment boom. The pro-competitive effect may powerfully magnify the medium-run growth effects from trade liberalization. Again, the pro-competitive effect is difficult to include in an endogenous growth model. With long-run growth, the number of firms keeps growing, shrinking market shares and markups of individual firms ever more. Consequently, as the profit rate keeps falling, the incentive to innovate vanishes and growth becomes unsustainable. That is why one must assume fixed markups that preclude pro-competitive effects from market integration.

Productivity-increasing knowledge spillovers are at the heart of every R&D-driven endogenous growth model. To sustain stable long-run growth, the research technology must be exactly linear in the knowledge stock. The authors specify a more realistic R&D technology that requires intermediate inputs in addition to highly skilled labour, but the condition for sustainable growth becomes rather special: the spillovers from the knowledge stock K must generate productivity increases exactly equal to

K^Ω with $\Omega = 1 + \alpha/(1-\sigma)$ (see equation (21), which assumes $\alpha = 1$). The cost share α of intermediates in R&D and the elasticity of substitution σ can be measured. The condition that spillovers should occur exactly at the rate dictated by Ω is a knife-edge case that one may find it hard to believe in. Admittedly, this is no more special than the case $\Omega = 1$ emphasized in the standard literature. However, the econometric evidence reported in Jones (1995) seems to reject the linear specification of knowledge creation and casts doubt on long-run growth rate effects, certainly not of the size suggested by the authors' calculations (see Tables 3.1 to 3.3). Maybe one should emphasize in CGE analysis the case of diminishing returns in the R&D technology. Even though this case would preclude long-run growth effects from integration, it would retain from the endogenous growth literature the theory of product development and firm entry based on profit-motivated R&D decisions. This approach is, of course, much more satisfactory than the standard formulation of firm entry based on a static zero-profit condition. The endogenous introduction of new products and the associated spillovers and productivity increases would still be potentially powerful magnifiers of medium-run growth effects.

Trade might facilitate international knowledge spillovers and, thus, boost long-run growth. Baldwin and Forslid capture international spillovers by postulating that an exogenous fraction λ of the foreign knowledge stock is available at home. An increase in the spillover rate λ boosts long-run growth, and might be a separate important element of an overall integration scenario. I do not find this entirely satisfactory, however, because it neglects the fact that increased international spillovers may be endogenously connected to increased import penetration. In tying spillovers to trade flows, they become an integral part of a trade liberalization scenario rather than being a separate exogenous element that is disconnected from trade flows.

Baldwin and Forslid focus on the effects of trade integration on long-run growth rates. The focus on steady-state solutions is quite limited, however, since one can solve only for growth rates relative to a given historically determined knowledge stock. Yet many aspects of the long-run equilibrium importantly hinge on the level of the knowledge stock; among the most important are the welfare implications of trade policy. In the simplest case, the economy would jump onto the new balanced growth path and start to grow from a given initial condition with a new constant growth rate. Then it is possible to infer the knowledge stocks at any point in time, and to derive the welfare implications of trade policy. More realistic models, however, would certainly involve non-trivial transitional dynamics, making it extremely difficult if not impossible to solve analytically for the levels. The long-run levels result from accumu-lated product innovations during the transition and can be determined only by solving jointly the long-run and transitional equilibria. It is also important to do so. Focusing only on the growth rate effects of trade policy tends to nourish the illusion that more growth is necessarily good. However, this is not automatically guaranteed in the second-best world of endogenous growth models where individual decisions suffer from several externalities. Many, but not all, types of growth models have the feature that growth is inefficiently low in the decentralized market equilibrium. If CGE analysis is to be useful for informed policy-making, it must deliver sound welfare calculations that other tools obviously cannot provide with the same rigour.

Focusing on the long-run implications of trade policy also tends to nourish the illusion that real income gains would become available immediately. At least these calculations do not provide any information about the timing of transitional adjustment and of the resulting welfare implications. For example, if trade liberalization boosts investment, it may take more than a decade until the full productive capacity of the trade-induced investments is actually installed. These investments early on must come from forgone consumption somewhere and require patience in waiting for the gains to materialize. In focusing on transi-tional adjustment, dynamic CGE analysis could make a valuable con-tribution to the informed trade policy debate. These issues are not fully explored in the analytical literature owing to the inherent complexity of the problem even in simple setups. In my view, the challenge of dynamic CGE analysis lies in transitional dynamics, where it can make the most useful and informative contributions.

To sum up, the paper presents and evaluates a number of modelling alternatives and how they may introduce or shut off long-run growth effects from trade integration. The discussion is geared to reveal a number of pitfalls that should be avoided in constructing an applied numerical model. It offers a lot of innovative and stimulating ideas that will prove most helpful in the further development of the dynamic CGE trade literature.

References

Jones, C. (1995), 'Time Series Tests of Endogenous Growth Models', *Quarterly Journal of Economics* 110: 495–525.

Keuschnigg, C. and W. Kohler (1996), 'Commercial Policy and Dynamic Adjustment under Monopolistic Competition', *Journal of International Economics* 40: 373–409.

4 Innovation, capital accumulation, and economic transition

CHRISTIAN KEUSCHNIGG
and WILHELM K. KOHLER

1 Introduction

The demise of communism in Central and East European countries (CEECs) has set the European continent on a path of rapid change, challenging economic policy makers not only in post-communist countries themselves but also in Western Europe. Having rid themselves of communist governments in 1989–90, people in the CEECs soon faced dubious rewards. Their economies experienced an unprecedented crisis, with successive double-digit annual reductions in real GDP and mass unemployment. Lacking both previous historical experience and an accepted theory of systemic transformation, observers had a hard time interpreting what was going on. Was it an unavoidable prelude to the formation of a capitalist system, something along the lines of Schumpeter's creative destruction? Were these countries actually heading towards a capitalist system of the Western type, or were they trying to go for some idiosyncratic mixture of communist–capitalist society? In the meantime, economists more or less unanimously agree that the CEECs will eventually emerge as market economies of the Western type, and that they will do so to their own great advantage. However, controversy still dominates as to the detailed policies of transformation. This holds true in particular with respect to privatization and industrial restructuring, while historical experience and theory seemingly offer somewhat more guidance on issues of macroeconomic stabilization.

Given the necessity of immediate action, it is not surprising that much of the discussion has so far centred on policies pertaining to systemic transformation, as for instance evidenced by Clague and Rausser (1992), and Blanchard et al. (1992). However, very soon economists also started to think about what the European economic map might look like in the post-transformation era, instead of focusing on the policy details of how to get there. Thus, very early on there was a great deal of interest in the

89

potential volume and pattern of trade between Western Europe and the CEECs, for the simple reason that any piece of reliable information would help policy makers in the West trying to anticipate likely adjustment problems. Evidence for this kind of interest can be found in the studies by Wang and Winters (1991), Collins and Rodrik (1991), Hamilton and Winters (1992), and Baldwin (1994). A preferred approach of these studies was to estimate a model that explains trade for West European countries, and then to apply this model to post-transformation CEECs, on the assumption that this same model will also fit the latter countries once they have completed their tranformation to market economies.[1] The most difficult step with this approach is to obtain reliable information on the relevant post-transformation characteristics for the Eastern countries (such as factor intensities, productivities, trade shares, and the like). The studies reveal enormous potential for increased trade beteen East and West. Using a calibrated partial equilibrium model for the European Union (EU) featuring scale economies and imperfect competition, Rollo and Smith (1993) explore the role of sensitive products in this picture by assuming a 400 per cent increase in CEEC exports to the EU. However, even for such an enormous trade shock they conclude that the threat of increased import competition from the East may have been exaggerated when designing the European Agreements with the CEECs. In contrast to Rollo and Smith, who abstain from any explicit modelling effort for the CEECs, Brown et al. (1995) incorporate CEECs in a static computable general equilibrium model of the world economy to estimate the trade and welfare effects of bringing some of them into the EU. Again, this approach basically assumes that the Eastern countries have been successfully transformed into market economies and that they may be modelled on an equal footing with Western countries. Instead of alluding to non-observable post-transformation country characteristics, they use 1992 observations on CEECs when calibrating their model. This avoids speculating about the future course of events, but it raises the question of whether post-transformation CEECs will continue to exhibit the structural characteristics of 1992. One of the conclusions from the experiment is that EU–CEEC integration holds sizeable welfare stakes for CEECs, but only minor gains for the EU. In an attempt to extend results pertaining to Austria's recent EU membership to the Visegrad countries, Keuschnigg and Kohler (1996b) similarly find that Eastern countries might obtain large welfare gains through EU integration. Somewhat surprisingly, however, Brown et al. (1995) conclude that the sectoral and distributional implications for EU countries are rather small in magnitude.

In this paper we present a thought experiment that is different from but complements the above-mentioned studies. Suppose that, contrary to all present experience, it were possible to install a Western-type economic system in the CEECs within a relatively short period. Although comparable in terms of how their economies work, Eastern countries would then still be faced with initial conditions that are vastly different from those of their Western counterparts, and different from what they would be if they had not had a communist past. Having successfully completed systemic transformation, they would, for instance, still find their physical capital stocks old and outdated. Part of the human capital that was specialized in operating within the old system would become obsolete in a modern market economy. Moreover, given a weak past record of innovation, the structure of production would be heavily biased towards standardized goods. These and several other related gaps must be seen as an economic legacy of the communist past, the common element being that they can be closed only through time. Formally speaking, they relate to stock variables where discrete jumps are impossible. This suggests a distinction between *systemic transformation* and *transition*. The former relates to a fundamental change in the way an economy operates, and in the present context it means the creation of a Western-type market economy – installing the logic of market incentives. The latter relates to initial conditions, and it means that, even with the logic of market incentives firmly in place, these economies would start from initial conditions that are grossly displaced from a balanced growth path, not unlike the West after World War II. Accordingly, they must be expected to reach their new steady-state paths only after a potentially long period of transition. Even if transformation is successfully accomplished, a balanced long-run growth equilibrium in the transformed CEECs will take a substantial time to materialize.

On the basis of this distinction, our thought experiment now runs as follows. Suppose that we have a suitably calibrated model of how Western-type market economies operate at any point in time, as well as how they evolve through time. Moreover, in line with the basic premise underlying some of the above-mentioned studies, suppose that, broadly speaking, the CEECs would be like average West European countries if they had had no communist past, and if they had participated in the post-war European integration. Resorting to some bold auxiliary assumptions it should then be possible to arrive at a very stylized, but numerically specified, model of how the pan-European economy might now look if there had been no communist past in the East. We take this as a reference path of balanced growth. Assuming successful *systemic transformation* and, therefore, keeping the structure of the (Western-type) model, we then introduce the economic legacy of Eastern communism by suitably adjusting several stock variables, and subsequently calculate the *transition* path from such unfavourable initial conditions to what might be called the post-transformation *steady state*.

The empirical claim of such an exercise is, of course, quite limited. For one thing, the distinction between transformation and transition, though helpful in organizing our thinking, is in some sense artificial. In particular, we cannot claim to portray the *actual* transition paths of the early phases where historical continuity in the realm of society and polity interacts with the more or less gradual encroachment of the logic of market incentives. Instead, what we propose to do with this kind of thought experiment is notionally to isolate those aspects of transition that arise purely because history donates very unfavourable economic stocks to transition economies. We do so by way of a numerical example relying on as much empirical information as possible. Moreover, by focusing on transition we restrict our attention to long-run growth and allocation, while problems of short-run stabilization (as a result of systemic transformation) are beyond the scope of our analysis.

Quite naturally, the usefulness of this exercise is limited by the structure of the model used and by the level of detail that it incorporates. The model will, almost by necessity, have to be rather stylized. What are the elements that one would none the less want to highlight, given that we concentrate on transition? There is probably no clear-cut answer to this, but we argue that international trade and capital flows should figure very prominently in the model structure. Further key elements should be accumulation of capital, both physical and human, as well as research and development (R&D) and innovation. And, finally, the model should provide for some role of economic policy regarding the aforementioned elements.

In developing such a model, we draw on recent literature on innovation-based growth in the context of a global economy, as well as on the literature emphasizing the role of human capital in growth. More specifically, we combine the models of horizontal product differentiation pioneered by Romer (1987, 1990) and Grossman and Helpman (1991) with models of endogenous accumulation of human capital, pioneered by Lucas (1988, 1993) and Chamley (1993). However, we assume that unbounded accumulation of human capital is prevented by the simple fact that human capital, unlike financial wealth, cannot easily be passed on from one generation to another. Old agents lose part of their skills in the process of ageing and eventually all may be lost by death. One way to incorporate bounded human capital accumulation in an aggregate growth model – short of explicitly modelling and aggregating the life-cycle education decisions of overlapping generations – is to assume diminishing returns to education with respect to the human capital stock. Consequently, we adopt the view that the general knowledge stock, the stored ideas from accumulated past R&D results, may grow without bounds whereas the human capital stock, or the quality of the highly skilled labour force, eventually stops growing. Nevertheless, the level of the human capital stock is endogenous and importantly determines the innovative capacity in the economy.

In the next section we present the details of such a model for a two-region world economy. Before we turn to a numerical implementation of the model, we derive several analytical results on long-run growth in section 3. Section 4 then discusses the procedure that we have chosen to calibrate our model towards the transition experiment mentioned above. Section 5 first presents the scenarios and then turns to the role that trade policy, R&D policy, and educational policy may play in the transition paths.

2   A growth model of the world economy

We now develop a two-region model of the world economy with educational investments and increasing product variety based on knowledge-driven innovation. Growth in the high-tech sector is driven by the innovations of profit-motivated entrepreneurs in the research sector who draw on a pool of highly skilled labour. The quality of the highly skilled labour force in each country hinges on past educational investments. Entrepreneurs pursue costly R&D efforts motivated by the prospect of subsequent monopoly profits from the production of newly invented products. An expanded product range contributes to productivity gains owing to increasing specialization and division of labour. These make investments in physical capital more profitable and thus provide incentives for continued capital accumulation. The model, formulated in discrete time, is a combination of Grossman and Helpman (1991; see also Ruffin (1994)) and Romer (1987, 1990).

2.1   Education and consumption

Consumers worldwide share common preferences over a range of sophisticated high-tech consumer goods as well as a homogeneous traditional good, C_Y. Given homogeneous preferences, demand for high-tech goods may be thought of as demand for a composite good $C_{\bar{X}}$ that is available at a price index $P_{\bar{X}}$ and is formed from a range of differentiated varieties c_x^j, as detailed below. Assuming homothetic preferences over the two broad types of consumer goods, $\tilde{u}(C_Y, C_{\bar{X}}) = u[\bar{C}(C_Y, C_{\bar{X}})]$, allows convenient aggregation of all demands into an overall commodity basket, $\bar{C}$. Then, overall consumer spending in any given period amounts to $\bar{C}\bar{P} = P_Y C_Y + P_{\bar{X}} C_{\bar{X}}$, where $\bar{P}$ is an exact consumer price index. Agents discount utility from future consumption with a factor ρ that equals one plus the subjective discount rate, and allocate consumption over time by maximizing a time-separable lifetime utility function:

$$U_t = \max \sum_{s=t}^{\infty} \rho^{t-s} u[\bar{C}(C_Y, C_{\bar{X}})]. \tag{1}$$

Agents accumulate financial assets A to achieve their preferred lifetime consumption pattern. The return on assets is reflected in the interest factor r, which equals one plus the interest rate. Savings out of interest income $(r-1)A_{-1}$ and disposable wage income $w_D = w_L L_L + [u + (1-u)\tau_E]w_H H_{-1} L_H - T$ determine the accumulation of wealth:[2]

$$A = rA_{-1} + w_D - \bar{P}\bar{C}, \quad H = g(e)H_{-1} + \delta_H H_{-1}, \quad e = (1-u)/H_{-1}. \tag{2}$$

The low-skilled labour force, L_L, performs standardized manufacturing tasks that do not require much training. It is in fixed supply and earns a wage w_L.[3] By way of contrast, highly-skilled labour, L_H, performs tasks that require specific training and schooling. Endowed with a time budget equal to unity, people belonging to L_H may work for a fraction of time u and earn an effective wage rate $w_H H_{-1}$ that depends on their skill level H_{-1}. They may enhance their skills and thus their future earnings potential by using the fraction $1 - u$ of their time for schooling and training. The government may subsidize this activity by paying a fraction τ_E of the forgone wage income, but levies a lump-sum tax, T, to cover its expenses. Given that skills deteriorate at a rate δ_H, continuous training and schooling are necessary to prevent skills from becoming obsolete. Educational technology is embodied in a function $G(1 - u, H_{-1}) = g(e)H_{-1}$, which is linearly homogeneous and increasing in both arguments. The intensive form satisfies $g'(e) > 0$ and $g''(e) < 0$. We impose a convenient normalization: $g(\bar{e}) = \bar{e}$ and $g'(\bar{e}) = 1$, where $\bar{e} = 1 - \delta_H$ is the education skill ratio that keeps constant the level of educational attainment in the long run.

Optimal consumption behaviour may be derived using Lagrangean methods. Details on the optimality conditions for consumption, schooling, and human capital accumulation are available upon request from a separate appendix. The agents' desire to balance the loss in marginal utility from forgone consumption today against the marginal benefit of future consumption determines the optimal rate of consumption growth. The level of consumption reflects lifetime wealth. With an intertemporal elasticity of substitution equal to γ, the Euler equation for consumption growth is:

$$\frac{\bar{C}}{\bar{C}_{-1}} = \left[\frac{r}{\rho}\frac{\bar{P}_{-1}}{\bar{P}}\right]^{\gamma}. \tag{3}$$

A similar consideration determines work effort and schooling. The optimal amount of time spent in school weighs the opportunity cost of forgone current income against the increase in future earnings potential from higher education,

$$V_H g'(e) = w_H H_{-1}(1 - \tau_E), \quad V_H = \sum_{s=t+1}^{\infty} y_s (\delta_H)^{s-t-1} R_{t+1,s}, \tag{4}$$

where $y = [u + (1 - u)\tau_E]w_H + [(g(e) - eg'(e))/(g'(e))](1 - \tau_E)w_H H_{-1}$
measures the increase in income from an additional unit of skills, and $R_{t+1,s} = \prod_{u=t+1}^{s}(1/r_u)$ is a discount factor. An additional hour spent in school increases skills by an amount $g'(e)$. Increased education, in turn, boosts lifetime earnings. The present value of this marginal income stream equals V_H. The increase in skills directly raises future effective wage income (see the first term in y). Furthermore, by increasing the skill level today, any given time spent in school in the future is more productive. Hence, future educational requirements are achieved with less time in school, and agents can afford to earn some income in the factory instead. This indirect effect is captured by the second term in y. Finally, the additional skills acquired today become partly obsolete through ageing, which erodes their future earnings potential at a rate δ_H. Hence, the value of acquiring an additional unit of skills today is the present value of future wage income per unit of skills, including the savings in future schooling efforts.

In a long-run equilibrium, agents spend a constant fraction of their time in school and in the factory. Owing to diminishing returns to education, the skill level remains constant but is otherwise endogenously determined in terms of technology, taste, and policy parameters. Consequently, the education ratio is a constant determined by the stationarity of the law of motion in (2), $\bar{e} = 1 - \delta_H$. Given the normalization of the schooling technology, wage income per unit of skills is $y = [u + (1 - u)\tau_E]w_H$, which grows with a factor $\hat{w}$ and thus attains a present value $V_H = [u + (1 - u)\tau_E]w_H/(r/\hat{w} - \delta_H)$. Anticipating the result proved later that consumption expenditure grows at a rate $\hat{w}$, the Euler equation (3) implies $r/\hat{w} = \rho$ when preferences are logarithmic.[4] Consequently, (4) simplifies to $(1 - \tau_E)H_{-1} = [u + (1 - u)\tau_E]/(\rho - \delta_H)$. Since the long-run education ratio is fixed at $\bar{e} = (1 - u)/H_{-1} = 1 - \delta_H$, we derive:

$$u = \frac{(1 - \tau_E)(\rho - \delta_H) - \tau_E\bar{e}}{\nabla} < 1 \qquad H_{-1} = \frac{1}{\nabla} > 0,$$

$$\nabla = (1 - \tau_E)(\rho - \delta_H + \bar{e}) > 0. \tag{5}$$

How does the effective supply of skilled labour respond to changes in important structural parameters? Starting from a position of $\tau_E = 0$, one derives:

$$\frac{\partial u}{\partial \rho} = \frac{1 - \delta_H}{\nabla^2}, \qquad \frac{\partial H_{-1}}{\partial \rho} = \frac{-1}{\nabla^2}, \quad \frac{\partial u H_{-1}}{\partial \rho} = -\frac{(\rho - 1)}{\nabla^3},$$

$$\frac{\partial u}{\partial \tau_E} = -\frac{(1 - \delta_H)}{\nabla^2}, \quad \frac{\partial H_{-1}}{\partial \tau_E} = \frac{1}{\nabla}, \quad \frac{\partial u H_{-1}}{\partial \tau_E} = \frac{(\rho - 1)}{\nabla^2}. \tag{6}$$

When agents are less patient, they prefer higher current income and spend more of their time working. Consequently, skills deteriorate and the supply of effective highly skilled labour diminishes. When the government introduces a small subsidy to education, agents find it attractive to spend more time in school rather than in the factory, thus increasing the long-run skill level. Even though time spent working is reduced, the net effect of the subsidy is to raise the effective supply of highly skilled labour services, uH_{-1}.

2.2   Investment

Part of demand for goods stems from investment in physical capital. Denoting the discount factor by $R_{t+1,s} \equiv \prod_{u=t+1}^{s}(1/r_u)$, maximization of the present value of cash flows determines the optimal rate of capital investments,[5]

$$\max\left\{\sum_{s=t}^{\infty}[w_K K_{-1} - \bar{P}\Psi(\bar{I}, K_{-1})]R_{t+1,s} \quad s.t. \quad K = \bar{I} + \delta_K K_{-1}\right\}. \tag{7}$$

The composite investment good, $\bar{I}$, is formed from the traditional and high-tech goods in exactly the same way as the composite consumption good. Hence, the two price indices are identical. Gross investment in each sector adds to the sectoral capital stock, K_{-1}, which is otherwise decaying by a factor δ_K.[6] A linearly homogeneous installation technology, $\Psi(\bar{I}, K_{-1}) = \psi(i)K_{-1}$, specifies the quantity of the investment composite that needs to be acquired in order to increase the capital stock by $\bar{I}$ units; $i = \bar{I}/K_{-1}$. The intensive form $\psi(\cdot)$ is increasing and convex (for details see appendix A at the end of the paper). The installation function reflects adjustment costs and makes it optimal to stretch investment over time rather than adjusting capital stocks instantaneously. Investment in physical capital maximizes the present value of rental earnings, $w_K K_{-1}$, in excess of investment outlays. Optimality requires that the return on investment including capital gains must match the return on other assets. In purchasing a unit of the capital good, investors pay an acquisition price, $\bar{P}$, and balance the marginal costs and benefits of investment. A unit increase in the capital stock generates a stream of future rental income equal to q in present value, but requires an effective investment outlay of $\psi'(i)\bar{P}$. Hence, optimal investment reflects a simple present-value criterion:

$$ q = \psi'(i)\bar{P}, \qquad rq_{-1} = w_K - [\psi(i) - i\psi'(i)]\bar{P} + \delta_K q. \tag{8} $$

2.3   Commodity demand

The overall level of demand for the composite good translates into derived demands for individual commodities. Specifically, differentiated goods are supplied by monopolistic producers that are located either at home or abroad. Suppose that new products become available only in the next period. Then, a total of $\bar{N}_{-1} = N^1_{-1} + N^2_{-1}$ of differentiated brands are available worldwide, with N^1_{-1} produced at home and N^2_{-1} produced abroad. Consumer preferences are characterized by love of variety in the spirit of Dixit and Stiglitz (1977). Then the composition of product demand derives from expenditure minimization, which yields an exact price index for the composite good,

$$ P^i_{\bar{X}} = \min_{c^{ij}_X} \left\{ \int_0^{\bar{N}_{-1}} (\tau^{ij}_B p^i_X) c^{ij}_X dj \quad s.t. \quad \left[\int_0^{\bar{N}_{-1}} (c^{ij}_X)^{\frac{1}{\beta}} dj \right]^\beta \geq 1 \right\}, $$

$$ \sigma = \frac{\beta}{\beta - 1} > 1, \tag{9} $$

where index j indicates one of the home- or foreign-produced varieties. Thus, c^{ij}_X is unit consumption demand originating in country i for country j's products. Note that producers charge the same price irrespective of where they sell their product. Demand prices for the same product may, however, differ across countries owing to a trade barrier on imports: $\tau_B^{ij} > 1$ for $i \neq j$ and $\tau_B^{ij} = 1$ for $i = j$.[7] Since demand and supply are completely symmetrical within the groups of home- and foreign-produced varieties, the price index may conveniently be calculated as

$$P_{\bar{X}}^i = \left[\int_0^{\bar{N}_{-1}} (\tau_B^{ij} p_x^j)^{\frac{1}{1-\beta}} dj \right]^{1-\beta} = \left[N_{-1}^1 (\tau_B^{i1} p_x^1)^{\frac{1}{1-\beta}} + N_{-1}^2 (\tau_B^{i2} p_x^2)^{\frac{1}{1-\beta}} \right]^{1-\beta}.$$

(10)

In the presence of trade barriers, the price index differs across countries. Country 1, for example, spends $P_{\bar{X}}^1 D_{\bar{X}}^1 = N_{-1}^1 p_x^1 D_x^{11} + N_{-1}^2 (\tau_B^{12} p_x^2) D_x^{12}$ on high-tech varieties. Adding up across different demand categories and countries, country i's expenditure is $\bar{P}^i \bar{D}^i = P_Y D_Y^i + P_{\bar{X}}^i D_{\bar{X}}^i$ and stems from consumption and investment demand: $\bar{D}^i = \bar{C}^i + \Psi_x^i + \Psi_y^i$.[8] It is important to distinguish carefully between sector x's demand for the composite investment good, Ψ_x^i, and derived demand for the high-tech sector's composite output, $D_{\bar{X}}^i$. This multiplies with unit demand to give the overall quantity that a producer in country j is able to sell in country i's market for high-tech products,

$$D_x^{ij} = [P_{\bar{X}}^i / (\tau_B^{ij} p_x^j)]^\sigma D_{\bar{X}}^i.$$

(11)

2.4   Monopolistic production

Each existing variety is produced by a single producer who owns an infinitely lived patent on his brand and, therefore, acts as a monopolist. His market power is limited, however, because varieties are close substitutes in demand. With perfect competition in factor markets, producers take factor prices as given. All producers have access to the same sector-specific production technologies, which are assumed linearly homogeneous in capital and labour. Per unit of output, producers choose minimizing factor inputs and incur unit costs equal to

$$\phi_x(w_H, w_K) = \min_{h_x, k_x} \{ w_H h_x + w_K k_x \quad s.t. \quad F_x(h_x, k_x) \geq 1 \},$$

$$\phi_y(w_L, w_K) = \min_{l_y, k_y} \{ w_L l_y + w_K k_y \quad s.t. \quad F_y(l_y, k_y) \geq 1 \}.$$

(12)

Both sectors use capital. However, low-skilled labour is employed only in the traditional sector whereas highly skilled labour finds employment either in the high-tech sector or in research and development. The derivatives of the unit cost functions give factor demands per unit of output in country i: $k_x^i, h_x^i, k_y^i, l_y^i$. Individual workshops may rent any amount of capital at a rental rate w_K^i, and may employ high- and low-skilled labour at wages w_H^i and w_L^i, where w_H^i is per 'skill unit'. Thus, capital and labour may be redeployed across workshops without friction.

In a well-diversified economy, the market for an individual variety is small compared with the size of aggregate demand. Consequently, individual producers have a negligible influence on the price index, $P_{\bar{X}}^i$, and on the state of aggregate demand in country i. Hence, they perceive an own-price elasticity of demand equal to σ. Given this estimate, they maximize profits $\pi^j = (p_x^j - \phi_x^j)x^j$, where $x^j = D_x^{1j} + D_x^{2j}$. In exploiting market power, producers in country j set a price in excess of marginal costs,

$$p_x^j = \beta\phi_x^j. \tag{13}$$

Because all producers face the same factor prices and because demand is symmetrical, implying a uniform price elasticity σ, all producers in country j end up charging identical prices. Markup pricing generates gross profits equal to

$$\pi = (\beta - 1)\phi_x x \tag{14}$$

in each period. The discounted flow of future profits creates monopoly wealth. The equity value of the workshop must generate a rate of return including capital gains that is equal to the economy-wide interest rate, to preclude any unexploited profits from financial arbitrage. Thus, the value of a patent on any variety must satisfy the no-arbitrage condition:

$$rv_{-1} = \pi + v. \tag{15}$$

Given a transversality condition, solving this equation forward in time shows that the stock market value of a new patent is equal to the present value of future profits. Because production of a new variety invented in period t commences only with the next period, the equity value, v_t, is defined ex current profits (use the discount factor $R_{t,s} \equiv \prod_{u=t}^{s}(1/r_u)$):

$$v_t = \sum_{s=t+1}^{\infty} \pi_s R_{t+1,s}. \tag{16}$$

2.5   Innovation

The prospects for future profits motivate current efforts in research and development. Innovation generates two basic benefits. It results in previously unknown blueprints for producing new varieties. With well-developed patent protection, a new blueprint gives an exclusive production right resulting in future monopoly profits. In addition, current innovation spills over to the remaining research community and adds to the general knowledge stock, which enhances the productivity of other researchers. This additional benefit, however, is non-rival in nature and not appropriable by private entrepreneurs. With immediate diffusion of innovative activity, the current knowledge stock reflects the cumulative experience of past innovations both at home and abroad and, by choice of units, may be equated to the worldwide stock of varieties $\bar{N}_{-1} = N^1_{-1} + N^2_{-1}$. For simplicity, research is assumed to be an activity of highly skilled labour only. The basic productivity in the research labs is $(\bar{N}_{-1}/a)$ and grows in line with the accumulated past research experience, $\bar{N}_{-1}$. Assuming a linear learning-by-doing technology, the labour input needed to generate $I_N = N - N_{-1}$ innovations, or new products, is given by

$$h_R = a I_N / \bar{N}_{-1}. \tag{17}$$

Research is motivated by profit opportunities from supplying the newly created product to a worldwide market. The value of a new patent reflects this profit stream. With free entry into R&D activities, agents devote efforts to innovative activities until the forgone wage income in producing existing goods matches the patent value,

$$v \lessgtr (1 - \tau_R) w_H a / \bar{N}_{-1}, \quad \Longleftrightarrow \quad I_N = N - N_{-1} \gtreqless 0. \tag{18}$$

If the value of a new patent fell short of the wage cost of the highly skilled labour input, then research would become unprofitable and all innovative activities would stop. The government may subsidize R&D costs at a rate τ_R.

2.6   Excess demand

We now close the model by adding an economy-wide portfolio condition. Define aggregate monopoly wealth in country i (i = $\{1,2\}$) by $V^i_m = v^i N^i$ and the value of the sectoral capital stocks by $V^i_x = q^i_x K^i_x$ and $V^i_y = q^i_y K^i_y$. Furthermore, agents may hold an internationally traded bond, B^i, which is denominated in terms of the traditional good. All assets are assumed to be perfectly substitutable and, therefore, must yield identical returns. The composition of financial wealth in the aggregate is then determined by the supply of assets: $A^i = V_x^i + V_y^i + V_m^i + B^i$. The excess demand system of the world economy is

$$\zeta_L^i = l_y^i Y^i - L_L^i,$$

$$\zeta_H^i = h_x^i x^i N^i_{-1} + h_R^i - u^i H^i_{-1} L_H^i,$$

$$\zeta^i_{K_x} = k_x^i x^i N^i_{-1} - K_{x,-1}^i,$$

$$\zeta^i_{K_y} = k_y^i Y^i - K_{y,-1}^i,$$

$$\zeta_x^i = N^i_{-1}[\sum_j (C_x^{ji} + I_x^{ji}) - x^i], \tag{19}$$

$$\zeta_y = \sum_i (C_y^i + I_y^i - Y^i),$$

$$\zeta_G^i = T^i + T_{\tau_B}^i - \tau_E^i(1 - -u^i)w_H^i H^i_{-1} L_H^i - \tau_R^i w_H^i h_R^i,$$

$$\zeta_A = \sum_i (A^i - V_m^i - V_x^i - V_y^i) = \sum_j B^j$$

In an integrated equilibrium of the world economy, all excess demands are zero. The first three equations show that factor markets clear separately in each country. Note that physical capital stocks in each country and sector are predetermined in every period, owing to adjustment costs of investment.[9] Commodity markets clear worldwide. Since each differentiated product is produced in only one location, there are two equilibrium conditions for home- and foreign-produced high-tech goods. Consumer demand originating in country j for a variety produced in country i is C_x^{ji}, and similarly for investment. The government budget constraint, ζ_G^i, restricts overall expenditure on subsidies to available revenues from lump-sum taxes, T^i, and from import tariffs, $T_{\tau_B}^i = (\tau_B^{ij} - 1)D_x^{ij}p_x^j N^j_{-1}$, $j \neq i$. Finally, there is a world-wide asset market. With perfectly substitutable assets, agents are indifferent with regard to their portfolio composition. By assumption, all equity issued at home is owned by domestic residents, which, in line with stylized facts, excludes cross-country equity holdings. Consequently, accumulated savings that exceed domestic equity value are invested in foreign-issued bonds. By definition, a claim of one country is the liability of the other: $B^1 = -B^2$.

The current account balance highlights the role of international capital mobility and its relation to the trade balance. Using budget constraints, pricing and cost equations, and the no-arbitrage conditions, the equation for the household sector's asset accumulation is equivalent to the current account equation $B^i = rB^i_{-1} + TB^i$. The trade balance may be viewed in two alternative ways:

$$(a) \quad TB^i = p^i_x x^i N^i_{-1} + P_Y Y^i + T^i_{T_B} - \bar{P}^i \bar{D}^i,$$

$$(b) \quad TB^i = P_Y(Y^i - D^i_Y) + N_{-1}{}^i p^i_x (x^i - D^{ii}_x) - N^j_{-1} p^i_x D^{ij}_x. \tag{20}$$

Version (a) reflects the difference between GDP and absorption in each country. Alternatively, (b) states the trade balance in terms of the value of exports minus imports. The first term captures one-way trade in the traditional good, while the remaining terms reflect two-way trade in differentiated goods, which are produced in only one location. The second term gives net exports of those varieties that are produced at home but not abroad, while the third term represents the imported varieties that are not produced at home. Finally, the equilibrium condition for the world capital market, $\sum_i B^i = 0$, amounts to the equality of world income and world spending.

3   Long-run growth

In a long-run equilibrium of balanced growth, prices and quantities grow at constant rates. The fact that these stationary growth rates differ across various types of variables imposes further restrictions on the production technology. Specifically, the factor prices for capital and labour will grow at different rates. Thus, constant factor shares require a unitary elasticity of substitution in production, hence we specialize the technology to

$$\phi^i_y = \phi^i_{0,y}(w^i_K/\alpha_{ky})^{\alpha_{ky}}(w^i_L/\alpha_{ly})^{\alpha_{ly}}, \quad l^i_y w^i_L = \alpha_{ly}\phi^i_y, \quad k^i_y w^i_K = \alpha_{ky}\phi^i_y,$$

$$\phi^i_x = \phi^i_{0,x}(w^i_K/\alpha_{kx})^{\alpha_{kx}}(w^i_H/\alpha_{hx})^{\alpha_{hx}}, \quad h^i_x w^i_H = \alpha_{hx}\phi^i_x, \quad k^i_x w^i_K = \alpha_{kx}\phi^i_x. \tag{21}$$

The same holds true for the allocation of consumption. Owing to ongoing product innovation and, consequently, the continuous introduction of new specialized varieties, the price index of the composite high-tech good grows at a rate different from that of the traditional good. To support a constant share of expenditure in a balanced growth equilibrium, one needs to specialize preferences to

$$\bar{P}^i = (P^i_{\bar{X}}/\alpha_{cx})^{\alpha_{cx}}(P_Y/\alpha_{cy})^{\alpha_{cy}}. \tag{22}$$

To pin down 'nominal' variables and their growth rates, we normalize the price of the traditional good to unity: $P_Y = 1$ and $\hat{P}_Y = 1$ (notice that $\hat{P} = P/P_{-1}$). We start by observing that all spending and income components at home and abroad must grow at a common rate that is identical across countries and equal to the growth rate of wages, $\hat{w}$. In particular, wages of high- and low-skilled labour must grow at the same rate because the effective supplies are constant in the long run. To support constant shares in the savings equation (2), financial wealth and consumption budgets must also grow at the same rate. If the net foreign asset position is to remain a constant share of domestic financial wealth, it must accumulate with the same speed. Perfect international capital mobility equates interest rates across countries. Hence, the current account equation in (20) implies that net foreign assets, GDP, and absorption grow at the same rate $\hat{w}$ in both countries. In particular, $\hat{N}^i \hat{x}^i \hat{p}^i_x = \hat{w}$. Could the components possibly grow at different rates? Since we require non-specialization in the high-tech sector with constant product shares $s^i_N = N^i_{-1}/\bar{N}_{-1}$, both countries must introduce new products with the same speed, $\hat{N}^i = \hat{N}$. Furthermore, the price index $P^i_{\bar{X}}$ given in (10) must grow at an identical rate in both countries, implying that the component prices must grow at the same rate, $\hat{p}_x$. Then, by virtue of $\hat{N}\hat{x}^i\hat{p}_x = \hat{w}$, factory output must increase at the same rate $\hat{x}$ in both countries. Finally, balanced growth in the world economy is supported only with identical demand shares in (22) and an identical cost share of capital in both countries. Hence, the α-parameters are identical.[10]

The solution in growth rates for iso-elastic intertemporal preferences is somewhat complicated and is obtained only in the numerical example below. The case simplifies considerably with logarithmic preferences, $\gamma = 1$, in which case the Euler equation in (3) gives a simple relation between the interest and growth rates,

$$r/\rho = \hat{w} = \hat{N}\hat{p}_x\hat{x}. \tag{23}$$

The resource constraint for highly skilled labour in (19) establishes an additional relationship between the world interest and growth rates. Use (17) and replace the unit demand for high-skilled labour, $h^i_x = \alpha_{hx}\phi^i_x/w^i_H$, to obtain:

$$\frac{\alpha_{hx}\phi^i_x x^i N^i_{-1}}{w^i_H} = u^i H^i_{-1} L^i_H + a^i s^i_N (1 - \hat{N}). \tag{24}$$

The valuation of monopoly wealth in (14) and (15) yields $(r/\hat{v} - 1)v^i = \pi^i = (\beta - 1)\phi^i_x x^i$, while the free entry condition (18) may be written as $v^i = (1 - \tau^i_R)w^i_H a^i s^i_N/N^i_{-1}$. Combining them, we have

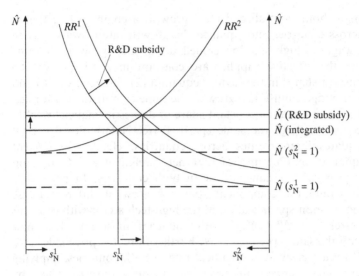

Figure 4.1   Innovation in the world economy.

$(r/\hat{v} - 1)[a^i s^i_N(1 - \tau^i_R)]/(\beta - 1) = \phi^i_x x^i N^i_{-1}/w^i_H$. Therefore, the resource constraint is:

$$\left(\frac{r}{\hat{v}} - 1\right) \frac{\alpha_{hx}(1 - \tau^i_R)}{\beta - 1} = 1 - \hat{N} + \frac{u^i H^i_{-1} L^i_H}{a^i s^i_N}. \tag{25}$$

The valuation equation of monopoly wealth implies $\hat{v} = \hat{p}_x \hat{x}$. Therefore, by using $\hat{w} = \hat{v}\hat{N}$, one may conveniently rewrite the Euler equation as $\rho\hat{N} = r/\hat{v}$. Upon collecting terms, the resource constraints of the two countries become:

$$\left[1 + \rho \frac{\alpha_{hx}(1 - \tau^i_R)}{\beta - 1}\right] \hat{N} = \frac{\alpha_{hx}(1 - \tau^i_R)}{\beta - 1} + 1 + \frac{u^i H^i_{-1} L^i_H}{a^i s^i_N}, \quad i = \{1,2\}.$$

The two constraints determine the two unknowns, the worldwide rate of product innovation, $\hat{N}$, and country 1's share in the product line, s^1_N. Note that the effective supply of skilled labour, $u^i H^i_{-1} L^i_H$ in each country is determined by preference and technology parameters, as well as by policy (see equations (5) and (6)). Figure 4.1 gives a graphic illustration, plotting the innovation rate on the vertical axis and the country share on the horizontal axis. The two curves represent the resource constraint of the two countries for highly skilled labour. The floor levels give the innovation rates that each country would have achieved as a closed economy, or in the absence of knowledge spillovers. The intersection of the two constraints determines the world innovation rate and pins down the country share in the worldwide number of products. Obviously, the innovation rate of the integrated world economy must exceed the autarkic rate of each country.

3.1   Education and R&D subsidies to promote growth

The total differential of (26) reveals how the two curves shift in response to government intervention,

$$
\hat{N}\left[1 + \rho\frac{\alpha_{\mathrm{hx}}(1 - \tau_{\mathrm{R}}^{i})}{\beta - 1}\right]\left(\frac{d\hat{N}}{\hat{N}}\right) = -\frac{u^{i}H_{-1}^{i}L_{\mathrm{H}}^{i}}{a^{i}s_{\mathrm{N}}^{i}}\left(\frac{ds_{\mathrm{N}}^{i}}{s_{\mathrm{N}}^{i}}\right)
$$

$$
+ (\rho\hat{N} - 1)\frac{\alpha_{\mathrm{hx}}}{\beta - 1}d\tau_{\mathrm{R}}^{i} + \left(\frac{\partial u^{i}H_{-1}^{i}}{\partial \tau_{\mathrm{E}}^{i}}\right)\frac{L_{\mathrm{H}}^{i}}{a^{i}s_{\mathrm{N}}^{i}}d\tau_{\mathrm{E}}^{i}, \quad i = \{1, 2\}. \quad (27)
$$

The first coefficient on the r.h.s. gives the slope of the resource constraints RR^{i} at the initial equilibrium position. The last two coefficients determine the upward shift of the resource constraints that is obtained when the government introduces either a subsidy to R&D or a subsidy to schooling. It is immediately apparent that both types of subsidies have quite similar long-run effects. If the other country remains passive, the activist country is able to capture a larger share of innovative products, thus boosting the common innovation rate at home and abroad.

3.2   Ineffectiveness of trade policy?

Perhaps somewhat surprisingly, trade policy affects neither the innovation rate nor the share of high-tech products, although there will be, of course, level effects on prices and quantities. Why would protection be ineffectual in raising a country's competitiveness in the high-tech industries? Trade barriers obviously raise the domestic demand price of imported brands and induce agents to shift demand into home-produced varieties. Output, prices, and, owing to fixed markups, unit costs rise at home. According to (14) to (16), profits and monopoly wealth rise in proportion to $\phi_x x$. If the wage for highly skilled labour were rising in proportion, $\widehat{\phi_x x} = \hat{v} = \hat{w}$, then protection would have no impact on the incentives to conduct R&D because the effects on benefits and costs would just offset each other. Similarly, higher wages would offset the increased demand of home producers for highly skilled labour, $h_x x N_{-1} = \alpha_{hx}(\phi_x x/w_H)N_{-1}$. Hence, wages rise by just enough to leave demand for highly skilled labour from production and R&D unchanged. In other words, protection raises the profitability of both manufacturing and research. By assumption, both activities compete for the same primary resource. Protection promotes both activities equally and, thus, enhances neither, but only bids up the equilibrium wage rate.[11] However, the ineffectiveness of trade policy is a rather special result, due to the fact that both research and manufacturing of high-tech products use exactly the same primary resource. If one were to allow for a different composition of factor demand, protection would surely affect the innovation rate and the home country's share of products. Still, the magnitude of the effects might remain small as compared with policies of directly promoting training and R&D. Furthermore, we have excluded any role that trade policy might play for the international dissemination of knowledge. We have assumed at the outset that the results of industrial innovation spill over to the international economy instantaneously and completely. Thus, trade policy has no role to play in facilitating access to the international knowledge stock.

4   Calibration to Western and CEEC countries

We now proceed with a numerical implementation of this model towards the kind of numerical thought experiment outlined in the introduction. We sketch the general procedure only as much as is necessary to understand the subsequent results, and relegate further details to appendix A at the end of the paper. Our approach assumes that the CEECs have successfully completed *transformation* to market economies of the West European type, so that the above model fits both the Western countries and the CEECs equally well. Moreover, our basic premise is that the CEECs would be in a situation broadly comparable to West European countries today if they had a capitalistic history in a pan-European economy instead of their communist past. On a fundamental level, this does not appear to be wholly unreasonable. After all, the stark separation of Europe that has characterized our perception up to 1990 did emerge primarily because of differences in the economic system.[12] What we now try to do is calibrate our two-region model to such a hypothetical pan-European economy without any communist past. In doing so, we assume a laissez-faire world. A suitable adjustment of key stock variables is then meant to reflect the unfavourable initial conditions that the communist past has in fact bequeathed to the CEECs. This allows us to calculate *transition paths*. We first calculate a laissez-faire transition path, which we then compare with adjustment under certain policy interventions.

The calibration procedure detailed in the appendix requires data on regional GDPs, flows of fixed capital formation, capital income shares, the structure of intra-industry trade between the two regions, the overall trade balance, as well as the size and breakdown (into high- and low-skilled) of each region's labour force. Among the key parameters to be specified exogenously are the real interest rate, the growth rate of wages, the elasticity of substitution between different varieties of the high-tech good (or, equivalently, the markup for these goods), the intertemporal elasticity of substitution, and an adjustment cost parameter for investment in physical capital. In line with our basic premise, we largely rely on observed data for the West European economies and use these, together with observations on the CEECs where available, to infer hypothetical data for the CEECs. For instance, we take the observed ratio of high- to low-skilled labour for Western countries and apply this to the observed overall labour force of the CEECs, to obtain the size of high- and low-skilled labour endowment of the CEECs. In a similar vein, the CEECs' GDP is obtained by applying the observed average labour productivity of West European countries to the CEECs' total labour force. The ratio of fixed capital formation to absorption as well as the capital income share are similarly taken from Western observations and assumed to hold for both regions in the benchmark equilibrium.

Perhaps the most difficult part of arriving at a meaningful stylized data set relates to trade flows. It might be tempting to look just at West European countries' external trade position (i.e. trade with non-European countries) to infer what trade between Western Europe and the CEECs might look like in the hypothetical pan-European benchmark equilibrium. There are, however, several problems with this, which led us to follow a different procedure. First, overall external trade of Western Europe is with countries that are quite different from our hypothetical 'non-communist' CEECs, both in terms of the degree of integration and in terms of structural characteristics. Secondly, the present volume of West European trade with the CEECs is way below its full post-transformation potential, as revealed by several empirical studies (see the survey by Baldwin (1994: 102)). And thirdly, any aggregation from some given commodity classification to our two-dimensional commodity space would appear to be highly arbitrary and, depending on where one drew the line between high- and low-tech goods, the calibrated structure of production could be quite different (and sometimes implausible). We therefore decided to resort to theoretical reasoning instead of trade statistics to arrive at the trade pattern of our two-region pan-European economy. In a world with identical and homothetic tastes, the share of high-tech exports in country 1's GDP is equal to the ratio of the other country's absorption in world GDP, $s_D^2 = \bar{P}^2\bar{D}^2/(GDP^1 + GDP^2)$, multiplied by the share of this commodity in domestic production, $s_X^1 = N_{-1}^1 p_X^1 x^1/GDP^1$.[13] Thus,

$$\frac{N_{-1}^1 p_X^1 (x^1 - D_X^{11})}{GDP^1} = s_D^2 s_X^1, \tag{28}$$

and analogously for the second region. The basic idea is simply to use s_D^i and s_X^i together with GDP data to infer exports of high-tech goods (the numerator of the l.h.s. above). We assume balanced trade between the two regions for our benchmark growth path, hence s_D^i coincides with the ratio of region-i GDP to world GDP. The justification is two-fold. First, if measured as a percentage of GDP, the observable deviation of absorption from GDP is very small for the group of Western countries as a whole (with an external surplus on goods *and services* of about 1 per cent of GDP in 1990, according to UN data).[14] Secondly, and more importantly, our benchmark growth path is a hypothetical construct with a very tenuous relationship to the current historical situation, in particular as regards aggregate trade balance. Hence, given GDP values obtained as mentioned above, all we need are reasonable figures for production shares in GDP to arrive at the high-tech trade figures that we require for calibration. By definition, $s_D^1 GDP^2 = s_D^2 GDP^1$, and the production shares are equal in both regions if and only if intra-industry trade in high-tech goods is balanced, i.e. if there is no inter-industry trade at all. In line with widely held expectations, we assume that the West continues to hold a comparative advantage in high-tech goods vis-à-vis post-transformation CEECs, and therefore is a net importer of standardized goods from the East in our benchmark equilibrium. We thus assume a larger production share of high-tech goods for the West (80 per cent) than for the East (60 per cent). More details on data sources are given in appendix B at the end of the paper, where Tables 4A.1 and 4A.2 give an overview of the values chosen for the various parameters and the calibration results obtained.

5   Transition path

Starting from a path of balanced growth for our hypothetical pan-European economy, we now introduce history by changing the initial conditions. Instead of being on this reference path, the CEECs start out with lower capital stocks, both physical and human. Moreover, reflecting a rather poor innovation record during their communist past, the degree of product diversity and the number of 'blueprints' available in the CEECs are assumed to fall short of their reference value by a significant amount. As with capital, the number of high-tech goods produced by CEECs must be seen as a stock variable that can adjust only through R&D, which requires time and resources.

5.1   Initial conditions

The extent to which the actual starting point of transition deviates from the benchmark balanced-growth path must be approximated by relying on indicative information rather than hard facts. Thus, looking at our data sources (see appendix B at the end of the paper), we observe that the (weighted) average ratio of high-tech exports (defined as SITC 5–9) to GDP for the West is more than twice the ratio of high-tech exports of the East to the West. In terms of our model, this must to a large extent be attributed to a much lower degree of product differentiation. We therefore scale down the *number of brands* produced by the East to half its benchmark balanced growth value. Turning to the physical capital stock, one might look at the observed differences in labour productivity between West and East to infer the extent to which the Eastern physical capital stock deviates from its hypothetical balanced-growth value. However, our data reveal that Eastern labour productivity is but a third of Western productivity and, taking any sensible value for the elasticity of output with respect to capital, this would amount to an enormous deviation. In their investigation of German unification, Sinn and Sinn (1992) suggest that the East German capital stock was devalued to about one-third of its book value upon unification. This is based on a direct confrontation with the West German economy. In our two-region model economy, the effect would appear to be somewhat more moderate, and it is certainly uneven across sectors. We therefore assume a 50 per cent gap for *physical capital* in the differentiated goods sector and a 30 per cent gap for the standardized goods sector. Our *human capital stock* largely relates to engineering knowledge. It is quite well known that Eastern countries do not lag behind as much in this regard as they do in terms of institutional knowledge. Hence, we assume a more modest lag of 10 per cent.

Starting from different initial conditions may, under certain assumptions, give rise to permanent effects in the sense of leading to a different steady-state level position, not only for the CEECs but also for West European countries. Thus, our model exhibits path dependence in terms of levels but not in terms of growth rates. In other words, starting out with grossly displaced initial conditions implies that East and West will permanently experience growth paths that are different in terms of *levels* from the hypothetical case of a 'non-communist history'. Long-run growth rates remain unaffected by initial conditions, but may be influenced by policy intervention (see below). With the help of our calibrated model, we now propose to quantify the implications of this difference in initial conditions. We first present the transition path emerging for a laissez-faire world. In section 6, we proceed to evaluate alternative ways of influencing transition by means of policy intervention, using the laissez-faire transition path as a reference case.

5.2   Physical capital

Table 4.1 gives percentage deviations for various selected periods between laissez-faire transition and the benchmark path of a pan-European economy without a communist history in the East. To obtain a better feel for the catching-up process, we decompose the displacement of initial conditions. Panel (a) turns to the fact that the East starts with a largely obsolete capital stock. Quite obviously, output and income must be very low compared with the long-run potential. Scarce capital depresses labour productivity and wages. Since the gap in the capital stock is more pronounced in the advanced X sector, highly skilled labour suffers from particularly strong wage pressure in the early transition phase, while the returns to capital should be large. This implies a more moderate wage spread early on compared with the long-run situation after the catching-up process. Large capital investments in the high-tech sector will also lead to wage increases for skilled labour. The prospect of relatively high wages in the future provides incentives for increased education. The effective supply of highly skilled labour is, therefore, relatively low in the short run because agents spend more time in school in order to acquire skills and supply less factory work. This presents an obstacle to the expansion of all skill-intensive activities. However, the brunt of adjustment is borne by the high-tech sector because employment will actually shift to R&D where labour productivity is largely unaffected. The output contraction in the high-tech sector strengthens prices, improving both the terms of trade and monopoly profits and thus the rewards to R&D, while the erosion of high-skilled wages saves research costs. Consequently, the speed of innovation picks up. Since the model abstracts from the use of physical capital in R&D, low initial capital stocks may thus indirectly favour product development. However, all of these are temporary phenomena. Once investment succeeds in closing the large initial gap in capital stocks, wage growth

Table 4.1   Transition in the East with laissez-faire

		Percentage changes in periods[a]			
		1	10	30	100
(a) Low initial physical capital stocks					
N_{-1}	Product range	0.000	1.989	1.423	−1.129
$K_{y,-1}$	Capital stock in Y sector	−30.000	−13.966	−2.705	−0.478
$K_{x,-1}$	Capital stock in X sector	−50.000	−22.440	−2.325	−0.473
H_{-1}	Skill level	0.000	1.955	0.672	−0.005
uH_{-1}	Effective supply of skills	−8.451	0.961	1.076	−0.006
$w_H H_{-1}/w_L$ Wage spread		−2.430	0.757	0.653	0.000
xN_{-1}	X-sector output	−27.656	−9.848	−0.037	−0.183
Y	Y-sector output	−10.076	−4.380	−0.813	−0.143
p_x^1/p_x^2	Terms of trade	10.289	3.632	0.465	−0.001
TB_Y	Y-sector trade balance[b]	−6.612	−1.535	1.593	2.145
TB_X	X-sector trade balance[b]	−12.991	−2.081	3.953	3.050
B_{-1}	Net foreign asset position[c]	0.000	−74.058	−101.046	−95.901
(b) Low initial human capital stock					
N_{-1}	Product range	0.000	−10.393	−5.985	−5.339
$K_{y,-1}$	Capital stock in Y sector	0.000	−0.703	−1.698	−2.264
$K_{x,-1}$	Capital stock in X sector	0.000	−4.404	−3.571	−2.262
H_{-1}	Skill level	−10.000	−4.358	−0.647	0.000
uH_{-1}	Effective supply of skills	−18.213	−7.166	−1.217	0.000
$w_H H_{-1}/w_L$ Wage spread		−6.650	−2.521	−0.487	0.001
xN_{-1}	X-sector output	−2.871	−6.774	−2.388	−0.865
Y	Y-sector output	0.000	−0.210	−0.509	−0.680
p_x^1/p_x^2	Terms of trade	0.529	−0.853	0.079	0.000
TB_Y	Y-sector trade balance[b]	1.809	1.489	0.987	0.909
TB_X	X-sector trade balance[b]	1.690	−4.239	0.137	1.558
B_{-1}	Net foreign asset position[c]	0.000	−10.434	−39.169	−45.872
(c) Low initial product range					
N_{-1}	Product range	−50.000	−14.518	710.519	710.070
$K_{y,-1}$	Capital stock in Y sector	0.000	72.205	73.890	74.343
$K_{x,-1}$	Capital stock in X sector	0.000	74.888	74.585	74.342
H_{-1}	Skill level	0.000	70.757	0.004	0.002
uH_{-1}	Effective supply of skills	6.988	71.359	70.124	0.002
$w_H H_{-1}/w_L$ Wage spread		5.251	70.595	70.118	0.000
xN_{-1}	X-sector output	721.053	74.272	71.953	71.671
Y	Y-sector output	0.000	70.662	71.175	71.313
p_x^1/p_x^2	Terms of trade	710.999	70.433	0.071	70.000
TB_Y	Y-sector trade balance[b]	2.725	1.486	1.218	1.187
TB_X	X-sector trade balance[b]	727.958	71.395	1.779	2.210
B_{-1}	Net foreign asset position[c]	0.000	749.071	761.885	763.485
(d) Overall initial conditions (a+b+c)					
N_{-1}	Product range	750.000	722.602	714.555	715.681
$K_{y,-1}$	Capital stock in Y sector	730.000	716.329	78.019	76.886
$K_{x,-1}$	Capital stock in X sector	750.000	730.426	710.193	76.878
H_{-1}	Skill level	710.000	73.169	0.077	70.003
uH_{-1}	Effective supply of skills	718.713	77.748	70.219	70.003

Table 4.1   (*cont.*)

		Percentage changes in periods[a]			
		1	10	30	100
$w_H H_{-1}/w_L$	Wage spread	74.253	72.510	0.046	0.002
xN_{-1}	X-sector output	745.008	720.428	74.334	72.672
Y	Y-sector output	710.076	75.170	72.458	72.102
p_x^1/p_x^2	Terms of trade	71.285	2.359	0.647	70.001
TB_Y	Y-sector trade balance[b]	72.216	1.296	3.630	4.075
TB_X	X-sector trade balance[b]	732.638	77.751	5.552	6.547
B_{-1}	Net foreign asset position[c]	0.000	7125.552	7194.586	7197.644

[a] Values indicate percentage differences vis-à-vis a hypothetical benchmark growth path with 'equal' initial conditions in East and West (no 'communist legacy').
[b] Real trade balance, difference from benchmark expressed as a percentage of benchmark sectoral outputs.
[c] As a percentage of benchmark GDP.

slows down to a more moderate speed in the long run, thus weakening education incentives. Both the schooling and the reallocation effects disappear. Indeed, the medium-run surge in innovative activities in the East is not sustained in the long run when diversity actually falls short of the undisturbed growth path. The most important and, indeed, the only significant long-run implication of initial capital shortage relates to foreign sector accounts. The CEECs accumulate a heavy debt position that must be serviced by returning to a trade surplus in the long run. Starting from depressed initial conditions, these countries should see rapid income growth during the catching-up period. The intertemporal consumption-smoothing motive implies that agents want to borrow against future income increases by going into debt abroad. The size of the foreign debt, of course, reflects the absence of any credit market imperfections and uncertainty about the future. In our model, countries have unlimited access to international capital markets as long as they satisfy intertemporal solvency conditions. In reality, however, access to international capital markets may be rather restricted, so that our results should be seen as an upper bound.

5.3   Human capital

Panel (b) of Table 4.1 turns to human capital, where the initial gap is a relatively modest 10 per cent. A lower overall supply of skills is felt in a higher wage per unit of skills (see the impact effect on the wage spread), but the opportunity cost of schooling ($w_H H_{-1}$) is none the less reduced. Weighing this cost against the present value of future income gains from additional education, agents decide to withdraw some of their time from factory work. As a result, the initial gap in the *effective* human capital stock is almost double the initial skill displacement. The CEECs cut back on high-tech manufacturing and innovation because these activities are particularly skill intensive. A smaller menu of specialized products depresses productivity and raises the acquisition price for capital. Investment incentives are further dampened by the skilled labour shortage, which depresses the marginal productivity of capital in the X sector, where short-run investment is particularly low. The severe medium-run contraction in high-tech output is reflected by a deterioration of the high-tech trade balance. Over the course of time, the CEECs will accumulate a significant foreign debt burden. Once they succeed in closing the skill gap, innovation and manufacturing pick up and the economy rebounds. However, capital stocks and the product range permanently remain below what they could have been if the CEECs had started out with initial conditions comparable to developed Western economies (the hypothetical benchmark case).

5.4 Knowledge stock

A further aspect of the 'communist legacy' relates to product diversification and the number of blueprints for differentiated goods. Panel (c) of Table 4.1 portrays the transition following a 50 per cent initial gap in the product range. Less product diversity implies lower productivity in forming capital goods and depresses investment incentives. Furthermore, a smaller knowledge stock retards the development of new varieties of sophisticated goods. Thus, the transition suffers from low physical capital stocks, which restrict production of both goods. However, contraction is much more severe in high-tech manufacturing. In the early adjustment phase, the CEECs are catching up in the research sector, creating a shortage of highly skilled labour. With a high wage rate today, the opportunity cost of education is high. Agents cut back on their schooling activities and devote more time to working, which eases the skilled labour shortage somewhat. Nevertheless, the innovation boom diverts highly skilled labour from skill-intensive manufacturing. High-tech production falls by more than 20 per cent initially, when capital stocks are still at their benchmark levels. Later on, when innovation returns to a more normal speed, wages for skilled labour yield somewhat as labour is released from research activities. The output decline in skill-intensive manufacturing is reversed to a large degree, but not completely. Because the initial gap in the product range is as much as 50 per cent, output per firm in the East must be much higher in these early phases of transition and prices of Eastern varieties therefore lower. The marked deterioration in the terms of trade also feeds into a large deterioration in the high-tech trade balance, whereas the trade balance in Y goods actually increases vis-à-vis the benchmark situation because there is no immediate contraction of output.

To complete the picture, panel (d) of Table 4.1 gives a flavour of how transition might look if all the initial gaps hold simultaneously. We may abstain from further explanations since we have already discussed the individual components of the transition scenario. Figures 4.2a–d allow for a convenient visual inspection of transition paths for key variables. Solid lines relate to the overall scenario, while broken lines show the decomposition. The figures also reveal that the catching-up process will never be complete if the scenario includes a displacement of Eastern knowledge stock and, thereby, implicitly of the world knowledge stock. As is clear from the analysis of section 3, the model does not endogenously determine the long-run level of the world knowledge stock. It depends on its own initial condition and developments during the transition. However, the model uniquely determines the long-run growth rates, interest rate, and also the *ratios* of capital stocks and country-specific knowledge stocks *relative* to the worldwide knowledge stock. Figure 4.2a shows that X-sector capital almost completely catches up if only its own initial condition is displaced (bold triangles). On the other hand, X-sector capital fails to converge back to the original growth path if the initial condition of either human capital or the Eastern knowledge stock is subject to an initial disturbance. In both cases, the innovations during the transition result in a permanently lower path of worldwide knowledge stocks. The argument is particularly clear from Figure 4.2c, where the initial displacement of Eastern (and, thus, worldwide) know-ledge capital cannot be made up for by innovation during the transition. In short, long-run income levels depend on what happens to innovation during the transition.

6   The role of policy

It is hard to conceive of transition without any government policy. Indeed, successful transition is widely regarded to be a matter of choosing the right policies, and it appears that transition economies are major attractions for economic policy advice. From the viewpoint of the neoclassical efficiency paradigm, policy needs to identify and correct market failures that may cause inefficiency along the adjustment path. In principle, such inefficiencies may be avoided and targeted by means of an appropriate corrective policy instrument. Unfavourable initial conditions

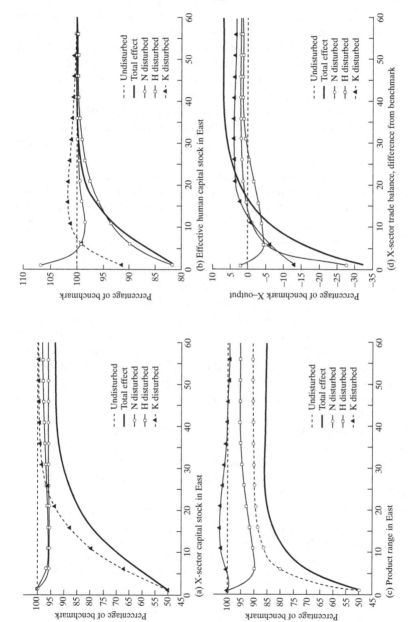

Figure 4.2 Transition paths under laissez-faire.

that are inherited from history are a matter of fact and, thus, unavoidable. Indeed, one of the principal messages from our results is that detrimental initial conditions do not, per se, provide any rationale for active government policy. Quite to the contrary, distortionary policies already in place may be important sources of inefficiencies. For example, trade between East and West is still heavily hampered by artificial tariff and non-tariff barriers, which are well known to cause static inefficiencies and are widely regarded as being detrimental to the transition process. Under certain conditions, trade policies may also influence the long-run growth performance even though we have ruled out such implications in the construction of our model (see above). It is none the less interesting to explore the role that commercial policy may play in our numerical calculations.

More fundamental distortions that we highlight in our model relate to R&D and high-tech manufacturing production. Product differentiation and monopolistic competition result in prices above marginal cost in the high-tech sector. Moreover, individual innovators produce knowledge spillovers to the rest of the economy. This positive externality is not rewarded by market prices, thus making private agents hesitant to invest in research and implying a lower than optimal rate of innovation.[15] Grossman and Helpman (1991) identify an R&D subsidy as a first-best policy to close the gap between the social and private returns to R&D. We investigate how transition might be affected by such a policy. Finally, given the importance of human capital in industrial research as well as in technologically sophisticated production, one might wonder if there is a case for subsidizing education. We therefore include a schooling subsidy in our policy scenarios. Tables 4.2 and 4.3 juxtapose the effects of these policies on the transition paths, and the panels in Figure 4.3 provide a concise visualization.

The preceding section demonstrated a catching-up scenario of an economy starting from unfavourable initial conditions. Table 4.1 and Figure 4.2 reported the transition in terms of deviations from a hypothetical balanced-growth equilibrium, which is indicated by the broken horizontal line in Figure 4.2. Once the historical stock variables are displaced from the steady-state path, path dependence in terms of levels may prevent the economy from ever again reaching the same long-run equilibrium path. The lines end up being horizontal because we have deflated all variables by their long-run growth rates. We interpreted the thick solid line as describing the laissez-faire transition path. We now shift our viewpoint and take this as our reference equilibrium. We ask how policy might cause the economy to follow an alternative path of development that deviates moderately from the thick solid lines of Figure

Table 4.2   Transition in the East with policy intervention

		Percentage changes in periods[a]			
		1	10	30	100
(a) 10 per cent tariff on high-tech imports in the East					
N_{-1}	Product range	0.000	70.126	0.031	0.218
$K_{y,-1}$	Capital stock in Y sector	0.000	73.785	75.589	75.859
$K_{x,-1}$	Capital stock in X sector	0.000	73.485	74.931	75.052
H_{-1}	Skill level	0.000	70.075	0.003	0.000
uH_{-1}	Effective supply of skills	0.507	70.091	70.021	0.001
$w_H H_{-1}/w_L$	Wage spread	70.114	0.452	0.805	0.858
xN_{-1}	X-sector output	0.387	71.337	71.936	71.950
Y	Y-sector output	0.000	71.142	71.698	71.782
p_x^1/p_x^2	Terms of trade	2.124	2.561	2.698	2.699
TB_Y	Y-sector trade balance[b])	73.389	74.301	74.699	74.741
TB_X	X-sector trade balance[b])	7.828	3.951	2.631	2.618
B_{-1}	Net foreign debt[c])	0.000	9.664	12.491	12.450
(b) 10 per cent tariff on standardized goods in the West					
N_{-1}	Product range	0.000	0.092	0.113	0.000
$K_{y,-1}$	Capital stock in Y sector	0.000	74.407	76.509	76.785
$K_{x,-1}$	Capital stock in X sector	0.000	2.265	3.272	3.275
H_{-1}	Skill level	0.000	0.136	0.050	70.000
uH_{-1}	Effective supply of skills	70.669	0.064	0.073	0.000
$w_H H_{-1}/w_L$	Wage spread	8.157	9.957	10.732	10.793
xN_{-1}	X-sector output	70.451	0.794	1.286	1.232
Y	Y-sector output	0.000	71.333	71.984	72.071
p_x^1/p_x^2	Terms of trade	0.144	70.248	70.431	70.459
TB_Y	Y-sector trade balance[b])	73.423	74.649	75.200	75.257
TB_X	X-sector trade balance[b])	5.716	4.498	4.299	4.213
B_{-1}	Net foreign debt[c]	0.000	79.640	712.580	711.884
(c) 10 per cent R&D subsidy in the East					
N_{-1}	Product range	0.000	5.965	9.862	21.039
$K_{y,-1}$	Capital stock in Y sector	0.000	70.216	0.145	3.960
$K_{x,-1}$	Capital stock in X sector	0.000	70.492	0.386	4.385
H_{-1}	Skill level	0.000	70.171	70.171	70.229
uH_{-1}	Effective supply of skills	1.106	70.083	70.042	70.093
$w_H H_{-1}/w_L$	Wage spread	4.644	3.969	3.986	4.000
xN_{-1}	X-sector output	74.748	72.918	72.170	70.687
Y	Y-sector output	0.000	70.064	0.043	1.163
p_x^1/p_x^2	Terms of trade	1.511	2.531	2.608	2.595
TB_Y	Y-sector trade balance[b])	0.182	0.045	0.031	0.295
TB_X	X-sector trade balance[b])	71.523	0.342	0.512	0.501
B_{-1}	Net foreign debt[c])	0.000	75.086	77.549	710.158
(d) 10 per cent education subsidy in the East					
N_{-1}	Product range	0.000	79.459	71.514	4.302
$K_{y,-1}$	Capital stock in Y sector	0.000	70.552	71.126	0.338
$K_{x,-1}$	Capital stock in X sector	0.000	73.879	70.464	3.355
H_{-1}	Skill level	0.000	6.459	10.351	10.975
uH_{-1}	Effective supply of skills	719.843	74.832	2.480	3.776

Table 4.2   (*cont.*)

		Percentage changes in periods[a]			
		1	10	30	100
$w_H H_{-1}/w_L$	Wage spread	3.519	7.659	9.676	10.170
$x N_{-1}$	X-sector output	72.970	75.790	1.020	3.605
Y	Y-sector output	0.000	70.165	70.337	0.101
p_x^1/p_x^2	Terms of trade	0.640	70.853	0.135	0.000
TB_Y	Y-sector trade balance[b]	0.946	0.467	70.102	70.036
TB_X	X-sector trade balance[b]	2.038	75.121	1.302	2.903
B_{-1}	Net foreign debt[c]	0.000	719.472	752.783	760.732

[a] Values indicate percentage differences vis-à-vis the laissez-faire transition path.
[b] Real trade balance, difference from laissez-faire transition as a percentage of laissez-faire sectoral outputs.
[c] Difference as a percentage of laissez-faire GDP.

4.2. Figure 4.3 and Table 4.2 show percentage deviations from the laissez-faire transition.

6.1   Trade policy

One of the main problems in East–West integration is the resistance of West European countries to opening their markets to traditional labour-intensive Y goods where the CEECs have a clear comparative advantage. The West continues to provide protection in these 'sensitive' sectors, which, in turn, might provoke a protectionist backlash in the CEECs against imports of high-tech, skill-intensive X goods from the West. We capture the essence of the problem by means of two scenarios: panel (b) of Table 4.2 shows how the East is affected if its exports to the West are discriminated against by a 10 per cent tariff; panel (a) shows some effects on the East if it imposes a 10 per cent tariff on high-tech, skill-intensive imports from Western Europe. In both scenarios, the tariff measures are unilateral. For lack of space we report results only for the East, which is identified as region 1. The effects are illustrated in Figures 4.3a and 4.3b.

Western protection against labour-intensive goods from the East reduces demand for the traditional good. The relative price of high-tech goods must increase, and more so in the West than in the East. Because the price of the imported goods in the East is p_x^2, while its export prices are p_x^1 and $p_Y = 1$, the terms of trade may be identified by the change in p_x^1/p_x^2. Consequently, the terms of trade move against the East, after a few periods at least. On the other hand, the East also produces the skill-intensive innovative good, which now sells at a price relatively higher than the traditional good. The prices of skilled labour and the rental

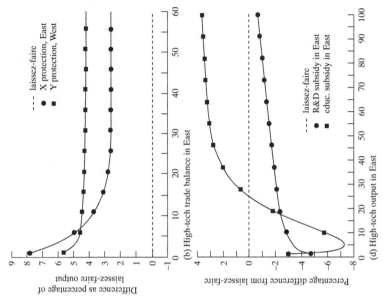

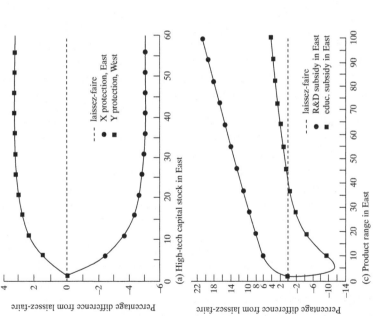

Figure 4.3   Transition paths: The role of government policy.

Table 4.3   Welfare and long-run growth effects

			Percentage change in:[b]			
		Bench-mark[a]	Tariff East	Tariff West	R&D subsidy	Education subsidy
EV-East	Equivalent variation[c]	0.000	1.070	70.757	1.233	70.967
r	World interest rate	1.040	0.000	0.000	0.041	0.022
$\hat{w}$	Wage growth rate	1.012	0.000	0.000	0.017	0.009
$\hat{C}$	Consumption growth rate	1.041	0.000	0.000	0.056	0.030
$\hat{N}$	Innovation rate	1.100	0.000	0.000	0.134	0.072

[a] Benchmark growth rates.
[b] Percentage changes from benchmark growth rates. Thus, if n_g is the percentage change in $\hat{N}$ for some policy, its new value is $\hat{N} \times (1 + n_g/100)$.
[c] The equivalent variation implied by the respective policies for the East, converted into a constant flow and expressed as a percentage of benchmark GDP.

price of X-sector capital rise because these factors are used in the high-tech industry. By the same reasoning, wages for the unskilled and the rental price of Y-sector capital must fall. Because both sectors purchase the same capital good, the increased rental rate of return in the X sector boosts capital accumulation, whereas investment in the Y sector is depressed. Higher future wages for highly skilled workers boost the returns to education and expand the skilled labour supply after a few periods. Such a shift in factor supplies clearly favours the expansion of the Eastern high-tech sector but shrinks its traditional sector. The East therefore generates a smaller trade surplus in Y goods but also relies less on net imports of the innovative good (note that the X-sector trade balance is negative in the base case transition). Obviously, the decline in export earnings also translates into higher foreign debt. Table 4.3 shows that Western protection inflicts welfare losses on the East. The terms-of-trade deterioration contributes importantly to these losses.

If the CEECs were to impose tariffs against skill-intensive Western high-tech imports, producer prices of innovative goods, p_x^1, would rise in the East while declining export demand would erode prices, p_x^2, in the West. Nevertheless, tariffs raise the demand prices of Western high-tech imports in the East and inflate the acquisition costs of the composite capital good. Investment conditions deteriorate relative to the base case transition. Since relative output prices move in favour of X manufacturing, the decline in capital investments is more pronounced in the traditional Y sector. Initially, a higher producer price, p_x^1, boosts wages for highly-skilled labour but eventually this effect is reversed as the lack of investment shrinks the capital stock. With a high opportunity cost today and low returns in the future, agents cut labour training and spend more time working in the factory instead. Consequently, the effective supply of highly skilled labour first expands before contracting later on. These changes in factor supplies explain the short-run expansion followed by a contraction after a few periods due to lower capital investment. Intuitively, as demand shifts away from imports towards home-produced high-tech goods and towards the traditional good, and as aggregate output of the X sector first expands before it contracts, the trade balance must improve quite vigorously in the short run. Over time, the improvement becomes more moderate. The trade surplus in traditional goods shrinks monotonically. Panel (a) in Table 4.2 reports the real trade balance. The increase in export prices gives even more weight to the improvement in the X-sector trade balance and explains why the net foreign asset position improves. The reduction in Eastern foreign indebtedness may also be viewed from a savings investment perspective. As agents anticipate the reduction in future income, they reduce consumption today and save more (consumption smoothing). The home economy also needs to finance less investment and, thus, relies less on foreign capital inflows. Finally, the East improves its welfare position (see Table 4.3), which may be largely explained by a terms-of-trade improvement. Western high-tech goods are the only imports of the Eastern economy. Thus, import prices fall relative to export prices for traditional goods and Eastern brands of the sophisticated good.

6.2 R&D subsidy

The R&D subsidy directly addresses the incentives for industrial innovation by reducing private research costs. As derived in our theoretical investigation, the common world innovation rate increases and the East captures a larger share of world production of innovative goods. More rapid innovation pushes up the interest rate as well as wage growth. From Table 4.3 we learn that the rise in the interest factor exceeds the change in wage growth, with the effect that the present value of future wages shrinks. Consequently, the incentives for labour training are diminished. Highly skilled agents redirect their activities from schooling to working in high-tech production or research labs. Therefore, the effective supply of skilled labour expands in the short run, but shrinks once skills deteriorate as a result of neglected labour training. Despite this favourable short-run supply effect, skill-intensive manufacturing actually declines. Highly skilled labour is released from manufacturing to accommodate the demand of a booming innovation sector. The productivity effect from the introduction of new specialized varieties reduces the resource cost per unit of capital. Capital becomes cheaper, which eventually attracts more investment to both production sectors and accommodates a slow revival of manufacturing output. The growth effects are illustrated in Figures 4.3c and 4.3d. Since all variables are deflated by their *initial* growth rates, more rapid growth after policy intervention tilts the time-paths upwards into the future. Finally, Table 4.3 shows that an R&D subsidy yields welfare gains that stem from two readily identified sources. First, the terms of trade change in favour of the East. The redirection of skilled labour towards innovation creates a supply shortage of the skill-intensive good in the East and raises the terms of trade in the X sector (see panel (c) of Table 4.2). In addition, more rapid innovation makes the prices of high-tech goods fall faster in both regions and decline relative to basic Y goods. Because the East is a *net* importer of high-tech goods but exports the basic good, it benefits from a dynamic terms-of-trade effect over time. A second channel for welfare gains is the fact that the R&D subsidy addresses a market failure that causes a suboptimally low innovation rate. A policy that accelerates innovation therefore yields first-order welfare gains on that account.

6.3   Education subsidy

The long-run consequences of an education subsidy are quite clear-cut and have already been discussed in the theoretical section. The general skill level and the effective supply of skilled labour expand in the long run and encourage both innovation and high-tech production. The most striking aspect of this scenario is that it demonstrates the possibility that things may get dramatically worse before they get better. In the short run, a considerable part of skilled labour is withdrawn from the active labour market, as agents respond to education incentives and spend more time on schooling. The skilled labour shortage strongly inhibits industrial research and, to a somewhat lesser extent, skill-intensive production. Once the skill upgrading in response to education incentives is completed, the shortage turns into a skilled-labour abundance that boosts innovation and high-tech manufacturing. Eventually, the available product diversity surpasses its laissez-faire value. The resulting productivity effects cut into investment costs and boost capital accumulation, which further expands production. Figures 4.3c and 4.3d demonstrate this dynamic adjustment pattern. Education shifts income into the future. In anticipation of future riches, agents spend on consumption now and reduce their savings. Consequently, domestic expenditure is partly financed by additional indebtedness abroad. The welfare implication of supporting education is not encouraging. The reason is that the schooling decisions of private agents correctly respond to market incentives. Rather than addressing an existing market failure, the subsidy introduces a new distortion between training and production activities. Although the education policy boosts the long-run growth rate and, thus, indirectly alleviates the R&D insufficiency, it does so by sacrificing output in the short run. Table 4.3 reports a non-negligible welfare loss.

7 Conclusions

In this paper, we have attempted to provide a quantitative treatment of the catching-up process that the Central and East European countries (CEECs) will experience once they have completed their transformation to market economies. Based on a conceptual distinction between systemic transformation and transition, the paper focuses on transition, which is identified as the dynamic adjustment following the very unfavourable initial conditions that their communist history has bequeathed to these countries. Towards this end, we have developed a two-region model of the world economy that highlights the importance of capital accumulation, both physical and human, as well as innovation for economic growth. We have characterized the equilibrium properties of such a world economy and how these may be influenced by economic policy. Economic transition is then viewed as a growth path that starts from initial conditions that are grossly displaced from a steady-state path. More specifically, we assume that the CEECs start out with much less physical capital, a lower level of manufacturing and research skills, as well as a lower product range than would be the case for a comparable Western-type economy. By relying on numerical techniques, we were able to pin down several important details of these transition paths. Moreover, we have compared the kind of transition emerging in a laissez-faire world with policy-influenced adjustment paths. The policies considered are tariff protection (by the CEECs themselves or by the West), as well as growth-oriented policies such as an R&D subsidy or an education subsidy.

One of the conclusions of this thought experiment is that, even if systemic transformation should go perfectly well, the time-horizon for catching-up is rather long. For instance, it may take more than four decades for transition economies to reach their steady-state levels of physical capital stocks. The time-horizon comes close to the economic life-span of a generation. Not only does catching-up take a long time, but it may also be incomplete. Detrimental initial conditions may have permanent effects. Our experiment shows that both physical capital and knowledge capital remain persistently below what they could have been without the unfortunate starting conditions bequeathed by the centrally planned economies. The long-run gaps are quite substantial – more than 15 per cent in the case of blueprints and more than 5 per cent in the case of human capital. A further aspect of the catching-up process is the unprecedented long-run levels of foreign debt. Our solutions may be seen as an upper bound for the borrowing requirements if these countries had unrestricted access to perfect international capital markets at a moderate interest rate. Our model does, of course, impose the condition that transition countries remain solvent and are in fact able to service the accumulated debt.

Transition is significantly affected by policies towards research and human capital accumulation, as well as by trade policies. We did not allow any influence of trade policy on the long-run growth rate, but protectionist policies nevertheless have important effects on levels. Our calculations show that continued import protection against labour-intensive goods by Western countries inflicts a welfare loss on the CEECs. The CEECs might be tempted to retaliate by discriminating against high-tech imports from the West. Even in the absence of retaliatory forces, such protection is sometimes advocated along the lines of an infant-industry argument. Our results reveal that the CEECs may, indeed, reap moderate welfare gains through such a trade policy. This is largely due to the familiar terms-of-trade effect.

Whether or not an active policy towards innovation or skill formation leads to a preferable transition path depends on the externalities that may be present in these activities. Our model captures such externalities in the form of knowledge spillovers. An R&D subsidy therefore gives rise to a positive welfare effect through more rapid product development during the transition. Moreover, such a policy also affects the long-run allocation of resources between R&D and manufacturing and, therefore, the long-run growth rate. However, for a 10 per cent subsidy the magnitudes of the welfare and long-run growth effects are less than impressive. An education subsidy will likewise raise the long-run growth rate by a moderate amount, but only at the cost of quite sizeable short-run output losses. Even though it helps to boost innovation, which is inefficiently low owing to knowledge spillovers, the model does not allow for a similar externality in the education decision. Rather than addressing an existing market failure, the subsidy introduces a new distortion and, thus, imposes a considerable welfare loss.

Appendix A: More on calibration

Calibration of an aggregate growth model that distinguishes only between standardized goods on the one hand and differentiated high-tech goods on the other proceeds along rather different lines from the familiar case of a static multi-sector model. Before turning to the details of the calibration procedure we need to specify some functional forms. Data sources will be given in appendix B.

Functional forms

Preferences
In a number of cases, balanced growth is possible only if the elasticity of the first derivative of some function, say $u(c)$, remains constant even though the argument grows at a constant rate. For example, we require the intertemporal elasticity of substitution in consumption, $\gamma = -(u'(c))/(cu''(c))$, to be constant over time. Upon integration, one derives the most general functional form satisfying this requirement,

$$u(c) = a \left(\frac{c^{1-1/\gamma}}{1 - 1/\gamma} \right) + b. \tag{A1}$$

One may now conveniently normalize the function by choosing values for the integration constants. Since nothing hinges on the normalization of the felicity function $u(\cdot)$, we set $a = 1$ and $b = 0$.

Schooling technology
The education technology is similarly implemented by choosing an iso-elastic form with an elasticity of marginal productivity equal to $\sigma_H = -eg''(e)/g'(e)$. One may normalize and set the integration constants a and b in two alternative ways. First, one may assume that it is impossible to improve skills without spending some time in school, $g(0) = 0$. Second, at the steady-state ratio, $\bar{e}$, implicitly determined by $g(\bar{e}) = 1 - \delta_H$ from (2), the marginal productivity of schooling in raising skill levels is unity, $g'(\bar{e}) = 1$. This normalization implies a form:

$$g(e) = (1 - \delta_H)^{\sigma_H} \left(\frac{e}{1 - \sigma_H} \right)^{1-\sigma_H}. \tag{A2}$$

It implies a stationary schooling ratio equal to $\bar{e} = (1 - \delta_H)(1 - \sigma_H)$ and satisfies $g(0) = 0$, $g(\bar{e}) = 1 - \delta_H$, and $g'(\bar{e}) = 1$. A problem with this is, however, that a sensitivity analysis of σ_H will change the schooling ratio $\bar{e}$. An alternative normalization would be to require $\bar{e} = 1 - \delta_H$ and, therefore, $g(\bar{e}) = \bar{e}$ and $g'(\bar{e}) = 1$. In this case, one would be left with a functional form:

$$g(e) = \left(\frac{1 - \delta_H}{1 - \sigma_H}\right)\left[\left(\frac{e}{1 - \delta_H}\right)^{1 - \sigma_H} - \sigma_H\right]. \tag{A3}$$

A drawback of this formulation, however, would be that the contribution of very small levels of educational effort to gross skill formation is negative. We therefore stick to the first alternative (A2).

Installation technology
We choose a quadratic form to parameterize the installation function for physical capital, $\psi(i)$,

$$\psi(i) = i + \psi_0 i^2. \tag{A4}$$

The installation function satisfies $\psi(0) = 0$ and $\psi'(0) = 1$. At a zero investment rate, a marginal unit of the capital good is transformed into a unit increase in the capital stock. With increasingly higher investment rates, the productivity of marginal investment in increasing the capital stock becomes rather low.

As a matter of experience, the computation of intertemporal equilibria is greatly facilitated by using $V = qK$ to replace the shadow price in the forward-looking investment equation (A4): $\psi'(i)\bar{P} = V/K$. Replacing the current value of K by the law of motion and using the quadratic form, the investment rate is implicitly determined by:

$$i^2 + \left(\delta_K + \frac{1}{2\psi_0}\right)i + \left(\delta_K - \frac{V}{\bar{P}K_{-1}}\right)\frac{1}{2\psi_0} = 0. \tag{A5}$$

Using shorthand notation, $a = \delta_K + (1/2\psi_0)$ and $b = [\delta_K - (V/\bar{P}K_{-1})]1/2\psi_0$; this quadratic function can be explicitly solved for the investment rate, $i_{1,2} = (-a \pm \sqrt{a^2 - 4b})/2$. We take, of course, the positive root to get the investment rate.

Fundamental identities

To start off it is useful to repeat a few accounting identities. Denoting effective demand for the composite capital good by $\bar{\psi} = \psi(i)K_{-1}$ and the current account by $CA = B - B_{-1}$, we have

(a) $CA + \bar{P}\bar{\psi} + vI_N = S = (r-1)B_{-1} + w_K K_{-1} + \pi N_{-1} + w_D - \bar{P}\bar{C}$,

(b) $\phi_x x N_{-1} + \phi_y Y = w_K K_{-1} + w_1 L_1 + w_H (H_{-1} u I_{,H} - h_R)$,

(c) $GDP = T_{\tau_B} + [\pi N_{-1} - w_H h_R + w_K K_{-1}] + w_L L_L + w_H H_{-1} u L_H$,   (A6)

(d) $GDP = TB + \bar{P}(\bar{C} + \bar{\psi}) = p_x x N_{-1} + P_Y Y + T_{\tau_B}$,

(e) $TB^i = GDP^i - \bar{P}^i \bar{D}^i = P_Y (Y^i - D_Y^i) + N_{-1}^i p_x^i (x^i - D_x^{ii}) - N_{-1}^j p_x^j D_x^{ij}$.

According to (a), household sector savings are channelled into financing the current account, domestic capital investments, and newly issued equity wealth from business formation. Since rental rates of capital are equalized across sectors in the long run and since capital is a homogeneous good, we simply write $w_K K_{-1} = w_K (K_{x,-1} + K_{y,-1})$ for the sum of rental payments of both sectors. Equation (b) gives the composition of value-added income at factor cost. By way of contrast, GDP at market prices also includes monopoly profits and indirect taxes as in (c). On the demand side, the trade balance and domestic absorption must add up to GDP, which is also equal to the sectoral outputs valued at producer prices plus indirect tax payments (see (d)). Finally, the trade balance in (e) may be viewed either as the difference between GDP and absorption or as the excess sum of exports over imports.

Demand

Relying on the above identities, we now use data on GDP, the aggregate trade balance, plus exports and imports of differentiated high-tech goods (see Table 4A.2) to calibrate the demand structure as follows. We start with cost normalizations $\phi_{x,0}^i = 1 = \phi_y^i$. Notice that the first of these equalities holds for the benchmark equilibrium only, while the second holds at all times owing to our choice of numeraire. The traditional good is priced at unit cost, $P_Y = 1$, while the price of the differentiated good reflects markup pricing, $p_{x,0}^i = \beta$. The markup factor is specified exogenously to reflect average results from econometric industry studies. The tariff rates chosen for differentiated goods, τ_B^{ij}, similarly reflect average values as reported in the literature. We fix units by setting an arbitrary value for $\bar{N}_{-1,0}$.

Given benchmark data for overall domestic absorption, $GDP_0 - TB_0$, of each region, we now determine the share s_N^1 of domestically produced varieties and the budget share α_{cx} for differentiated goods in total spending, such that the implied demand structure reproduces export and import data in the innovative sector, $EXP_{x,0}$ and $IMP_{x,0}$. The procedure is iterative and based on the following sequence of computations. First, we set $s_N^2 = 1 - s_N^1$ and $N_{-1,0}^i = s_N^i \bar{N}_{-1,0}$. Utilizing the above price normalization and the tariff barriers, one may then compute price indices, $P_{\bar{X}}^i, 0$, from (10) and the top-level Cobb–Douglas price indices, $\bar{P}_0^i$, using a guess for the expenditure share α_{cx}. This allows to determine the *quantity* of absorption as $\bar{D}_0^i = (GDP_0^i - TB_0^i)/\bar{P}_0^i$. The quantities of the standard and differentiated goods used in each region, $D_{Y,0}^i$, $D_{\bar{X},0}^i$ and $D_{x,0}^{ij}$, are then readily available from the demand functions. These quantities, in turn, imply benchmark tariff revenues $T_{\tau_B,0}^i$. Market clearing determines output of a representative firm in the high-tech sector, $x_0^i = \sum_j D_{x,0}^{ji}$. Going back to GDP data, we obtain production levels in the traditional sectors as $Y_0^i = (GDP_0^i - T_{\tau_B,0}^i - N_{-1,0}^i p_{x,0}^i x^i)/P_Y$. Moreover, the difference between domestic production and domestic use of differentiated goods implies a unique structure of intra-industry trade in the differentiated goods sector: $N_{-1,0}^1 p_{x,0}^1 (x^1 - D_{x,0}^{11}) = EXP_{x,0}^1$ and $N_{-1,0}^2 p_{x,0}^2 D_{x,0}^{12} = IMP_{x,0}^1$, and analogously for region 2. We now iterate on s_N^1 and α_{cx} until these equalities hold to a specified level of accuracy. The whole procedure boils down to finding the zeros of a two-dimensional non-linear function.

Production

Because all factors except unskilled labour are in endogenous supply, calibration of production needs to take into account factor accumulation and must be carried out jointly with calibration of growth rates. Two crucial figures that have to be specified exogenously are the real interest rate and the rate of real income growth. Barring any more reliable information, we choose a real interest rate of 4 per cent to reflect an average over the past two decades. Similarly, judging from past experience of West European countries, we specify the growth rate, $\hat{w}$, of wages to be 1.2 per cent. Notice that in our framework this wage growth is in terms of the standardized good, whereas in terms of the overall commodity bundle wage growth is higher according to $\hat{w}/\hat{\bar{P}}$ ($\hat{\bar{P}} < 1$). Our model identifies product innovation as the only source of long-run wage growth, and our choice of $\hat{w}$ ultimately also pins down the benchmark rate of innovation according to $\hat{w} = \hat{N}^{-(1-\beta)\alpha_{cx}\alpha_{ky}/A}$, where $A \overset{\text{def}}{=} \alpha_{cx}(\alpha_{ky} - \alpha_{kx}) + (1 - \alpha_{ky}) > 1$ and the various parameters have yet to be calibrated.

In the following we now omit country indices whenever possible without creating confusion. We first note that both sectors use the same type of capital good, which is available at a price $\bar{P}_0$. We know from above that both capital stocks grow at a common rate $\hat{K} = \hat{w}/\hat{\bar{P}}$. Noting that $\hat{\bar{P}} = \hat{w}^{-(1-\alpha_{ky})/\alpha_{ky}}$, we take a guess for α_{ky} and calculate the associated $\hat{\bar{P}}$ from our specified value for $\hat{w}$. Denote this by $\hat{\bar{P}}(\alpha_{ky})$ and the associated growth of the capital stock as $\hat{K}(\alpha_{ky})$. Assuming identical rates of decay for both capital stocks, the steady-state investment ratio is $i = \hat{w}/\bar{\hat{P}}(\alpha_{ky}) - \delta_K$. Denote this by $i(\alpha_{ky})$ to indicate dependence on the initial guess for α_{ky}. Turning to the Euler equation, we may write:

$$\left(\frac{r}{\bar{\hat{P}}} - \hat{K}\right) q K_{-1} = w_K K_{-1} - \bar{P}\psi(i)K_{-1}$$

$$\left(\frac{r}{\bar{\hat{P}}} - \hat{K}\right) \frac{\psi(i)\bar{P}K_{-1}\psi'(i)}{\psi(i)} = w_K K_{-1} - \alpha_I \bar{P}\bar{D} \qquad (A7)$$

$$\left(\frac{r}{\bar{\hat{P}}} - \hat{K}\right) \frac{\psi'(i)}{\psi(i)}\alpha_I = \frac{w_K K_{-1}}{\bar{P}\bar{D}} - \alpha_I$$

We may write $(w_K K_{-1})/(\bar{P}\bar{D}) = \alpha_K g$, where g is the ratio of GDP to absorption: $g = GDP/\bar{P}\bar{D}$ and α_K is the share of capital income in GDP. Since g is already known from above, all we need to complete calibration of α_{ky} is a benchmark observation on α_K. We may then write:

$$\left[\frac{r}{\bar{\hat{P}}(\alpha_{ky})} - \hat{K}(\alpha_{ky})\right] \frac{\psi'[i(\alpha_{ky})]}{\psi[i(\alpha_{ky})]}\alpha_{I,0} = g_0\alpha_{K,0} - \alpha_{I,0} \qquad (A8)$$

and iterate on α_{ky} until this equation is satisfied.

Benchmark investment expenditure may be written as $\bar{P}_0\psi[i(\alpha_{ky})]K_{-1,0}$. Having calibrated total absorption $\bar{P}_0\bar{D}_0$ above, we may now equate

$$\bar{P}_0\psi(i_0)K_{-1,0} = \alpha_{I,0}\bar{P}_0\bar{D}_0, \qquad (A9)$$

where $\alpha_{I,0}$ is the observed benchmark ratio of investment expenditure to domestic absorption and i_0 is the ratio of investment to capital stock as obtained with the calibrated value of α_{ky} (see above). We solve for the aggregate benchmark capital stock:

$$K_{-1,0} = \frac{\alpha_{I,0}\bar{D}_0}{\psi(i_0)\bar{P}_0}. \qquad (A10)$$

From the first-order condition on investment we now calculate

$$q_0 = \psi'(i_0)\bar{P}_0, \qquad (A11)$$

and we note that $\hat{q} = \bar{\hat{P}}$. Returning to the steady-state version of the Euler equation for investment, we write:

$$\frac{r}{\hat{q}} = \frac{w_K}{q} - \frac{\psi(i)\bar{P}}{q} + \frac{i\psi'(i)\bar{P}}{q} + \delta_K$$

$$q\frac{r}{\hat{\bar{P}}} = w_K - \psi(i)\bar{P} + \hat{K}, \qquad\qquad\qquad (A12)$$

where $\bar{P}/q$ was replaced by $1/\psi'(i)$ from the first-order condition and i was replaced from the equation of motion for the capital stock. We may now use this last equation to solve for the benchmark value of the capital rental:

$$w_{K,0} = \left(\frac{r}{\hat{\bar{P}}} - \hat{K}\right)q_0 + \bar{P}_0\psi(i_0), \qquad\qquad (A13)$$

where $\hat{\bar{P}}$ and $\hat{K}$ follow from the above procedure to calibrate α_{ky}. Given the functional form of $\psi(\cdot)$ and $\hat{K} = i + \delta_K$, this may equivalently be written as:

$$w_{K,0} = \left(\frac{r}{\hat{\bar{P}}} - \delta_K\right) - \phi_0(i_0)^2. \qquad\qquad (A14)$$

Knowledge of $w_{K,0}$ now allows us to calibrate the capital share of the differentiated goods sector:

$$\alpha_{kx} = \frac{w_{K,0}K_{-1,0} - \alpha_{ky}P_Y Y_0}{\phi_{x,0}x_0 N_{-1,0}}. \qquad\qquad (A15)$$

All of this is carried out separately for each of the two regions, but we note that all α-parameters are equal in both regions. Moreover, $\alpha_{ly} = 1 - \alpha_{ky}$ and $\alpha_{hx} = 1 - \alpha_{kx}$. We are now in the position to calculate the rate of innovation as:

$$\hat{N} = \hat{w}^{A/[-(1-\beta)\alpha_{cx}\alpha_{ky}]}. \qquad\qquad (A16)$$

Labour supply and education

We specify a value for the intertemporal elasticity of substitution γ as suggested by available econometric studies and invoke the Euler equation to calibrate the rate of time preference as $\rho = r\hat{w}^{-1/\gamma}\hat{\bar{P}}^{(1-\gamma)/\gamma}$ identically for both regions. Having specified $g(\cdot)$ such that its steady-state value is $1 - \delta_H$, we may now specify δ_H and τ_E to calibrate the steady-state levels of educational effort u_0^i and the steady-state level of human capital $H_{-1,0}^i$. These are the same in both regions provided the educational subsidy and depreciation are the same. We then observe the size of the low-skill labour force in both regions to calculate the wage rate $w_L^i = \alpha_{ly}^i P_Y Y_{i,0}/L_{i,0}^i$ that is consistent with wage payments of the traditional sector. The next task is to calibrate the size of the workforce with variable skills. To do so, we take a guess value for the wage spread s^i, which determines the high-skill wage rate as

$$w_{H,0}^i(s^i) = s^i w_{L,0}^i / H_{-1,0}^i, \tag{A17}$$

where we explicitly indicate that this wage rate depends on our guess of s^i. From the above procedure we already know monopoly profits $\pi_0^i = (\beta - 1)\phi_{x,0}^i x_0^i$. We invoke the free-entry condition for R&D and the no-arbitrage condition to calibrate the productivity parameter:

$$v^i = \pi^i / \left(\frac{r}{\hat{v}} - 1\right)$$
$$v^i = (1 - \tau_R^i)w_H^i a^i / \bar{N}_{-1}$$
$$a^i(s^i) = \frac{\pi_0^i \bar{N}_{-1,0}}{(r\hat{w}/\hat{N} - 1)(1 - \tau_R^i)w_{H,0}^i(s^i)}, \tag{A18}$$

where the last equation uses $\hat{v} = \hat{w}/\hat{N}$ and indicates that the calibrated value of a^i depends on our guess for the wage spread. Note that $\hat{N}$ is known from above. Given the benchmark number of varieties, $N_{-1,0}^i$, the number of new products created in the benchmark period is $I_{N,0}^i = (\hat{N} - 1)N_{-1,0}^i$ and the skilled labour requirement is therefore

$$h_{R,0}^i(s^i) = a^i(s^i)I_{N,0}^i / \bar{N}_{-1,0}. \tag{A19}$$

Multiplying the full employment condition for human capital by w_H, and remembering that $w_H h_x = \alpha_{hx}\phi_x$, we may write this as:

$$L_H^i = \frac{w_{H,0}^i(s^i)h_{R,0}^i(s^i) + \alpha_{hx}\phi_{x,0}^i x_0^i N_{-1,0}^i}{w_{H,0}^i(s^i)u_0^i H_{-1,0}^i}. \tag{A20}$$

We observe the size of the skilled labour force in either region, insert this on the l.h.s. and iterate on s^i until the above equation is satisfied.

A few final steps complete the calibration exercise. Knowing all factor prices, we evaluate the unit cost functions, and enforce the normalizations $\phi_x^i = \phi_y^i = 1$ by appropriately fixing the scaling coefficients $\phi_{0,x}^i$ and $\phi_{0,y}^i$. The government budget constraint yields lump-sum taxes or transfers T_0^i. The value of net foreign assets follows from the current account balance and is tied to the trade balance by $B_{-1,0}^i = TB_0^i/(\hat{w} - r)$.

Equity values and net foreign debt add to household sector financial wealth, A_0^i. With all budget identities holding exactly, the value for consumption implied by the savings equation must reproduce the value given in the data set.

Appendix B: Data sources

1. The **West European countries** are: Austria, Belgium, Denmark, Finland, France, Germany, Greece, Ireland, Italy, Luxembourg, the Netherlands, Norway, Portugal, Spain, Sweden, Switzerland, and the United Kingdom.
2. The **Central and East European countries** (CEECs) are: Bulgaria, Croatia, the Czech Republic, Hungary, Poland, Romania, the Slovak Republic, and Slovenia. All data for these countries are taken from the Vienna Institute for Comparative Economic Studies (1995). The most comprehensive coverage is for 1993. The 1992 data for the West have been appropriately scaled up to maintain consistency. Because our hypothetical benchmark assumes the counterfactual case of favourable initial conditions, we scale up the Eastern labour force by 20 per cent to take account of currently unemployed labour.
3. 1992 GDP as well as absorption data for the West European countries are from United Nations (1994). These are given in national currencies and we convert them into US$ million using nominal exchange rates as reported in *OECD Economic Outlook*.
4. 1992 capital income shares for these countries are similarly taken from *OECD Economic Outlook* (1994), and we take a GDP-weighted average of the above-mentioned economies for our hypothetical benchmark equilibrium.
5. The labour force breakdown is taken from various issues of the International Labour Office, *Yearbook of Labour Statistics*. Occupational categories 0/1–5 are identified as high-skill, while categories 6–X are identified as low-skill labour.
6. Finally, trade data for Western countries have been taken from the UN 'Global Trade Matrix' in machine-readable form.

For the whole set of parameters chosen and/or calibrated, see Table 4A.1, and, for the underlying data set, see Table 4A.2.

Table 4A.1   Basic parameters

		East	West[a]
Taste and technology parameters			
r	World interest factor	1.040	
ρ	Subjective discount factor[b]	1.010	
γ_c	Intertemporal elasticity of substitution	0.700	
α_{cx}	Share of x consumption[b]	0.676	
β	Markup factor	1.400	
σ_H	Elasticity education	0.300	
δ_H	Depreciation factor skills	0.960	
δ_K	Depreciation factor capital	0.900	
ψ_0	Adjustment cost parameter	10.000	
α_{ky}	Capital share y sector[b]	0.298	
α_{kx}	Capital share x sector[b]	0.380	
L_L	Low-skilled labour force	15.917	64.652
$\frac{w_H H_{-1}}{w_L}$	Wage spread[b]	1.344	2.091
u	Fraction of time at work[b]	0.628	0.628
H_{-1}	Skill level[b]	9.288	9.288
L_H	High-skilled labour force	26.645	108.224
a	Productivity R&D[b]	2450.118	2633.111
s_N	Share of product range x[b]	0.209	0.791
$\bar{N}_{-1}$	Worldwide product range	10.000	
Growth factors			
$\hat{w}$	Wages and income components	1.012	
$\hat{N}$	Innovation rate[b]	1.100	
$\hat{x}$	Output high-tech goods[b]	0.923	
$\hat{p}_x$	Price high-tech goods[b]	0.997	
$\hat{D}_{\bar{X}}$	High-tech composite[b]	1.055	
$\hat{P}_{\bar{X}}$	PI high-tech goods[b]	0.959	
$\hat{C}$	Total consumption composite[b]	1.041	
$\hat{P}$	Total consumer price index[b]	0.972	

[a] Empty second column: same parameter for both regions.
[b] A calibrated parameter.

Table 4A.2   Macroeconomic identities

		East	West
Trade balance and absorption			
Trade balance Y	+	7.641	−7.641
Exports X	+	45.847	53.489
Imports X	+	−53.489	−45.847
Trade balance	=	0.000	0.000
Consumption	+	78.704	255.607
Investment	+	21.296	68.345
GDP	=	100.000	323.952
Demand structure[a]			
Demand for country 1 goods	+	14.153	45.847
Demand for country 2 goods	+	53.489	173.278
Demand for goods X	=	67.641	219.125
Demand for goods Y	+	32.359	104.827
Absorption	=	100.000	323.952
Output structure[a]			
Output Y	+	40.000	97.186
Output X	+	60.000	226.767
Indirect taxes	+	0.000	0.000
GDP	=	100.000	323.952
Cost structure[a]			
Depreciation		12.552	40.283
Accounting profits	+	19.631	65.274
Capital income NA	=	32.183	105.557
Rental capital income		28.196	90.488
Monopoly profits	+	17.143	64.790
R&D costs	−	13.156	49.722
Capital income NA	=	32.183	105.557
Low-skilled wages	+	28.089	68.247
High-skilled wages	+	39.728	150.149
Indirect taxes	+	0.000	0.000
GDP	=	100.000	323.952

[a] Calibrated values.
NA: National Accounts

Notes

Financial support by the Austrian Ministry of Science and Research is gratefully acknowledged. Keuschnigg appreciates financial support from the Erwin Schrödinger Foundation for a visiting research fellowship at Princeton University. We appreciate generous support on the data side by Mirela Ursulescu, Jarko Fidrmuc, Helmut Hofer, and Michael Pfaffermeyer. Thanks are also due to Christian Pierdzioch who has provided valuable research assistance.

1. Throughout this paper, 'Western' and 'West European' are used synonymously.
2. To avoid cluttered notation, we suppress time and country indices whenever possible without confusion. An undated variable such as N refers to the current period, while N_{-1} refers to the previous period. When necessary, superscripts 1 and 2 identify the home and foreign economies.
3. For a model in which the composition of the labour force responds to the wage spread, see Keuschnigg (1996).
4. The main text focuses on some analytical results and, thus, specializes to the logarithmic case with $\gamma = 1$. The simulation model implements the more general case. A detailed treatment of this case is described in a separate appendix, which is available upon request.
5. Further details may again be found in the separate appendix.
6. The same type of investment problem applies in each sector at home and abroad. At this stage, we suppress country and sector indices.
7. The computational model incorporates trade barriers also in the traditional good.
8. Notice that any increase in the number of varieties affects the acquisition price for the capital good, thus raising the productivity of investment. In Keuschnigg and Kohler (1996a), we show how this may give rise to an investment multiplier if the introduction of new goods in turn relies on physical capital.
9. If capital could be costlessly transferred across sectors but not across countries, one would be left with a consolidated country-specific resource constraint, $\zeta_K^i = k_y^i Y^i + k_x^i x^i N_{-1}^i - K_{-1}^i$.
10. With $\hat{P}_Y = 1$, the consumer price index increases with $\hat{P}^i = (\hat{P}_{\bar{X}})^{\alpha_{cx}^i}$. The cost function in the Y sector implies $\hat{w}_K^i = \hat{w}^{-\alpha_{ly}^i/\alpha_{ky}^i}$. Since the no-arbitrage relation (8) implies $\hat{w}_K^i = \hat{P}^i$, one equates the two equations to obtain $\hat{P}_{\bar{X}} = \hat{w}^{-\alpha_{ly}^i/(\alpha_{ky}^i \alpha_{cx}^i)}$. Except for a coincidence, this cannot hold for diverging α-shares. Other cases would inevitably give rise to specialization. Note, however, that in a more general framework, where both sectors use high- and low-skilled labour, only the cost share of capital needs to be identical, while the shares of the two types of labour may differ because their prices grow at a common rate.
11. Grossman and Helpman (1991: 66) note the same result for the effect of an output subsidy in a simplified version of the model.
12. In this connection, Baldwin (1994: 106) reports on an interesting observation from 1928 League of Nations statistics where Czechoslovakia was listed under 'Industrial Continental Europe', whereas Denmark, Spain, Norway, and Finland were listed under 'Other Continental Europe'.
13. See Helpman and Krugman (1985: Ch. 8) for a detailed treatment of the volume of trade in models such as ours.

14. On goods alone, West European countries exhibit an external deficit of about 0.7 per cent of GDP.
15. This outcome is specific to the case of growth driven by horizontal product differentiation and does not necessarily carry over, for instance, to growth based on quality improvements (Grossman and Helpman 1991).

References

Baldwin, Richard E. (1994), *Towards an Integrated Europe*. London: Centre for Economic Policy Research.

Blanchard, Olivier Jean, Kenneth A. Froot, and Jeffrey D. Sachs (1992), eds. *The Transition in Eastern Europe*, vols. I and II. Chicago: University of Chicago Press.

Brown, Drusilla K., Alan V. Deardorff, Simeon D. Djankov, and Robert M. Stern (1995), *An Economic Assessment of the Integration of Czechoslovakia, Hungary, and Poland into the European Union*. Ann Arbor: University of Michigan Research Forum on International Economics, Discussion Paper No. 380.

Chamley, Christophe (1993), 'Externalities and Dynamics in Models of "Learning or Doing" ', *International Economic Review* 34: 583–609.

Clague, Christopher and Gordon C. Rausser (1992), eds., *The Emergence of Market Economies in Eastern Europe*. Cambridge, Mass. and Oxford: Basil Blackwell.

Collins, Susan M. and Dani Rodrik (1991), *Eastern Europe and the Soviet Union in the World Economy*. Washington D.C.: Institute for International Economics.

Dixit, Avinash K. and Joseph E. Stiglitz (1977), 'Monopolistic Competition and Optimum Product Diversity', *American Economic Review* 67: 297–308.

Grossman, Gene M. and Elhanan Helpman (1991), *Innovation and Growth in the Global Economy*. Cambridge, Mass.: MIT Press.

Hamilton, Carl and L. Alan Winters (1992), 'Opening up Trade with Eastern Europe', *Economic Policy* 14: 77–116.

Helpman, Elhanan and Paul R. Krugman (1985), *Market Structure and Foreign Trade*. Cambridge, Mass.: MIT Press.

Keuschnigg, Christian (1996), 'Labour Training, Innovations, Trade, and Growth', Discussion Paper No. 9604, University of Saarland, Europa Institute.

Keuschnigg, Christian and Wilhelm Kohler (1996a), 'Commercial Policy and Dynamic Adjustment under Monopolistic Competition', *Journal of International Economics* 40: 373–409.

(1996b), 'Austria in the European Union', *Economic Policy* 22: 157–211.

Lucas, Robert E. (1988), 'On the Mechanics of Economic Development', *Journal of Monetary Economics* 22(1): 831–44.

(1993), 'Making a Miracle', *Econometrica* 61: 251–72.

Rollo, Jim and Alasdair Smith (1993), 'The Political Economy of Eastern European Trade with the European Community: Why So Sensitive?' *Economic Policy* 16: 139–81.

Romer, Paul M. (1987), 'Growth Based on Increasing Returns Due to Specialization', *American Economic Review* 77: 56–62.

(1990), 'Endogenous Technological Change', *Journal of Political Economy* 98: S71–102.

Ruffin, Roy J. (1994), 'Endogenous Growth and International Trade', *Review of International Economics* 2: 27–39.

Sinn, Gerline and Hans-Werner Sinn (1992), *Jumpstart: The Economic Unification of Germany*. Cambridge, Mass.: MIT Press.

United Nations (1994), *National Accounts Statistics: Main Aggregates and Detailed Tables*. Parts I and II.

Vienna Institute for Comparative Economic Studies (1995), *Countries in Transition 1995 (Handbook of Statistics)*. Vienna: WIIW.

Wang, Zhen Kun and L. Alan Winters (1991), 'The Trading Potential of Eastern Europe', CEPR Discussion Paper No. 610.

5 Multinational production, skilled labour, and real wages

JAMES R. MARKUSEN
and ANTHONY J. VENABLES

1 Introduction

International trade has a long tradition of explaining trade flows and international differences in sectoral production levels by differences in relative factor endowments among countries. Dual results relate real factor rewards to international prices and trade barriers. But factor-proportions trade theory, at least in its traditional competitive formulation, is not well suited to discussions about the role of trade in technologies and knowledge capital in determining real wages and national standards of living. Because of problems relating to the public goods nature of knowledge or to the firm-specific character of knowledge and skills, the services of these assets are often exploited internally within multinational firms in serving foreign markets.

Many theoretical and empirical developments have improved our understanding of which firm-level characteristics lead to industries dominated by multinationals. More recently, we have begun to incorporate these firm-based models into the general equilibrium theory of international trade so that we understand, for example, which country characteristics lead to international activity dominated by direct investment rather than trade.[1]

The purpose of this paper is to exploit these recent developments in order to improve our understanding of how multinationals in turn influence certain variables in equilibrium, outputs and factor prices in particular. While previous work has given us a basis for understanding how country characteristics such as size, relative endowments, and trade costs lead to multinational firms, we now turn to the question of how the introduction of multinational production alters the inter-country distribution of production and the intra-country distribution of income.[2]

We adapt our two-country, two-sector, two-factor static model developed in Markusen and Venables (1995a, 1996). Here factors are skilled

138

and unskilled labour. One sector of the economy (X) is composed of three distinct activities: (1) creating firm-specific capital, (2) creating plant-specific capital, and (3) final production. Skilled labour is required in the production of firm-specific knowledge capital ('blueprints', etc.) and is also combined with unskilled labour in the creation of plant-specific fixed costs (producing capital equipment). Production of final output of X requires only unskilled labour. Our other work focuses almost entirely on the determinants of what types of firms are active in equilibrium and trade volume issues, assuming that all three of these activities use factors in the same proportion, or indeed use only one composite factor.

There are two countries, and the nationality of a firm corresponds to the location of its firm-specific capital. There are four firm types. There are two types (nationalities) of single-plant firms, corresponding to locations in the two countries. Each single-plant firm may or may not export to the other country. There are similarly two types (nationalities) of multinational enterprises (MNEs), each maintaining plants in both countries. The term 'regime' denotes the set of firm types active in equilibrium. We review, with appropriate modifications, our earlier results on how differences between countries in relative endowments of skilled labour and in country size (absolute endowments), along with trade barriers, determine the equilibrium regime.

Multinationals fragment production geographically, locating skilled-labour-intensive activities and one production plant in their home country and an additional production plant in the host country. To put it differently, these firms change the nature of what is traded, from commodity exports to skilled-labour-intensive producer services. Assessing the consequences of multinationals, however, requires a well-defined counterfactual. An equilibrium with multinationals can be compared with one in which (a) parameters (e.g. country sizes, trade barriers) are altered such that national firms displace multinationals, or (b) those parameters are held constant, but direct investment is simply banned. We will concentrate mostly on the latter situation, so that 'the effects of multinationals' compares a case in which multinationals exist in equilibrium with one in which there is a prohibitive investment barrier, all other parameters being equal.

When the two countries have asymmetric relative endowments but are of similar size, the entry of multinationals as a result of the removal of a prohibitive investment barrier has several effects. For the skilled-labour-abundant country (also referred to as the 'advantaged' or 'high-income' country), two results are of interest. First, final production of X decreases in the advantaged country, so in a relevant sense multinationals do export less skilled jobs. Secondly, the entry of multinationals raises the real wage of skilled labour and increases the skilled–unskilled wage gap in the advantaged country.

The unskilled-labour-abundant ('disadvantaged' or 'low-income') country gains production from the entry of multinationals. But the effects on the real wage of skilled labour and on the skilled–unskilled wage gap are ambiguous. On the one hand, MNEs export skilled-labour-intensive producer services (knowledge capital) that indirectly substitute for host-country skilled labour, thereby lowering the latter's relative return. On the other hand, national firms in the disadvantaged country may be severely handicapped by the scarcity of skilled labour so that few or possibly none of them can enter when investment is banned. In such cases, the entry of MNEs headquartered in the advantaged country increases the demand for skilled labour in the disadvantaged country and raises the skilled-labour wage. The latter possibility is likely when the difference in the relative endowments of the two countries is large. The entry of multinationals then raises the real wage of skilled labour in both countries; intuitively, branch plants requiring significant skilled-labour inputs replace transport costs, which use only unskilled labour.[3]

The effects of multinational entry when the countries differ in absolute size is somewhat different. Again, multinationals transfer production from the advantaged to the disadvantaged country (in this case 'advantaged' and 'disadvantaged' referring to large and small). But the effects on the wage of skilled labour can be reversed, with the disadvantaged country's wage rising and the advantaged country's wage falling. Both results can be understood in terms of effects identified in the trade industrial organization literature. In the absence of multinationals, national firms headquartered in the advantaged country have a significant home-market advantage that allows them to dominate in equilibrium out of proportion to country-size differences. The entry of multinationals shifts ownership and therefore the demand for skilled labour more towards the smaller country.

Three final sections generate additional results. Section 6 notes that a convergence in country sizes can raise the skilled–unskilled wage gap in both countries as multinationals displace national firms. A country that is both large and skilled-labour abundant will initially experience an increasing wage gap as the countries converge in both size and relative endowments.

Section 7 considers trade costs. By inducing the entry of multinationals, we show a case in which trade costs protect the abundant factor in each country. This result is opposite to traditional theory, in which trade barriers protect the country's scarce factor. If skilled-labour requirements in branch-plant fixed costs are high however (our central case), then the regime shift to multinationals raises the wage of skilled labour in both countries. Section 8 considers some dynamic extensions, which suggest that a small and/or skilled-labour-scarce country will likely have its steady-state supply of skilled labour increased by investment liberalization.

2   Model structure

The model has two countries (h and f) producing two homogeneous goods, Y and X. There are two factors of production, L (unskilled labour) and S (skilled labour). L and S are mobile between industries but internationally immobile. Y will be used as numeraire throughout the paper. Skilled labour is used for the firm-specific fixed cost of producing X, and plant-specific fixed costs use a combination of the two labour types. Unskilled labour is used in variable costs, and in addition there are transport costs between countries, specified as units of unskilled labour per unit of X exported.

Subscripts (i, j) will be used to denote the countries (f, h). The output of Y in country i is a constant elasticity of substitution (CES) function, identical in both countries. The production function for Y is:

$$Y_i = [aL_{iy}^\varepsilon + (1-a)S_{iy}^\varepsilon]^{1/\varepsilon} \quad i = h, f, \tag{1}$$

where L_{iy} and S_{iy} are the unskilled and skilled labour used in the Y sector in country i. The elasticity of substitution $(1/(1-\varepsilon))$ is set at 5.0 in the simulation runs reported later in the paper.

Superscripts (n, m) will be used to designate a variable as referring to national firms and multinational firms respectively. (m_i, n_i) will also be used to indicate the number of active m firms and n firms based in country i. We hope that it will always be clear from the context what is being represented (e.g. n_i as a variable in an equation always refers to the number of national firms in country i).

In order to enter X production with one plant, a firm must incur a fixed cost in units of skilled labour, denoted F, and a fixed cost in units of unskilled labour, G: national-firm fixed costs are thus $L_i = G$, $S_i = F$.

A two-plant multinational headquartered in country i incurs additional fixed costs in both countries. These include both skilled and unskilled labour costs in the branch plant in country j, and possibly additional skilled-labour costs in the source country i. Total fixed costs for a two-plant multinational headquartered in country i are:

$$L_i = G, \; L_j = \beta G, \; S_i = F + \gamma F, \; S_j - \delta F, \; 1 \geq \beta > (\gamma + \delta).$$

The inequality on the right expresses the assumptions that the second plant is more unskilled-labour intensive than the first, and that there are multi-plant economies of scale arising from the joint-input nature of knowledge capital. γ can be thought of as a technology-transfer cost. Later in the paper our central case uses $\beta = 0.75$, $\gamma = 0.1$, $\delta = 0.4$.[4]

Marginal factor requirements are constant in units of unskilled labour.[5] X_{ij}^n denotes the sales in country j of a national firm based in country i. Let w_i and v_i denote the prices of unskilled labour and skilled labour respectively in country i. A national firm undertakes all its production in its base country, so the cost function of one national firm in country i is given by:

$$w_i L_i^n + v_i S_i^n = w_i [c X_{ii}^n + (c + \tau) X_{ij}^n + G] + v_i F, \quad i, j = h, f, i \neq j, \quad (2)$$

where c is the constant marginal production cost. c, F, and G are identical across countries. τ is the amount of unskilled labour needed to transport one unit of X from country i to country j, which we assume to be the same in both directions. In our calibration, national firms in the X sector are moderately more skilled-labour intensive than Y-sector firms. However, this is not particularly important in our model since we are focusing on the switch between national and multinational X-sector firms.

A multinational based in country i has sales in country j, X_{ij}^m. It operates one plant in each country, incurring fixed costs $(G_i, (1 + \gamma) F_i)$ in its base country, and fixed costs $(\beta G_j, \delta F_j)$ in country j. Sales are met entirely from local production not trade. $L_{ij}^m (S_{ij}^m)$ denotes a country-i multi-national firm's demand for unskilled (skilled) labour in country j. A firm type m_i thus has a cost function:

$$w_i L_{ii}^m + w_j L_{ij}^m + v_i S_{ii}^m + v_j S_{ij}^m = w_i [c X_{ii}^m + G] + w_j [c X_{ij}^m + \beta G]$$
$$+ v_i (1 + \gamma) F + v_j \delta F. \quad (3)$$

In our calibration, multinational firms are generally more skilled-labour intensive than national firms, using more skilled labour for branch-plant fixed costs versus the additional unskilled labour for transport costs used by national firms. This depends, however, on firm scale.[6]

Let $\bar{L}_i$ and $\bar{S}_i$ denote the total labour endowments of country i. Adding labour demand from n_i national firms, m_i multinationals based in country i, and m_j multinationals based in country j gives country-i factor market clearing:

$$\bar{L}i = L_{iy} + n_i L_i^n + m_i L_{ii}^m + m_j L_{ji}^m$$

$$\bar{S}_i = S_{iy} + n S_i^n + m_i S_{ii}^m + m_j S_{ji}^m \tag{4}$$

In equilibrium, the X sector makes no profits, so country-i income, denoted M_i, is:

$$M_i = w_i \bar{L}_i + v_i \bar{S}_i \quad i = h, f. \tag{5}$$

p_i denotes the price of X in country i, and X_{ic} and Y_{ic} denote the consumption of X and Y. Utility of the representative consumer in each country is Cobb–Douglas:

$$U_i = X_{ic}^\alpha Y_{ic}^{1-\alpha}, \quad X_{ic} \equiv n_i X_{ii}^n + n_j X_{ji}^n + m_i X_{ii}^m + m_j X_{ji}^m, \tag{6}$$

giving demands:

$$X_{ic} = \alpha M_i / p_i, \quad Y_{ic} = (1 - \alpha) M_i. \tag{7}$$

Equilibrium in the X sector is determined by pricing equations (marginal revenue equals marginal cost) and free-entry conditions. We denote proportional markups of price over marginal cost by $e_{ij}^k(k = n, m)$, so, for example, e_{ji}^m is the markup of a country-j multinational in market i. Pricing equations of national and multinational firms in each market are (written in complementary-slackness form with associated variables in brackets):

$$p_i(1 - e_{ii}^n) \le w_i c \quad (X_{ii}^n) \tag{8}$$

$$p_j(1 - e_{ij}^n) \le w_i(c + \tau) \quad (X_{ij}^n) \tag{9}$$

$$p_i(1 - e_{ii}^m) \le w_i c \quad (X_{ii}^m) \tag{10}$$

$$p_j(1 - e_{ij}^m) \le w_j c \quad (X_{ij}^m) \tag{11}$$

In a Cournot model with homogeneous products, the optimal markup formula is given by the firm's market share divided by the Marshallian price elasticity of demand in that market. In our model, the price elasticity is one (see equation (7)), reducing the firm's markup to its market share. This gives (also using demand equations (7)),

$$e_{ij}^k = \frac{X_{ij}^k}{X_{jc}} = \frac{p_j X_{ij}^k}{\alpha M_j} \quad k = n, m, \quad i, j = h, f. \tag{12}$$

There are four zero-profit conditions corresponding to the numbers of the four firm types. Given equations (8)–(11), zero profits can be written as the requirement that markup revenues equal fixed costs.

$$p_h e_{hh}^n X_{hh}^n + p_f e_{hf}^n X_{hf}^n \leq w_h G + v_h F \qquad (n_h) \tag{13}$$

$$p_f e_{ff}^n X_{ff}^n + p_h e_{fh}^n X_{fh}^n \leq w_f G + v_f F \qquad (n_f) \tag{14}$$

$$p_h e_{hh}^m X_{hh}^m + p_f e_{hf}^m X_{hf}^m \leq w_h G + v_h (1 + \gamma) F + w_f \beta G + v_f \delta F \quad (m_h) \tag{15}$$

$$p_f e_{ff}^m X_{ff}^m + p_h e_{fh}^m X_{fh}^m \leq w_f G + v_f (1 + \gamma) F + w_h \beta G + v_h \delta F \quad (m_f) \tag{16}$$

To summarize the X sector in the model, the eight inequalities (8)–(11) are associated with the eight output levels (two each for four firm types), the eight equations in (12) are associated with the eight markups, and the four inequalities in (13)–(16) are associated with the number of firms of each type. Additionally, goods prices are given by (7), income levels from (5), and factor prices from factor-market-clearing equation (4) together with labour demand from the Y sector.

The model is quite complex and inherently involves inequalities, making traditional analytical, comparative-statics methods of limited value. The problems introduced by inequalities are compounded by the fact that we have four different production activities (Y, X-sector output, national-firm fixed costs, multinational-firm fixed costs), all using factors in different proportions. In the next section, we will try to gain some intuition by reviewing analytical results from our earlier papers, and later in the paper simulate the full model, which involves fifty-one non-linear inequalities.[7]

3   Forces at work

In our related papers (Markusen and Venables 1995a, 1996) we were able to make considerable analytical progress, although partly at the expense of assuming the same factor intensity in all of the X-sector activities. Rather than re-derive some of the previous results here, we will simply explain the intuition behind them, and conjecture on some extensions to the case of differing factor intensities considered in this paper. The focus of the section will be on the equilibrium regime as a function of relative and absolute factor endowments and trade costs.

Suppose that the two countries are absolutely identical. Suppose also that we calibrate fixed costs and trade costs so that all four firm types could exist together in equilibrium. The higher total fixed costs of national firms are exactly balanced by the higher trade costs of the national firms. Our previous work then establishes the following results.

(a) An increase in both countries' size $(\Delta M_h = \Delta M_f > 0)$ will imply that only multinational firms exist in equilibrium. Large markets favour high-fixed-cost multinational firms over high-variable-cost national firms.

(b) An increase $v\Delta F = -w\Delta G > 0$ will imply that only multinational firms exist in equilibrium. This shift leaves national firms unaffected, but benefits multinationals (the second plant is more unskilled-labour intensive: $\beta > (\gamma + \delta)$).

(c) An increase in trade costs will imply that only multinational firms will exist in equilibrium. High trade costs favour two-plant firms that pay no trade costs.

We thus have the result that multinationals are more likely to exist in equilibrium when incomes are high, skilled-labour requirements in fixed costs are more important relative to unskilled-labour requirements, and trade costs are relatively high.

Now consider the two countries differing in relative endowments, and assume that the countries are large, F is large relative to G, and trade costs are sufficiently high that multinationals dominate in equilibrium when the two countries are initially identical. As the countries begin to diverge somewhat in relative endowments, with h becoming more skilled-labour abundant, the regime should stay fixed at (m_h, m_f). Firm numbers should adjust, with more firms headquartered in country h, but there is no reason to expect the regime to shift for relatively small differences. But eventually relative factor prices in the two countries will begin to diverge along with the divergence in relative endowments. Holding the regime fixed, skilled labour will become more expensive in the skilled-labour-scarce country. This in turn disadvantages multinational firms, which must purchase skilled labour in both countries, relative to (potential) national firms headquartered in the skilled-labour-abundant country. At some point, type-n_h firms will enter and type-m_f firms will exit (not necessarily at the same parameter values), leaving a regime of type-m_h and/or type-n_h firms in equilibrium. Although production in country f may continue, we would expect all firms to be headquartered in country h for sufficiently large differences in relative endowments.

Next, consider the effects of country size, making country h larger and country f smaller. Assume again that initially only multinational firms exist in equilibrium. As the country sizes begin to diverge, there is no inherent disadvantage created for type-m_f multinationals, although they should be fewer in number. If factor prices are the same in the two countries (consistent with $0 < m_f < m_h$), then type-m_f and type-m_h firms are in fact in a perfectly symmetrical position. Each incurs the same total fixed costs, and produces the same amount in a given country's plant, with simply a larger output in the country-h plant than in the country-f plant.

As the country sizes diverge further, type-n_h firms gain a potential advantage. Their (potential) sales are concentrated in their low-cost (zero transport cost) market, whereas multinationals must incur fixed costs in country f to serve an ever-shrinking market there. Eventually, some type-n_h firms should be able to enter in competition with the multinationals.

Eventually, there will come a point where only type-n_h firms can exist in equilibrium. As country f's size and therefore demand become very small, it is simply not profitable for a firm to build a plant in f. Markup revenue cannot cover fixed costs.

Taken as a whole, these arguments suggest that country-h firms will dominate when the countries are very different in size or in relative factor endowments, that there will be a mixed regime (in both types and nationalities) as the countries converge, and that eventually only multi-nationals of both countries will exist, provided transport costs and/or income levels are sufficiently high.

It seems rather obvious that skilled-labour-intensive activities, which translate here into firm ownership, should be concentrated in the skilled-labour-abundant country, although the role of country size is perhaps less obvious. But the concentration of firm ownership in the large and/or skilled-labour-abundant country does not lead to any simple predictions about the effects of multinational entry as a result of the removal of an investment ban. For example, the entry of multinationals may decrease the X-sector demand for skilled labour in the large or skilled-labour-abundant country h as branch plants are built in country f and/or type-m_f firms are able to enter. Alternatively, country-h X-sector skilled-labour demand could increase as type-m_h firms replace type-n_f firms. Similarly, intuition suggests contradictory effects of multinational entry on skilled-labour demand (and hence wages) in host countries, as we noted earlier. Exports of skilled-labour-intensive producer services by multinationals to branch plants may substitute for host-country skilled-labour demand by local firms. But if there are few or no local firms in the absence of multinationals, then multinational entry is likely to correspond to an increased demand for local skilled labour. With strong analytical results unavailable, we thus turn to simulation analysis in the next two sections.

4   Entry of multinationals as a result of investment liberalization: countries differ in relative endowments

In this section, we assume that countries differ in relative endowments, but that they are of the same size, meaning that their GDP levels are about the same. A numerical model using Rutherford's (1994) non-linear complementarity algorithm solves a model of fifty-one non-linear equations and inequalities. Our central case uses the values $\beta = 0.75$, $\gamma = 0.1$, $\delta = 0.4$. A second plant requires 75 per cent as much unskilled labour as the first plant, all drawn from the host country. The second plant also requires 50 per cent as much skilled labour as the first plant, 10 per cent drawn from the country of headquarters and 40 per cent in the country in which the branch plant is located. If the S/L ratio in Y is normalized to 1.0, the calibration implies an overall S/L ratio in the X sector between about 2.1 and 2.6 in case 1, depending on what firm types are active in equilibrium.[8]

In almost all experiments conducted, we found the results qualitatively robust with respect to significant variations in these values. One exception occurred with respect to increased trade costs, which induce multinational entry, so section 7 presents an interesting result using alternative values: $\beta = 1.0$, $\gamma = \delta = 0.1$. In this case the branch plant uses more unskilled labour and less skilled labour relative to the central case.

Figure 5.1 presents qualitative results on the equilibrium regime for the relative endowment experiment (all results are 'central case' unless otherwise noted). The countries are identical in the top row and their difference is maximized in the bottom row. The unit of measurement on the vertical axis is country f's endowment of skilled labour as a proportion of its initial endowment. Moving down a column, S is transferred from country f to country h, and L is transferred in the opposite direction in amounts needed to maintain approximate parity in the two countries' GDP levels.[9] The horizontal axis measures the transport cost variable τ as a proportion of marginal production costs (both use unskilled labour only). Results would be similar using a tariff variable except for a relatively small income effect. When the two countries are relatively similar and trade costs are low, the equilibrium regime involves intra-industry trade competition between national firm types n_h and n_f (region b). When trade costs are higher, the regime involves intra-industry investment competition between type-m_h and type-m_f multinational firms (region i).

Consider moving down the column for $\tau = 0.15$ in Figure 5.1. As country f becomes relatively more scarce in skilled labour, we expect that v_f/v_h eventually rises, making country h more suitable and country f less

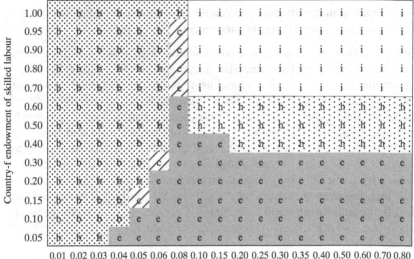

Figure 5.1   **Relative endowment experiment.**
Note: countries are identical in the top row.

suitable as the location for corporate headquarters. This is what we see in Figure 5.1 moving down column $\tau = 0.15$, with a regime shift to type-m_h firms only at row 0.60. Continuing the spread in relative endowments by moving further down this column should further raise v_f/v_h, making country f less suitable even for branch plants of type-m_h firms. Alternatively, potential type-n_h firms become more profitable (they use no S_f), serving country f by exports. This occurs in Figure 5.1 with a second regime shift to type (m_h, n_h) firms at row 0.40. Moving down a column for moderate transport costs, such as $\tau = 0.15$, we see a sequence about the same as that suggested in the previous section:

$$(m_h, m_f) \rightarrow (m_h) \rightarrow (m_h, n_h).$$

In order to understand exactly how multinationals affect variables of interest, we re-ran the model suppressing multinational firms (e.g. a prohibitive investment barrier), comparing the resulting values with those in which multinationals are endogenous. Figure 5.2 plots ratios of variables with and without multinationals, where the subscript 'n' indicates 'no multinationals'. v_i now denotes the real wage of skilled

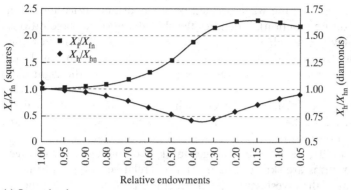

(a) Output levels

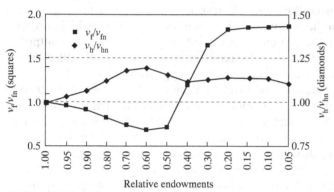

(b) Wage of skilled labour

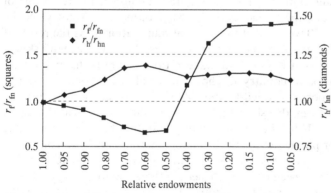

(c) Relative wages

Figure 5.2   **Effect of removing an investment barrier: differences in relative endowments, $\tau = 0.15$.**

labour in country i, the wage divided by the consumer price index (the unit expenditure function). r_i denotes the skilled–unskilled wage ratio v_i / w_i in country i. The values run down the column for $\tau = 0.15$ in Figure 5.1, so countries are identical on the left-hand side of each panel, and their relative endowment differences are maximized on the right-hand side.[10]

Looking at the left-hand side of each panel (countries identical) of Figure 5.2, we see that the removal of an investment barrier has virtually no effect on outputs in the two countries or on the real wages of skilled labour. Actually, these 'zero' changes mask two counteracting changes. The type-m firms are skilled-labour intensive relative to type-n firms, so the removal of the investment barrier generates an increased demand for skilled labour at constant firm scale. But the removal of the investment barrier (and given the moderate transport costs) has a pro-competitive effect in which the multinational firms have a significantly higher output per firm than the national firms that they displace. Since output is unskilled-labour intensive, this tends to reduce the overall skilled-labour intensity of the X sector. The two effects approximately cancel.

Now consider relative endowments values in the range 0.95 to 0.50 in Figure 5.2. Entry of multinationals as a result of the removal of a trade barrier raises X production in country f and lowers it in country h (the top panel). Exports of knowledge capital by type-m_h firms compensate for the shortage of skilled labour in country f, and production (which is unskilled-labour intensive) is transferred from country h to country f. In some sense, the entry of multinationals does result in the 'export' of unskilled jobs from the high-income country.

The middle and bottom panels of Figure 5.2 consider the real wage of skilled labour and the skilled–unskilled wage ratio respectively. Over the range 0.95 to 0.50 we see that the entry of multinationals as the result of the removal of an investment barrier raises the real wage of skilled labour and the skilled–unskilled wage ratio in country h, and lowers these same ratios in country f. The removal of the investment barrier permits the export of skilled-labour-intensive producer services (knowledge capital) from the skilled-labour-abundant to the skilled-labour-scarce country. Thus the result is fairly intuitive but of considerable importance for public policy. For example, multinationals do contribute to raising the skilled–unskilled wage gap in the high-income country, something that has been of great concern in these countries.

These results are reversed for country f (but not for country h) when the difference in relative endowments becomes larger – values 0.40 to 0.05 in Figure 5.2. In such a situation, country f is so short of skilled labour that its national firms are uncompetitive in the absence of multinationals and production in country f is close to zero. The removal of the investment barrier removes this constraint on production, and the number of plants (type-m_h multinationals) is 3.5 times as large as the number of type-n_f firms displaced. Hence the aggregate demand for S_f increases substantially even though each plant of a type-m_h firm demands less S_f than did a type-n_f firm in the absence of direct investment. In this region, the removal of an investment barrier increases the real wage of skilled labour and the wage ratio in *both* countries, and home-country exports of skilled-labour-intensive producer services become a complement rather than a substitute for foreign-country skilled labour.

To summarize this section in which countries are of roughly equal GDP but differ significantly in relative factor endowments, we see several results. The entry of multinationals as the result of the removal of a prohibitive investment barrier transfers production from the high-income to the low-income country, and raises the real wage of skilled labour and the skilled–unskilled wage ratio in the high-income country. The one ambiguous result relates to the real wage of skilled labour and the skilled–unskilled wage ratio in the low-income country. If the difference in the relative endowments between the countries is not too large, then the entry of multinationals harms skilled labour in the low-income, skilled-labour-scarce country. The result is reversed if the relative endowment differences are large. In the latter case, exports of skilled-labour-intensive producer services by the high-income country are complementary to skilled labour in the low-income country. Another way of thinking about this result is that, when the countries are very similar, the entry of branch plants into the low-income country displaces local national firms in the X sector, which are more skilled-labour intensive than the branch plants. But, if the countries are very different, then the branch plants draw factors from the Y sector, which is less skilled-labour intensive than those branch plants.

5 Entry of multinationals as a result of investment liberalization: countries differ in size (absolute endowments)

Now consider pure country-size effects, in which we hold the total world endowment constant but transfer factors in equal proportion from country f to country h, beginning with the two countries identical. The equilibrium regime is shown in Figure 5.3. As in the case of Figure 5.1, the two countries are identical in the top row and their size difference is maximized in the bottom row. The scaling on the vertical axis is country f's factor endowment as a proportion of its initial endowment. The horizontal axes of Figures 5.1 and 5.3 are the same. Results in the top

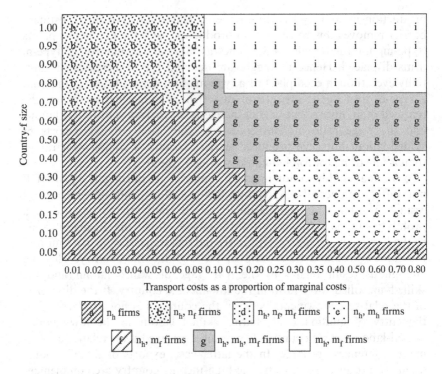

Figure 5.3   Absolute endowment experiment.
Note: countries are identical in the top row.

halves of Figures 5.1 and 5.3 are similar. When the countries are not too
different, intra-industry trade competition between national firm types
occurs when trade costs are small, and intra-industry investment competition between multinational firm types occurs when trade costs are
higher.

Figures 5.1 and 5.3 differ substantially in their middle and bottom
sections, when relative endowment and size differences are moderate to
large. Consider low trade costs, and compare points in row–column
(0.50, 0.05) in the two diagrams. When the difference between countries h
and f is in relative endowments (Figure 5.1), some country-f-owned
(type-n_f) firms can exist. A small endowment of S_f will restrict the
number of firms, but they are not hampered by a small domestic market.
When the difference between countries h and f is in relative size (Figure
5.3), no country-f-owned firms can exist. The small domestic market size
in country f disadvantages country-f firms sufficiently that they cannot
be supported in equilibrium.

Now consider high trade costs and compare points in row–column (0.50, 0.15) in Figures 5.1 and 5.3. Here it is in the case of relative endowment differences (Figure 5.1) that no country-f-owned firms can exist in equilibrium. Once endowment differences become sufficiently large that factor-price equalization cannot hold, type-m_f and type-m_h firms cannot coexist with $v_f > v_h$. But when countries differ only in size (Figure 5.3), the two multinational firm types are in a symmetrical position and the real wage of skilled labour can remain equalized across the countries despite the large difference in country size. Moving down a column of Figure 5.3 such as $\tau = 0.15$, we see a sequence of regime shifts similar to that suggested by the partial equilibrium analysis of section 3:

$$(m_h, m_f) \rightarrow (m_h, m_f, n_h) \rightarrow (n_h).$$

Figure 5.4 plots the same ratios as Figure 5.2, but this time for the column $\tau = 0.15$ of Figure 5.3. The two countries are identical at the left-hand edge of each panel of Figure 5.4 as before, with their size differences being maximized at the right-hand edge. The top panel gives production ratios with and without multinationals banned, as in earlier figures. The ratio X_f / X_{fn} quickly goes off to infinity as the denominator goes to zero with a moderate difference in country size: with multinationals banned, the smaller country specializes in good Y. As in the case of the countries differing in relative endowments, the removal of an investment barrier shifts production from country h to country f, in this case from the larger to the smaller country.[11]

The country-size experiment, however, yields rather different results from the relative-endowment experiment in Figure 5.2 with respect to the real wage of skilled labour and the skilled–unskilled wage ratio. In the present case, the removal of an investment ban raises v_f and r_f and lowers v_h and r_h.[12] The reason for this is familiar from the industrial-organization approach to trade. With the countries different in size and multinationals banned, type-n_h firms have a significant advantage over type-n_f firms in that the former have their sales concentrated in their low-cost (no transport costs) domestic market, whereas type-n_f firms have a small domestic market. Thus, in equilibrium, country f generally has fewer firms than its relative size would predict. Even after accounting for size, X-sector demand for skilled labour is greater in country h than in country f, and the real wage of skilled labour is higher in the former. The introduction of multinationals removes country size as a 'determinant of comparative advantage', shifts production and firm ownership to country f, and thus increases v_f and decreases v_h.[13] Conversely, one could say that the removal of the investment barriers causes country h to 'lose

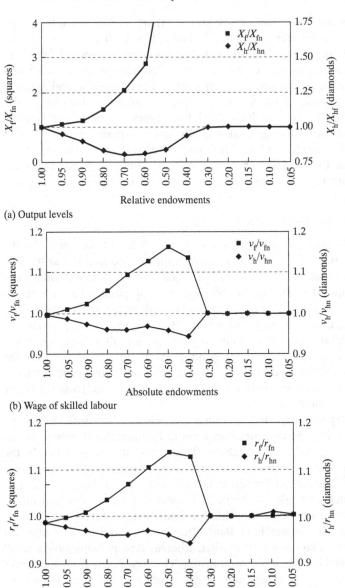

(a) Output levels

(b) Wage of skilled labour

(c) Relative wages

Figure 5.4   Effect of removing an investment barrier: differences in absolute endowments, $\tau = 0.15$.

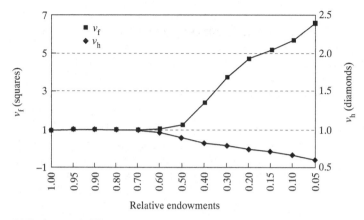

(a) Real wage of skilled labour

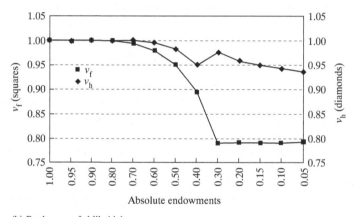

(b) Real wage of skilled labour

Figure 5.5   **Effect of endowments on the real wage of skilled labour: $\tau = 0.15$ (multinationals permitted).**

competitiveness', not only as the favoured site for production (also true in Figure 5.1) but as the favoured site for firm headquarters.

6   The real wage of skilled labour

The analysis of the preceding two sections focused on the effects of multinationals by comparing a situation in which they are present with one in which they are excluded by a direct investment ban. But the fact that the removal of such a ban, for example, raises v_h and lowers v_f does not imply that $v_h > v_f$ post liberalization. In this section, we directly examine v_f and v_h when multinationals enter endogenously.

Figure 5.5 has two panels corresponding to the two experiments shown in Figures 5.1 and 5.3. These panels move down the column for $\tau = 0.15$, as in the case of Figures 5.2 and 5.4. In both panels of Figure 5.5, we see that there is a region of factor-price equalization when the two countries are similar. We see the intuitive result in the top panel that, as country f becomes increasingly scarce in skilled labour, the return to skilled labour in country f rises and that in country h falls. Combining these results with those of Figure 5.2 suggests that multinationals reduce the difference in v_h and v_f, except possibly when the countries are very different in relative endowments (in which case direct investment increases both v_h and v_f).

In the bottom panel, we see that the large country has a high real wage for skilled labour and the small country a low real wage, even though their relative endowments are the same. This is an effect that is familiar from the new trade theory, as noted in the previous section. In this model, country size is itself a source of comparative advantage and the small country will have firm numbers less than in proportion to its size when multinationals are not present. Referring back to Figure 5.3, multinationals disappear in the column $\tau = 0.15$ at absolute endowment ratio 0.4–0.3, and it is here we see the large divergence in v_h and v_f in the bottom panel of Figure 5.5. This is a rather startling finding with implications for a dynamic analysis or even a static one with factor migration. If countries are identical in relative endowments but differ so significantly in size that multinationals do not enter, factor trade or accumulation may produce a divergence in relative endowments, with the small country becoming skilled-labour scarce: a brain-drain phenomenon.

Finally, note in the bottom panel of Figure 5.5 that the real wage of skilled labour is lower in both countries when they are of very different size, even though total world endowments are constant. This is a reflection of the fact that multinational firms are more skilled-labour intensive than national firms. Moving from right to left (convergence in country size), the wage of skilled labour rises in both countries as multinational firms displace national firms. Considering both panels of Figure 5.5 together, we see that a convergence in both relative and absolute endowments tends to raise the wage of skilled labour in the initially large and skilled-labour-abundant country.

Combining these results with those of the previous two sections, the general conclusion is that multinationals create a tendency toward factor-price equalization relative to a situation where they are exogen-

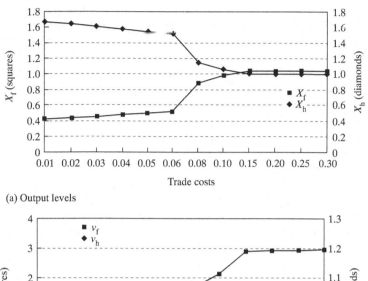

(a) Output levels

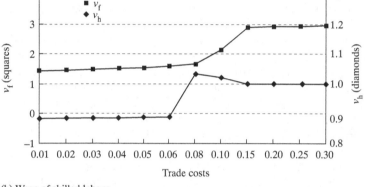

(b) Wage of skilled labour

Figure 5.6 **Effects of trade costs: relative endowment experiment, central case (multinationals permitted, relative endowment = 0.40).**

ously excluded. The possible exception occurs when the countries are very different in relative endowments but similar in size, in which case the removal of an investment ban might increase the (positive) difference between v_f and v_h.

7 Trade costs

Some of the same questions we have addressed above can also be asked with respect to trade costs, insofar as multinationals are associated with moderate to high trade costs relative to the size of the market. Thus multinationals can also be induced to enter by raising trade costs from an initial low level. Figure 5.6 shows the effects of trade costs on the real wage of skilled labour for row 0.40 of Figure 5.1, the relative endowment experiment. The effects are pretty much as expected: trade barriers reduce the degree of specialization in production, moving the output levels together. But the 'togetherness' is much more dramatic here in that the production levels are in fact equalized, whereas in the Heckscher–Ohlin model they would remain well apart given the differences in relative endowments. The key to understanding the result here is that, although production levels converge, the firm numbers do not converge, m_h being the only firm type in equilibrium (see Figure 5.1). Exports of skilled-labour-intensive producer services by country h compensate for the low endowment of S in country f.

The lower panel of Figure 5.6 plots the real wages of skilled labour. Here we see something that is rather different from the Heckscher–Ohlin model. In the HO model, trade costs drive the prices of a factor apart across countries. Here the effect of trade costs is to raise the price of skilled labour in both countries. The intuition lies in the regime shift induced by the higher trade costs. The entry of multinationals actually increases the demand for skilled labour in country f. The larger number of branch plants that are established by type-m_h firms generates more demand for country-f skilled labour than was generated by its smaller number of type-n_f firms when trade barriers were very low. Although we do not show it here, a similar effect of trade barriers on v_f occurs when the countries differ in size: trade barriers raise v_f when multinationals enter or, in other words, the 'brain-drain' problem referred to above is worse when trade barriers are low than when they are high.

The analysis of trade barriers is one case where a somewhat different parameterization yielded qualitatively different results, and because they are interesting we report them in Figure 5.7. In Figure 5.7 the parameterization is $\beta = 1.0$, $\gamma = \delta = 0.1$, so that a branch plant is much more unskilled-labour intensive than in our central case. The upper panels of Figures 5.6 and 5.7 are not much different. The interesting result is in the lower panel of Figure 5.7, where we see something that is completely opposite from the Heckscher–Ohlin model. In the latter, free trade tends to equalize factor prices, whereas trade barriers drive factor prices *apart* as just noted. Here we see the opposite, with trade barriers nearly *equalizing* the return to skilled labour in the two countries. The left-hand region in this lower panel can be thought of as a competitive effect familiar in the trade industrial organization literature. Despite (almost) free trade, the difference in the endowments of the two countries leads to significantly fewer firms in country f, and hence to differences between countries in markups and in the price of X. With multinationals induced

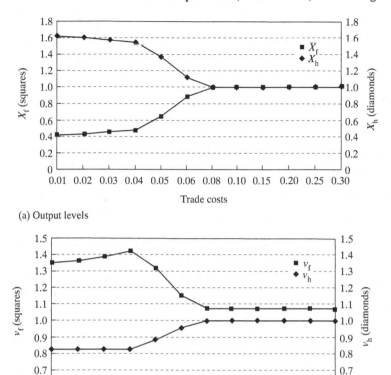

(a) Output levels

(b) Wage of skilled labour

Figure 5.7   **Effects of trade costs: relative endowment experiment, $\beta = 1.0$, $\gamma = \delta = 0.1$ (multinationals permitted, relative endowment = 0.40).**

to enter at higher trade costs, the markups and prices are the same in the two countries and the real returns to skilled labour are almost the same.

Finally, results shed light on the following question: do trade barriers protect unskilled labour in the skilled-labour-abundant country? Although we do not plot the price of w_h, it moves in the opposite fashion to v_h. Trade barriers do not protect unskilled labour in country h, another result that seems opposite to that of traditional factor-proportions trade theory in which trade barriers protect the scarce factor. The reason is that trade barriers encourage the entry of multinationals, which are skilled-labour intensive and which tend to headquarter in the skilled-labour-abundant country. Thus trade barriers actually raise the return to the *abundant* factor by altering the trade regime.

8   Comparative steady-state analysis

Results suggest a number of dynamic implications, which are of interest both from the point of view of positive economics and from the point of view of policy analysis. In particular, does the entry of multinationals due to the removal of an investment barrier (or an increase in a trade barrier) stimulate or retard the development of a skilled labour force? This question is surely of particular interest in developing countries, where debates over the effects of multinationals often focus on the possibilities of technology spillovers, learning, and human capital accumulation.

Several approaches to this question are possible, all of which likely reflect reality in some measure. We could for example consider learning-by-doing within multinational firms. Skills are accumulated by workers in the course of production, and the rent to that learning may or may not be captured by the multinationals in terms of the wage schedule paid to new workers.

Instead, we rather arbitrarily focused on a simple market model of skilled labour, closely related to traditional models of productive physical capital. We assume that there is a competitive 'education' sector that converts unskilled workers to skilled workers and, sticking with a representative agent model, those skills depreciate over time. Multinationals do not directly train workers within the firm; the 'learning' technology is an independent competitive sector of the economy. Multinationals influence the level of skilled labour in the economy through their demands for skilled labour and the resulting general-equilibrium effects on factor prices.

The technology for producing skilled labour is quite simple: $z > 1$ units of L produce one new unit of S. Time is discrete, and the depreciation rate of the stock of skilled labour per period is $\delta < 1$. The rate of time preference is denoted $\rho > 0$. The steady-state condition for the accumulation of skilled labour is given:

$$v = \left[1 - \frac{1-\delta}{1+\rho}\right]zw = \left[\frac{\rho+\delta}{1+\rho}\right]zw, \tag{17}$$

where the term in brackets is the difference between the value of one unit of S at the beginning of a period and the present value of what is left at the end of that period. In the comparative steady-state simulations to follow, the supply of S is endogenously adjusted following a parameter change to ensure that (17) is satisfied.

We performed the analysis using the same parameter values used throughout the paper (except in Figure 5.7, which uses alternative fixed costs). The procedure is as follows:

1. Suppress multinational firms, and run the model for both the case in which relative endowments differ and the case in which absolute endowments differ.
2. Assume that, for each initial parameter value, the solution represents a steady-state equilibrium: (17) is satisfied at the equilibrium levels of w_i and v_i.
3. We choose ρ exogenously, and then calibrate z and/or δ so that (17) holds at the equilibrium values of w_i and v_i. Note that this implies that a country with a higher v_i/w_i ratio has a 'poorer' technology for producing skilled labour.[14]
4. Remove the implicit investment ban, and allow S_i to adjust to maintain (17), holding δ, ρ, and z constant at their calibrated (or exogenously chosen) levels.

Figures 5.8 and 5.9 show the effects of removing the investment barrier when the countries differ in relative endowments, fixed costs are as in our central case, and transport costs $\tau = 0.15$. This experiment is thus the comparative steady-state equivalent of the static results shown in Figures 5.3 and 5.4. The notation is similar to that of the body of the paper, with the subscript 'n' denoting a variable with multinationals banned, no additional subscript to the country subscript (h,f) denoting a variable with multinationals permitted but skilled labour exogenously fixed. But we now have the additional subscript 'e', denoting a variable with multinationals permitted and skilled labour endogenous.

The top panel of Figure 5.8 shows the effect of removing the investment ban on the steady-state stock of skilled labour in the two countries. For small initial relative endowment differences, the removal of the barrier increases the stock in country h and decreases it in country f. This reflects the factor-price effects discussed in connection with Figures 5.3 and 5.4. This is an interesting result insofar as the removal of the investment ban drives the relative endowments of the two countries further apart.

But, when initial endowment differences are large, the removal of the ban leads to an increase in the steady-state stock in both countries, reflecting our earlier finding in Figure 5.4 that the removal of the ban increases v_i/w_i in both countries. The substitution of more-skilled-labour-intensive multinational firms for less-skilled-labour-intensive national firms raises the steady-state stock of S in both countries.

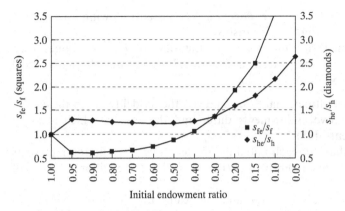

(a) Steady-state supply of skilled labour

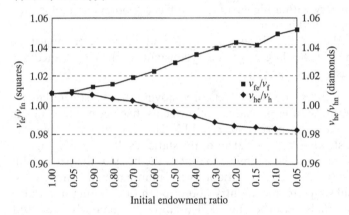

(b) Steady-state wage of skilled labour

Figure 5.8   Steady-state effects of removing an investment barrier: relative endowment experiment, $\tau = 0.15$.

The bottom panel of Figure 5.8 gives the effect of the removal of the investment ban on the steady-state real wage of skilled labour. Although it follows from (17) that v/w does not change when the skilled labour stock adjusts endogenously, the price index does, implying that some of the change shown in this bottom panel is due to the change in the steady-state stock.

Figure 5.9 shows the proportional steady-state consumption effects of removing the investment ban (again, $\tau = 0.15$). Subscripts 'n' and 'e' have the same meanings as just defined for Figure 5.8. The top panel shows the overall effect, while the middle and bottom panels decompose

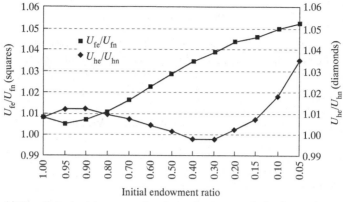

(a) Overall steady-state consumption change due to removal of an investment barrier

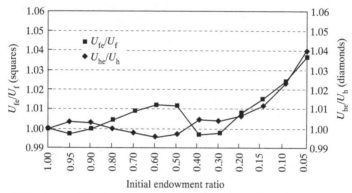

(b) Component of steady-state consumption change due to change in skilled labour supply

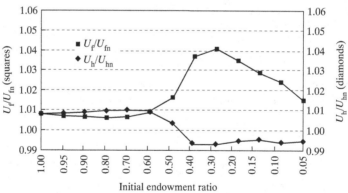

(c) Component of consumption change due to change in regime, holding skilled labour constant

Figure 5.9   **Steady-state effects of removing an investment barrier on welfare: relative endowment experiment, $\tau = 0.15$.**

that effect into two changes. The bottom panel shows the effect on welfare of holding the stock of S constant in each country (the 'impact effect'), and the middle panel shows the added effect due to the change in the steady-state stock of S (the 'labour-force adjustment effect').

There almost seems to be a negative correlation for these two components of consumption change for each country. When the initial endowment difference is large, country h is harmed by the impact effect but is helped by the labour-force adjustment effect. The former is a result of the 'home-market' effect we talked about earlier. When the countries are quite different, country h benefits from an investment ban, in that production is concentrated in country h, resulting in a low price (high real income). Removal of the ban causes a negative impact effect for country h. But removal of the ban also leads to an increase in the real wage of S_h owing to effects discussed earlier in connection with Figures 5.3 and 5.4. Thus the labour-force adjustment effect increases steady-state consumption in country h.

Country f on the other hand is helped by the impact effect and, while not harmed by the labour-force adjustment effect, the latter appears to be negatively correlated with the impact effect.[15] The impact effect is maximized for country f when the difference in relative endowments is in the range 0.40–0.30. Above this range, country f is not severely damaged by the home-market advantage of country h and, below this range, country f cannot attract as much multinational investment when the ban is removed. But it is also in this intermediate range that the labour-force adjustment effect is minimized for country f: removing the investment ban has little impact effect on v_f.

Figures 5.10 and 5.11 conduct the same experiment when countries differ in size, again using the parameterization of our central case and the transport cost $\tau = 0.15$. Results in the top panel of Figure 5.10 reflect results discussed in connection with Figure 5.4 that removal of the investment ban harms skilled labour in country h and raises its real wage in country f (recall that the investment ban becomes non-binding at size difference 0.30, so removing it has no effect). Results in the lower panel of Figure 5.10 reflect a price-index effect of the type discussed earlier.

Figure 5.11, giving changes in steady-state consumption, is the equivalent of Figure 5.9 for the present case of differences in absolute endowments. The top panel gives the total effect, the bottom panel the 'impact effect', and the middle panel the 'labour-force adjustment effect'. Removal of the investment ban helps country f overall and hurts country h in most of the region in which the ban is binding. Furthermore, and unlike the case of relative endowments, the two components of this welfare change are now positively correlated. The impact effect harms country h owing to the loss

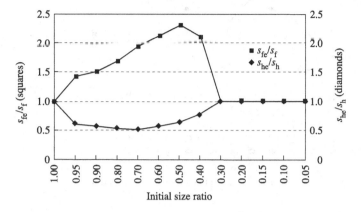

(a) Steady-state supply of skilled labour

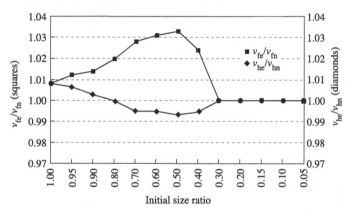

(b) Steady-state wage of skilled labour

**Figure 5.10   Steady-state effects of removing an investment barrier: absolute
endowment experiment, $\tau = 0.15$.**

of its home-market advantage, and that impact effect involves a fall in v_h. Thus the labour-force adjustment effect reinforces the impact effect. Similar but opposite comments apply to country f.

Overall, the results suggest favourable welfare effects for the small and/or skilled-labour-scarce country from direct investment. The introduction of direct investment has a positive impact effect on such countries by removing the home-market advantage of the large and/or skilled-labour-abundant country. Direct investment thus lowers the price index in the disadvantaged country but may raise it in the advantaged country. Analytical foundations for these results are derived in our earlier papers

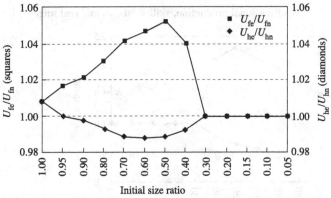

(a) Overall steady-state consumption change due to removal of an investment barrier

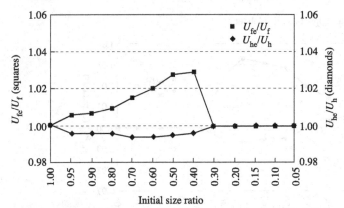

(b) Component of steady-state consumption change due to change in skilled labour supply

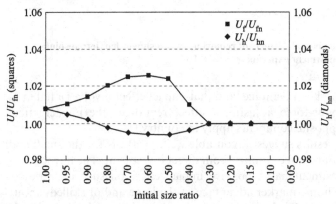

(c) Component of consumption change due to change in regime, holding skilled labour constant

Figure 5.11 Steady-state effects of removing an investment barrier on welfare: absolute endowment experiment, $\tau = 0.15$.

(Markusen and Venables 1995a,b). The labour-force adjustment effect reinforces the impact effect for both countries if they differ initially in size, but has more complicated effects if the countries differ initially in relative endowments. But, even in the latter case, both effects act to increase steady-state consumption in the skilled-labour-scarce country if the initial endowment difference is large.

9   Conclusions

The general findings and implications of the paper can be summarized as follows.

(1) The industry of interest in this paper is characterized by both firm-level and plant-level scale economies. The value-added of this paper is explicitly to introduce human capital, and to model human capital as necessary for the creation of firm-specific knowledge capital and, to a lesser extent, for plant fixed costs as well. Final production is assumed to use unskilled labour.

(2) The entry of multinationals corresponds to a change in the nature of what is traded between countries. National firms engage in the export of goods, which are bundles of skilled- and unskilled-labour services. Multinationals are exporters of skilled-labour-intensive producer services (or services of knowledge capital). Accordingly, multinationals should have important implications for factor returns in addition to their implications for the volume and composition of trade.

(3) When countries differ in relative endowments of factors, we found that the entry of multinationals as the result of the removal of a barrier to direct investment shifts production from the skilled-labour-abundant (advantaged) to the unskilled-labour-abundant (disadvantaged) country. By being able to segment activities geographically, multinationals lead to more concentration of knowledge-capital production in the advantaged country and more concentration of unskilled-labour-intensive production in the disadvantaged country.

(4)   The entry of multinationals when countries differ in relative endowments raises the return to skilled labour in the advantaged country because more firms are 'headquartered' in this country and raises the skilled–unskilled wage gap, an issue of considerable interest to public policy.[16] The effect of multinational entry on the disadvantaged country is however ambiguous. We found that entry was more likely to raise the return to skilled labour in the disadvantaged country when the relative endowment difference between the countries is moderate to large. Multinational branch plants draw labour from the (unskilled-labour-intensive) composite sector rather than displacing (skilled-labour-intensive)

national X-sector firms. In these circumstances, multinationals raise the return to skilled labour in both countries.[17] Intuitively, the regime shift replaces less-skilled-labour-intensive national firms with more-skilled-labour-intensive multinational firms.[18]

(5) When countries differ in size, multinational entry shifts production from the large to the small country. But now the return to skilled labour falls in the large country and rises in the small country. The intuition here is a home-market effect familiar from the trade industrial organiza-tion literature. In the absence of multinationals, most national firms are headquartered in the large country where most of their sales are in their low-cost domestic market. The entry of multinationals eliminates this locational advantage, and firm ownership (headquarters) and/or plants become geographically dispersed in proportion to country size.

(6) A comparison of the real wage of skilled labour between countries reveals that the entry of multinationals creates a tendency toward factor-price equalization. Although multinational entry might lower the wage of skilled labour in the skilled-labour-scarce country f, entry does not lower it below the wage in country h. In other cases (particularly size differences) multinational entry eliminates a 'brain-drain' possibility in which the skilled-labour wage in the disadvantaged country is signifi-cantly below that in the advantaged country. The one exception to the tendency of multinationals to create factor-price equalization occurs when the countries are very different in relative endowments.

(7) Figure 5.5 also suggested that a convergence in country character-istics has interesting implications for the wage of skilled labour and the skilled–unskilled wage gap. Beginning with one country both large and skilled-labour abundant, convergence in characteristics should lead to a rising skilled–unskilled wage gap in that country as the other country 'catches up'.

(8) Section 7 looks at the effects of trade costs when the countries differ in relative endowments. Trade costs generally raise X production in the disadvantaged country and raise the return to skilled labour in the advantaged country (its multinationals are the dominant firm type when trade costs are high). By inducing a regime shift, trade barriers thus protect the *abundant* factor in the skilled-labour-abundant country. Trade protection lowers the return to skilled labour in the small country (i.e. also protecting the abundant factor) if host-country skilled labour is relatively unimportant in plant fixed costs but raises its real wage if skilled labour is important (our central case).

(9) Results suggest some important dynamic extensions, considered in section 8. Much recent literature has stressed favourable effects of multi-nationals on host countries via the transfer of technology, knowledge,

and skills. Some of these effects are present here (the transfer of firm-specific knowledge capital raises X output and welfare), but there may also be adverse factor-price effects on skilled labour, resulting in a slower rate of skill and knowledge accumulation. Such adverse effects are unlikely (a rise in the steady-state level of S_f owing to multinational entry is likely) when the host country is small and/or poorly endowed with S.

Notes

This paper was prepared simultaneously for two conferences with rather different themes. One was the conference 'Dynamic Issues in Applied Commercial Policy Analysis', Geneva, 26–28 January 1996, organized by the Centre for Economic Policy Research, London. The other was the conference 'Creation and Transfer of Knowledge: Institutions and Incentives', Rome, 21–23 September 1995, organized by the Fondazione Eni Enrico Mattei (FEEM) of Milan. The latter version is entitled 'The International Transmission of Knowledge by Multinational Firms' and will be published by FEEM. The analytical sections of the two papers are similar, with the introductory and summary sections written to reflect the very different focuses of the two conferences. Results reported and discussed differ for the same reason.

1. Some examples are Brainard (1993a,b,c), Ekholm (1995), and Markusen and Venables (1995a,b, 1996). Brainard and Markusen and Venables do not address human capital issues. Ekholm addresses them empirically, but theory of exporting versus direct investment in relation to human capital endowments is not developed. Theoretical results in this paper are consistent with Ekholm's empirical findings that outward direct investment is closely associated with a country's human capital endowment. Helpman and Krugman (1985) model a separation of headquarters and production activities. However, there is no endogenous choice of single- versus multi-plant production and their factor-price equalization framework makes their approach unsatisfactory for the policy issues addressed here.
2. Technologies and skill levels will be taken as exogenous in this paper. In a later paper, we hope to examine how multinational firms in turn endogenously determine international differences in skills by transferring technologies and other forms of knowledge capital. See Blomstrom and Kokko (1995) for an excellent review of existing work in this area.
3. Rising skilled–unskilled wage gaps in both North and South have been discussed and modelled, and hypotheses tested, in a number of papers, including Feenstra and Hanson (1995a,b), Hanson and Harrison (1995), Cragg and Epelbaum (1995), and Berman et al. (1995). Feenstra and Hanson model a continuum of intermediate inputs for an industry, ranked in terms of skilled–unskilled labour intensity. Investment liberalization moves capital to the South, and shifts the dividing line in the continuum in favour of more inputs produced in the South. The shifted inputs are skilled-labour intensive in the South, but unskilled-labour intensive from the North's point of view, hence the relative demand for skilled labour rises in both countries. Hanson and Harrison find evidence that foreign-owned firms and joint ventures in Mexico pay higher wages to skilled workers and demand more skilled labour

than other firms. Cragg and Epelbaum focus on capital mobility and skill-biased technical change, while Berman et al. also find evidence of skill-biased technical change.

4. Reiterating what we noted above, our earlier papers either assume that all X-sector activities use factors in the same proportion (Markusen and Venables 1995b) or use just a single factor (Markusen and Venables 1995b, 1996). Labour-market effects are of only second-order importance in those papers and not addressed. The technology-transfer cost ($\gamma > 0$) is motivated by empirical results, especially those of Teece (1977, 1986), that direct invest-ments require significant further investments in skilled-labour-intensive activ-ities for multinational firms.

5. Skilled workers could be used in X production (and in G) but they enjoy no productivity advantage over unskilled labour: engineers are no better on the assembly line than unskilled workers. Since skilled workers are differentiated from unskilled workers in the composite Y sector, all 'excess' skilled workers not needed in fixed costs will be allocated to the Y sector in equilibrium.

6. An exception can occur when the two countries are *very similar*. The removal of an investment barrier leads, in equilibrium, to multinational firms with significantly higher output per firm than the national firms they displace, a type of pro-competitive effect. Since final output is unskilled-labour intensive, the difference in equilibrium firm scale contributes toward making the multi-national firms less skilled-labour intensive. In the simulation results we report, this firm-scale effect approximately cancels out the fixed-cost effect (making multinationals more skilled-labour intensive at common scale) so that the equilibrium skilled-labour wage and the skilled–unskilled wage gap are essentially unaffected by the removal of an investment ban when the countries are identical.

7. Reviewing points made separately earlier, multinational firms are moderately more skilled-labour intensive than national firms, which are moderately more skilled-labour intensive than Y production in our calibrations. But many of the interesting factor-market effects that we identify are driven by geogra-phical rearrangement of activities when multinationals are allowed to enter rather than by the skilled-labour intensities of type-n firms versus type-m firms versus Y production per se.

8. If multinationals are banned, this can result in an inefficiently large number of firms in protected markets producing at small scale, resulting in a significantly higher S/L ratio in the X sector, as we shall note later.

9. Note that the vertical axis of Figure 5.1 gives S_f as a proportion of its initial value. Skilled labour is transferred to country h, holding the world endow-ment constant. Thus the row 0.4 in Figure 5.1 has a ratio of $S_f/S_h = 0.4/1.6$, or 0.25. The vertical axis in the later regime diagram (Figure 5.3) is similarly defined.

10. Apologies for the different scales for the two ratios in each of the panels of Figure 5.2. The fact that one of the ratios generally changes much more than the other makes the change in the smaller one difficult to evaluate if the two ratios are plotted on the same scale. We calibrated the two scales such that the ratios have the same position when the countries are initially identical and the ratios are equal.

11. Of course, we see from Figure 5.3 that, when size differences are very large, multinationals do not enter even in the absence of an investment barrier.

12. As we shall see shortly, this does not imply that $v_f > v_h$! We are referring here only to the change in these prices when an investment barrier is removed.
13. When the difference in size becomes very large, we see from Figure 5.3 that multinationals do not produce in country f even though they could. Thus all of the ratios in Figure 5.4 become equal to 1 when the absolute endowment number is less than or equal to 0.30.
14. A 'poor' technology could mean a higher z for a given δ, or a higher δ for a given z. The two alternatives seem equivalent in steady-state analysis. In the simulations to follow, we rather arbitrarily calibrate δ and hold z exogenously fixed.
15. It is of course consistent for the two components to be negatively correlated at the same time that they both contribute positively to welfare.
16. The role of trade in explaining the growing gap in skilled–unskilled wages has been an important policy issue. An excellent discussion of the evidence and conceptual arguments is present in articles by Freeman, Richardson, and Wood in the summer 1995 issue of the *Journal of Economic Perspectives*. No role for multinationals is identified by these authors. The paper suggests that such a role should be considered, especially owing to the empirical fact that direct investment has grown much more rapidly than trade over the past two decades.
17. As we noted earlier, the puzzle of the rising wage gap in both North and South has been documented and modelled by Feenstra and Hanson (1995a,b), with the rising gap in the South a particular focus of Cragg and Epelbaum (1995), Hanson and Harrison (1995), and Berman et al. (1995). Capital mobility from North to South has been a focus of the first two papers in particular. Physical capital acts in a complicated way as a general equilibrium complement to Southern skilled labour, just as Northern exports of skilled-labour-intensive producer services can be a general equilibrium complement for Southern skilled labour in the present paper.
18. This result is consistent with the empirical findings of Hanson and Harrison (1995).

References

Berman, Eli, Stephen Machlin, and John Bound (1995), 'Implications of Skill Biased Technological Change: International Evidence', Working Paper.
Blomstrom, Magnus and Ari Kokko (1995), 'Multinational Corporations and Spillovers to the Host Country', Working Paper, Stockholm School of Economics.
Brainard, S. Lael (1993a), 'A Simple Theory of Multinational Corporations and Trade with a Trade-off between Proximity and Concentration', NBER Working Paper No. 4269.
(1993b), 'An Empirical Assessment of the Factor Proportions Explanation of Multinationals' Sales', NBER Working Paper No. 4583.
(1993c), 'An Empirical Assessment of the Proximity-Concentration Tradeoff between Multinational Sales and Trade', NBER Working Paper No. 4580.
Caves, Richard E. (1996), *Multinational Enterprise and Economic Analysis*, 2nd edn. London: Cambridge University Press.

Cragg, Michael Ian and Mario Epelbaum (1995), 'The Premium for Skills in LDCs: Evidence from Mexico', Working Paper.

Eaton, Jonathan and Akiko Tamura (1994), 'Bilateralism and Regionalism in Japanese and US Trade and Direct Foreign Investment Patterns', *Journal of the Japanese and International Economies* 8: 478–510.

Ekholm, Karolina (1995), *Multinational Production and Trade in Technological Knowledge*. Lund Economic Studies No. 58.

Feenstra, Robert C. and Gordon H. Hanson (1995a), 'Foreign Investment, Outsourcing, and Relative Wages'. In *Political Economy of Trade Policy: Essays in Honor of Jagdish Bhagwati*. Cambridge, Mass.: MIT Press.

(1995b), 'Foreign Direct Investment and Relative Wages: Evidence from Mexico's Maquiladoras', Working Paper.

Freeman, Richard B. (1995), 'Are Your Wages Set in Beijing?' *Journal of Economic Perspectives* 9: 15–32.

Hanson, Gordon H. and Ann Harrison (1995), 'Trade, Technology, and Wage Inequality', NBER Working Paper No. 5110.

Helpman, Elhanan and Paul Krugman (1985), *Market Structure and Foreign Trade*. Cambridge, Mass.: MIT Press.

Keller, Wolfgang (1994), 'Absorptive Capacity: Understanding the Creation and Acquisition of Technology in Development', Working Paper, Yale University.

Leamer, Edward E. (1994), 'American Regionalism and Global Free Trade', NBER Working Paper No. 4763.

(1995), 'A Trade Economist's View of US Wages and Globalization', manuscript.

Markusen, James R. (1995), 'The Boundaries of Multinational Enterprises and the Theory of International Trade', *Journal of Economic Perspectives* 9: 169–89.

Markusen, James R. and Anthony J. Venables (1995a), 'Multinational Firms and the New Trade Theory', Working Paper.

(1995b), 'The Theory of Endowment, Intra-Industry and Multinational Trade', Working Paper.

(1996), 'The Increased Importance of Direct Investment in North Atlantic Economic Relationships: A Convergence Hypothesis'. In Matthew B. Canzoneri, Wilfred J. Ethier, and Vittorio Grilli (eds.), *The New Transatlantic Economy*. Cambridge: Cambridge University Press, pp. 169–90.

Motta, Massimo (1992), 'Multinational Firms and the Tariff-Jumping Argument', *European Economic Review* 36: 1557–71.

Richardson, J. David (1995), 'Income Inequality and Trade: How to Think, What to Conclude', *Journal of Economic Perspectives* 9(3): 33–56.

Rutherford, Thomas F. (1994), 'Applied General-Equilibrium Modelling with MPS/GE as a GAMS Subsystem', Working Paper.

Teece, David (1977), 'Technology Transfer by Multinational Firms: The Resource Cost of Transferring Technological Know-How', *Economic Journal* 87: 242–61.

(1986), *The Multinational Corporation and the Resource Cost of International Technology Transfer*. Cambridge, Mass.: Ballinger.

Wood, Adrian (1995), 'How Trade Hurt Unskilled Workers', *Journal of Economic Perspectives* 9: 57-80.

Discussion

TIMOTHY J. KEHOE

Although average real wages in the United States have increased since 1980, the real wages of the less educated have fallen. In fact, the wage gap – the difference between the median real wage of college-educated workers and the median real wage of other workers – rose by 35 per cent between 1980 and 1995 (*Economic Report of the President*, 1997). In the intense political and economic debate referred to by Markusen and Venables over the causes of, and possible remedies for, this sharp increase in the wage gap, two competing stories have emerged for explaining this increase. The first is that competition from workers in less developed countries, in the form of increased trade and investment flows between the United States and these countries, has driven down the wages of the less educated workers. The second is that changes in technology have occurred in the US workplace, particularly with the introduction of computers and robotics, that have driven down the demand for workers who lack the education to use this technology.

The Stolper–Samuelson theorem of Heckscher–Ohlin trade theory offers an appealing explanation of the increasing wage gap based on increases in trade flows between the United States and less developed countries: the United States has relatively more educated workers than does a developing county such as Mexico. According to the Heckscher–Ohlin theory, the United States will export to Mexico goods that use these educated workers intensively. Mexico, on the other hand, will export to the United States goods that use the less educated workers intensively. The Stolper–Samuelson theorem says that the resulting increase in the demand for educated workers in the United States will drive up their real wages, and the resulting decline in demand for less educated workers will drive down their real wages.

So far, so good. There are three problems with this explanation, however. First, Heckscher–Ohlin theory predicts that the increase in demand for the education-intensive goods, the goods that the United States exports, should have driven up their prices. Instead, as Lawrence and Slaughter (1993) have shown, the prices of the goods that the United States exported actually fell slightly during the 1980s compared with the prices of the goods that it imported. Secondly, the Stolper–Samuelson theorem predicts that the opposite movement in relative wages should occur in Mexico – that the wage gap there should shrink as that in the

United States grows. In fact, the wage gap in Mexico has grown in a similar way to that in the United States (see, for example, Alarcon and McKinley (1996)). Thirdly, the timing is wrong. Whereas the 1980s were the period with most of the increase in the wage gap, the 1990s have been the period with most of the increase in trade between the United States and less developed countries.

A more convincing explanation of the increase in the wage gap in the United States has been provided by Krusell et al. (1997): a sharp decline in equipment prices in the 1980s, due largely to a fall in computer prices, led to an increase in demand for educated workers, who are complements for this equipment in production, and a decline in demand for less educated workers, who are substitutes. In a carefully calibrated model, Krusell et al. show that the timing of the fall in equipment prices and the increase in the wage gap is right. Furthermore, their theory predicts the fall in the prices of the US export goods and the increase in the wage gap in Mexico.

Where do Markusen and Venables stand on all this? What they have done is to propose an ingenious, yet plausible, new explanation of the increase in the wage gap based on increases in trade with developing countries. It is now trade in services within multinational corporations that is the culprit. A multinational firm in the United States opens a plant in Mexico. The education-intensive services connected with the operations of the plant are conducted at the headquarters in the United States, but the less-education-intensive production work is done in Mexico. Real wages of educated workers in the United States go up, and real wages of less educated workers go down. What about the wages of workers in Mexico? The effects are ambiguous because the multinational firm has access to a different technology than do Mexican firms. As Markusen and Venables explain:

> In our calibration, multinational firms are generally more skilled-labour intensive than national firms, using more skilled labour for branch-plant fixed costs versus the additional unskilled labour for transport costs used by national firms. This depends, however, on firm scale.

The opening of plants in Mexico that are subsidiaries of multinationals can actually increase demand for educated workers there, who will be managers at these plants rather than working in the Mexican firms in the same sector or in the other sector, which is less education intensive.

Markusen and Venables' model is capable, therefore, of explaining the increasing wage gap in both the United States and Mexico. There are parts of their story that ring true, and I hope that either they or others spend more effort on following it up. Where this effort is needed is in looking at the data. I still think that the timing is wrong in their story: the explosion of foreign direct investment into Mexico occurred in the 1990s, but the increase in the wage gap in both the United States and Mexico occurred mostly in the 1980s. The differences in technologies between multinational branch plants and Mexican firms in the same sector, while plausible, also need some study.

What I like about Markusen and Venables' paper is the way it mixes an imaginative insight with theoretical ingenuity to produce a thought-provoking new take on an important debate. I am nervous, however, that this might end up being as far as this new take goes. The 'new trade' literature – which, over the past two decades, has introduced scale economies, product differentiation, and imperfect competition into the study of international trade and investment, and in which Markusen and Venables, along with people such as Paul Krugman, are the leaders – is short on confrontation with data.

To make this point, I will mention a paper by Markusen – not because it is a bad paper; quite the opposite. (And Jim is such a good friend of mine that I do not think that he will take offence at my good-natured criticism; if he does, I can make up for it by buying him a beer.) Markusen (1986) proposes a simple model to explain some of the stylized facts of international trade from, say, 1950 to 1985: world trade has grown faster than world income; most of this growth in trade has been trade between developed countries; and most of the trade between developed countries is intra-industry trade. In Markusen's model, developed countries trade among themselves for the typical reasons in the new trade literature: scale economies and product differentiation. Developed countries trade with less developed countries for the reasons in Heckscher–Ohlin theory: differences in factor endowments. Trade between developed countries grows faster than income because the goods they trade are superior goods. The key assumption in Markusen's model is the non-homotheticity of consumers' preferences. At first glance, this seems to match the facts, because the primary goods that developed countries have traditionally imported from less developed countries are inferior goods.

Bergoeing (1996) takes this model to the data and finds that it does not work. Specifically, he makes a number of heroic assumptions to calibrate Markusen's model, but finds that it cannot come close to explaining the increase in trade. The sticking point is that the goods that developed countries trade are not superior enough, and their share in consumption has not been increasing. The product category most traded between developed countries is automobiles and auto parts for example, but consumer expenditures on automobiles and auto parts have not increased at anywhere near the rate at which trade in this product category has increased. Furthermore, suppose, ignoring the data, that we assume that these goods are actually very superior. Then their share in consumption in poor countries should have risen even faster than that in richer countries as the poor countries became richer, driving up trade between developed and less developed countries even faster than the trade between developed countries. There may be something of an escape clause here, because trade between developed and less developed countries has recently begun to expand more quickly than that between developed countries, but this is the opposite of the result that Markusen set out to establish.

Bergoeing's work suggests many exciting directions for future research, and I think it is an example of something that is all too rare in the new trade literature: research that takes seriously the sort of models that Markusen and Venables are so good at building, where I mean 'take seriously' in the sense of carefully calibrating a model and then comparing its results with the data along a number of dimensions. Krusell et al. have done this with their story of technological change driving the increase in the wage gap. Somebody – maybe Markusen and Venables themselves – will need to do something similar before I can accept their story of the culprit being the expansion of foreign direct investment by multinationals.

References

Alarcon, Diana and Terry McKinley (1996), 'The Rising Contribution of Labor Income to Inequality in Mexico', unpublished manuscript, American University.

Bergoeing, Raphael (1996), 'Studies on Trade', unpublished PhD dissertation, University of Minnesota.

Krusell, Per, Lee E. Ohanian, Jose-Victor Rios-Rull, and Giovanni L. Violante (1997), 'Capital–Skill Complementarity and Inequality: A Macroeconomic Analysis', Staff Report No. 239, Federal Reserve Bank of Minneapolis.

Lawrence, Robert Z. and Matthew J. Slaughter (1993), 'International Trade and American Wages in the 1980s: Giant Sucking Sound or Small Hiccup?' *Brookings Papers on Economic Activity*, Microeconomics 2: 161–210.

Markusen, James R. (1986), 'Explaining the Volume of Trade: An Eclectic Approach', *American Economic Review* 76: 1002–11.

6 Economic policy and the manufacturing base: hysteresis in location

ANTHONY J. VENABLES

1 Introduction

Discussion of industrial policy often refers to the importance of maintaining a 'manufacturing base', and suggests that there may be some level of activity below which contraction of manufacturing may be difficult to reverse. In simple economic models it is difficult to make sense of this line of reasoning. An adverse shock to industry in one country may cause exit or relocation of firms, but, if the shock is reversed, then those remaining earn a higher return than in the original equilibrium. Entry will occur, and the equilibrium will revert to the initial position.

There are several circumstances in which this need not be the case. One is when there are sunk costs associated with entry and exit (as in the 'beachhead' models of Baldwin and Krugman (1989) and Dixit (1989)). It may take a large shock to attract new entrants (importers, in the literature referred to), but once they have paid their fixed costs they are difficult to dislodge. Another circumstance is when there are positive 'linkages' between firms in the industry, these linkages causing profits to be an increasing, rather than decreasing, function of the number of firms in the location. With such linkages there is a high degree of interdependence between the location decisions of different firms, and this creates the possibility of agglomeration of activity. An adverse shock may then destroy one centre of activity and cause others to form, in which case, even if the shock is reversed, its effects may not be.

Positive linkages between firms may take the form of either technological or pecuniary externalities, and pecuniary externalities can be driven by a variety of different mechanisms (see Krugman (1991) for a discussion of some possibilities). The pecuniary externalities we explore in this paper arise from the interaction between imperfect competition, transport or trade costs, and an input–output structure in production. The idea is simple. Each firm uses the products of other firms as intermediates

177

in production, and some of each firm's output is used as an intermediate good by other firms. If there are a number of possible production locations and shipping goods between these locations is costly, where do firms choose to produce? If there are final consumers in each location, then firms will tend to disperse, in order to serve these final consumers. But the input–output structure creates an incentive for firms to locate close to each other. Cost linkages occur because firms will have lower intermediate input prices if they locate close to their suppliers. And demand linkages occur because firms will have larger local markets if they locate close to firms demanding their output. In a perfectly competitive model such linkages are of no significance, but if we combine them with imperfect competition they generate positive pecuniary externalities, encouraging agglomeration of activity.

Venables (1996) and Krugman and Venables (1995, 1996) have analysed the structure of equilibria that can arise in a benchmark model in which locations are identical in underlying cost and demand primitives. It turns out that trade is 'symmetry breaking' in the sense that at high trade barriers economies will be identical, but at lower trade barriers industry will agglomerate in a subset of locations. This creates international differences in industrial structure and in wages and income and generates inter-industry trade.

In this paper we turn emphasis away from economies with identical structures to asymmetric economies. In particular we consider the effects of policy that changes costs of firms in just one country. How does policy affect industrial location, and is it the case that contraction of the industrial base can reach some point at which it becomes 'catastrophic' and difficult to reverse?

Section 2 of the paper sets out the model we use to address these questions. In section 3 we specialize this down to a particularly simple form that illustrates the range of equilibria that may arise, and the different possible responses of industrial location to policy change. Section 4 calibrates our model to the chemical industry – an industry in which there are quite strong input–output linkages between different activities. We consider the effects of one group of countries taxing energy input in the sector.

Two main messages come from the study. The first is that a 'manufacturing base' matters, and we shall see examples where policy reduces the number of firms below the 'critical mass' level necessary for survival of the sector. As firms exit or relocate, remaining firms benefit from a relaxation of competitive pressure (they get a larger share of local demand). However, they suffer from now having lower demand for any intermediate products they produce and from having to pay a higher price for intermediates, more of which are now imported (with a transport cost) rather than being locally supplied. Withdrawal of the benefits arising from these demand (backwards) and cost (forwards) linkages can cause collapse of the entire sector. There may be multiple equilibria and consequent hysteresis. Policy measures may therefore have effects that are difficult to reverse.

The second message that comes from the paper is that it is extremely difficult for economists to predict the effect of policy change. In some regions of a parameter space, policy changes may have very small effects on location of firms. Precisely because of the existence of demand and cost linkages, industrial structure may be very robust to adverse shocks or policy changes. However, in other regions of parameter space the same policy changes will have dramatic effects, tipping the equilibrium through a critical point. Even in cases in which catastrophic change does not occur, we shall observe widely differing responses to policy change. Although the model is constructed with isoelastic ingredients, the elasticity of output with respect to the policy instruments we employ will vary enormously according to the point at which the policy change is evaluated. These possibilities pose new challenges for the ways in which economists endeavour to evaluate the effects of policy.

2   The model

We consider a world consisting of M economies, and $N + 1$ industries, each using H primary factors. The last sector is perfectly competitive and has constant returns to scale technology. Its output is freely traded and will be used as the numeraire. All other sectors are imperfectly competitive, and produce differentiated products. Following Dixit and Stiglitz (1977), constant elasticity of substitution (CES) price indices for the output of industry k in location i, P_i^k, are defined as:

$$(P_i^k)^{(1-\sigma^k)} = \sum_{j=1}^{M} n_j^k (p_{ji}^k \tau_{ji}^k)^{(1-\sigma^k)}, \quad i, j = 1 \ldots M, \ k = 1 \ldots N. \quad (1)$$

In this and following equations, superscripts denote industries, and subscripts denote locations, with the first subscript giving the location of production and the second the location of sale. Thus, the location i price index depends on producer prices of products produced in j and shipped to i, p_{ji}^k, times an iceberg trade cost factor, τ_{ji}^k. n_j^k is the number of k-industry firms located in country j (all assumed to be symmetric). σ^k is the elasticity of demand for a single firm's output. Demand for the output of a single country-j firm in market i, x_{ji}^k, can be derived as:

$$p_{ji}^k x_{ji}^k = (p_{ji}^k \tau_{ji}^k)^{1-\sigma^k} (p_i^k)^{\sigma^k-1} E_i^k, \qquad (2)$$

where E_i^k is the total location-i expenditure on industry-k products.

Turning to the cost side, we assume that firms use a composite input. They have increasing returns to scale, so use the composite input according to:

$$\beta^k x_j^k + \alpha^k, \qquad (3)$$

where x_j^k is the total sales of a firm located in j (the sum over markets i of x_{ji}^k), α^k is a fixed input, and β^k is input per unit output. The composite is composed of primary inputs and intermediate inputs with input–output coefficients b^{ik} and a^{ik} respectively. Denoting the price of primary factor i in location j by w_j^i, this gives a total cost function, tc_j^k:

$$tc_j^k = (\beta^k x_j^k + \alpha^k) \left(\sum_{i=1}^{H} b^{ik} w_j^i + \sum_{i=1}^{N+1} a^{ik} P_j^i \right). \qquad (4)$$

Notice that the intermediate prices in the cost functions are the price indices, (1), and for the numeraire good, $P_j^{N+1} = 1$. Use of CES price indices in the cost functions follows Ethier (1982), and captures the idea that a greater range of input varieties, other things being equal, will lower costs.

Firms are engaged in 'large-group' monopolistic competition. The equality of marginal revenue to marginal cost therefore takes the form:

$$p_{ji}^k (1 - 1/\sigma^k) = mc_j^k, \qquad (5)$$

where mc_j^k denotes marginal cost. Long-run equilibrium is established where numbers of firms have adjusted to give zero profits (or, if no firms are active, non-positive profits). As usual in this type of model, zero profits establishes a unique firm size:

$$x_j^k = (\sigma^k - 1)\alpha^k/\beta^k. \qquad (6)$$

To complete the description of equilibrium we have to determine primary factor prices and total expenditures. We assume that primary factor prices are exogenous. This reflects our partial equilibrium focus on a group of industries rather than the entire economy. Total expenditures on each industry in each location, E_i^k, are derived from two sources. One is demand for the industry's output from the rest of the economy – consumer demand and intermediate demand from the perfectly competitive sector; we denote this $E_i^k(c)$, and assume it is exogenous. The other is demand for the product as an intermediate from the N industries on which we are focusing. This can be derived by using Shepard's lemma, so:

$$E_i^k = E_i^k(c) + P_i^k \sum_{j=1}^{N} n_i^j (\alpha^j + \beta^j x_i^j) \alpha^{kj}. \tag{7}$$

This model differs from a standard monopolistic competition trade model in only one respect – the presence of input–output linkages between imperfectly competitive firms. As we shall see in what follows, this has dramatic implications for the structure of equilibria generated by the model. The reason for this can be seen by asking, how does adding a firm in one location affect the profitability of other firms in the location? There are three channels. The first is the standard one: an extra firm reduces the industry price indices (equation (1)), thus shifting demand curves down (equation (2)) and hence reducing scale and profitability (equations (2) and (6)). The second and third channels operate through input–output linkages. The reduction in price indices associated with an increased number of firms now reduces total and marginal costs (in (4) and (5)), thus raising firms' profits. This is a *cost* or *forwards linkage* between firms. An increase in the number of firms also increases expenditure (equation (7)), thus raising demand and profits (equations (2) and (6)). This is a *demand* or *backwards linkage* between firms. It is the presence of these linkages that generates the effects we describe in this paper.

3   One industry, two countries

The qualitative structure of equilibria is best illustrated by stripping the model down to essentials. We do this by assuming that there are just two locations ($M = 2$), one primary factor ($H = 1$), and one industry ($N = 1$). The input–output structure therefore reduces to a single element, in which the industry uses some of its own output as an input to production. Figures in this section are drawn with the further assumptions that transport costs, τ, are the same in both directions, and that the cost function is Cobb–Douglas between the primary factor and the intermediate, so (4) becomes:

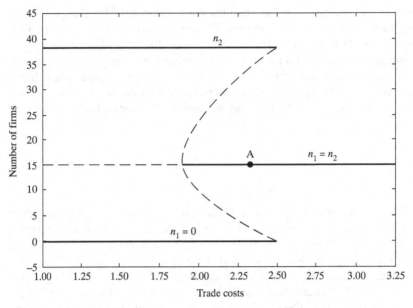

Figure 6.1 Trade costs and industrial location.

$$tc_j = (\alpha + \beta x_j) w_j^{1-\mu} P_j^{\mu}. \tag{8}$$

μ is the value share of the intermediate in costs, and superscripts have been dropped (since there is a single industry).

3.1 Symmetrical locations

The structure of equilibrium in this model depends critically on the relative strengths of trade costs, τ, and the intermediate linkage, μ. At high trade costs, industry must be divided between locations in order to meet final consumer demand, but at lower trade costs agglomeration forces become relatively more powerful and will lead to agglomeration of industry in one location. Figure 6.1 illustrates possibilities. The horizontal axis is the trade cost factor, τ ($\tau = 1$ being completely free trade), and the vertical axis the number of firms in each location, n_1 and n_2. Solid lines illustrate stable equilibria, and dashed lines unstable ones. At high τ, $n_1 = n_2$, as illustrated; this is the unique equilibrium and has production diversified between locations. At very low τ, all industry is concentrated in one location. Since it could be either location, there are two stable equilibria, and a third unstable one between. (The figure is constructed with labels such that $n_1 = 0$ and $n_2 > 0$.) At intermediate values of τ, both the diversified and agglomerated outcomes are equilibria, thus giving five equilibria (three stable, two unstable). Linkages are powerful enough to support agglomeration, but if the economy is at a diversified equilibrium (such as point A) then no firm has an incentive to relocate.

We have demonstrated elsewhere (Venables 1996, Krugman and Venables 1995) that, in this symmetrical case, $\mu > 0$ and $1/\sigma > 0$ are sufficient for there to be an interval of τ, $(0, \tau^*)$, in which the diversified equilibrium is unstable, and we refer to τ^* as the critical value of τ. This critical value is higher (giving larger ranges of τ within which there are multiple equilibria) the stronger are linkages (higher μ), and the greater the price–marginal cost markup (lower σ).

3.2   Taxation and trade costs

We now consider the case in which the industry has higher costs in location 1 than it does in location 2. We think of this as arising because of taxation of costs at *ad valorem* tax rate $\tau - 1$. It must be noted that this tax is borne only by the industry under study, and not by other industries in location 1; if it were borne by all sectors, it would be shifted to labour and would not be a source of *comparative* disadvantage. The effects of setting $t = 1.1$ are illustrated in Figures 6.2 and 6.3; Figure 6.2 gives the 'strong linkage' case ($\mu = 0.5$) and Figure 6.3 the 'weak linkage' case ($\mu = 0.25$); both figures have $\sigma = 5$. In Figure 6.2, the case when $t = 1$ is illustrated by bold lines (identical to Figure 6.1), and $t = 1.1$ is illustrated by the lighter lines. We can see from the figure that the tax has two important effects. First, the diversified equilibrium is no longer symmetrical; as would be expected, $n_2 > n_1$, and this gap is larger the lower are trade costs. Secondly, the level of trade costs at which the diversified equilibrium becomes unstable is shifted upwards (from around $\tau = 1.9$ to $\tau = 2.3$).

What is the effect of the tax on the location of industry? The answer depends crucially on the level of trade costs. If the initial equilibrium was at point A, and the equilibrium remains diversified, then taxation changes n_1 to point A'. However, if the initial equilibrium was at B, then taxation renders diversification unstable; the equilibrium flips to points B', at which $n_1 = 0$. In this case the tax induces sufficient firms to relocate from location 1 to 2 that 1 loses the benefits of cost and demand linkages, 2 gains them, and 1 ceases to be a viable location for the industry.

Figure 6.3 is analogous, but constructed for the weak linkage case. If $t = 1$, then the structure of equilibria is illustrated by the bold lines. This is

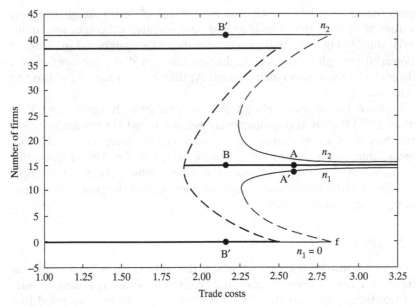

Figure 6.2   Strong linkages.

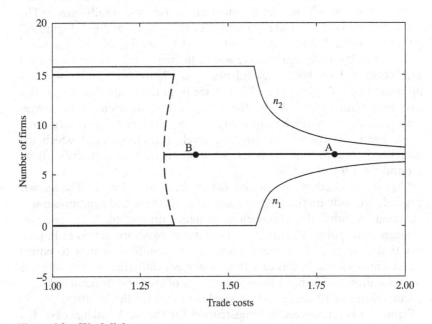

Figure 6.3   Weak linkages.

qualitatively as in Figure 6.2, although the critical value of τ is much lower than in the strong linkage case, and the interval in which there are five equilibria is much narrower. Lighter solid lines illustrate the equilibrium with $t = 1.1$. Two points should be noted. First, with taxation there is no longer a region of multiple equilibria. And secondly, as in the previous figure, the effects of the tax depend crucially on the value of trade costs; at point A the equilibrium remains diversified, whereas the same tax at point B forces $n_1 = 0$. As before, taxation reduces the number of firms at location 1, transferring the benefits from the linkages to location 2, and leaving 1 unviable.

Although policy change drives n_1 to zero in both Figures 6.2 and 6.3, the distinction between the 'strong' and 'weak' linkage cases is important. In the 'weak' case there is a unique equilibrium, this equilibrium varies continuously with the tax instrument, and hysteresis does not occur. In the strong case there are multiple equilibria and discontinuities in the response to small tax changes, and, as we shall see, there is also hysteresis. The presence of multiple equilibria in this case raises difficult questions concerning the selection of equilibrium. If one equilibrium becomes unstable as a parameter changes then there are generally at least two stable equilibria. Which becomes the actual new equilibrium of the economy? Throughout the paper we shall let simple myopic dynamics – entry and exit of firms in response to current profits and losses – determine the equilibrium to which the economy goes.

3.3 Taxation and hysteresis

Whereas Figures 6.2 and 6.3 are constructed for given values of the tax rate, t, with trade costs, τ, on the horizontal axis, Figures 6.4 and 6.5 are constructed at given values of τ, with t on the horizontal. The vertical axis gives the number of firms in country 1. Figure 6.4 gives the strong linkage case ($\mu = 0.5$). The solid lines give equilibrium values of n_1 as t varies, given $\tau = 2.2$ (as at point B on Figure 6.2). Looking first at the solid lines, we notice that $n_1 = 0$ is an equilibrium for all values of t illustrated. However, at lower values of t there is also an equilibrium with $n_1 > 0$, but this becomes unstable at t approximately equal to 8 per cent. The hysteresis story is apparent. Starting at point E, tax increases bring continuous adjustment up to point F, at which point n_1 and production in location 1 go to zero. Reversing the tax policy leads the equilibrium back to point G; once all production is concentrated in location 2 there is no incentive for any firm to relocate to 1, even as the tax rate is returned to zero.

The dashed lines tell a similar story given $\tau = 2.6$ (as at point A on Figure 6.2). The higher level of trade costs dramatically increases the

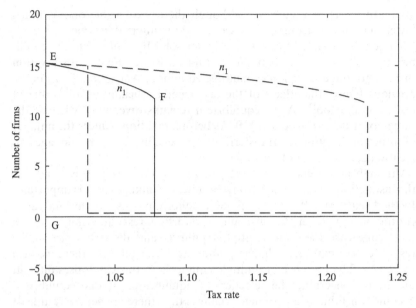

Figure 6.4   Taxation with strong linkages.

range within which the tax can be varied without precipitating a
catastrophic change. Thus, starting at point E, the diversified equilibrium
remains stable until the tax reaches around 23 per cent. At higher tax
rates there is a unique equilibrium, which has $n_1 = 0$. Tax rates in the
interval $t \in (1.03, 1.23)$ are consistent with two equilibria – either $n_1 > 0$
or $n_1 = 0$ – so this interval marks out the region of hysteresis in location.
However, returning the tax rate to zero ($t = 1$) will, in this case, restore
the initial (unique) equilibrium at E.

Figure 6.5 is the analogous figure for the weak linkage case, with the
solid line mapping out n_1 when $\tau = 1.4$ (point B on Figure 6.3), and the
dashed line giving the case when $\tau = 1.8$ (point A on Figure 6.3). For all
values of the tax rate the equilibrium is unique, but the point to note is
that (as in Figure 6.4) the effects of the policy are extremely sensitive to
trade costs. The tax shifts industry towards location 2, and agglomeration forces amplify this, giving the concave shape of the curves. The
extent of this amplification depends on the level of trade costs.

3.4   Regions of discontinuous change

As the previous figures make clear, the equilibrium response to tax
changes depends critically on the value of trade costs, τ, and of the

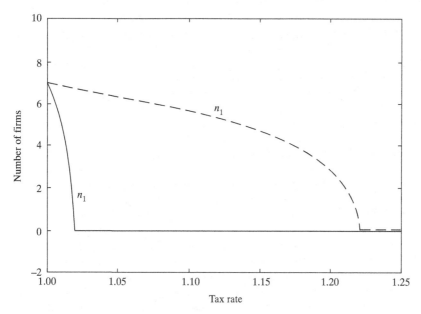

Figure 6.5   Taxation with weak linkages.

intermediate linkage, μ. Figures 6.6a–c summarize some of the information about the response to tax changes. Each of these figures has the tax rate, t, on the horizontal axis, and trade costs, τ, on the vertical; panels 6.6a, 6.6b, and 6.6c are drawn for $\mu = 0.5$, 0.4, and 0.3 respectively.

The curve ss maps out values of t and τ at which, when $n_1 = 0$, entry of a firm in 1 becomes profitable. Below the line, this entry is unprofitable, so there is an equilibrium with $n_1 = 0$. Above it, trade barriers are high and/or the country 1 tax disadvantage is small, so entry in 1 is profitable and concentration of production in 2 is not an equilibrium. The curve dd gives values at which the diversified equilibrium with production in both countries becomes unstable. Above dd there is a stable equilibrium with production in both countries. Below dd there is no stable equilibrium with $n_1 > 0$. In between the ss and dd curves there is a stable equilibrium with $n_1 = 0$ and another with $n_1 > 0$. Hysteresis occurs as we cross this region.

The effects of a tax change can be seen by moving horizontally on the figures. Thus, suppose that $\mu = 0.5$ (Figure 6.6a) and that $\tau = 2.0$. A diversified equilibrium exists at $t = 1$, but raising the tax to approximately 3 per cent causes specialization, $n_1 = 0$. If the tax is reversed, $n_1 = 0$ remains an equilibrium, so the system does not revert

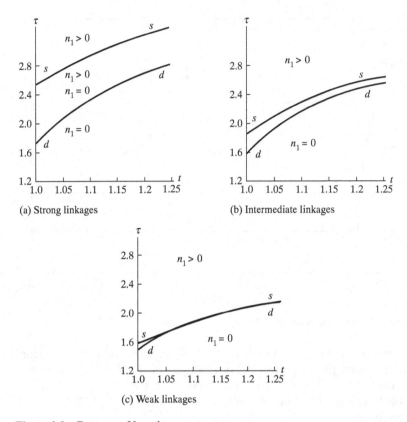

(a) Strong linkages   (b) Intermediate linkages

(c) Weak linkages

Figure 6.6   Patterns of location.

to the initial diversified position. Alternatively, if $\tau = 2.0$ but $\mu = 0.4$ (Figure 6.6b), then the initial equilibrium must be diversified, and specialization occurs when the tax goes to approximately 7 per cent. Hysteresis occurs in the interval 3–7 per cent, but returning the tax to zero restores the original equilibrium. If $\tau = 2.0$ and $\mu = 0.3$ (Figure 6.6c), then the diversified equilibrium persists up to tax rates of approximately 17 per cent, and the hysteresis band is extremely narrow.

Comparison of the figures confirms our distinction between 'weak' and 'strong' linkage cases. The greater is the intermediate goods linkage, the greater is the region of $\{t, \tau\}$ space in which specialization ($n_1 = 0$) is the unique equilibrium (below ss), and the greater is the region in which there are multiple equilibria (below ss and above dd). This region disappears for low enough μ and/or high τ.

4   Energy taxation in the chemical industry: a calibrated example

In the preceding section we illustrated the sensitivity of tax response to parameters of the system. If we draw parameters from an actual industry, then what can we expect to happen? In this section we report results of a calibration/simulation exercise undertaken on data from the chemical industry. We choose the chemical industry for two reasons. The first is the presence of relatively strong input–output links within the sector. The second is that the sector is a relatively heavy user of energy. The experiment we undertake is the taxation of energy in one location, this motivated by concern about the effects of environmental policy on the location of the industry.

We have aggregated the chemical sector into two industries: basic industrial chemicals (ISIC), which we refer to as industry 1; and manufacture of other chemicals (ISIC), referred to as industry 2. We assume that firms in both these sectors have increasing returns to scale and that the sectors are imperfectly competitive; we model this as described in section 2 above. For both industries the initial scale elasticity (marginal cost divided by average cost) is set at 83 per cent and the demand elasticity (σ) at 6, these in combination giving a base equilibrium with zero profits. (Alternative specifications of imperfect competition and product differentiation are discussed in section 5 below.)

Input–output coefficients (derived from 1984 UK input–output tables) are given in Table 6.1. The top two rows give inter-industry linkages; about 26–27 per cent of each industry's inputs come from the chemical sector as a whole. Over 30 per cent of inputs are intermediates coming from the rest of the economy, excluding energy. Rows 4–8 give inputs of coal, etc., mineral oil and natural gas, mineral oil processing, electricity, and gas. In industry 1 these account for 13.6 per cent of costs, and in industry 2 a mere 3.5 per cent. The bottom row gives primary factor inputs.

We divide the world into four country blocs: USA and Canada – USC (1); Japan, Australia, and New Zealand – JANZ (2); the European Union and the European Free Trade Association – EUR (3); and the rest of the world – ROW (4). Trade and production data were obtained for these blocs, although rest of the world production data are not satisfactory. The calibration procedure uses observed trade flows to impute tariff-equivalent trade barriers. These are reported in Tables 6.2 and 6.3, where an element gives τ_{ij}^k, the barrier on exports from the row country to the column. The tariff equivalents are mainly in the range 1.5–2.0. These numbers seem large, but it should be remembered that they are constructed from actual trade flows, and should be thought of as

Table 6.1   Input–output coefficients

	Industry 1	Industry 2
Industry 1	0.248	0.169
Industry 2	0.022	0.090
Rest of economy	0.315	0.344
Coal and solid fuels	0.005	0.002
Oil and natural gas	0.004	0.001
Oil processing	0.082	0.009
Electricity	0.031	0.018
Gas	0.014	0.005
Primary factors	0.280	0.362

Table 6.2   Tariff-equivalent trade barriers: Industry 1

	USC (1)	JANZ (2)	EUR (3)	ROW (4)
USC (1)	1.00	2.14	1.22	1.57
JANZ (2)	1.57	1.00	1.65	1.23
EUR (3)	1.69	2.29	1.00	1.23
ROW (4)	2.02	2.46	1.59	1.00

Table 6.3   Tariff-equivalent trade barriers: Industry 2

	USC (1)	JANZ (2)	EUR (3)	ROW (4)
USC (1)	1.00	2.34	1.73	1.80
JANZ (2)	1.74	1.00	1.61	1.86
EUR (3)	1.69	2.38	1.00	1.25
ROW (4)	2.48	2.87	1.80	1.00

incorporating *all* possible reasons firms have smaller market shares in export markets than they do in their home market. The imputed barriers are consistently high on imports to the Japan, Australia, and New Zealand bloc.

4.1   Experiment 1

The first experiment we conduct is energy taxation in Europe (3) alone. Firms are allowed to relocate between locations 1, 2, and 3, although we hold the number of firms in the rest of the world (location 4) constant, because of the rather crude modelling of the rest of the world necessitated

Table 6.4   EUR energy tax

Tax (%)	n_1^1	mc_1^1	n_2^1	mc_2^1	n_3^1	mc_3^1	n_1^2	mc_1^2	n_2^2	mc_2^2	n_3^2	mc_3^2
5	1.03	1.00	1.00	1.00	0.91	1.01	1.00	1.00	1.00	1.00	0.97	1.01
10	1.06	1.00	1.01	1.00	0.83	1.02	1.01	1.00	1.00	1.00	0.94	1.01
15	1.09	0.99	1.01	1.00	0.74	1.04	1.01	1.00	1.00	1.00	0.91	1.02
20	1.13	0.99	1.01	1.00	0.64	1.05	1.02	1.00	1.01	1.00	0.87	1.02
25	1.07	0.99	1.02	1.00	0.54	1.06	1.02	0.99	1.01	1.00	0.84	1.03
30	1.22	0.99	1.02	1.00	0.44	1.07	1.03	0.99	1.01	1.00	0.81	1.04
35	1.28	0.99	1.02	1.00	0.32	1.08	1.03	0.99	1.01	1.00	0.77	1.04
40	1.35	0.98	1.02	1.00	0.18	1.10	1.04	0.99	1.01	1.00	0.73	1.05
45	1.44	0.98	1.03	1.00	0.02	1.11	1.05	0.98	1.01	1.00	0.68	1.06
50	1.45	0.98	1.03	1.00	0	1.12	1.05	0.98	1.02	1.00	0.67	1.06
75	1.45	0.98	1.03	1.00	0	1.15	1.05	0.98	1.02	1.00	0.63	1.07
100	1.45	0.98	1.03	1.00	0	1.19	1.05	0.98	1.02	1.00	0.59	1.08
200	1.44	0.98	1.03	1.00	0	1.33	1.06	0.98	1.03	1.00	0.41	1.12

by data availability. Results are presented in Table 6.4, the first column of which gives the tax rate imposed on energy inputs.

Consider the number of industry-1 firms in Europe, n_3^1. This declines rapidly, going to zero at a tax rate of 47 per cent. Qualitatively, the decline in n_3^1 is very similar to that illustrated in Figure 6.5, the 'weak linkages' case of section 3. That is, it is concave, but not catastrophic, and there is no region of hysteresis. This is as the examples of section 3 would lead us to expect: in industry 1, input–output linkages account for 27 per cent of costs (close to the 'weak linkage' case of section 3), and trade costs are substantial. The relocation of firms in industry 2 (n_3^2) is much less dramatic, primarily because of the lower energy share in costs. However, n_3^2 is a concave function of the tax rate and goes, eventually, to zero. It is worth noting that the rate of decline of n_3^2 is greatest when n_3^1 is falling fastest (as the tax rate goes from 40 per cent to 45 per cent); this is precisely because of the linkage between the industries.

The relocation of industry away from region 3 is driven by three forces. The first is the direct effect of the higher taxes. The second is the demand linkage: as firms relocate so they take their input demand with them, thus reducing the profits of firms that are left. The third is the cost linkage, and the marginal cost figures reported in Table 6.4 illustrate this. The *direct* effect of a 50 per cent energy tax is to increase industry-1 marginal costs in country 3, mc_3^1, by around 6.5 per cent, and to leave marginal costs in other countries unchanged. However, there is also a change in costs created by movement of intermediate suppliers, so that the actual change in marginal costs is a 12 per cent increase in mc_3^1 and a 2 per cent decrease in mc_1^1 (Table 6.4). Cost linkage effects therefore raise the

Table 6.5   EUR and USC energy tax

Tax (%)	n_1^1	n_2^1	n_3^1	n_1^2	n_2^2	n_3^2
10	0.98	1.02	0.89	0.99	1.01	0.95
20	0.96	1.03	0.78	0.99	1.01	0.90
30	0.94	1.05	0.67	0.98	1.02	0.85
40	0.92	1.07	0.56	0.97	1.02	0.80
50	0.90	1.09	0.45	0.97	1.03	0.75
60	0.88	1.11	0.34	0.96	1.04	0.70
70	0.86	1.13	0.22	0.95	1.04	0.65
80	0.83	1.16	0.08	0.95	1.05	0.60
90	0.79	1.19	0	0.94	1.06	0.55
100	0.72	1.21	0	0.92	1.06	0.53
200	0	1.42	0	0.80	1.16	0.36

international cost differential opened up by the policy from 6.5 per cent (direct effects alone) to 14 per cent (direct plus induced). The same effect is present in industry 2. The direct effect of the policy is to raise mc_3^2 by less than 2 per cent, but the actual increase is 6 per cent, coupled with a 2 per cent reduction in mc_1^2. Whereas in a standard model the relocation of firms would absorb some of the direct cost effect, here it amplifies it, and by a considerable amount – a factor of approximately 2 in industry 1 and 4 in industry 2.

4.2   Experiment 2

The second experiment we undertake is to impose the energy tax in two locations – chosen to be EUR (location 3) and USC (location 1). The results of this experiment are reported in Table 6.5. As would be expected, taxing two locations reduces the extent to which industry relocates out of the taxed regions. Industry 1 in Europe survives up to a tax rate of 83 per cent, and industry 1 in USC survives up to 175 per cent. The difference in the performance of industry in Europe relative to that in USC is accounted for by inspection of Table 6.2, which gives tariff-equivalent trade barriers for industry 1. Comparing column 1 with column 3, it is apparent that the USC market is, on average, slightly less open to imports than is the EUR market. These higher trade costs have the effect of making USC industry somewhat less vulnerable to cost changes than is EUR industry.

Experiments 1 and 2 were both undertaken holding the number of firms in the rest of the world constant. Simulations have also been run letting these numbers change. Although we have little confidence in our data describing the rest of the world, it is worth noting how these affect the results of Tables 6.4 and 6.5. In both cases the value of the tax rate at which EUR production in industry 1 goes to zero is reduced. With tax in EUR only, this rate drops to 42 per cent (compared with 47 per cent). With tax in EUR and USC, the rate drops to 71 per cent (compared with 83 per cent). As would be expected, relocation effects are larger, the more places there are to relocate to.

5   Cournot competition

We have so far ignored oligopolistic interaction between firms by making the 'large-group assumption' that price–cost markups depend only on σ^k, the demand elasticity reflecting the degree of product differentiation. The cost linkage then works through relocation of firms changing the set of products that bear transport costs at each location, and hence changing price indices.

In this section we add the possibility that firms are Cournot oligopolists, so that price–cost markups depend on the market shares of each firm. Pricing equations (5) are then replaced by:

$$p_{ji}^k \left(1 - \frac{1 - s_{ji}^k}{\sigma^k} - \frac{s_{ji}^k}{\eta^k} \right) = mc_j^k, \tag{9}$$

where s_{ji}^k is the share of a single firm from country j in the market at location i for industry k, and η^k is the elasticity of expenditure with respect to the price index. (This collapses to the previous case if market shares are perceived to be small, i.e. $s_{ji}^k = 0$.) This provides an additional way in which the cost linkage may work. A location with many firms will have intense competition, low price–cost markups, and lower prices, thus raising the profits of downstream firms. This creates a further force encouraging agglomeration (see Combes (1993) for analysis of this possibility).

Satisfactory empirical implementation of this case is difficult, both because we require industrial organization detail to give market shares, and because the elasticity η^k must include derived demands (through (7)). Here we simply make some rather ad hoc assumptions about these parameter values in order to illustrate possible effects. We set Herfindahl concentration indices at 0.1, and let $\sigma^k = 10$ in each industry. We assume that η^k is unity. The selection of these values is arbitrary, but has the effect of holding base profits close to zero. The effect is to reattribute some of firms' market power from product differentiation to oligopolistic behaviour.

Table 6.6   EUR energy tax with Cournot competition

Tax.(%)	n_1^1	mc_1^1	n_2^1	mc_2^1	n_3^1	mc_3^1	n_1^2	mc_1^2	n_2^2	mc_2^2	n_3^2	mc_3^2
10	1.06	1.00	1.01	1.00	0.76	1.02	1.01	1.00	1.00	1.00	0.92	1.01
20	1.13	1.00	1.01	1.00	0.48	1.05	1.02	1.00	1.01	1.00	0.82	1.02
30	1.23	0.99	1.02	1.00	0.09	1.07	1.03	0.99	1.01	1.00	0.71	1.04
40	1.25	0.99	1.02	1.00	0	1.09	1.04	0.99	1.01	1.00	0.67	1.04
50	1.25	0.99	1.02	1.00	0	1.10	1.04	0.99	1.01	1.00	0.64	1.05

The effects of energy taxation in EUR alone are given in Table 6.6. They are qualitatively similar to those in Table 6.4. Quantitatively, the additional cost linkage mechanism has the effect of increasing the sensitivity of location to tax differences, implying that specialization occurs at a somewhat lower tax rate than with the 'large-group assumption'. Of course, the value of the Herfindahl index we are working with – 10 – implies a very unconcentrated industry. Results can be made much more dramatic if industries are made more concentrated.

6   Conclusions

Despite its historical origins (including, for example, extensive work by Marshall), the study of locational agglomeration of economic activity has, for a long time, been outside mainstream economics. This is changing, owing to the recent work of Krugman and others. Recent literature explores ways in which different sorts of linkages between economic agents can support agglomeration of activity, and investigates the structure of multiple equilibria that may arise in such circumstances. The present paper extends this line of research to an investigation of the effects of policy change on industrial location and agglomeration.

The possible effects of policy change on industrial location were outlined in section 3 of the paper. Two conclusions come from this section. The first is that an 'industrial base' matters; policy can lead to catastrophic changes in location of industry, and there can be hysteresis in location. The second conclusion is that the results of policy are extremely sensitive to the parameters of the model and the values of the policy instruments. At some values, linkages are a force that reduces the incentive to relocate (firms stay where their suppliers and markets are), but at other values abrupt change occurs.

Section 4 draws some of the key parameters of the model from data on the world chemical industry, and investigates the effects of energy taxation on industrial location. It turns out that linkages are weak enough for catastrophic change not to occur. However, as tax rates are increased, so linkages amplify the direct effects of policy. Thus, giving one location a cost disadvantage causes relocation of firms, thus further disadvantaging the location, because more intermediates have to bear transport costs and more customers (of intermediate goods) are far away. Complete exit of the industry from a location occurs at quite modest tax rates.

Clearly, the results presented in this paper are highly speculative, and much is left out of the model – for example, forward-looking dynamics, general equilibrium effects, and industry-specific factors. Even so, it is hoped that the possibilities outlined in this paper pose a challenge to more neoclassical methods of policy analysis.

Note

This research is supported by UK ESRC grant no. Y320 25 3038, and is part of the International Economic Performance programme of the UK ESRC-supported Centre for Economic Performance at the London School of Economics.

References

Baldwin, R. E. and P. R. Krugman (1989), 'Persistent Trade Effects of Large Exchange Rate Shocks', *Quarterly Journal of Economics* 104: 635–54.
Combes, P.-P. (1993), 'Regional Industry Location under Cournot Competition', CREST Working Paper No. 9449, Paris.
Dixit, A. K. (1989), 'Hysteresis, Import Penetration and Exchange Rate Pass-through', *Quarterly Journal of Economics* 104: 205–28.
Dixit, A. K. and J. E. Stiglitz (1977), 'Monopolistic Competition and Optimum Product Diversity', *American Economic Review* 67: 297–308.
Ethier, W. J. (1982), 'National and International Returns to Scale in the Modern Theory of International Trade', *American Economic Review* 72: 389–405.
Krugman, P. R. (1991), *Geography and Trade*. Cambridge, Mass.: MIT Press.
Krugman, P. R. and A. J. Venables (1995), 'Globalization and the Inequality of Nations', *Quarterly Journal of Economics* 110: 857–80.
(1996), 'Integration, Specialization and Adjustment', *European Economic Review, Papers and Proceedings* 40: 959–67.
Venables, A. J. (1996), 'Equilibrium locations of vertically linked industries', *International Economic Review* 37: 341–59.

Discussion

J. PETER NEARY

This paper contributes to the rapidly growing literature in the exciting new field of economic geography. This 'new' economic geography is a sub-field of international trade theory (though perhaps with ambitions to outgrow its parent!) and has rather little in common with economic geography as practised by geographers, a field whose lack of behavioural underpinnings has, for all its achievements, made it unattractive to mainstream economists. The basic ingredients of the new economic geography – increasing returns and imperfect competition – have been around for some time. However, the models that have been developed recently add some extra features, which gives rise to a distinctive prediction: the possibility of endogenous agglomeration of economic activity in a model with maximizing agents. In the work of Paul Krugman (1991), the extra feature is factor mobility. By contrast, Tony Venables has emphasized inter-industry linkages as a force encouraging agglomeration. The result is a rich new framework that formalizes the insights of Hirschman (1987) and others while also inviting further theoretical elaboration and empirical implementation.

In my comments, I first present an alternative exposition of the model that shows that its basic qualitative predictions do not depend on special functional forms. I then consider the calibration results, and finally comment on the general issues raised.

I

The model is presented in the paper for many goods and countries but for special functional forms, mostly of the CES (or Dixit–Stiglitz) type. I prefer to reverse this hierarchy of generality, considering only one industry and two countries but, initially at least, imposing no restrictions on functional forms. For the most part I use the same notation as in the paper, with an asterisk to denote variables relating to the foreign country.

The problem facing a representative home firm is to choose the prices at which it sells on the home and foreign markets. With these prices chosen optimally, we may write the firm's profits as the sum of revenues from home and foreign sales, r and r^*, respectively, less total costs c:

$$\pi = r(P, E) + r^*(P^*, E^*, \tau) - c(P, t). \tag{1}$$
$$\quad\ \, {}_{+\ \ +}\qquad\ \, {}_{+\ \ \ +\ \ \ -}\qquad {}_{+\ \ +}$$

Revenue in each market depends positively on the industry price index (P and P^*) and on the level of expenditure (E and E^*) there, while revenue in the foreign market also depends negatively on the level of trade costs τ. Since every firm sells in both markets, each price index depends negatively on the number of firms (n and n^*) producing in both markets (because greater variety benefits consumers) and depends positively on trade costs:

$$P = P(n, n^*, \tau), \quad P^* = P^*(n^*, n, \tau). \tag{2}$$
$$\quad\ \, {}_{-\ \ -\ \ \ +}\qquad\qquad\ \ {}_{-\ \ -\ \ \ +}$$

So far, this is a standard model of trade with monopolistic competition, of the kind developed by Krugman and others in the late 1970s and early 1980s. (Once it would have been called 'new trade theory', but 'middle-aged' is probably more appropriate now!)

The distinctive features of the Venables variant of economic geography enter through the expenditure and cost functions. The model is partial equilibrium, so consumer demand and factor prices are given. However, each firm uses some of the output of every other firm as an input, which implies two significant changes to the usual structure. First, demand in each country depends positively on the number of firms located there and on the local price index:

$$E = E(n, P), \quad E^* = E^*(n^*, P^*). \tag{3}$$
$$\quad\ \, {}_{+\ \ +}\qquad\qquad {}_{+\ \ \ +}$$

Secondly, as the last term in (1) shows, costs depend positively on the local price index and on the production tax rate t.

What are the implications of these assumptions for the existence of an agglomerated equilibrium? To answer this, go through the same thought experiment as in the paper. Assume the economy is initially in a diversified long-run equilibrium, and consider how the entry of one extra home firm affects the profits of existing firms (which of course are initially zero because of free entry). If they fall, then the diversified equilibrium is stable: losses force at least one firm to exit and the initial equilibrium is restored. However, if profits rise, the initial equilibrium is unstable and more firms are encouraged to enter. If this happens at every diversified equilibrium, the world economy moves towards an equilibrium with agglomeration: the whole industry locates in the home country.

From the above equations, the effects of entry are easily deduced:

$$\frac{d\pi}{dn} = \left[\frac{dr}{dP}P_n + \frac{dr^*}{dP^*}P_n^*\right] - c_P P_n + r_E E_n, \tag{4}$$

(where subscripts denote partial derivatives). The first effect, represented by the bracketed terms on the right-hand side, is that an extra firm reduces the industry price index both at home and abroad, which reduces revenue and hence profits. This effect is standard and encourages stability of the diversified equilibrium. By contrast, the two other effects tend to encourage instability and so lead to agglomeration. The reduction in price has a *cost* or *forward* linkage (represented by the middle term on the right-hand side of (4)), as the cost of the composite intermediate input is reduced for all firms, so raising profitability. Finally, the last term in (4) reflects a *demand* or *backward* linkage. An extra firm raises demand for the output of every other firm and so also raises profitability.

Setting equation (4) equal to zero imposes a restriction on the parameters such that the equilibrium is on the threshold between agglomeration and diversification. It makes sense to view this restriction as defining the threshold level of trade costs $\hat{\tau}$ at which the diversified equilibrium switches from stability to instability. Such a threshold level must exist provided there is some incentive for agglomeration, represented in the paper as a positive value for the parameter μ, the share of intermediate inputs in the cost of the composite factor of production. For sufficiently high τ (possibly infinite), imports are so expensive that home production becomes profitable; while, for sufficiently low τ (possibly zero), diversification is ruled out because the countries are *ex ante* identical (neither has a comparative advantage). Then we can write the threshold value of τ as a function of the other parameters of the model:

$$\hat{\tau} = \hat{\tau}(\underset{-}{\sigma}, \underset{+}{\mu}, \underset{+}{t}). \tag{5}$$

It is evident that $\hat{\tau}$ must be increasing in μ: the greater the importance of intermediate inputs, the larger the range of trade costs at which diversification is not an equilibrium. It is also increasing in t because this tax on production at home encourages agglomeration abroad. Finally, the threshold value of τ is negatively related to σ, the elasticity of substitution in demand. This effect is the only one that hinges on Dixit–Stiglitz preferences. Higher σ means that consumers view different varieties as closer substitutes. Such a reduced preference for diversity leads (other things equal) to an equilibrium with fewer varieties and a higher output of each. As a result, both countries are more likely to hold on to some production at lower trade costs.

The final step is to repeat the derivation of equations (4) and (5) for the case where there are no home firms. This leads to a new threshold, τ^0, which defines the level of trade costs at which agglomeration abroad is on the margin of being an equilibrium. This new threshold has the same relationship to the underlying parameters as $\hat{\tau}$:

$$\tau^0 = \tau^0(\underset{-}{\sigma}, \underset{+}{\mu}, \underset{+}{t}) \geq \hat{\tau}. \tag{6}$$

Crucially, τ^0 may (though need not) be higher than $\hat{\tau}$: if μ is large, so agglomeration economies are substantial, there will be some trade costs at which it would be profitable for a group of firms to locate in the home country but not for a single firm to enter on its own. It is differences between τ^0 and $\hat{\tau}$ that open up the possibilities of multiple equilibria and hysteresis that are discussed in the paper. Within the range where $\tau^0 > \tau > \hat{\tau}$, *both* agglomeration and diversification are possible equilibria, so history and policy have a potential role in influencing which equilibrium prevails.

II

Having explored the theoretical properties of the model, the paper then calibrates a four-country, two-industry variant of it to the world chemical industry. Such an exercise is always brave, yet arguably the assumptions made fit this industry reasonably well. For example, it is unrealistic to ignore comparative advantage altogether. Yet this may not matter so much in the chemical industry, where technology is close to best-practice worldwide and where location-specific factors are probably relatively unimportant (however much they may have influenced the evolution of the current industry structure). Similarly, a restrictive feature of the model is that it takes wages as exogenous and so removes a stabilizing influence. Endogenous wages would add an extra negative term, $-c_w w_n$, to (4), moderating the cataclysmic effects of any loss of competitiveness. Yet the chemical industry is so capital intensive that this too may not matter very much.

A more serious problem with the calibration exercise arises from data limitations. No data on tariffs or quotas are available, so tariff-equivalent trade barriers are imputed from the model. This means that they are set at the levels that would generate the actual trade flows in the initial equilibrium, given the assumed values for the parameters. The problem with this is that all the specification error in the model is pushed onto the estimates of τ. Admittedly trade economists from other traditions have been doing this sort of thing for years. (For example, an influential study by Leamer (1988) uses the residuals from Heckscher–Ohlin trade regressions as a measure of trade barriers in a competitive general equilibrium model.) And it is probably inevitable that some element of arbitrariness must creep into any calibration exercise if the initial diversified production structure is to be pinned down. Nevertheless, it is an unsatisfactory feature and the results (given in Tables 6.2 and 6.3) are not very persuasive. The implied trade barriers for Japan, Australia, and New Zealand are all well over 100 per cent. Even less plausibly, the USA and Canada have higher levels of trade barriers than Europe in four out of six cases and similar levels in the other two.

The other key feature of the calibration model is the estimated strength of input–output linkages. With two industries, there are four different intermediate-input cost shares, but probably the most relevant figures are the total cost shares in each sector of inputs from both sectors combined. Drawn from UK data, these come out at 27.0 per cent and 25.9 per cent. Although probably higher than would be found in many industries, these estimates nevertheless place the chemical industry firmly in the 'weak linkages' category. In the terminology introduced above, $\tau^0 = \hat{\tau}$, so multiple equilibria and hysteresis effects are ruled out. As a result, the simulations exhibit behaviour that is consistent with more orthodox models. Energy taxes lead to a steady decline in the size of the industries located in the tax-imposing countries, at a faster rate for the more energy-intensive sector.

III

Finally, what do we learn from this exercise? Tony Venables suggests two lessons, one substantive and the other methodological: first, he concludes that 'an "industrial base" matters', and, secondly, he hopes that 'the possibilities outlined ... pose a challenge to more neoclassical methods of policy analysis'. I am sympathetic to both, but not entirely convinced.

The model is of course prejudiced in favour of a manufacturing base, in the sense that the prior existence of other firms at one location lowers the costs of entry for a new firm there. Yet this feature alone does not seem to capture many of the issues that arise in discussions of industrial policy. The problem is that, because all firms in the model are footloose, the manufacturing base itself is completely footloose. There are no externalities or local public goods (such as R&D spillovers) that might lock an industry into a location even after the factors that encouraged it to locate there have disappeared (though hysteresis effects might lead to observationally equivalent behaviour). Further, the myopic Chamberlinian firms used in most of the paper cannot engage in industrial strategies to shore up their position. They cannot make strategic commitments to create artificial barriers to entry, or vertically integrate to internalize the externalities arising from the combination of intermediate inputs with increasing returns.

As for questioning neoclassical policy analysis, I have already noted that the relatively low shares of intermediate inputs in the calibrated model lead to smooth adjustment paths that would not be out of place in a neoclassical model. This is all the more striking, since the model abstracts from traditional sources of comparative advantage, which might be expected to dilute further the potential for hysteretic behaviour. This needs to be investigated: for example, whereas location-specific factors would presumably weaken the propensity to agglomerate, factor mobility would presumably strengthen it. However, as it stands the paper provides little evidence to convince a sceptic that agglomeration effects are important at the economy-wide level (as opposed to the local level, where they are clearly crucial).

In summary, the paper performs a useful service by highlighting how cumulative processes driven by inter-industry linkages can lead countries to acquire, or lose, a manufacturing base. Moreover, the possibility of hysteresis shows that the smooth monotonic adjustment paths of simple neoclassical models may be misleading. However, these conclusions need to be reviewed in models that extend the present one to allow for more sophisticated firm behaviour, on the one hand, and differences in comparative advantage, on the other.

References

Hirschman, A. O. (1987), 'Linkages'. In J. Eatwell, M. Milgate, and P. Newman (eds.), *The New Palgrave: A Dictionary of Economics*, vol. III. London: Macmillan, pp. 206–11.

Krugman, P. (1991), 'Increasing Returns and Economic Geography', *Journal of Political Economy* 99: 483–99.

Leamer, E. E. (1988), 'Measures of Openness'. In R. E. Baldwin (ed.), *Trade Policy Issues and Empirical Analysis*. Chicago: University of Chicago Press, pp. 147–200.

7 Trade liberalization and investment in a multilateral framework

JOSEPH F. FRANCOIS,
BRADLEY J. MCDONALD,
and HÅKAN NORDSTRÖM

1 Introduction

The gains from trade in static models stem from the increased efficiency of resource allocation and improved consumption possibilities. With the addition of imperfect competition, gains from trade may also follow from pro-competitive effects related to increasing returns to scale, the erosion of market power, and increased product and input variety. Numerical estimates of basic static efficiency effects tend to be relatively small as a percentage of gross domestic product (GDP). For example, static assessments of the Tokyo Round and Uruguay Round typically pointed to income effects of less than 1 per cent of base GDP.[1] This is hardly consistent with cross-country studies of trade and income, which suggest linkages between trade policy and incomes, through investment, much stronger than those identified in static numeric studies. Nor are such modest estimates easily reconciled with the expectations held about trade reforms of this magnitude.

One shortcoming of the basic static story is that it fails to account for the positive relationship between trade, investment, and growth, a linkage that is fairly well established empirically (see, e.g., Edwards (1992), and Levine and Renelt (1992)). Also, on a theoretical level, classical growth theory suggests the potential for a medium-run growth or accumulation effect through induced changes in savings and investment patterns.[2] The magnitude and possible direction of such effects depend on whether savings are assumed to be exogenously fixed or endogenously derived from intertemporal optimization.[3]

On the basis of this literature, we explore the interaction between trade policy and capital accumulation in a multi-sector, multi-country setting. The trade policy reforms considered are the basic elements of the Uruguay Round. As expected, the results turn out to be sensitive to the savings specification. The medium-run impact of the Round tends to be a

202

simple multiple of the static impact when saving rates are fixed, although terms-of-trade changes may upset this direct relation. In contrast, with endogenous savings – determined by the condition that the opportunity cost of postponed consumption (as given by the rate of time preference) should equal the net marginal return of capital – the medium-run impact can differ quite substantially from the static impact. The induced impact on capital formation may reinforce or weaken the static impact, or even *reverse* the short-term impact if returns to investment fall. We conclude that the traditional focus on static effects is potentially misleading, and that more attention needs to be given to savings behaviour in assessments of trade policy reforms.

The discussion is organized as follows. We start with a conceptual discussion of classical trade–investment linkages under fixed and endo-genous savings rates. We show that the two specifications have identical steady-state implications for certain parameter values in the most simple, one-sector growth model. This is a very special case, however. A more general treatment using duality theory reveals that the steady-state implications of policy reforms hinge critically on the savings specifica-tions. This is shown in the appendix. The theoretical discussions are followed by a case-study of the Uruguay Round. The modelling exercise confirms the sensitivity of steady-state implications to the underlying savings behaviour. For example, for some regions, such as the European Union and North America, the basic story of the Round remains intact when accumulation effects are accounted for. Individual numbers differ, but not the overall qualitative results. In contrast, qualitative results for a number of developing countries hinge critically on our representation of savings and investment.[4]

2   Accumulation theory

2.1   Accumulation effects with fixed saving rates

Some of the basic features of capital-accumulation effects been illustrated nicely in a one-sector neoclassical growth model by Baldwin (1989, 1992). The first element is an aggregate production function linking output, Y_t, at time t to the amount of capital, K_t, and labour, L_t, employed:

$$Y_t = AK_t^\alpha L_t^{1-\alpha}; \qquad 0 < \alpha < 1, \tag{1}$$

where A is an overall productivity parameter, and α and $1 - \alpha$ are the elasticities of output with respect to capital and labour, respectively. The

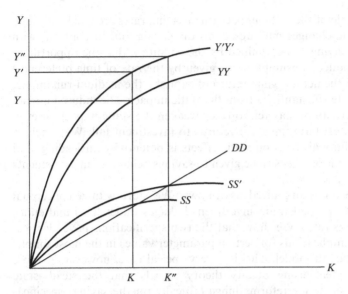

Figure 7.1   Short-run and long-run effects of an income shock.

relation between the stock of capital and output is plotted as YY in Figure 7.1. Note the curvature of YY, reflecting diminishing returns to capital when the labour force is held constant.

For a given flow of investment, the capital stock evolves over time according to:

$$K_{t+1} = (1 - \delta)K_t + I_t; \quad 0 < \delta < 1, \tag{2}$$

where δ is the fraction of the capital stock that depreciates each year (owing to wear and tear), and I_t is the flow of gross investment. The capital stock will be higher next period if today's investment is sufficiently large both to replace worn-out capital and to add new units to the stock.

To complete the model, we must specify how much of current output is set aside for savings and investment. For the moment, we adopt the classical assumption that consumers save a fixed share (s) of income,

$$S_t = sY_t, \tag{3}$$

where S_t is total saving. Abstracting from international capital flows, knowing savings means we also know investment. Furthermore, since savings depend on income that in turn depends on the capital stock, savings depend (indirectly) on the stock of capital.[5] The savings function is plotted as SS in Figure 7.1. The final relation plotted in Figure 7.1 is $DD = \delta K_t$, the amount of investment needed to replace worn-out capital in each period. The capital stock grows over time if savings and investment are larger than the rate at which capital depreciates ($SS > DD$), it is constant if savings and investment are just enough to replace depreciated capital ($SS = DD$), and it falls otherwise ($SS < DD$).

Starting from a low capital stock with high returns on investment, income will grow over time as capital is accumulated through savings and investment. In the absence of technical progress, this process will eventually come to an end because of the diminishing returns of adding more capital per worker. In the long run, growth in per capita income will stop at the point where savings are just enough to replace depreciated capital. The 'steady-state' capital stock and output (distinguished by absence of time subscripts) are given by:

$$K = \left(\frac{s}{\delta}\right)^{\frac{1}{1-\alpha}} A^{\frac{1}{1-\alpha}} L; \quad Y = \left(\frac{s}{\delta}\right)^{\frac{\alpha}{1-\alpha}} A^{\frac{1}{1-\alpha}} L. \tag{4}$$

Now, consider the impact of efficiency-enhancing reform, here referred to as trade liberalization. We assume that the region we are modelling is initially in a steady state, and that trade liberalization enhances the efficiency of capital and labour by moving resources into sectors where they are more valuable at the margin. In Figure 7.1, this is represented by an increase in the economy-wide productivity parameter A, which shifts out the production function from YY to $Y'Y'$ for any given level of capital and labour. That is, the same amount of labour and capital can now produce more than before, as illustrated by the difference between Y' and Y in the figure. This is the short-run or static gain. Part of the additional income will be saved and invested in new capital, which in turn yields an additional income gain. (Note the positive difference between $S'S'$ and DD for the initial capital stock K, implying positive net investments.) The economy will, over time, move up to a new higher steady-state capital stock and corresponding higher output, marked in the figure by K'' and Y'' respectively.

Decomposing the total income gain into static and induced (medium-run) gains we have:

$$(Y'' - Y)/Y = (Y' - Y)/Y + (Y'' - Y')/Y, \tag{5}$$

where the first part is the static income gain and the second part is the induced (medium-run) gain. It turns out that the latter is simply a multiple of the static gain:

$$(Y'' - Y')/Y = (\alpha/1 - \alpha)(Y' - Y)/Y. \tag{6}$$

That is, for each percentage increase in static income, one gets an additional fraction in induced income gain over the medium run. (Of course, *any* policy change that improves productivity will induce higher incomes with a savings–investment linkage.) The size of the induced income gain depends on the curvature of the YY schedule, which in turn depends on the elasticity of output with respect to capital, measured by the parameter 'α' in the production function. The larger the output–capital elasticity, the less the curvature of the YY schedule, and the larger the induced gain in income. For example, an 'α' of 0.25 (low estimate) implies an accumulation-related growth multiplier of one-third on top of the initial income gain, and an 'α' of 0.4 (high estimate) implies a multiplier of two-thirds.[6]

2.2   Accumulation effects with endogenous savings rates

Endogenizing the savings rate does not change the basic story in this simple, one-sector Cobb–Douglas economy. Using standard dynamic optimization, it is easy to show that steady-state levels of capital and income (abstracting from exogenous technological progress and population growth) are simply,

$$K = \left(\frac{\alpha}{\delta + \rho}\right)^{\frac{1}{1-\alpha}} A^{\frac{1}{1-\alpha}} L, \quad Y = \left(\frac{\alpha}{\delta + \rho}\right)^{\frac{\alpha}{1-\alpha}} A^{\frac{1}{1-\alpha}} L. \tag{7}$$

Comparing (4) and (7), note that the steady-state capital stock and income with endogenous savings rates are identical to the fixed savings rate case for certain sets of parameters: $s = \alpha(\delta/\delta + \rho)$. However, this 'equivalence' between fixed and endogenous savings may break down if additional sectors are introduced, if the aggregate production function is not Cobb–Douglas, or if the relative price of capital in terms of consumption goods changes as a result of the trade reforms. Indeed, a more general, dual treatment reveals that the steady-state effects of trade policy reforms depend critically on the savings specification. This is demonstrated mathematically in the appendix at the end of the paper and graphically below.

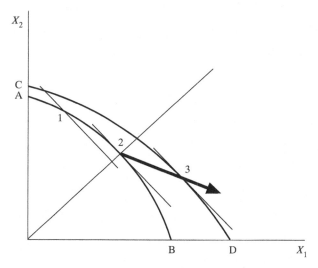

Figure 7.2   A capital-friendly liberalization.

2.3   *Accumulation effects with fixed and endogenous savings in a two-sector model*

So far, we have discussed capital-accumulation effects with reference to neutral shocks to an aggregate Cobb–Douglas GDP function. However, a number of complicating factors should also be kept in mind. We have shown that accumulation effects can compound initial output and welfare effects over the medium run, and can magnify income gains or losses. However, how much these accumulation effects will actually supplement static effects depends on a number of other factors as well. These include the economy-wide marginal product of capital, underlying savings behaviour, sectoral interactions, and terms-of-trade effects. Results will also depend on the pattern of underlying distortions embedded in the GDP function.

To illustrate some of these factors, we have represented a capital-friendly tariff reform for a two-good model in Figure 7.2, where we assume that goods X_1 and X_2 are combined into a composite good used for consumption or investment. The initial equilibrium is at the tariff-distorted production point 1, with the world price line intersecting the production possibility frontier (PPF). Trade liberalization, in the short run, implies a shift in production from point 1 to point 2, with an expansion of capital-intensive production of X_1 and a contraction of

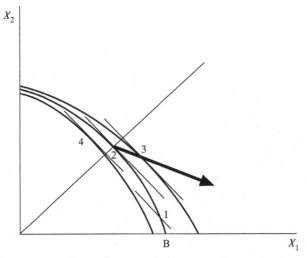

Figure 7.3   Divergence between effects with fixed and endogenous savings rates.

labour-intensive production of X_2. The result is an increase in the return to capital and investment, and an induced expansion of the capital stock under both a fixed savings rate and endogenous savings rate specification. The result is continued expansion of production of X_2, as the PPF expands from AB to CD. The economy embarks on a new dynamic path, converging on the new steady state at point 3.

Alternatively, the income and/or factor price effects of trade liberalization may also signal a draw-down of the capital stock. This is represented in Figure 7.3. Tariff reform moves us, in the short run, from point 1 to point 2. The increase in income leads, under fixed savings rates, to a rise in investment, and a further shift in production to point 3, with a rise in X_1 production as we move from point 2 to point 3. However, the short-run effects of the tariff reform also imply a fall in the return to investment. With a savings rate sensitive to real returns, this induces a draw-down of the capital stock, with production shifting from point 2 to point 4, implying a further contraction of X_1 production. Note, however, that, even with the draw-down in GDP, welfare should increase. This is because the earlier allocation of income to investment reflected distorted private returns relative to the social return of deferred consumption. Hence, in Figure 7.3, welfare associated with production at point 4 will be higher than at point 1.

3 A numerical example: the Uruguay Round

We next turn to numerical examples. We use a multi-region general equilibrium model to examine the possible investment-related effects of the Uruguay Round. Our policy simulations include industrial tariff liberalization, the elimination of the multi-fibre arrangement (MFA), the elimination of a number of other industrial non-tariff barriers (NTBs), and reductions in protection for agriculture. The specifics of these agreements have been detailed elsewhere (see the World Bank volume edited by Martin and Winters (1995)) and are not repeated here.

3.1 The model

We work with a ten-sector, ten-region computable general equilibrium (CGE) model of the world economy. There are three factors: land, labour, and capital. The sectoring scheme, along with parameters, is detailed in Tables 7.1 and 7.2. Social accounting data are based on a modified version of the basic GTAP version 2 database (Hertel et al. 1997). Initial protection data, for the present application, are representative of the world as of 1992 (i.e. pre-Uruguay Round), with MFA protection and various industrial non-tariff barriers represented as export taxes. Our basic pre- and post-Round protection data are described in Francois et al. (1995), and include both tariffs and industrial and agricultural NTBs.

Composite household demand is specified, at the upper tier, as Cobb–Douglas between government spending and private spending. Government spending therefore involves a fixed share of temporal consumption. Consumption across goods is determined by constant difference elasticity (CDE) preferences. Under the reference specification, the capital stock is fixed. Alternatively, with steady-state capital accumulation, investment, savings rates, and the capital stocks adjust as described below. Factor markets are competitive, with labour and capital being mobile between sectors but *not* between countries.

Capital markets are modelled as regional markets, with capital fully mobile between sectors (and countries making up the relevant 'regions'). We do not model changes in international (interregional) financial capital flows induced by trade policy changes. Rather, our capital market closure involves fixed net capital inflows and outflows.

Trade is modelled in one of two ways. In the constant-returns-to-scale (CRTS) specification, traded goods are treated as differentiated by country of origin (the Armington assumption). Different country varieties are combined through a constant elasticity of substitution (CES)

Table 7.1   Model aggregation

Regions	Sectors
Australasia	Agriculture
North America	Extraction
Japan	Processed Food
European Union	Textiles
Asian NIEs	Clothing
ASEAN	Iron and Steel
China	Machinery and Equipment
South Asia	Transport Equipment
Latin America	Other Manufactures
Rest of world	Services

Table 7.2   Trade and scale elasticities

Sector	Substitution between imports and domestic	Substitution between different imports	CDR
Agriculture	2.48	4.72	*
Extraction	2.80	5.60	0.05
Processed food	2.38	4.77	0.15
Textiles	2.20	4.40	0.14
Clothing	4.40	8.80	*
Iron and steel	2.80	5.60	0.14
Machinery and equipment	5.20	10.40	0.15
Transport equipment	2.80	5.60	0.15
Other manufactures	2.27	4.86	0.12
Services	1.94	3.92	*

aggregator into a composite good used as intermediates (in other sectors) or for final consumption. Alternatively, we assume that products in some sectors are differentiated by firms. This assumption is adopted in the monopolistic competition, increasing-returns-to-scale (IRTS) specification of the model. Imperfect competition is specified as a stylized version of large-group monopolistic competition for specialized production, with CES-based demand for variety (see Francois and Roland-Holst (1997)). Under this approach, scale/variety effects and the degree of product substitutability are determined by the inverse of the cost disadvantage ratio (CDR), a measure of scale economies. The CDR values we work with are reported in Table 7.2.

To highlight capital-accumulation effects, we adopt three alternative closure rules for the capital market. Our benchmark closure is the standard static specification with fixed aggregate capital stocks:

$$K_1 = K_0 = \overline{K}, \tag{8}$$

where sub-indexes 0 and 1 denote pre- and post-reform values. This static closure is contrasted with two steady-state closures. Under the assumption of fixed savings rates, a fixed proportion of the static income gain will be saved and invested, leading to additional income, of which part is saved, and so forth. The steady-state capital stock is related to the initial GDP according to $K_0 = [s/(g + \delta)](Y_0/P_0)$, where s is the fixed savings rate, g is the steady-state growth rate (equal to the exogenous rate of technical progress), δ is capital depreciation, P is the relative price of the investment good in terms of the composite consumption good, and the composite consumption good is the numeraire. Similarly, in the post trade liberalization steady state, the associated new steady-state capital stock is $K_1 = [s/(g + \delta)](Y_1/P_1)$. Together these two steady-state relations, two for each region, allow us to solve for the post-reform capital stocks:

$$K_1 = K_0(Y_1/Y_0)(P_0/P_1). \tag{9}$$

The change in steady-state capital stocks, following a shock to the regional GDP functions, is proportionate to the change in the steady-state GDP functions, controlling for changes in the relative prices of the composite investment goods. The crucial assumption is that all regions are initially in steady state – a convenient although admittedly unrealistic assumption.[7]

Turning next to the endogenous saving specification, and again assuming the composite consumption good is the numeraire, the equation for consumption (derived from standard dynamic optimization) is given by:

$$\frac{\dot{C}}{C} = \sigma\left[\frac{r}{p} + \frac{\dot{P}}{P} - \delta - \rho\right]. \tag{10}$$

That is, growth in consumption is a function of the difference between the net *private* return to capital in terms of the consumption good $(r/P - \delta)$ plus capital gain, and the rate of time preferences, ρ. In steady state, consumption grows at a constant rate g and the relative price between investment and consumption growth is constant.

Thus, comparing the pre- and post-reform steady states, we have:

$$\frac{r_0}{P_0}\delta = \rho + \frac{g}{\sigma} = \frac{r_1}{P_1}\delta$$

$$\therefore r_1 = r_0 x(P_1/P_0). \tag{11}$$

Under this endogenous savings closure, if a trade reform boosts the return to capital, it will induce further capital accumulation. New investments will take place until the marginal return falls back to the steady-state level. Conversely, a trade reform that reduces the return to capital will bring about capital decumulation, because depreciated capital is not replaced.

Of course, a global trade reform may raise the returns in one country while reducing them in another. The country-specific impact hinges on the interaction between the trade reform (which sectors are liberalized) and the specialization pattern (which, in turn, depends on factor endowments and initial trade barriers).

3.2   Results

Tables 7.3–7.7 present short- and medium-run changes in capital returns, capital stocks, terms of trade, wages, and GDP under the alternative assumptions of (i) a fixed capital stock; (ii) a fixed savings rate; and (iii) a fixed steady-state return on capital (endogenous savings). We also offer a comparison of steady-state welfare (based on a comparison of steady-state consumption levels) in Table 7.8.[8]

Note first in Table 7.3, columns 1 and 4, that the Uruguay Round boosts the short-run returns to investment in some regions, while returns fall in others. With endogenous savings, this initial impact induces accumulation or decumulation of capital to bring returns back to their steady-state levels. The corresponding changes in steady-state capital stocks are reported in columns 3 and 6 of Table 7.4. Compare this with the fixed savings rate specification. In the latter case, investments are unrelated to what happens to capital returns. Instead, investments are proportional to the static income gain. What is critical in this case is the change in income relative to capital goods prices. Hence, in the Asian NIE region, income gains are positive, based on GDP valued at base-period prices (see Table 7.7). However, rising capital goods prices dominate, leading to a fall in the capital stock (Table 7.4, columns 2 and 5).

3.3   How well does the Baldwin multiplier analysis hold up?

A rule of thumb for assessing potential medium-term accumulation effects is the Baldwin multiplier, which is defined in equation (6) above. In Figure 7.4, we compare estimates based on the multiplier approach, for constant returns specifications, with those based on explicit accumulation mechanisms. For marginal trade reforms the multiplier analysis should yield identical results to the fixed and endogenous savings

Table 7.3 Change in real returns to investment (%)

	CRTS			IRTS		
	Static	Endogenous K, fixed s	Endogenous K and s	Static	Endogenous K, fixed s	Endogenous K and s
Australasia	3.3	1.8	*	3.5	2.1	*
North America	2.2	1.8	*	2.8	2.3	*
Japan	−0.8	−1.0	*	−0.7	−0.8	*
European Union	2.6	1.5	*	4.7	3.8	*
Asian NIEs	1.1	1.3	*	−0.5	0.4	*
ASEAN	2.2	0.7	*	−2.5	−8.8	*
China	−2.6	−9.3	*	−3.1	−7.8	*
South Asia	−3.7	−4.2	*	−7.5	−7.6	*
Latin America	2.7	1.9	*	3.1	2.1	*
Rest of world	2.5	2.3	*	3.2	2.8	*

Table 7.4 Change in capital stock (%)

	CRTS			IRTS		
	Static	Endogenous K, fixed s	Endogenous K and s	Static	Endogenous K, fixed s	Endogenous K and s
Australasia	*	1.8	4.4	*	2.4	4.7
North America	*	0.4	3.0	*	1.4	3.9
Japan	*	0.2	−1.5	*	0.1	−1.3
European Union	*	1.4	3.3	*	1.5	6.0
Asian NIEs	*	−0.3	2.0	*	−1.1	−2.1
ASEAN	*	3.7	6.1	*	29.2	−7.8
China	*	8.7	−3.4	*	5.0	−2.5
South Asia	*	0.5	−4.5	*	−2.3	−11.7
Latin America	*	1.7	6.2	*	2.2	7.5
Rest of world	*	0.1	3.8	*	0.5	5.2

Table 7.5 Change in real wages (%)

	CRTS			IRTS		
	Static	Endogenous K, fixed s	Endogenous K and s	Static	Endogenous K, fixed s	Endogenous K and s
Australasia	3.2	3.2	3.2	2.7	0.6	2.8
North America	2.0	2.0	2.1	2.7	3.1	2.8
Japan	-0.8	-0.9	-1.2	-0.9	-0.8	-1.2
European Union	2.4	2.4	2.3	3.8	3.9	3.6
Asian NIEs	0.9	1.0	1.4	-0.6	-0.0	-1.9
ASEAN	4.1	5.7	7.0	10.5	30.3	4.8
China	-1.5	-0.4	-2.0	-2.0	-1.8	-2.3
South Asia	-3.1	-3.0	-3.8	-4.5	-6.0	-8.2
Latin America	2.7	3.0	4.9	2.9	3.7	6.0
Rest of world	2.1	2.1	2.6	2.9	2.9	3.9

Table 7.6 Change in terms of trade (%)

	CRTS			IRTS		
	Static	Endogenous K, fixed s	Endogenous K and s	Static	Endogenous K, fixed s	Endogenous K and s
Australasia	-0.2	-0.3	-0.6	-0.3	-0.0	-0.5
North America	0.7	0.8	0.7	1.5	1.7	1.6
Japan	0.5	0.6	1.6	0.6	0.8	0.8
European Union	1.6	1.6	0.9	1.8	1.9	1.8
Asian NIEs	-1.5	-1.4	-1.6	-0.7	-0.5	-0.8
ASEAN	-1.7	-2.0	-2.2	-3.5	-4.5	-3.4
China	-1.2	-1.6	-1.0	-2.5	-2.2	-2.8
South Asia	-2.2	-2.2	-1.8	-5.0	-5.4	-5.7
Latin America	-1.1	-1.3	-1.7	-1.3	-1.3	-1.4
Rest of world	-1.4	-1.4	-1.7	-1.4	-1.4	-1.6

Table 7.7 Change in real GDP (%)

	CRTS			IRTS		
	Static	Endogenous K, fixed s	Endogenous K and s	Static	Endogenous K, fixed s	Endogenous K and s
Australasia	0.2	0.9	1.8	0.4	1.4	2.4
North America	0.1	0.3	1.2	0.2	0.7	1.7
Japan	0.1	0.8	−0.5	0.2	0.2	−0.4
European Union	0.3	0.2	1.4	0.4	1.0	2.7
Asian NIEs	0.2	0.1	1.1	−0.4	−0.8	−1.4
ASEAN	2.3	4.7	6.3	12.7	34.9	7.2
China	1.6	4.9	0.3	1.5	3.7	0.6
South Asia	1.2	1.4	−0.4	1.7	0.9	−3.2
Latin America	0.1	1.0	3.6	0.3	1.7	4.9
Rest of world	0.0	0.1	1.7	0.0	0.3	2.6

Table 7.8 Change in welfare from personal consumption (%)

	CRTS			IRTS		
	Static	Endogenous K, fixed s	Endogenous K and s	Static	Endogenous K, fixed s	Endogenous K and s
Australasia	0.2	0.7	1.2	0.5	1.4	1.8
North America	0.3	0.5	1.1	0.6	1.0	1.7
Japan	0.0	1.6	-0.0	0.1	0.2	-0.1
European Union	0.9	1.2	1.6	1.3	1.7	2.6
Asian NIEs	-1.1	-0.6	-1.0	-0.9	-1.0	-1.8
ASEAN	0.4	4.6	3.1	6.4	25.4	7.7
China	0.1	6.9	0.6	-0.1	1.5	-0.2
South Asia	-0.0	6.6	-0.6	-0.3	-1.1	-3.4
Latin America	-0.1	-0.4	2.6	0.1	1.3	4.0
Rest of world	-0.4	-1.7	0.6	-0.4	-0.1	1.4

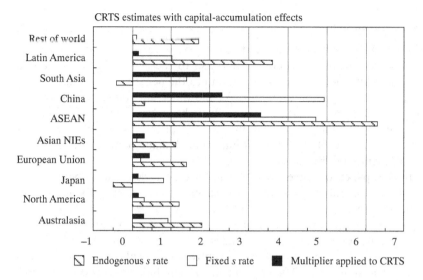

Figure 7.4 Estimated changes in GDP: CRTS estimates with capital-accumulation effects.

specifications. Yet, for discrete changes, the three approaches can and *do* lead to divergent results quantitatively, and sometimes also qualitatively. Clearly, marginal calculus is not always a good guide for assessing discrete policy changes in a general equilibrium framework.

The information reported in the tables can also be used to decompose the factors driving the divergence in results. Consider, for example, the set of results for Latin America. From Table 7.8, with a fixed capital stock there is a slight increase in income (at base-period prices) under both CRTS and IRTS specifications. At the same time, though, a fall in the cost of capital, under fixed savings rates, leads to a relatively large increase in the steady-state capital stock (Table 7.4). Yet, there is still a residual increase in the return to investment, even with this initial increase in capital (Table 7.7). This leads to a further expansion of the capital stock, as indicated in Table 7.4. The result is a further expansion in production as measured by GDP (Table 7.8), and a slight worsening of the terms of trade as production for export expands (Table 7.6). A similar tracing of effects can be made for the other regions as well.

4   Conclusions

The implications of trade and trade policy relate not only to static resource allocation efficiencies, but also to the accumulation of capital (human, knowledge, and physical) and to the negative accumulation (i.e. depletion) of natural resources. As the older and more recent growth literatures have emphasized, such effects have very real implications for the level and the growth of income. Empirical evidence also points (Levine and Renelt 1992) to an important linkage between trade policy, investment, and the path of income.

In this paper we have examined linkages between trade liberalization and multilateral investment, emphasizing effects related to investment and the accumulation of capital. Trade and investment linkages have been explored in the context of simple steady-state closure rules, where we specify explicit stylized linkages between investment and income levels, and between investment incentives (i.e. real factor prices) and capital accumulation. The importance of these linkages is shown to hinge on the sensitivity of savings rates with respect to real returns. Empirical evidence points to a sensitivity of the *level* of savings to income, such that income shocks can be magnified by induced savings (see Carroll and Weil (1993)). However, we remain sceptical about whether we should expect trade policy shocks to induce first-order changes in the *rate* of savings (see Kotlikoff (1989)).

The one consistent pattern to emerge from our results is the occasional lack of consistency. In particular, for some regions, such as the EU and North America, the basic story told by our Uruguay Round simulations remains unchanged under a range of model structures. Clearly, capital-accumulation effects and scale economies imply potential gains greater than those suggested by static, constant returns models. However, the story remains one of gains. The same cannot be said for all other regions. Estimated effects for a number of developing countries hinge critically on our representation of investment effects. As resulting shifts in the resource base interact with the terms of trade and potential scale economies, the order of magnitude and even the sign of estimated results can be affected. Hence, while we have not addressed here how likely it is that savings rates will increase in response to shifting incentives, it is clear that this response matters. At the same time, compared with explicit fixed or endogenous savings specifications, it is also clear that, at least for multilateral liberalization, multiplier-type analysis can be a poor guide to potential accumulation effects.

Appendix: A dual treatment of accumulation effects

Consider a multi-sector, small economy that trades at given world market prices. The outputs of the different sectors are combined, through a linear homogeneous aggregation function, into a composite good that can be either consumed or saved/invested. Formally, we can represent this economy by replacing equation (1) with the following reduced-form GDP function:

$$Y = G(K', L' : P); \quad K' = \alpha_K K, \quad L' = \alpha_L L. \tag{A1}$$

In equation (A1), Y still represents national income, measured in units of the composite consumption/investment good. The α_i terms represent factor-specific efficiency parameters and P the vector of world market prices. A trade policy reform is analogous to a shock to the α vector. It can be shown that, in steady state, a shock to the efficiency parameters will lead to the following change in steady-state GDP under fixed and endogenous savings, respectively.

Fixed savings rates:

$$\frac{dY}{Y} = (1 - \theta_{K'})^{-1} \left[\theta_{K'} \frac{d\alpha_k}{\alpha_K} + \theta_{L'} \frac{d\alpha_L}{\alpha_L} \right] \tag{A2}$$

Endogenous savings (fixed net real return to capital):

$$\frac{dY}{Y} = \left[\theta_{K'} \frac{d\alpha_K}{\alpha_K} + \theta_{L'} \frac{d\alpha_L}{\alpha_L} \right] + \left[\theta_{K'} (-G_{K'K'})^{-1} G_{K'} (K')^{-1} \frac{d\alpha_K}{\alpha_K} \right]$$
$$+ \left[\theta_{K'} (-G_{K'K'})^{-1} G_{K'L'} (K')^{-1} \frac{d\alpha_L}{\alpha_L} \right]; \quad \theta_i = \frac{G_i}{G}, \quad G_{K'} = \frac{\partial G}{\partial K'}. \tag{A3}$$

With a Hicks-neutral shock to the GDP function, and with a composite GDP function that is Cobb–Douglas, both equations (A2) and (A3) collapse to equation (6), the simple Baldwin multiplier. Under other, more general, conditions, we can expect to see divergence in steady-state income effects between the two savings specifications.

Notes

This paper represents the opinion of the authors. It is not meant to represent, in any way, the opinions or official position of the WTO Secretariat or its Members.
1. As a rule of thumb, economy-wide trade reforms yield a 1 per cent static

impact on GDP. This observation is sometimes referred to as 'Markusen's law'.

2. Accumulation effects of trade policy have been explored by, among others, Samuelson (1975), Smith (1976, 1977), Srinivasan and Bhagwati (1980), Baldwin (1989, 1992), Baldwin and Venables (1995), and Francois et al. in Chapter 2 of this volume.

3. It should be noted that the medium-run effects are qualitatively different from long-run effects arising from dynamic externalities. For an exposition of the more recent literature on endogenous linkages between trade policy, investment, and steady-state growth, see, for instance, Grossman and Helpman (1991, 1995).

4. We do not explore overlapping-generations models in this paper. However, because such models exhibit relatively rigid savings rates (at least with regard to changes in relative returns), the contrast between our fixed and endogenous savings rate specifications suggests potentially significant differences between the qualitative results of infinite horizon and overlapping-generations models.

5. Of course, the savings–investment link need not hold exactly for individual countries that can borrow abroad to finance their investment, though it must hold globally.

6. The endogenous growth literature suggests substantially higher capital–output elasticities. Indeed, the simplest AK models assume an elasticity of 1 for a broad concept of capital, including human capital. In this limiting case, trade reform will lead to permanent growth effects because capital is not subject to diminishing return. Note that the 'medium-run' growth bonus approaches infinity (i.e. a permanent growth effect) as 'α' approaches 1.

7. Francois, Nordström, and Shiells (Chapter 2 in this volume) show in a one-sector growth model that trade policy reforms during transition to steady state will spur growth temporarily, bringing the fruits of policy reform forward to an earlier date. Trade liberalizations are therefore potentially more important for developing countries than for developed countries, assuming that developing countries are further away from their steady-state incomes.

8. The preferred welfare measure would be a comparison of the intertemporal equivalent variation. However, this approach is relevant only for the endogenous savings case where the time profile of consumption and savings is determined from intertemporal optimization. This would also require numerical solutions for transition dynamics.

References

Baldwin, R. E. (1989), 'The Growth Effects of 1992', *Economic Policy* 9(2): 247–81.

(1992), 'Measurable Dynamic Gains from Trade', *Journal of Political Economy* 100(1): 162–74.

Baldwin, R. E. and A. J. Venables (1995), 'Regional Economic Integration'. In G. M. Grossman and K. Rogoff (eds.), *Handbook of International Economics*, vol. III. Amsterdam: North-Holland/Elsevier.

Carroll, C. D. and D. N. Weil (1993), 'Saving and Growth: A Reinterpretation', NBER Working Paper No. 4470, September.

Edwards, Sebastian (1992), 'Trade Orientation, Distortions, and Growth in Developing Countries', *Journal of Development Economics* 39(1): 31–57.

Francois, J. F. and D. Roland-Holst (1997), 'Scale Economies, Imperfect Competition, and Commercial Policy in Applied Models'. In J. F. Francois and K. A. Reinert (eds.), *Applied Methods for Trade Policy Analysis: A Handbook*. Cambridge: Cambridge University Press.

Francois, J. F., B. McDonald, and H. Nordström (1995), 'Assessing the Uruguay Round'. In W. Martin and L. Alan. Winters (eds.), *The Uruguay Round and the Developing Economies*, World Bank Discussion Paper No. 307. Washington D.C.: World Bank.

Grossman, G. M. and E. Helpman (1991), *Innovation and Growth in the Global Economy*. Cambridge, Mass.: MIT Press.

(1995), 'Technology and Trade', CEPR Discussion Paper No. 1134, February.

Hertel, T. W., E. Ianchovichina, and B. McDonald (1997), 'Multi-Region General Equilibrium Modeling'. In J. F. Francois and K. Reinert (eds.), *Applied Methods for Trade Policy Analysis*. New York: Cambridge University Press, Chapter 9.

Kotlikoff, L. J. (1989), *What Determines Savings?* Cambridge, Mass.: MIT Press.

Levine, R. and D. Renelt (1992), 'A Sensitivity Analysis of Cross-Country Growth Regressions', *American Economic Review* 82(4): 942–63.

Martin, W. and L. Alan Winters (1995), eds., *The Uruguay Round and the Developing Economies*, World Bank Discussion Paper No. 307. Washington D.C.: World Bank.

Samuelson, P. (1975), 'Trade Pattern Reversals in Time-Phased Ricardian Systems and Intertemporal Efficiencies', *Journal of International Economics* 5: 209–364.

Smith, M. A. M. (1976), 'Trade, Growth and Consumption in Alternative Models of Capital Accumulation', *Journal of International Economics* 6: 385–88.

(1977), 'Capital Accumulation in the Open Two-Sector Economy', *Economic Journal* 87: 273–82.

Srinivasan, T. N. and J. N. Bhagwati (1980), 'Trade and Welfare in a Steady State'. In J. S. Chipman and C. P. Kindleberger (eds.), *Flexible Exchange Rates and the Balance of Payments*. Amsterdam: North-Holland.

Discussion

IAN WOOTON

This paper is an investigation into the links between trade liberalization, capital accumulation, and economic growth. It falls into two parts. The main part is a numerical exercise to determine the potential dynamic impact of the trade liberalization resulting from the Uruguay Round.

The results are shown to be sensitive to the specification of savings behaviour. Consequently, the authors provide a discussion of a simple theoretical model that illustrates the effects of different assumptions about capital accumulation in a dynamic model of trade liberalization. They adopt Baldwin's (1989, 1992) neoclassical growth model. Because this model represents the economy as a single sector, it is unable to capture effects arising from differences in relative capital intensities in different sectors of the economy. These can be dealt with only in the full numerical model of the latter part of the paper.

In my discussion, I wish to provide a complementary analysis of savings behaviour and accumulation in a one-sector model. Specifically, I shall demonstrate the sensitivity of results to the elasticity of substitution between factors in production. This requires a departure from the Cobb–Douglas specification in the paper and the adoption of production technology allowing for non-unitary substitution elasticities. Suppose then that production is according to a CES production function, with inputs of labour and capital, where the labour supply remains fixed over time:

$$Y_t = A\{K_t^\alpha + \overline{L}^\alpha\}^{\frac{1}{\alpha}},$$

where $\alpha < 1$ and is non-zero. The elasticity of substitution is $\sigma \equiv 1/(1-\alpha)$. I will use a per capita representation of the model, assuming that the initial equilibrium represents a steady state under each of the rules. Output per worker is then:

$$y_t = A\{k_t^\alpha + 1\}^{\frac{1}{\alpha}}, \tag{1}$$

where $k_t \equiv K_t/\overline{L}$. The behavioural assumptions that I investigate are: (a) the maintenance of a constant capital stock; (b) agents having a fixed savings rate; and (c) savings activity that keeps constant the real return to capital.

The first task is to determine the steady state for each of these assumptions. The marginal productivity of capital is the derivative of (1) with respect to k_t:

$$f'(k_t) = A^\alpha \left\{\frac{y_t}{k_t}\right\}^{1-\alpha}. \tag{2}$$

(a) With constant capital stock $\overline{K}$ and unchanging labour population, the per capita stock of capital will be constant in the steady state. This is:

$$k^* = \bar{k} \tag{3}$$

and hence per capita income remains at its initial levels throughout time.

(b) With a fixed saving rate, s, as a proportion of per capita income, we must take into account the depreciation rate of capital, δ. The steady state is achieved where saving is just sufficient to cover the depreciation of the existing stock of capital:

$$\frac{y^*}{k^*} = \frac{\delta}{s}. \tag{4}$$

(c) When the real return to capital, ρ, is fixed in the steady state then, from (3), this will yield the following relationship between the steady-state income and capital levels:

$$\frac{y^*}{k^*} = \left\{ \frac{\rho}{A^\alpha} \right\}^{\frac{1}{1-\alpha}}. \tag{5}$$

In order to facilitate a comparison, I assume that the initial equilibrium is consistent with all three steady-state conditions. Therefore the right-hand sides of (4) and (5) are equal. Taking the two expressions and manipulating them slightly yields:

$$\left(\frac{As}{\delta} \right)^\alpha = \left(\frac{A}{\rho} \right)^{\frac{\alpha}{1-\alpha}} \equiv \phi, \tag{6}$$

where the first term is the condition from (b), the second term that of (c), and the final term $\phi > 0$ will be used later. Rewriting (1) in steady-state terms:

$$y^* = A \{ k^{*\alpha} + 1 \}^{\frac{1}{\alpha}}. \tag{1'}$$

The effects of trade liberalization are characterized in the paper as an exogenous (positive) productivity shock. This is captured in an increase in A. The impact on the steady state will arise from two sources: the initial productivity shock; and the induced change in capital accumulation, if any. Let a technology shock of $\hat{A} \equiv dA/A$ induce a change in per capita income in the steady state of $\hat{y}_j^* \equiv \hat{y}^*/dy^*$ for each of the cases $j \in \{a, b, c\}$.

(a) When the capital stock is fixed, the effect of the productivity shock is found from differentiating (1') and solving, using (3). This yields:

$$\hat{y}_a^* = \hat{A}. \tag{7}$$

Because the capital stock is assumed to remain unchanged, the steady-state income is a linear function of A and so per capita output rises in proportion to the size of the shock.

(b) When the savings rate is fixed, (4) is used in the solution and hence:

$$\hat{y}_b^* = \frac{1}{1 - \phi} \hat{A}. \tag{8}$$

The expression in the denominator is positive and less than 1, hence $\hat{y}_b^* > \hat{A}$. The increase in productivity raises per capita incomes, inducing additional capital accumulation, and raising per capita incomes more than proportionately.

(c) It is easy to demonstrate that, for the case of a Cobb–Douglas production function (unitary elasticity of substitution), a productivity shock of the type considered here will result in the same steady-state equilibrium for cases (b) and (c). However, when the elasticity is different from unity, the steady states differ. Finding a general solution for the case of a fixed real return to capital is more difficult as, from (5), it is clear that the output/capital ratio is not constant. I therefore examine two representative cases.

Consider initially $\alpha = 0.5$ (an elasticity of substitution $\sigma = 2$). Differentiating (1′) and using (5) and (6) yields:

$$\hat{y}_c^* = \left(\frac{1 + \phi}{1 - \phi} \right) \hat{A} > \hat{A}. \tag{9}$$

Thus, for a positive productivity shock, $\hat{y}_c^* > \hat{y}_b^*$.

Now let $\alpha = -1$ (elasticity of substitution of 0.5). Performing the same type of manipulations yields:

$$\hat{y}_c^* = \left(\frac{1 - \dfrac{\phi}{2}}{1 - \phi} \right) \hat{A} > \hat{A}. \tag{10}$$

In this instance, a positive productivity shock leads to $\hat{y}_c^* < \hat{y}_b^*$.

Why does this difference arise? From (4), the steady-state output/capital ratio does not change as a result of productivity shocks when the savings rate is constant. However, the shock changes the return to capital. Differentiating (2) with respect to A, and rearranging:

$$\frac{df'(k_t)}{dA} = \frac{\alpha}{A} f'(k_t).$$

The real return to capital will rise or fall depending on whether α is positive or negative. A rise in the real return will induce capital accumulation, whereas a fall will result in a reduction in capital holdings. Such a shock will induce a change in the output/capital ratio under the assumption of a fixed real return to capital. Differentiating (5) with respect to A yields:

$$\frac{d(y^*/k^*)}{dA} = \left(\frac{-\alpha}{1-\alpha}\right)\left(\frac{\rho}{A}\right)^{\frac{1}{1-\alpha}}. \tag{11}$$

This is negative for $0 < \alpha < 1$. Thus $\hat{k}^* > \hat{y}^*$ when $\sigma > 1$, that is, the production function is elastic. When $\sigma < 1$, the production function is inelastic and $\hat{k}^* < \hat{y}^*$.

Thus the greater the elasticity of substitution between labour and capital, the greater accumulation of capital in the new steady state when the production function receives a positive shock from an event such as trade liberalization. Consequently, production functions with high elasticities of substitution will yield larger steady-state gains when agents accumulate capital so as to maintain its real rate of return than when the savings rate is fixed.

References

Baldwin, R. E. (1989), 'The Growth Effects of 1992', *Economic Policy* 9(2), 247–81.
    (1992), 'Measurable Dynamic Gains from Trade', *Journal of Political Economy* 100(1), 162–74.

8 Investment creation and investment diversion: simulation analysis of the Single Market programme

RICHARD E. BALDWIN, RIKARD FORSLID,
and JAN I. HAALAND

1 Introduction

The European Union's Single Market programme altered commercial realities in Europe, making it easier for firms based in one European Union (EU) market to compete in other EU markets. This had a generally positive effect on EU economies yet, because the programme initially applied only to EU nations, it unintentionally threatened firms based in non-EU nations. The threat is easy to understand. By lowering the cost of doing business on an intra-EU basis, without lowering costs for non-EU firms, the programme altered the relative competitiveness of EU and non-EU firms in EU markets. This loss of competitiveness constituted a severe problem for the nations of the European Free Trade Association (EFTA) because 60 per cent of EFTA exports go to EU markets.

Many EFTA firms decided to adjust by becoming EU-based firms. The result was a well-documented outflow of direct investment from EFTA nations to EU nations.[1] Moreover, after 1989, total investment in the EFTA countries slumped faster and farther than it did in EU nations, and the Single Market programme may have had something to do with this. EFTAns also experienced a deeper and longer recession than the EU nations. In stark contrast, the two European economies that were rapidly integrating with the EU during the mid- to late 1980s – Spain and Portugal – experienced exactly the opposite pattern. Net foreign direct investment flowed in at an increasing pace, and they experienced investment-led surges in their GDP growth.

Of course, many factors were responsible for these trends. One factor that is often mentioned, however, is the impact of the Single Market programme. That is, it is asserted that the closer integration of the EU economies *diverted investment* from European nations that did not participate and *created investment* in those that did.

228

This paper is an attempt to investigate the investment creation and diversion effects of the Single Market. The paper has five sections, beyond the introduction. Section 2 presents details of the Single Market programme, the European Economic Area (EEA) agreement, and the *prima facie* case that investment creation and diversion did occur in Europe in the 1980s and early 1990s. Section 3 presents a simple, illustrative model that allows us to trace out the economic channels by which closer integration in the EU could trigger investment creation and diversion. Although the illustrative model is useful, the assumptions that are necessary for tractability imply that it has very few points of contact with the real world. Section 4 discusses a slightly modified medium-sized simulation model, the Haaland–Norman model (Haaland and Norman 1992). This model is far too complex to study analytically; however, it does bear a closer resemblance to the world economy than the illustrative model. Section 5 discusses the simulation results from the following scenarios. We simulate the effects of the 1992 Single Market programme (EU92) on EFTA and EU economies – including the steady-state capital stocks – when EFTA is excluded from EU92 and when it is included. The final section presents some concluding remarks.

2 The *prima facie* case for investment diversion

This section presents evidence that suggests that the Single Market programme might have led to investment creation and diversion. The evidence is far from conclusive and indeed no formal tests are performed. The point of this section is to provide an empirical basis for the belief – widely held in EFTA nations during the late 1980s and early 1990s – that the Single Market favoured investment in the EU at the expense of EFTA.

2.1 The Single Market programme: policies and chronology

In 1985 the European Commission, under the leadership of Jacques Delors, started a massive microeconomic liberalization programme aimed at turning the Common Market into a Single Market. Vickerman (1992) and Emerson (1988) provide a detailed list of the policy measures, but in general terms the programme consisted of three elements: goods trade liberalization, factor trade liberalization, and general deregulation and promotion of competition. The main elements of the trade liberalization involved streamlining and/or elimination of border formalities, liberalization of government procurement, and mutual recognition of technical standards in production, packaging, and marketing (with minimum harmonization). The principal element of factor trade liberalization consisted of increased capital market integration and liberalization of cross-border market-entry policies (rights of establishment, etc.), including mutual recognition of approval by national regulatory agencies. Lastly, although not formally part of the 1992 package, the European Commission engaged in a tighter enforcement of existing policies concerning anti-competitive practices and state aids to industry.

The lack of opposition to the Single Market measures stimulated the Commission to pursue liberalization of sectors excluded from the Single European Act. Although these are not strictly speaking part of the 1992 programme, they have affected or soon will affect the operation of the Single Market. These extra sectors include air transport, telecommunications, energy, and insurance.

As far as this paper is concerned, the main implication of the Single Market was that it made it easier for EU-based firms to compete in other EU markets. It did not, however, do the same for firms based in non-EU countries. In the late 1980s, this was especially difficult for firms based in EFTA nations because the EU market was very important to them.

The timing of events from the mid-1980s to the mid-1990s is critical to understanding the *prima facie* evidence we present below. The sequence, which is somewhat involved, concerns three types of policy change: the adoption and implementation of EU92, the Iberian enlargement of the EU, and the EFTAns' evolving response to EU92.

2.1.1   Chronology of the European integration since 1985

The first formal step towards the Single Market programme was a June 1985 White Paper by Lord Cockfield. This listed 282 measures necessary to complete the Single Market. The Single European Act treaty was signed in February 1986 by EU heads of government. After being ratified by all member state parliaments, it came into force in July 1987.

Adopting the Single European Act, however, was far from sufficient for the creation of a Single Market. Most of the measures had to be adopted individually by member states because they often involved detailed changes in existing member state legislation. This process is still going on, although most member states have adopted most of the measures. Additionally, the Single Market programme continues to develop. New measures and initiatives are being added continuously.

It is important to note that, until the late 1980s, many analysts were very sceptical about the likelihood of the Single Market programme being implemented on time. Pointing to the many other major EU initiatives that had failed (e.g. several monetary arrangements), these observers suggested that widespread opposition from domestic special interest groups would delay or dilute EU92. Consequently, the credibility of the Single Market gradually grew as more measures were passed by member state parliaments.

2.1.2 Chronology of the Iberian enlargement
Accession talks with the countries from the Iberian peninsula (Spain and Portugal) began formally in 1980. These accession talks were quite difficult and lasted six years. None the less, from as early as 1984, a successful conclusion was widely anticipated.

2.1.3 Chronology of the EEA and the EFTA enlargement
The Single Market's threat was recognized even before the White Paper was adopted, and in the mid-1980s EFTA governments had decided that they must react. The idea of countering the threat with a new plurilateral agreement was first suggested at a meeting of EFTA and EU ministers in Luxembourg in 1984. This produced the so-called Luxembourg Declaration, but the difficulties of such an initiative, and the EU's preoccupation with the Single European Act and the Maastricht Treaty, led to long delays. Negotiations were at a standstill until January 1989 when Jacques Delors proposed the European Economic Area (EEA) agreement (initially called the European Economic Space agreement). Talks on the EEA began informally in 1989, continuing more formally in 1990 and 1991.

The first version of the EEA was signed in 1991. It was, however, rejected by the European Court of Justice in December 1991. The Court ruled that this first version was inconsistent with the Treaty of Rome. The problem was the so-called EEA Court, which was supposed to have jurisdiction over Single Market cases involving EFTA and EU firms. This was found to violate the primacy of the European Court of Justice over all EU legal matters. To get around this, a new EEA was devised with an awkward 'two pillars' legal system.[2]

Negotiations were reconvened and the second version of the EEA was signed in May 1992. While acceptable to the European Court, it was rejected by Swiss voters in a December 1992 referendum. Since this version of the treaty presumed that all EFTAns would join, the Swiss 'no' required a technical rewriting of the agreement. More importantly, the EEA obliged the EFTAns to make financial transfers to poor EU regions, so the withdrawal of Switzerland also forced a renegotiation of the size of these transfers. The final version of the EEA was signed in 1993, with implementation starting in January 1994.

Two aspects of the EEA are truly extraordinary. First, the EEA is unbalanced as to the rights and obligations of EFTAns when it comes to future EU legislation. In essence, it forces the EFTAns to accept future

EU legislation (the *Acquis Communautaire*) concerning the Single Market, without formal participation in the formation of these new laws.[3] Second, the EEA creates a good deal of supranationality among the EFTAns.[4] This supranationality is extraordinary for two reasons. First, it was the EU that imposed this supranationality on the EFTAns to simplify the task of keeping the Single Market homogeneous. Second, the EFTAns have resisted such supranational authority since the end of World War II, so it is astounding that they said they would accept it.

As it turns out, few of the EFTAns were willing to live with the EEA. Even before the final version was adopted, all the EFTAns (except Iceland and Liechtenstein) had applied for full EU membership. Applications were received from Austria (July 1989), Sweden (July 1991), Finland (March 1992), Switzerland (May 1992), and Norway (November 1992). For these countries, the EEA was viewed as a transitional arrangement, not a long-term solution. Note that the EU froze the Swiss application in response to the negative outcome of their EEA referendum and Norwegian voters rejected membership in November 1994.

As of 1995, the EU side of the EEA consists of fifteen countries (population 367.5 million) while the EFTA side consists of two: the micro-states Liechtenstein and Iceland (populations 0.03 and 0.3 million respectively) and Norway with its 4.3 million citizens.

2.2   The prima facie case

Investment is difficult to explain empirically since expectations are notoriously difficult to account for empirically, yet they are at the very heart of the investment decision. The importance of this is that investment flows may respond before policy changes actually occur and may respond to changes in the private sector's opinion about the viability of policy changes. Keeping this in mind, we look at three types of evidence: net foreign direct investment (FDI) flows, net FDI flows disaggregated by source and destination, and total investment/GDP ratios. As the aim of this paper is to illustrate how investment incentives may be affected by trade policies, each of these variables may contribute to the overall picture. This evidence is not conclusive, but it does suggest that there is a phenomenon worth looking into.

2.2.1   Net foreign direct investment flows

The first piece of evidence that the EU92 programme caused investment diversion in the EFTA nations is presented in Figure 8.1. This shows net foreign direct investment flows (positive numbers indicate a net inflow) for the EFTA5 (Austria, Finland, Norway, Sweden, and Switzerland),

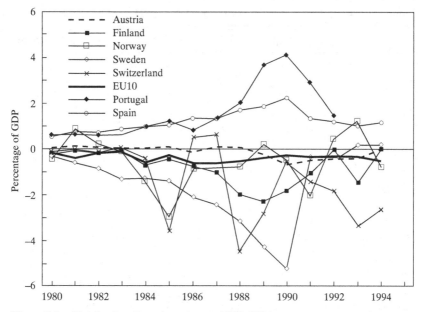

Figure 8.1 **Net foreign direct investment, 1980–1994.**

Spain, and Portugal, and the average of the EU10 (France, Germany, Italy, the United Kingdom, Belgium, the Netherlands, Luxembourg, Denmark, Ireland, and Greece). The EU10 (shown with a heavy solid line) account for the bulk of the output and purchasing power in the European economy, so we can think of their behaviour as a benchmark. That is, apart from issues of European integration and idiosyncratic national shocks, the Iberians and EFTAns should have roughly been subject to the same macroeconomic shocks as the EU10 and should therefore have experienced roughly the same FDI paths.

Given this, the widely differing behaviour of FDI flows is very suggestive. Roughly speaking, those nations that participated, or were expected to participate, in EU92 experienced rising net FDI inflows. Those that did not participate experienced deterioration of their FDI balances until their governments took action that made it likely that they would participate. FDI flows continue to worsen for the only West European nation, namely Switzerland, that has not arranged to participate in the Single Market. The break-point seems to come in 1987, the year the Single European Act was ratified by all member state parliaments.

The behaviour of the Iberian aggregate provides the clearest evidence of investment creation. These nations experienced above-average FDI inflows throughout the 1980s and early 1990s. There also appears to be a

Table 8.1   Economic indicators of the EFTA6, 1991

	Austria	Finland	Iceland	Norway	Sweden	Switzerland
Share of EFTA6 total GDP (%)	19	14	0.7	12	27	27
Population (millions)	7.8	5.0	0.3	4.3	8.6	6.9
Manufacturing GDP share (%)	25	24	18	14	22	25
Exports to EU12 as % of GDP	17	9	16	21	13	16
Manufactures as % of total exports	91	85	14	40	86	95

Sources: World Bank, *World Tables 1993* and EFTA (1992).
Note: Data for Liechtenstein (population 29,000) are included in the Swiss data.

rise in the rate between 1987 and 1990. A similar, but muted pattern occurs in the EU10 as a whole. Although they started from a negative position, they experienced a mild upward trend around 1987.

In contrast, the figures for most EFTAns turned sharply downwards in 1987 or 1988. Although there may be other explanations, it is highly suggestive that the EFTAns' direct investment flows turned around in the year that the negotiations that eventually led up to the EEA agreement were announced in January 1989.

2.2.2   FDI flows by nation

Studying the individual EFTAns' FDI figures provides additional information because the EFTA economies did not all adjust in the same way to the threat of the Single Market. However, before turning to the country FDI data, it is important to understand that the EFTAns are far from homogeneous economically. Table 8.1 shows that Switzerland, Sweden, and Austria are the largest EFTA economies, together accounting for 73 per cent of all EFTAn output. These three and Finland rely heavily on manufacturing, whereas Iceland and Norway depend more on natural resources. Since the EU92 programme affects the manufacturing sector more heavily than industries based on natural resources, the experiences of Switzerland, Sweden, Finland, and Austria are particularly relevant. Finally, notice that the EU market is much less important for Finland than for the other economies, reflecting Finnish trade with other Nordics and with Eastern Europe.

The EFTAns also differ in their policy response to the Single Market's threat. At one extreme, Austria applied for membership as early as 1989. Since there was a strong possibility that it would join the EU eventually, Austrian industry experienced much less uncertainty than did that of other EFTAns over the solution to the threat of the Single Market. At the other extreme, Switzerland's rejection of the EEA and the freezing of its application have created continuing uncertainty over its competitiveness in EU markets.

The Swedish data in Figure 8.1 show the clearest evidence of FDI diversion. Swedish flows were negative in the early 1980s, and the magnitude of the outflows increased sharply around the time that EU92 was adopted. The flows turned around quite clearly between 1990 and 1991. As usual, many factors were at work, but it is suggestive that the Swedish membership application was handed in mid-1991. By 1993, Sweden had become a net importer of FDI. Finnish data show a similar pattern, although the changes are somewhat muted. This may be partially because a lower fraction of Finnish exports consists of manufactured products, so they are less affected by EU92.

The Austrian case is more muted still, as might be expected given that its 1989 EU membership application received widespread popular support. Austrian FDI fluctuated around zero until 1988, at which time it turned negative and remained negative up to the end of the available data series. A slow improvement, however, is apparent from 1990 onwards.

The Swiss case is especially interesting. Switzerland is now the only West European country that does not have access to the Single Market. The Swiss government had put in an EU membership application before this, but the EU Commission ruled that rejection of the EEA amounted to a rejection of membership. The Swiss figures are also quite noisy, but there is some evidence of FDI diversion after 1990. Note that the referendum results were widely anticipated. Norway's investment figures, which are dominated by the idiosyncratic oil and shipping industries, are quite noisy too.

2.2.3 Bilateral FDI flows

The data on FDI flows by source and destination are quite sketchy. Data reaching back to the 1970s are available for some nations (Austria and Finland). They were collected in Switzerland only from 1986 so aggregate figures can be had only from that date. Figure 8.2

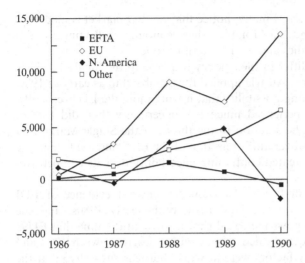

Figure 8.2   EFTA6's net FDI flows by region, 1986–1990 (US$ million).

shows the net bilateral flows from the EFTA6 to other EFTA
countries, the EU, North America, and the rest of the world. The fact
that EFTA's flow to itself is not zero gives us some idea of the
imperfections in these data.

The evolution of the bilateral FDI balance with the EU is the most
relevant feature of the figure. Starting from a position of approximate
balance in the mid-1980s, EFTA turned into a net exporter of capital to
the EU. EFTA's balance with the rest of the world also increased,
although not as sharply. In contrast, EFTA's balance with North
America became slightly negative.

2.2.4   Gross fixed investment flows
The data that we have reviewed so far have dealt only with a specific
type of international capital flow. This seemed to indicate that the EU,
and especially Spain and Portugal, had become relatively more attractive locations for investment. However, FDI is only a fraction of total
investment. For instance, at their maximum, net FDI inflows
amounted to 2 per cent of the Iberians' GDP, while their gross fixed
capital formation/GDP ratio was about 23 per cent of GDP. Thus, if
investment creation and diversion are to have large effects on a
nation's medium-term growth rate, then they must also affect domestic
investment. This is what we turn to next. As we shall see, the evidence
of investment diversion in the EFTA economies is much less clear,

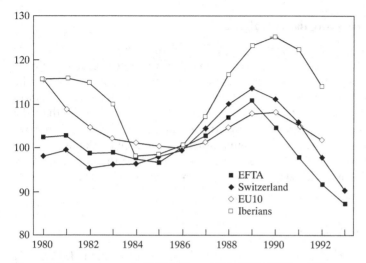

Figure 8.3   Investment to GDP indices, 1980–1993 (1986 = 100).

although evidence for investment creation in the Iberian economies is quite strong.

Figure 8.3 shows the time-paths of total investment (gross fixed capital formation) as a ratio of GDP. To emphasize the changes in the levels, all ratios are rebased to 100 in 1986, which is the year that the Single Market programme was adopted and the Iberians acceded to the EU. First, reflecting the general macroeconomic upswing of the late 1980s, all investment ratios rose (investment is pro-cyclical). Notice that the Iberians experienced a rise that was well above that of other European economies. Although it has fallen since 1990, the cumulative rise is certainty still positive. The EFTAns' ratio also rose more than that of the EU10 during the late 1980s; however, starting in 1990, their investment ratio declined much more steeply than that of the EU10 or the Iberians.

Again this provides weak evidence that EU92 improved the investment climate in those countries that participated in it, and worsened the climate in the countries that did not participate. This evidence, however, is greatly clouded by macroeconomic events. Most EFTAns experienced a three-year recession starting in 1990 or 1991. It is hard to tell whether the output fall lowered investment or vice versa. Moreover, these EFTA recessions were longer and more severe than those in EU nations. Although some of this may be related to EU92, most analysts cite purely domestic factors (e.g. domestic interest rate policies) as the main explanation of the EFTA recessions.

3   An illustrative theoretical model

In this section, we present a simple model that helps us organize our thinking about the investment diversion and investment creation effects of closer integration in the EU. At the end of this section we discuss the logical links in our model that are essential for our main results. This will make it obvious that theoretical implications are more general than the model. Since the purpose of the theory in this paper is to improve understanding of real-world events rather than to explore the limits of an existing theoretical framework, we do not undertake the important task of formally characterizing the class of models in which our main results hold.

3.1   The basic model

Consider a model with three symmetrical countries (denoted H, P, and R for home, partner, and rest of world), each with two factors and two sectors. One sector (the X sector) is marked by decreasing average costs, imperfect competition between differentiated products in segmented markets, and free entry. In the other sector (the Z sector), a homogeneous product is produced under constant returns by perfectly competitive firms. Trade in X is hindered by frictional trade barriers of the 'iceberg' type, with τ_i^j being the tariff-factor equivalent of the barrier hindering the sale of goods made in country i and sold in j (i.e. $\tau_i^j \geq 1$, $\tau_i^i = 1$, $\forall$ i, j). Trade in Z is unhindered by manmade or natural trade barriers. Countries' labour supplies are fixed, but investment and therefore the capital stocks are endogenous.

Preferences for the representative consumer in a typical country are given by a three-level utility function. The top level concerns intertemporal allocation of aggregate consumption. The second level specifies a consumption index, C, where C is a Cobb–Douglas index of consumption of differentiated products, C_X, and the homogeneous goods, C_Z, while the third level gives the sub-utility of differentiated products, C_X, as a constant elasticity of substitution (CES) index of all industrial varieties. Namely,

$$U_j = \int_0^\infty e^{-\rho t} \ln C(t) dt, \quad C = C_X^\alpha C_Z^{1-\alpha}, \quad C_X \left(\sum_{i=1}^N C_{Xi}^{(\sigma-1)/\sigma} \right)^{\frac{\sigma}{\sigma-1}}, \quad (1)$$

where N is the total number of varieties produced globally (the summation runs over all industrial goods because we assume that trade barriers are low enough to ensure that all goods are sold in all countries), and C_{Xi} and ρ are consumption of variety i and the subjective discount rate respectively. Where clarity permits, we drop the time argument to lighten the notation. For welfare calculations and various other purposes, it is convenient to express the instantaneous utility function in its indirect form. The indirect utility function for a typical country is $V[E,P] = \ln(E/P)$, where the E is national consumption expenditure and P is the perfect price index. We take consumables C as the numeraire, so $P = 1$.

The preferences permit three-stage utility maximization. The first stage determines the optimal time-path of consumption expenditure, E. The following steps determine the optimal temporal allocation of E. With free entry, national income is $rK + wL$, where r and w are the prices of capital K and labour L. Thus, the Hamiltonian for the first-stage is:

$$H[E, K, \lambda, t] = e^{-\rho t}\ln(E/P) + \lambda[rK + wL - E]. \tag{2}$$

The standard necessary conditions that characterize the evolution of the state variables K and λ are:

$$\frac{\partial H}{\partial E} = 0 \Leftrightarrow e^{-\rho t}(P/E) = \lambda P$$

$$\dot{\lambda} = -\frac{\partial H}{\partial K} \Leftrightarrow \dot{\lambda} = -\lambda r$$

law of motion $\Leftrightarrow \dot{K} = Y - E$

transversality condition $\Leftrightarrow \lim_{t\to\infty}\lambda(t)K(t) = 0 \tag{3}$

With some manipulation (involving total differentiation of the first necessary condition with respect to time and using the second condition to eliminate λ from the system), we transform these into a two-equation system with E and K as the state variables, namely:

$$\frac{\dot{E}}{E} = r - \rho, \ \dot{K} = Y - E. \tag{4}$$

These are the standard Euler equation and K's law of motion. In steady state, r equals ρ and income equals expenditure.[5] The second and third stages of utility maximization define the demand functions for a typical X variety and Z taking E as given.

Technology is defined by the Z- and X-sector cost functions:

$$b_X[w, r](\phi + x) \quad b_Z[w, r]Z, \tag{5}$$

where b_X and b_Z are the marginal cost functions, w and r are the nominal prices of labour and capital services, and $b_X[w, r]\phi$ is a fixed cost. The marginal cost functions are defined as:

$$\begin{pmatrix} b_X[w, r] \\ b_Z[w, r] \end{pmatrix} \equiv A \begin{pmatrix} w \\ r \end{pmatrix}, \quad A \equiv \begin{pmatrix} a_{xL} & a_{xK} \\ a_{zL} & a_{zK} \end{pmatrix}, \tag{6}$$

where A is the matrix of constant unit input coefficients.

X-sector firms choose a price in each market to maximize profits, ignoring the impact of their pricing decisions on aggregate variables (the price index and total expenditure). This implies that the perceived elasticity facing each X firm in each market is σ. With a fixed markup (equal to $\sigma/(\sigma - 1)$), each firm needs to sell exactly:

$$\bar{x} = \phi(\sigma - 1) \tag{7}$$

units to cover its fixed costs. Notice that $\bar{x}$ is invariant to trade policy.

In the Z sector, perfect competition and constant returns render firm size indeterminate. As usual, the indeterminacy is removed by treating the entire output of each nation's Z sector as being produced by a single price-taking firm.

Investment is quite literally assumed to be forgone consumption in this model. When we assume no international capital mobility, the national capital stock evolves as:

$$\dot{K} = Y - E \quad s.t. \ Y = rK + wL + n\Pi, \tag{8}$$

where Y and Π are national income and the profit of a typical industrial firm respectively. Note that free entry forces Π to zero in equilibrium. These relationships hold at all moments in time. We have dropped the time argument to lighten the notation.

3.2   Symmetrical steady-state equilibrium

Focusing on the symmetrical equilibrium, the equilibrium marginal costs in the X and Z sectors are given by (6). Given the competition assumptions, the producer prices of a typical X variety and Z are:

$$\begin{bmatrix} q_X \\ q_Z \end{bmatrix} = \begin{bmatrix} \frac{\sigma}{\sigma-1} & 0 \\ 0 & 1 \end{bmatrix} \begin{bmatrix} b_X \\ b_Z \end{bmatrix}. \tag{9}$$

Consumer prices are proportional to producer prices where the factor of proportionality is the trade cost that must be incurred. Note that this is zero for all Z sales and home market sales of X goods; for export sales of X varieties it is the trade cost τ.

With symmetrical countries, all countries produce some of both Z and X. Notice that, since Z is freely traded and r equals ρ in all nations, (6) implies that the w's are also equalized across nations. Consequently, all marginal costs and therefore all producer prices are equalized across nations.

Given that firm output is fixed by the zero profit condition, we can find the equilibrium number of varieties and Z production per country as a function of national labour and capital stocks:

$$\begin{bmatrix} (\phi + \bar{x})n \\ Z \end{bmatrix} = (A^{\mathrm{T}})^{-1} \begin{bmatrix} L \\ K \end{bmatrix}. \tag{10}$$

This expression turns out to be quite useful. Notice that if we know K and L in each nation, then we can uniquely determine that country's n and Z. Conversely, if we know what n must be and assume that L is fixed, then we can uniquely determine what K and Z must be. In particular, since we assumed that X is capital intensive, if a nation's n rises (with no change in L) then its K will rise and its Z will fall.

The equilibrium number of firms is simple to derive. It is easy to show that a firm's operating profits (total profit gross of fixed costs) are simply $1/\sigma$ times consumer expenditure on its goods. Given the symmetry of countries and firms, it is obvious that consumer expenditure per variety is $\alpha E/n$ where E and n are the typical expenditure and the number of firms in each nation. Zero profits require that n is such that $\alpha E/n$ equals fixed costs times σ.

3.3   Discriminatory liberalization and investment diversion

Consider the impact of forming a perfect economic union between the H and P countries. This turns the three-symmetrical-country model into a two-asymmetrical-country model. In particular, one country – which we call the economic union (EU) – has twice the population of the R country.

3.3.1   The simplest case: Perfect international capital mobility and repatriated profits

It is easy to show that, as long as factor price equalization holds, the global number of varieties of X goods implied is invariant to changes in τ.[6]

Consideration of this result and the fixity of labour stocks implies that the world capital stock is invariant to changes in τ. The importance of this fact is the following. If we assume that capital is perfectly mobile internationally *and* that all payments to foreign capital are repatriated (i.e. spent in the capital's country of origin), then the changes in capital stocks do not alter expenditure patterns. The only impact of protection will be on the location of X-sector production.

Production shifting

With all this assumed, we now turn to the analysis. We start by looking at the production-shifting effect, i.e. the fact that regional liberalization of the X sector tends to shift production of X into the liberalizing region. Denoting the equilibrium operating profit, n's, and E's for a typical EU country as $O\Pi_{EU}$, n_{EU}, and E_{EU}, and the corresponding variables for the ROW country as $O\Pi_{ROW}$, n_{ROW}, and E_{ROW}, the post-integration free-entry conditions are:

$$\phi b_X = O\Pi_{EU} = \frac{1}{\sigma}\left(\frac{2\alpha E_{EU}}{2n_{EU} + \tau^{1-\sigma}n_{ROW}} + \frac{\tau^{1-\sigma}\alpha E_{ROW}}{n_{ROW} + 2\tau^{1-\sigma}n_{EU}}\right)$$

$$\phi b_X = O\Pi_{ROW} = \frac{1}{\sigma}\left(\frac{2\tau^{1-\sigma}\alpha E_{EU}}{2n_{EU} + \tau^{1-\sigma}n_{ROW}} + \frac{\alpha E_{ROW}}{n_{ROW} + 2\tau^{1-\sigma}n_{EU}}\right) \quad (11)$$

Recall that, before integrating, $n_{EU} = n_{ROW}$. The first thing to do is to check whether this division is still an equilibrium in the post-integration steady state. To this end, we ask whether (11) holds when all E's and n's are equal to the pre-integration levels. Keeping in mind the fact that $\tau^{1-\sigma}$ is less than unity, inspection of (11) reveals that, if $n_{EU} = n_{ROW}$, then $O\Pi_{EU}$ would be greater than $O\Pi_{ROW}$. Since this would violate the equality between operating surplus and fixed costs in one or both regions, it cannot be that the EU has two-thirds of the X varieties.

Intuition for this result is as follows. The integration leads to an incipient change in a typical EU firm's sales. If the n's and E's are unaltered, then there would be no change in its sales to the ROW market. The discriminatory liberalization would, however, lower its home market sales and expand its intra-EU export sales. The important point is that the rise in intra-EU export sales outweighs the loss of home market sales. This happens because the price of all EU-produced goods falls relative to that of non-EU goods. Thus, all EU firms gain in sales from the loss of relative competitiveness experienced by ROW firms. Obversely, ROW firms experience no change in home sales, but experience an unambiguous loss of export sales. Since operating profits are proportional to sales and were initially equal to fixed costs, this incipient change in sales would produce pure profits for EU-based firms and pure losses for non EU firms. Clearly this would result in a rise in the number of EU firms and a drop in the number of ROW firms. The total number of varieties produced worldwide does not change. Another way to say this is that the discriminatory liberalization has induced production shifting in the X sector, with n_{EU} rising and n_{ROW} falling.

Investment creation and diversion
Finally we are ready to turn to investment creation and investment diversion. From (10) we see that the increase in n_{EU} would cause the EU's capital stock to rise because X is capital intensive. This is investment creation. The decrease in n_{ROW} would lower ROW's capital stock. This is investment diversion. In fact, in the simple model at hand, we could think of this as a pure diversion scenario, since the net result is nothing more than a reallocation of a constant global capital stock. However, in slightly more complex models there may be changes in the global capital stock as well; hence, investment creation will be something more than just a reallocation of a given capital stock.

Notice that investment creation and diversion are accompanied by a change in the trade pattern. The EU becomes a net exporter of X and an importer of Z.

3.3.2   No international capital mobility
Now we switch to the polar assumption of no international capital mobility. Here, similar changes in n's and K's will occur, but there are two important differences. First, since the induced capital formation in the EU must come from domestic savings, the EU's income as well as output would change. Second, since expenditure equals income in steady state, the investment creation and diversion will shift expenditure patterns. This is important because it will kick off a 'circular causality' of the type discussed in the economic geography literature (Krugman 1991). The first half-circle is the expenditure-shifting effect of the production shifting. The second half-circle concerns the way in which expenditure shifting tends to lead to more production shifting. The net result is that the total production shifting, and therefore the total investment creation and diversion, is amplified. Depending upon parameter values, this circular causality may lead all firms to leave ROW. This is the core–periphery outcome that has been heavily emphasized in the economic geography literature. As Krugman (1991) demonstrates, using a model not too unlike our model, this extreme result depends upon scale economies being strong enough and trade costs being low enough. Here

we assume that parameters are such that both regions continue to produce some X and Z goods.

It is interesting to consider the impact of the integration when capital stocks are fixed in the short run. From the full employment conditions, fixity of K and L implies fixity of n and Z. Thus, the integration cannot lead to production shifting immediately. The incipient production shifting appears as a shift up in the EU's derived demand for capital and a shift down in the ROW's demand for capital. The result is a short-run increase in r_{EU} and a short-run fall in r_{ROW}. The nominal EU wage should fall and that of the ROW should rise, owing to free trade in Z. The impact on the real wage in the EU is ambiguous, because the price of X goods tends to fall as a result of the reduction in intra-EU trade costs. Real wages in ROW should unambiguously rise in the short run, because there is no immediate change in goods prices.

3.4   Generality and ambiguities

Our main result is that discriminatory trade liberalization will raise the steady-state capital stocks in the integrating countries and reduce them in excluded countries. The economic logic of this is simple. Trade policy changes typically shift a nation's derived demand for capital and labour. If labour stocks are fixed, the result is factor price changes à la Stolper–Samuelson. If the capital stock is endogenous, then the result is induced capital accumulation or decumulation. In general, the mapping between trade policy changes and the derived demand for capital is extremely complex. In the highly structured illustrative model, the map is easily characterized. While this was useful for fixing ideas, it is certainly too simplistic to provide a useful description of the real world.

There are three important sources of ambiguity. The first has to do with the existence of more than two factors. Once we allow for capital and skilled and unskilled labour, then the mapping between trade liberalization and the demand for capital becomes ambiguous. Indeed, all we can really say is that when factor supplies are held constant at least one factor will experience a rise in its demand and at least one will experience a fall.

The second concerns the existence of more than two sectors. The discriminatory liberalization raised the relative price of ROW X-sector exports to the EU and so forced a change in the ROW trade and production pattern. In the simple model the Z sector was the only alternative use for ROW resources, so ROW labour shifted into the Z sector. This reduced the overall demand for ROW capital and thereby induced a reduction in ROW's capital stock. However, if we allow another export sector, call it the Y sector, then ROW labour may shift from the X sector to the Y sector, expanding ROW's production and exports of Y. If it is also true that the Y sector is more capital intensive than the X sector, then this shift may raise the demand for ROW capital and thereby trigger an endogenous rise in the ROW capital stock.

This is particularly important in the case of Europe because Finland, Norway, and Sweden export natural-resource-based products, such as oil, paper pulp, and minerals. As it turns out, these industries are even more capital intensive (in the sense that they have very high capital value-added shares) than most manufactured goods.

Third, allowing a more complete model of strategic interactions results in price–cost margins that depend endogenously on the market shares of firms. This introduces an additional influence on ROW and EU capital stocks stemming from changes in firm size. The point is that, when market shares affect perceived elasticities, liberalization may change equilibrium firm size. Forming the free trade area (the EU) tends to defragment two-thirds of the world market in this three-country model. This may reduce the average price and marginal cost markup charged by EU firms, forcing down the number of firms and raising the equilibrium firm size. Larger firms mean lower average cost and lower prices. This increases total X-sector output in the EU. Consequently, this pro-competitive mechanism unambiguously raises the demand for EU capital. The impact on ROW capital, by contrast, is ambiguous.

Introducing these sources of ambiguity is essential to bring the model closer to the real-world situation. Unfortunately, they also render the interactions far too complex to solve analytically. Hence, we turn now to a simulation model that allows us to resolve the ambiguities.

4   The simulation model

The simulation model employed in this paper is a variant of the Haaland–Norman simulation model. Originally presented in Haaland and Norman (1992), the Haaland–Norman model is closely related to the Gasiorek, Smith, and Venables (1992) model, which was in turn inspired by the path-breaking paper by Smith and Venables (1988).

4.1   Description of the model

The model contains four main regions: the EU, EFTA, the USA, and Japan. Production and consumption in the rest of the world are not modelled explicitly. Trade flows between our four main regions and the rest of the world are taken as fixed and invariant to policy changes. Since market integration and intra-regional trade costs play an important role, we divide the EU region into six identical markets and EFTA into five identical markets. Japan and the USA are treated as individual countries.

The production structure in each country consists of fourteen traded sectors and one non-tradable sector. The non-traded sector and one traded-good sector are modelled as perfectly competitive with constant returns. The other thirteen traded-goods sectors consist of differentiated products produced under imperfect competition and increasing returns. There are three primary factors: capital, unskilled labour, and skilled labour.

Final demand is quite similar to the theoretical model described above in that consumers are assumed to have a two-level utility function determining the pattern of consumption each period. The top level is a Cobb–Douglas function enforcing constant expenditure shares on non-traded goods, the perfect competition traded goods, and each of the thirteen differentiated goods sectors. The principal difference is that we allow for home market biases in the thirteen differentiated goods sectors. This is accomplished by including a multiplicative constant in the CES second-tier utility function.

Goods are produced using capital, skilled labour, unskilled labour, and an intermediate goods aggregate. Marginal costs in all sectors are given by nested CES functions. For the typical sector, the top level is a CES combination of a factor price index and an intermediate goods price index. Both of these indices are themselves nested CES functions. In particular, the CES factor price indices reflect sector-specific factor intensities. The intermediate goods index (which is country specific) reflects the local price of intermediate goods.

More specifically, the total and marginal cost functions for a firm in an imperfect competition sector are given by:

$$TC_k^i = MC_k^i(x_k^i + F), \quad MC_k^i = b_k^i[\omega_k^i(PV_k)^{1-\theta} + \phi_k^i(Q_k)^{1-\theta}]^{\frac{1}{1-\theta}}, \quad (12)$$

where F is the fixed cost, and x_k^i is the total quantity produced by a sector-i firm in country k. Also PV and Q are the price indices for factor prices and intermediate goods facing firms in country k, and b, ω, and ϕ are country-specific, sector-specific parameters.

The price indices in country j for factors and intermediate goods are:

$$PV_j = [\beta_j^K (w_j^K)^{1-\lambda} + \beta_j^L (w_j^L)^{1-\lambda} + \beta_j^H (w_j^H)^{1-\lambda}]^{1/(1-\lambda)},$$

$$Q_j = \left\{ \sum_{i=1}^{13} \gamma_i \left[\left(\sum_{r=1}^{N} n_r \Psi_r (p_{rj}^i)^{1-\xi} \right)^{1/(1-\xi)} \right]^{1-\mu} + \sum_{i=14}^{15} \gamma_i (p_j^t)^{1-\mu} \right\}^{1/(1-\mu)} \quad (13)$$

where w^K, w^L, and w^H are the factor prices for capital, unskilled labour, and skilled labour respectively (the subscript j indicates the producing country). Notice that Q is a nested CES price index of goods prices p. For the differentiated goods sectors ($i = 1$ to 13), goods from different origins are combined to a first-level CES aggregate (there are n_r symmetrical firms in region r, and N regions). These in turn are combined together with the two perfectly competitive sectors ($i = 14$ and 15) to the top-level CES aggregate. The parameters β, γ, and Ψ are country specific, while the elasticities λ, ξ, and μ are not country specific.

In the constant-returns-to-scale sectors, marginal cost equals average cost and prices are set at marginal cost.

The fragmentation of EU markets and the wide cross-country dispersion of prices for similar products are key aspects that EU92 was designed to address. More specifically, home firms typically have higher market shares than foreign firms. Unfortunately, the simple imperfect competition framework used in the illustrative model – namely, large-group monopolistic competition – cannot capture this market fragmentation unless one assumes unrealistically high trade costs (e.g. 50–100 per cent). The basic problem is that pricing, even to segmented markets, does not depend upon market shares, so producer prices are equalized across all markets (assuming identical demand elasticities).

To incorporate market fragmentation we assume that firms in the differentiated goods sectors play Cournot. With segmented markets, this involves firms choosing submarket-specific sales, taking as given their rivals' sales. The first-order condition for the sales of a typical country-j firm to a typical submarket k can be written as:

$$p_{jk}(1 - t_{jk}) = \left(\frac{\varepsilon_{jk}}{1 - \varepsilon_{jk}} \right) MC_j, \quad (14)$$

where ε_{jk} is the firm's perceived elasticity, t_{jk} is the cost of selling country-j goods in market k, and we drop the industry superscript to simplify the notation. With segmented markets these perceived elasticities depend on market-specific shares and elasticities of substitution. In particular, referring to the share of a country-j firm in market k as ms_{jk}, the top-level elasticity (i.e. between different industries) in country k as s_k, and the elasticity of substitution between different varieties within a typical industry as σ_k, the Nash–Cournot perceived elasticity is given by:

$$\frac{1}{\varepsilon_{jk}} = ms_{jk}\frac{1}{s_k} + (1 - ms_{jk})\frac{1}{\sigma_k}. \tag{15}$$

Firms sell their output as final goods and intermediate inputs. In this version of the model, we assume that firms do not distinguish these two sources of demand, so firms will choose a single level of sales to each submarket.[7] As a result, each variety will have a common price when sold as a final good or as an intermediate and the variables s_k and σ_k are weighted averages of the elasticities in the final demand and the intermediate markets. As we can safely assume that $\sigma_k > s_k$, firms charge higher prices where they have higher market shares. The result is reciprocal dumping.

Following Smith and Venables (1988), one of our policy experiments assumes that markets become fully integrated in the sense that firms are forced to treat all the integrating markets as a Single Market. In other words, firms cannot control the quantity sold in each submarket; they can control only total sales to the integrated market. As a result, producer prices are equalized in all such markets. Consumer prices may differ owing to bilateral trade cost differences. The threat of arbitrage via unrestricted re-exports, an end to exclusive dealerships, the emergence of international trading houses, and so on are some justifications that are provided for this switch between segmented and integrated markets.

Playing Cournot in such an integrated market implies that each firm decides its total sales to the integrated market taking as given its competitors' total sales to the same market. However, the distribution of sales between the submarkets is given by an arbitrage condition that ensures that the consumer prices differ only by the trade costs. In the integrated market case, the perceived demand elasticities depend on average market shares – rather than the position in each submarket – but 'average' is defined in a rather complicated manner.[8] As we shall see, prices are typically lower and firms typically sell larger quantities in their home markets with integrated markets. This tends to reduce trade in the integrated market, since exports based on reciprocal dumping disappear. Given that trade involves real costs, this trade reduction tends to be welfare enhancing.

As an alternative, the model could also be solved under an assumption of small-group monopolistic competition with all firms playing Bertrand.

In that case, the general first-order condition (14) still holds, but the perceived elasticity of demand is:

$$\varepsilon_{jk} = m s_{jk} s_k + (1 - m s_{jk}) \sigma_k. \tag{16}$$

Comparison of the Bertrand and Cournot perceived elasticities illuminates three important features. First, with much competition or no competition Bertrand and Cournot are equivalent. That is, as the number of firms rises and market shares approach zero, both elasticities approach σ_k. Thus, at this extreme the two approaches are equivalent to the large-group monopolistic competition framework. Moreover, when there is only a single active firm, $ms = 1$ and the two perceived elasticities are identical, this time equal to s_k. Second, for all intermediate market shares, the Bertrand elasticity exceeds the Cournot elasticity. Hence, Cournot prices will exceed Bertrand prices. Third, inspection of the formulas (using the fact that $\sigma_k > s_k$) reveals that Cournot elasticity is more sensitive to changes in the market share ms_{jk} when no firm's market share is greater than one half (as is the case in our simulation model). Therefore, producer prices are also more responsive to trade cost changes under Cournot than under Bertrand. This is particularly important when it comes to the policy experiment that assumes a switch from segmented to integrated markets, because this change directly equalizes all market shares (apart from trade cost considerations) in the integrating markets.

Previous model experiments (e.g. Smith and Venables 1988) indicate that the type of competition assumed has important implications for the results obtained. We have experimented with both Bertrand and Cournot assumptions and found that nearly all changes are much more pronounced with Cournot conjectures.

The capital stock in the model is endogenous. In particular, it is assumed to adjust to the level where the steady-state condition holds. From (10) this implies that $dE/dt = 0$, and $r = \rho$. There are no international capital flows; in that respect, the model resembles the version of the theoretical model discussed in section 3.3.2 above. We do not investigate transitional dynamics.

4.2   Calibration

The model is calibrated to the data set used in Haaland (1993). The calibration procedure is complicated, but essentially it solves the model in reverse, treating the endogenous variables (trade flows, market share, concentration, etc.) as exogenous and treating the parameters as endo-

Table 8.2   Key characteristics, base case

Model sectors	Sectoral GDP shares				Herfindahl	
	Japan	EC	EFTA	USA	EC	EFTA
NT Non-traded goods	0.579	0.621	0.619	0.678	n.a.	n.a.
N13,15 Mining, ores, & minerals	0.044	0.040	0.052	0.031	n.a.	n.a.
N17 Chemical products	0.025	0.024	0.021	0.019	0.129	0.443
N19 Metal products	0.039	0.020	0.036	0.016	0.019	0.104
N21 Agricultural & industrial machinery	0.023	0.023	0.026	0.016	0.019	0.217
N23 Office machines & precision instruments	0.012	0.008	0.012	0.016	0.308	0.270
N25 Electrical goods	0.044	0.023	0.018	0.019	0.094	0.302
N28 Transport equipment	0.029	0.025	0.015	0.028	0.359	0.199
N36 Food products	0.031	0.036	0.019	0.021	0.034	0.114
N42 Textiles, clothing, and leather	0.023	0.020	0.016	0.010	0.010	0.109
N47 Paper and printing products	0.008	0.018	0.025	0.022	0.033	0.146
N48 Timber and other n.e.s.	0.015	0.011	0.019	0.010	0.011	0.102
N49 Rubber and plastic products	0.012	0.009	0.007	0.007	0.082	0.263
N6X Transportation services	0.037	0.046	0.046	0.036	0.060	0.060
N69 Financial services	0.079	0.076	0.069	0.071	0.048	0.060

	Factor cost shares				
	Skilled labour	Unskilled labour	Capital	Scale elasticity	Elasticity of substitution
NT Non-traded goods	0.285	0.531	0.185	0	n.a.
N13+N15 Mining, ores, & minerals	0.275	0.409	0.316	0	n.a.
N17 Chemical products	0.389	0.280	0.331	0.30	3.94
N19 Metal products	0.312	0.491	0.197	0.14	8.65
N21 Agricultural & industrial machinery	0.376	0.458	0.166	0.14	8.41
N23 Office machines & precision instruments	0.536	0.301	0.163	0.30	5.83
N25 Electrical goods	0.413	0.431	0.156	0.20	7.30
N28 Transport equipment	0.303	0.463	0.234	0.24	8.97
N36 Food products	0.307	0.397	0.296	0.08	17.10
N42 Textiles, clothing and leather	0.299	0.507	0.194	0.06	18.84
N47 Paper and printing products	0.334	0.423	0.243	0.26	4.34
N48 Timber and other n.e.s.	0.322	0.510	0.168	0.10	11.42
N49 Rubber and plastic products	0.312	0.451	0.237	0.10	20.79
N6X Transportation services	0.110	0.538	0.352	0.10	23.30
N69 Financial services	0.824	0	0.176	0.10	19.61

genous. Table 8.2 shows several key aspects of the data set that we shall refer to below.

5   Results

This section discusses the results from two standard policy experiments (see, for example, Smith and Venables (1988), Gasiorek et al. (1992), Haaland and Norman (1992, 1995)). The first experiment assumes that real trade costs fall by 2.5 per cent. The second experiment assumes that, besides the trade cost reduction, firms treat the integrating markets as an integrated market rather than as segmented markets. We run two sets of simulations with these policy experiments. The first investigates discriminatory liberalization by assuming that the policy changes affect only intra-EU trade and markets. In the second set of simulations, we suppose that these policy changes apply to all EU and EFTA markets. In both sets we calculate changes with fixed and with endogenously determined (i.e. steady-state) capital stocks.

The mapping between these two sets of simulations and real-world policy is fairly straightforward. The intent of the 1992 European Economic Area (EEA) agreement was to grant Single Market status to firms based in EFTA economies. Thus, one interpretation of our results is that the difference between the two scenarios represents the gains from the EEA. As events actually evolved, Swiss voters refused to accept the EEA, and Austria, Finland, and Sweden acceded to the EU. Thus, there is a slight problem in this interpretation, since in our second scenario we assume that the Single Market covers Switzerland as well. It should, however, be emphasized that the results should not be viewed as a direct evaluation of any particular policy changes. The aim of this part of the paper is to use the simulation to learn about investment creation and diversion in a model that is too complicated to solve analytically.

5.1   Closer EU integration with EFTA6 excluded

We turn first to the scenario of discriminatory integration of the EU12, i.e. a lowering of real trade costs and a switch between segmented market pricing and integrated market pricing that affect only intra-EU12 trade. In keeping with the focus of this paper, the issue of investment creation and diversion is addressed first.

5.1.1   Investment creation and diversion
The second column of Table 8.3 presents the capital stock effects when European integration is presumed to alter firms' pricing strategies in the

Table 8.3   Changes in steady-state capital stock: EU12 integration with
EFTA6 excluded (% change from base case)

	Trade cost reduction	Integrated market pricing and trade cost reduction
EFTA	0.20	−0.64
EU12	0.26	1.66
USA	0.02	−0.01
Japan	0.01	−0.01

EU12. Investment diversion occurs in the EFTA6 and investment creation occurs in the EU12. The USA and Japan are projected to experience tiny investment diversion effects. These findings are entirely in line with the predictions of the simple model. A discriminatory liberalization leads to production shifting that tends to lower the demand for capital in the non-integrating region, raising it in the integrating region. In the short run, this should show up as a fall in the return to capital in the non-integrating regions and a rise of that in the integrating region. In the long run, capital stocks respond in order to restore the rate of return to its normal, steady-state level. The fact that the impacts on the USA and Japan are negligible is also expected since only a tiny fraction of these countries' capital stocks is dependent upon conditions in the European market.

Comparing the results in the two columns reveals two striking differences. First, the investment-creation effect in the EU12 is 540 per cent larger with market integration. Second, the EFTA6 are projected to experience a moderately large loss of capital, namely about two-thirds of 1 per cent of their initial capital stock. The impact on the USA and Japan switches signs between the two columns, but the effects are vanishingly small.

The first column of the table shows the impact of the scenario of trade cost reduction only. The most striking feature of the first column results is the lack of investment diversion. Steady-state capital stocks are projected to rise in all regions including the USA and Japan. The investment creation, however, is not evenly distributed. It is fairly small in the EU12 and EFTA – about a fourth and a fifth of 1 per cent for the EU12 and the EFTA6 (respectively) – but it is trivially small for the USA and Japan – 2 and 1 basis points, respectively.

The absence of investment diversion in the first-column scenario is unexpected and we shall explore this result in more detail below. In contrast, the huge differences in magnitudes between the column-one and

Table 8.4   Real factor price changes: EU12 integration with EFTA6 excluded and fixed capital stocks (% change from base case)

	Factor	Trade cost reduction	Market integration and trade cost reduction
EU12	Skilled labour	0.45	1.47
	Unskilled labour	0.35	1.51
	Capital	0.30	1.61
EFTA6	Skilled labour	−0.34	−0.06
	Unskilled labour	−0.13	−0.43
	Capital	0.16	−0.55

column-two results are entirely expected and found in the other simulation models of this type. For example, Smith and Venables (1988), Gasiorek et al. (1992), and Haaland and Norman (1992) have all found that market integration has a big impact on nearly all aspects of the equilibrium.

Accounting for investment creation and diversion
Changes in the steady-state capital stock can be thought of as driven by the demand for capital. If a policy change raises the demand for capital, in the sense that it raises capital's price, the steady-state supply of capital will rise. More specifically, trade policy shifts production patterns and this can alter the return to capital by the standard Stolper–Samuelson logic. Changes in the return to capital alter the return to forgone consumption and therefore lead to medium-term changes in the steady-state level. This line of reasoning directs us to investigate factor price and production pattern changes when capital stocks are held constant. The factor prices are dual measures of the changes in factor demands generated by the policy changes. The production patterns help us understand the source of the dual effects on factor prices. That is to say, using our knowledge of the capital intensity of the various sectors, alteration of the production pattern will indicate what the incipient pressures are on the EU and EFTA capital stocks.

Table 8.4 shows the impact on EU12 and EFTA6 factor prices. In the EU12, all three factor prices rise in both policy experiments; however, the magnitudes of the changes are about five times larger with market integration. In the EFTA6, capital's rental rate rises when only trade costs are reduced, but the return on EFTA labour falls. When the cost reductions are accompanied by a switch to integrated market pricing, the rental rate on EFTA capital falls significantly. The impact on labour is mixed. In the EU, both types of labour gain in both scenarios, with each group gaining approximately an equal amount. In EFTA, both types lose in both scenarios; in the market integration scenario, however, the drop in the real wage of unskilled labour is seven times larger than that of skilled workers. Furthermore, the drop in EFTA6 wages for unskilled workers is much greater with market integration than with trade cost reductions only. The opposite is true for EFTA6 skilled labourers' wages. These results are simply summary statistics for the changes in the derived demand for EFTA6 skilled and unskilled labour. As we shall see below, the pattern of factor price changes can be understood from shifts in the EFTA6 production pattern under the two policy experiments. In the first experiment (trade cost reductions only), the shrinking sectors – such as office machines and agricultural and industrial machinery – tend to be heavy users of skilled labour. In the second policy experiment, the sectors that experience the largest decline in output – especially the transport equipment sector – are quite intensive in their use of unskilled labour.

Production pattern shifts
The economics of discriminatory integration are highly complex and have not been thoroughly explored at a theoretical level. In particular, a great deal of intricacy arises from the interactions between free entry, declining average costs, and the variable markups that come with small-group monopolistic competition. Allowing endogenous capital accumulation adds an additional factor, but most of the complexity stems from the allocation, rather than the accumulation, effects. Lastly, since we calibrate the base case to data, the degree of scale economies, the initial degree of competition, and the initial level and distribution of market shares differ across the fifteen sectors. With this in mind, we turn to the projected production pattern shifts from discriminatory EU liberalization.

Figure 8.4 shows the changes in the EU and EFTA production patterns (relative to the base case) stemming from discriminatory liberalization in the EU. The fifteen sectors are arranged with the most capital intensive listed first. For instance, capital's initial factor cost share is 0.331 in chemicals, 0.194 in textiles and apparel, and only 0.18 in non-traded goods (see Table 8.2 above). The EFTA economy-wide average capital cost share (weighted by sectoral GDP shares) is about 20 per cent and lies between transport equipment and metal products. The top panel shows changes for the EU12 and EFTA6 when only trade costs are reduced. The bottom panel shows the changes for the scenarios with integrated market pricing and trade cost reduction.

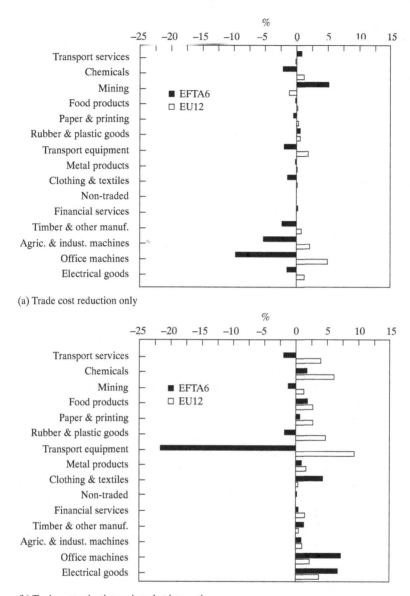

(a) Trade cost reduction only

(b) Trade cost reduction and market integration

Figure 8.4   Production changes: EU12 integration with EFTA6 excluded and fixed capital stocks.

The figure helps us explain the presence of investment diversion in the market integration case and its absence in the trade cost reduction only case. In the latter case (top panel), EFTA generally experiences an expansion of the more capital-intensive sectors and (especially) a contraction of the least capital-intensive sectors. Generally speaking, the opposite pattern appears when market integration accompanies the cost reductions. That is, EFTA's production pattern shifts towards the more capital-intensive sectors. The projected impact on EFTA transport equipment is spectacular, with a drop of over 20 per cent indicated. Given the size of this drop, it is important to note that this sector is more capital intensive (as measured by capital's factor cost share) than the average sector.

Accounting for production shifting

Theoretical analysis in Haaland and Wooton (1992) and Baldwin and Venables (1995) suggests two mechanisms by which discriminatory integration can reduce EFTA production in imperfectly competitive sectors. The first is quite simple and might be called the direct competitiveness effect. Holding constant the number of firms, discriminatory liberalization harms the competitiveness of EFTA-based firms in the EU and this reduces the optimal level of exports to the EU and output in the affected sectors. The second, which is more involved, can be called the pro-competitive mechanism or the market defragmentation mechanism.

To understand the second mechanism, consider the thought experiment of switching from segmented to integrated market pricing in a two-symmetrical-country world. Owing to trade costs, a typical firm initially has a larger share in its local market than in its export market. An immediate effect of the switch to integrated market pricing is to even out the distribution of a typical firm's market shares (as far as pricing is concerned). Because a firm's profit is convex in its shares in its various markets, the defragmentation of the two markets harms profits in both countries. The resulting exit of firms produces an industry restructuring that ends up lowering average cost and prices. That is to say, although fewer firms operate in each country, the markets are more competitive and so firms operate at a higher scale of output. In a sense, the market integration has lessened the trade-off between competition and scale economies by increasing the competitive pressures from foreign firms.

Things become more complicated when we expand this simple model to three initially symmetrical countries and consider a discriminatory market integration. As before, market integration tends to even out a typical firm's distribution of market shares in the integrating countries.

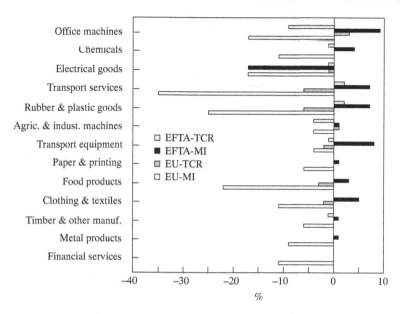

Figure 8.5   Changes in the number of firms: EU12 integration with EFTA6 excluded and fixed capital stocks.

In these countries, integration tends to lower profits, forcing exit and increasing the exploitation of scale economies, as in the two-country model. This mechanism affects the non-integrating country in a novel way. The reduction in the number of firms in the integrating countries lowers the degree of competition facing firms based in the non-integating country. With fewer foreign competitors, the non-integrating firms experience an increase in the dispersion of their local and export market shares. Convexity of profits implies that this increases their profitability and induces a rise in the number of firms in the non-integrating countries. The result of all this is a decrease in firm size in the non-integrating country, a negative scale effect, and therefore a rise in prices in the non-integrating countries.

This change in the number of firms shows up very clearly in our simulation, as Figure 8.5 demonstrates. In the figure, four bars are shown for each industry. The top two show the change in the number of EFTA firms in the two policy experiments (trade cost reduction (TCR) and market integration plus trade cost reduction (MI)). The bottom two bars show the same thing for EU firms. In all cases, capital stocks are held constant (in fact the number of firms is little influenced by allowing the capital stocks to vary endogenously). The sectors are listed according to

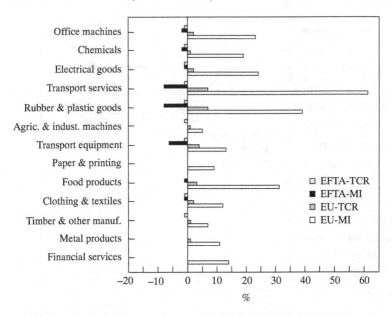

Figure 8.6   Changes in firm size: EU12 integration with EFTA6 excluded and fixed capital stocks.

scale economy elasticities, with the industries marked by the greatest scale economies listed first.

In most sectors, the number of EU firms drops and the number of EFTA firms rises, with the electrical goods sector being an exception. Generally speaking, the biggest production shifting occurs in those sectors that are subject to the largest scale economies. Moreover, it is very apparent that the EFTA6 gain the most firms in exactly the sectors that the EU loses the most firms.

Figure 8.6 shows the change in equilibrium firm sizes in the EU12 and EFTA6. Again there are four bars for each sector, ordered as in the previous figure. As we can see, EU12 firms generally enjoy increased scale in both policy experiments, while the opposite holds for EFTA6 firms. The changes in EU12 scale are remarkably large under market integration, with the average firm size in the rubber and plastic goods and transport services sectors rising more than 40 per cent.

5.1.2   Real income gains and losses

The aggregate real income effects for the discriminatory liberalization case are shown in Table 8.5. In the fixed capital stock cases, these numbers can be viewed as welfare effects. However, as Baldwin (1992)

Table 8.5   Changes in aggregate real income: EU12 integration with EFTA6 excluded (% change from base case)

	Trade cost reduction with segmented market pricing		Trade cost reduction with integrated market pricing	
	Fixed capital stock	Endogenous capital stock	Fixed capital stock	Endogenous capital stock
EU12	0.35	0.41	1.42	1.79
EFTA6	−0.13	−0.08	−0.12	−0.25
USA	−0.01	−0.00	−0.03	−0.03
Japan	−0.02	−0.02	−0.04	−0.04

pointed out, allowing for capital accumulation clouds the link between real income and welfare. The point is that some consumption must be forgone in order to accumulate capital, so the present value of utility is not well measured by the present value of real income.

Three aspects of the real income results stand out. First, the EU12 gain and the EFTA6 lose always. We could not say that this pattern of gains and losses was inevitable *a priori*. It is not unexpected, however, because the discriminatory liberalization in the EU boosts the competitiveness of EU-based firms at the expense of EFTA-based firms. The USA and Japan also lose, but their losses are trivial because only a very small fraction of US and Japanese economic activities depends upon the situation in the EU12. Second, allowing for the endogenous accumulation of capital amplifies the gain to the EU in both policy experiments. The ratio of the gains with and without endogenous capital – what Baldwin (1989) called the medium-run growth bonus – is about 1.2 for the EU in both policy experiments. In the trade cost reduction case, capital accumulation mitigates the EFTA welfare loss by about 40 per cent. In the market integration case, investment diversion doubles the EFTAns' loss.

Third, the switch between segmented and integrated market pricing has an enormous impact on real income. For instance, the EU12's gain is typically four times larger when the switch from segmented to integrated market pricing accompanies the trade cost reduction.

5.2   Results for non-discriminatory European integration

We turn now to the results of our simulations for the non-discriminatory scenario, i.e. when EU92 is extended to the EFTA6. As usual there are two policy experiments: trade cost reduction with and without a switch

Table 8.6   Changes in steady-state capital stock: EU12 integration with EFTA6 included (% change from base case)

	Trade cost reduction	Integrated market pricing and trade cost reduction
EFTA6	1.12	4.65
EU12	0.28	1.62
USA	0.02	−0.02
Japan	0.01	−0.01

from segmented to integrated market pricing. For both experiments, we consider the short-run (fixed capital stocks) and medium-run (endogenous capital stocks) cases.

5.2.1   Investment creation

Table 8.6 shows the percentage changes in capital stocks under the two policy experiments. The table has three salient features. First, in contrast to the discriminatory liberalization case, the EFTA6 experience investment creation in both experiments. Second, the magnitude of EFTA's capital stock increase is truly remarkable in the market integration experiment (almost 5 per cent of their initial capital stock). In other words, the decision to participate in the Single Market via the European Economic Area agreement (or membership) has very important economic consequences for the EFTAns. The difference between having and not having Single Market status (assuming this involves market integration as well as trade cost reductions) amounts to a change in EFTA6 capital stock of 5.3 per cent. Third, the economic impact on the EU12 is almost identical in the discriminatory and non-discriminatory cases. This latter fact results from the smallness of the EFTA6 economies. As usual, the impacts on the USA and Japan are negligible.

Figure 8.7 shows the impact of market integration on production patterns in the EU12 and EFTA6 economies. The EU12 experience an expansion in virtually every industry (this is possible with scale economies), but the expansion is biased towards capital-intensive sectors. The EFTA6 experience expanded production in all but two sectors (mining, minerals and ores, and office machines). Although mining is the second most capital-intensive sector in the model, the production pattern changes do have a bias towards capital-intensive sectors. Further evidence for this is found in the fact that the real return to EFTA6

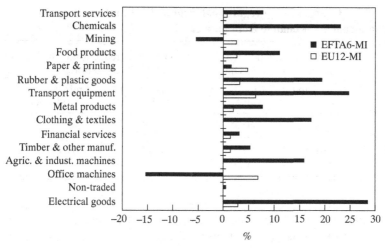

Figure 8.7 **Production changes with pan-European trade cost reduction and market integration: fixed capital stocks.**

capital jumps almost 5 per cent in the fixed capital stock case. Note that the corresponding figure for the EU12 is 1.6 per cent. The figures (not shown) are quite similar for the trade cost reduction only experiment; however, the magnitudes of the changes are muted.

5.2.2   Aggregate real income results
Table 8.7 shows the real income effects of including the EFTA6 in the EU integration. Comparing the first row of this table with that of Table 8.5, we see that including the EFTA6 in the EU's liberalization has very little impact on the EU12's real income in any of the four scenarios. The impact on the EFTA6, however, is dramatic. Looking at the scenario of market integration with endogenous capital stocks, we see that, instead of losing a small amount of incomes (-0.25 per cent), the EFTA6 gain 5.2 per cent. The same comparison holds for the other three scenarios. The impacts on the USA and Japan become slightly more negative when the EFTA6 are included; however, the change is never more than one or two basis points and the absolute size of the effects is tiny.

The importance of capital endogeneity can also be seen in Table 8.7. In the trade cost reduction only experiment, investment creation adds 15 per cent to the EU's income gains and 43 per cent to the EFTAns' income gain. For the market integration experiment, the figures are 27 per cent and 25 per cent, respectively.

Table 8.7   Changes in aggregate real income: EU12 integration with EFTA6 included (% change from base case)

	Trade cost reduction with segmented market pricing		Trade cost reduction with integrated market pricing	
	Fixed capital stock	Endogenous capital stock	Fixed capital stock	Endogenous capital stock
EU12	0.39	0.45	1.38	1.75
EFTA6	0.60	0.86	4.13	5.16
USA	−0.01	−0.01	−0.03	−0.04
Japan	−0.03	−0.02	−0.05	−0.05

It is interesting that the switch from segmented to integrated market pricing has a much larger effect on EFTA than it does on the EU. For instance, when capital stocks are endogenous, switching to integrated market pricing raises the EFTA6 income gains six-fold. The increase is even greater for the fixed capital stock case, with EFTA6 gaining 6.9 times more under integrated market pricing than under segmented market pricing. The corresponding figures for the EU are 3.9 and 3.5. It is difficult to trace the causes of such differences exactly, given the complexity of our simulation model. However, it seems likely that differences in the initial degree of concentration play an important role (see the Herfindahl indices in Table 8.2). Moreover, in most sectors, a typical EFTA6-based firm faced a larger difference between its home market share and its shares in export markets. Consequently, the market integration had a more important impact on the distribution of these shares. As explained above, narrowing a firm's market shares distribution tends to drive down profits and induce exit of firms. This industrial restructuring is typically associated with more efficient firm sizes and greater scale economies.

Evidence for this explanation is found in Figure 8.8, which shows the changes in equilibrium firm size for EFTA6 and EU12 firms in the various sectors. The figure shows that, in most sectors, the switch to integrated market pricing results in a greater expansion of the typical EFTA6 firm than the typical EU12 firm.

Bertrand conjectures

An earlier version of this paper simulated the eight scenarios (two EU policy experiments, with or without endogenous capital stocks and with the EFTA6 included or excluded) using Bertrand conjectures instead of Cournot conjecture in the thirteen sectors marked by small-group mono-

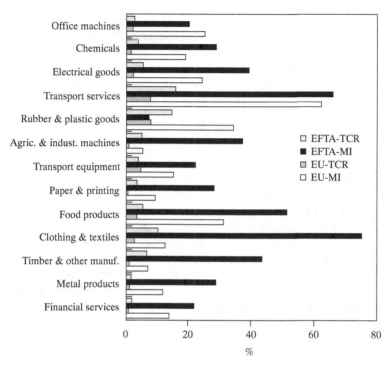

Figure 8.8 **Firm size changes with pan-European integration and fixed capital stocks.**

polistic competition. As expected, the simulation results are quite different for the Bertrand case. In particular, we find that investment diversion never occurs and all of the real income effects are small. Capital stocks in the EU, EFTA, the USA, and Japan all rise as a result of closer integration among the EU12, although the rise in the EU's capital stock is much more pronounced.

6 Summary and concluding remarks

In this paper we looked at the investment creation and investment diversion effects of the EU's Single Market programme in three ways. First we presented suggestive, but not conclusive, evidence indicating that the EU's Single Market programme may have led to investment diversion in the EFTA countries and investment creation in Spain and Portugal.

Secondly, we presented a simple model that allows us to illustrate the main channels through which discriminatory integration could lead to investment creation and diversion. The model shows that, if capital-intensive traded goods are subject to discriminatory liberalization, the resulting shift in production tends to increase the steady-state capital stock of the integrating region and decrease it in the rest of the world. This unambiguous result depends heavily on the specific structure of the model. In a more general model, many other effects arise and these may reverse the conclusion. A more detailed computable equilibrium model (which is closely related to the well-known Haaland–Norman model) is used to simulate the investment creation and diversion effects of European integration.

The simulations confirm the possibilities of investment diversion; however, the effects depend strongly both on the structure of the model and on the structural changes that take place in the economies. Hence, the simulations emphasize the need for general equilibrium simulation studies. The results show that for the EFTA countries the investment effects of EU92 vary from investment diversion, when staying outside the Single Market, to fairly strong investment creation, when EFTA is part of the Single Market. In all cases, the EU experiences investment creation, while the effects on the USA and Japan are trivially small.

Notes

Baldwin and Forslid thank the Swiss National Science Foundation (Subsidy #12-33801) and the CEPR's MIRAGE project for supporting this project. We also thank the Research Council of Norway for financial support. Many thanks to Victor Norman, Tony Venables, Elhanan Helpman, and Gene Grossman for helpful comments and suggestions.
1. See Oxelheim (1994) and Andersson and Fredriksson (1993).
2. See Baldwin (1994: 13–15) for details.
3. See Baldwin (1994) for further analysis of the EEA agreement. The *Acquis Communautaire* is the term for primary EU law. This includes the Treaty of Rome, subsequent treaties, and secondary law adopted under the Treaty of Rome. This concerns regulations, directives, and decisions as well as the relevant case law of the EU Court of Justice. Each year approximately 2,000 new legal acts, decisions, and directives are added to the *Acquis*.
4. See Baldwin (1994: Ch. 1) and CEPR (1992) for details.
5. In a model with an exogenous force driving growth, the steady-state growth rate and the evolution of the price index would enter the steady-state condition.
6. Operating surplus is proportional to sales in this model and expenditure on each sector is fixed by the Cobb–Douglas preferences. Consequently, total operating surplus – and therefore the number of fixed costs that can be paid for – is invariant to trade policy.
7. In previous versions of the model, there has been a clear distinction between the markets for final demand and for intermediates, with Cournot competi-

tion in the final demand market and (large-group) monopolistic competition in the intermediate markets (see Haaland and Norman (1992)).

8. See Haaland and Norman (1992) for a version of the model specification in this case, and Haaland and Wooton (1992) for a discussion of the market conditions with integrated markets.

References

Andersson, Thomas and T. Fredriksson (1993), 'Sveriges val, EG och directinvesteringar', IUI, Bilaga 7 till EG-Konsekvensutredningen, Samhallsekönomi.

Baldwin, Richard E. (1989), 'Growth Effects of 1992', *Economic Policy* 9(2): 247–81.

(1992), 'Measurable Dynamic Gains from Trade', *Journal of Political Economy* 100(1): 162–74.

(1994), *Towards an Integrated Europe*. London: CEPR.

Baldwin, Richard E. and Anthony Venables (1995), 'Regional Economic Integration'. In G. Grossman and K. Rogoff (eds.), *Handbook of International Economics*, vol. III. Amsterdam: North-Holland.

CEPR (1992), *Is Bigger Better? The Economics of EC Enlargement*, Monitoring European Integration 3. London: Centre for Economic Policy Research.

EFTA (1991), *EFTA Trade 1990*. Geneva: EFTA Secretariat.

(1992), *EFTA Trade 1991*. Geneva: EFTA Secretariat.

Emerson, Michael (1988), *The Economics of 1992*. Oxford: Oxford University Press.

Gasiorek, Michael, Alasdair Smith, and Anthony Venables (1992), '"1992": Trade and Welfare – A General Equilibrium Analysis'. In L. Alan Winters (ed.), *Trade Flows and Trade Policy after '1992'*. Cambridge: CEPR and Cambridge University Press.

Haaland, Jan I. (1993), 'Welfare Effects of 1992: A General Equilibrium Assessment for EC and EFTA Countries', *Empirica* 20: 107–27.

Haaland, Jan I. and Victor D. Norman (1992), 'Global Production Effects of European Integration'. In L. Alan Winters (ed.), *Trade Flows and Trade Policy after '1992'*. Cambridge: CEPR and Cambridge University Press.

(1995), 'Regional Effects of European Integration'. In R. Baldwin, J. Kiander, and P. Haaparanta (eds.), *Expanding Membership of the European Union*. Cambridge: Cambridge University Press.

Haaland, Jan I. and Ian Wooton (1992), 'Market Integration, Competition and Welfare'. In L. Alan Winters (ed.), *Trade Flows and Trade Policy after '1992'*. Cambridge: CEPR and Cambridge University Press.

Krugman, Paul (1991), *Geography and Trade*. Cambridge, Mass.: MIT Press.

Oxelheim, Lars (1994), *The Global Race for Foreign Direct Investment*. Bonn: Springer-Verlag.

Smith, Alasdair and Anthony Venables (1988), 'Completing the Internal Market in the European Community: Some Industry Simulations', *European Economic Review* 32: 1501–25.

Vickerman, R. W. (1992), *The Single European Market*. London: Harvester Wheatsheaf.

Discussion

ALASDAIR SMITH

This paper embeds an analysis of European integration based on imperfect competition in a model in which capital accumulation takes place. The task is accomplished with elegance and the possible links between microeconomic change and long-run dynamics are clearly established.

The motivation for the analysis is provided by the striking data on foreign direct investment flows shown in Figure 8.1, which strongly suggests that European integration has significant effects on foreign direct investment flows. The underlying model combines imperfect competition with a Heckscher–Ohlin approach. Capital and labour are intersectorally mobile and there are intersectoral differences in factor intensities. The Single Market is modelled as having the same impact effect in all sectors but, because of differences in trade patterns and in the competitive structure of sectors, intersectoral resource movements take place. The model then has the third layer of endogenous capital accumulation, so the effects of policy on steady-state capital stocks can be derived. (Most of the interpretation of the results is presented in terms of the effects on factor demand for given capital stocks, so the endogeneity of capital does not have a major role in the analysis.)

This approach sees the impact of European integration on capital flows as resulting from differential sectoral effects of integration. For example, Tables 8.3 and 8.4 present the striking result that the Single Market programme has a positive effect on the demand for capital in EFTA countries excluded from the programme if the Single Market is seen just as reducing intra-EU trade barriers, whereas it has a negative effect if the Single Market results in firms treating the EU as an integrated market in which price discrimination is impossible. The difference in the two cases depends on the complex interaction of market structures, trade patterns, and factor intensities, but the broad result is that simple trade cost reduction has its most adverse effects for EFTA in the less capital-intensive sectors, while market integration has its most adverse effects for EFTA in the more capital-intensive sector.

However, it is questionable whether the data in Figure 8.1 should be interpreted as showing the effect on capital-intensive Single-Market-sensitive sectors in the EFTA countries of the Single Market programme and its extension to the EEA. The literature on foreign direct investment cautions strongly against treating FDI as a vehicle for international capital mobility and instead emphasizes the importance of firm specific advantages. Perform the thought experiment of imagining that the Single Market programme was known to have its main impact on labour-intensive service sectors. According to the model presented here, the effect of excluding the EFTA countries from the Single Market would then be to transfer resources into capital-intensive sectors and to generate an investment *boom* in the excluded countries. In reality it is much more plausible that exclusion would cause an outflow of sector-specific FDI from service sectors in EFTA and a macroeconomic depression, and the transfer of resources to other sectors would follow much later only after factor prices had adjusted and macroeconomic conditions recovered.

The other big question I have about the analysis concerns the sensitivity of the results to parameters on which we are ill informed. The policy experiments assume that the impact of the change on trade costs is uniform across sectors, even though we now have information (for example, from Buigues et al. (1990), and from the European Commission's 1990 *ex post* study) on the intersectoral impacts of the programme. The results are driven by the sectoral distribution of the full effects of the Single Market programme, and must therefore be quite sensitive to assumptions about the sectoral distribution of the impact effects.

Thus, the broad prediction of Table 8.3 that market integration in the EU would have adverse effects on the demand for capital in excluded EFTA countries could first be questioned on the grounds that the Single Market might well have bigger impacts in less capital-intensive sectors such as financial services. Then the role of the transport equipment sector in the analysis deserves scrutiny. It is the most concentrated sector and therefore the one in which market integration has the most pro-competitive effects in the EU, so a small negative effect for EFTA from trade cost reduction becomes a large negative effect in the case of market integration. But the renegotiated restrictions on Japanese car imports and the consequent renewal of the block exemption for car distribution arrangements cast doubt on whether market integration will actually be achieved in the transport equipment sector.

Furthermore, given that the assumed impact of the policy change is the same in all sectors, the intersectoral differences in final effects are generated by the interaction of trade patterns, factor intensities, market structure, and scale economies. The latter three are captured by parameters in which we cannot have a high degree of confidence and their effects on the pattern of results must be quite sensitive also to the degree of sectoral aggregation. The analysis must therefore be read as using the example of the Single Market programme to illustrate the properties of the model rather than as providing particularly credible estimates of the impact of the programme in reality.

References

Buigues, P., Ilzkovitz, F., and Lebrun, J.-F. (1990), 'The Impact of the Internal Market by Industrial Sector: The Challenge for the Member States', *European Economy*, special issue.

European Commission, Directorate-General for Economic and Financial Affairs (1990), 'Economic Evaluation of the Internal Market', *European Economy*, no. 4.

9 Blueprints, spillovers, and the dynamic gains from trade liberalization in a small open economy

THOMAS F. RUTHERFORD
and DAVID G. TARR

1 Introduction

International trade economists have typically argued that an open trade regime is very important for economic development. This view has been based partly on neoclassical trade theory, which generally finds that a country improves its welfare from trade liberalization; partly on casual empirical observation that countries that remain highly protected for long periods of time appear to suffer significantly and perhaps cumulatively; and partly on systematic empirical work that also finds trade liberalization beneficial to welfare and growth (e.g. World Bank (1987) and Sachs and Warner (1995)). What has been troubling is that the numerical estimates of the impact of trade liberalization have generally found that trade liberalization increases the welfare of a country by only about 1 per cent of GDP, gains that are small in relation to the paradigm.[1]

With the development of endogenous growth theory (for example, Romer (1990), Grossman and Helpman (1991), and Segerstrom et al. (1990)) a clear theoretical link has been provided from trade liberalization to economic growth. Owing to the complexity of the models, the theoretical literature has necessarily been based on rather aggregated models, and has focused on the steady-state growth path. In this paper we develop a dynamic numerical, which allows us to derive a number of interesting properties. One contribution of our paper relative to the theoretical literature is that we trace out the dynamic adjustment path of all the variables in the model and evaluate the welfare consequences of a change in policies; i.e. two policies that achieve the same steady-state growth path could have very different welfare consequences as a result of the dynamic adjustment path.

The basic features of our dynamic small open economy model are as follows. The model is defined over a thirty-one-year horizon, from 1990

269

to 2020. There are two sectors, X and Y. The Y sector produces only final goods and produces under constant returns to scale (CRTS). Inputs into Y are labour, capital, and a pure intermediate good X. The good X is produced by both foreign and domestic firms under the large-group monopolistic competition assumption and increasing returns to scale (IRTS).[2]

We employ the by now standard assumption that inputs of X affect the production of Y according to a Dixit–Stiglitz function. This means that additional varieties of X reduce the cost of producing Y. Domestic firms in the IRTS sector must incur a once-and-for-all fixed cost of a 'blueprint' in order to introduce a new product; and both domestic and foreign firms incur a fixed cost in any period in which they operate. All agents in the model, including firms in the IRTS sector, optimize over the infinite horizon with perfect foresight apart from unanticipated policy changes. Following Grossman and Helpman and others, in our benchmark steady-state equilibrium growth path and our basic scenarios we assume that an increase in the number of foreign varieties has the spillover effect of reducing the costs of blueprints for domestic firms. (See Keller (1995) for an analysis of R&D spillovers and a survey of the empirical literature.)

The sole distortion in the economy in the benchmark data set is a 10 per cent tariff on imports in the X sector. We establish a benchmark steady-state growth path and after removing the tariff compare all variables with their benchmark value in the counterfactual.

Some of our most important results are as follows. In our basic scenario we find that welfare (Hicksian equivalent variation) increases by 7.2 per cent of the present value of consumption, a rather large increase for a tariff rate of only 10 per cent in an economy with less than 15 per cent of its GDP coming from imports. With higher tariff rates, as exist in many developing economies, the gains from liberalization would be much larger because the gains from liberalization increase with the tariff cut. Moreover, the dynamic path of consumption is increasing, so that in later years of the model the economy is consuming at more than 8 per cent higher than the benchmark steady-state level. Thus, we believe these results support the paradigm that trade liberalization leads to significant income increases. As a result of increased competition from foreign varieties, the domestic industry declines sharply in the first four years, but owing to spillovers it begins to recover subsequently.

Perhaps our most striking result is that we do not need spillovers to generate the large welfare gains. What is crucial to the large welfare gains is the availability of increased varieties (see Romer (1994) for a similar view). We construct a model identical in all respects to our basic model, but in which there are no spillovers through which additional foreign varieties reduce blueprint costs of domestic firms. Not surprisingly, the domestic industry declines monotonically and by 2020 is dramatically reduced. What may be surprising is that the welfare benefit to the economy does not decrease in this case (it is about 8.2 per cent of the present value of consumption), and the growth path of consumption increases faster. The reason is that the economy still obtains the benefits of increased varieties of X, deriving entirely from increased foreign varieties (in fact it obtains additional total varieties because foreign firms do not need to cover blueprint costs), and domestic resources shift to the CRTS sector in greater quantities. Since our model employs the Chamberlinian large-group assumption, the markup over fixed costs remains unchanged; i.e. there are no rationalization gains. Thus, this scenario shows that the Ethier–Dixit–Stiglitz characterization of production, where additional varieties lower costs, is sufficient to generate the large welfare gains and increase in consumption. Since whether or not there are spillovers is somewhat controversial, this provides stronger support for the trade liberalization paradigm.

We investigate the impact of pre-announcement in 1990 of the tariff cut in 1995. Contrary to what is sometimes alleged, it is not clear that adjustment costs are reduced by pre-announcement. Although forward-looking firms start to adjust immediately before the implementation of the tariff cut (reducing adjustment costs between 1990 and 1992), another sharp drop in domestic production occurs in the year of implementation of the tariff cut. Moreover, the welfare gain is reduced because the economy lives with the tariff for an additional five years, and the rapid adjustment is optimal because all adjustment costs are internalized by the firms. In another model variant we allow capital flows. This has the opposite impact: it slightly increases the welfare gains and increases the adjustment costs.

We also investigate the impact of two alternative modelling assumptions for firm behaviour sometimes employed in the literature: myopic firms, i.e. firms that operate for only one period, and competitive firms. Myopic firms do not capitalize the stream of quasi-rents into the indefinite future, and consequently the rate of entry of foreign firms in the early years is less dramatic. Thus, we find that the welfare gains, growth rate of consumption, and adjustment costs are all muted compared with the model with forward-looking firms. None the less, welfare gains remain at close to 7 per cent of the present value of consumption. With competitive firms, we must drop the Dixit–Stiglitz variety assumption and the welfare gains over the thirty-year horizon fall to 0.3 per cent.

Based on the econometric estimates of Roberts et al. (1995), we have chosen the value of 3 for the Dixit–Stiglitz elasticity of substitution among intermediate varieties. The results are sensitive to this elasticity. We have found that, with a Dixit–Stiglitz elasticity this small, even the comparative static analog to our dynamic model produces large estimates of the welfare gain – about one-third of the gains in the dynamic model.

2   The model

We consider a two-sector economy. The Y sector produces exports and final goods for the domestic market under constant returns to scale and perfect competition. The X sector, which is composed of both domestic and foreign firms, produces intermediate goods under increasing returns to scale and imperfect competition with a Dixit–Stiglitz representation of the impact of increases in the number of products on productive efficiency in the Y sector. Markups of goods in the IRTS sector are based on the Chamberlinian large-group assumption – that is, the elasticity of demand facing the representative firm is equal to the elasticity of substitution between varieties.

2.1   Consumer behaviour

The intertemporal utility function of the infinitely lived representative consumer equals the discounted sum of the utility of consumption over the horizon:

$$U = \left(\sum_t \Delta^t C_t^\rho \right)^{\frac{1}{\rho}}.$$

In this equation, parameter ρ controls the intertemporal elasticity of substitution[3] and Δ is the single-period discount factor. Aggregate consumption in a given period (C_t) is a Cobb–Douglas aggregate of consumption of domestic and imported final goods:

$$C_t = CD_t^{\alpha_D} CM_t^{1-\alpha_D}.$$

We assume that imported final goods cannot be produced in the home market, owing to technical limitations of the domestic final goods sector. The intertemporal and within-period consumption decisions are weakly separable. Thus, the typical static first-order condition applies on consumption decisions within a time-period, given a decision on how much to spend on consumption in any period. In the standard manner, the intertemporal decision is based on the maximization of the intertemporal utility function subject to the constraint that the present value of income less expenditures is zero:

$$\max U = \left(\sum_t \Delta^t CD_t^{\alpha_D \rho} CM_t^{(1-\alpha_D)\rho} \right)^{\frac{1}{\rho}}$$

s. t.

$$p_{K0} K_0 + \sum_t w_t L_t + \Pi_0^D + \sum_t T_t - \sum_t p_{Dt} CD_t - \sum_t p_{Mt} CM_t = 0.$$

In this expression, all prices are defined in present-value terms, discounted to period 0 (= 1990). The present value of income includes the value of the entering (period 0) capital stock, the present value of wage income, and the value of any pure profits or losses that accrue to existing domestic firms. In a steady-state equilibrium, there are no pure profits, but along an adjustment path moving to a new steady state these profits may be non-zero. In other words, pure profits and losses are associated only with current (extant) firms. All firms formed during the model horizon earn zero economic profit.

2.2   Sales and production of the final good

Good Y is produced as differentiated products for sale in the domestic and international markets. Products destined for these markets are differentiated and the relative magnitude of sales at home and abroad is determined by relative prices. This is in effect an Armington-style differentiation of products in the export market. A constant elasticity of transformation (CET) function relates the composite output level in a given period to domestic and export sales. Firms producing the final good maximize profit subject to the constraint:

$$Y_t = \left[\theta_D \left(\frac{D_t}{\bar{D}_t} \right)^{1+\eta} + (1 - \theta_D) \left(\frac{E_t}{\bar{E}_t} \right)^{1+\eta} \right]^{\frac{1}{1+\eta}}.$$

In this equation, parameters $\bar{D}$ and $\bar{E}$ are the base-year (benchmark) levels of output to the domestic and export markets, and θ_D is the value share of domestic sales in total sales.

Production of this composite is associated with a nested production function whose three inputs are composite intermediates (X), capital, and labour. Given prices of intermediate goods, capital, and labour, firms minimize the costs of producing any output level:

$$Y = \min\left(\frac{X(X_D, X_F)}{\bar{X}}, \frac{V(LY_t, KY_t)}{\bar{V}}\right).$$

In this function, the intermediate input composite and value-added enter in fixed proportion to their base-year input. At the second level, we account for substitution between domestic and foreign varieties of X:

$$X = (X_D^\rho + X_F^\rho)^{1/\rho},$$

in which the effective supply of X from all type-f firms is described by:

$$X_f \equiv \left(\sum_{i=1}^{n_f} x_{if}^\rho\right)^{1/\rho} = (n_f x_f^\rho)^{1/\rho} = n_f^{\frac{1-\rho}{\rho}} \tilde{X} \qquad f \in \{D, F\}$$

in which $x_{if} = x_f$ (by symmetry) is output of a representative type-f firm, $\tilde{X} = n_f x_{if}$ is the total output from type-f firms, and $n_f^{(1-\rho)/\rho} = n_f^{1/(\sigma-1)}$ is the 'variety effect multiplier' which depends on $\sigma > 1$, the elasticity of substitution between firms. The second equation in this expression reflects our assumption of symmetrical firm structure.

The value-added composite for the production of Y is a simple Cobb–Douglas aggregate of labour and capital inputs:

$$VA(KY, LY) = KY^\alpha \, LY^{1-\alpha}.$$

Output of the good Y supplied to the domestic market can be consumed or invested. Investment in the X_D, X_F, and Y sectors involves forgone consumption of domestic output. The market clearance for Y-sector output sold in the domestic market is given by:

$$D_t = CD_t + I_t^Y + I_t^{XD} + I_t^{XF}.$$

In this equation, I_t^{XD} and I_t^{XF} are demands for domestic inputs to capital investments for domestic and foreign firms producing good X. Domestic firms make investments in plant and equipment, whereas foreign firms, which generally import all the key components, invest solely in distribution facilities such as warehouses and transportation equipment.

2.3   Investment and physical capital formation

We follow Uzawa (1969) among others by assuming that investment in all sectors (X_D, X_F, and Y) reflects adjustment costs of installation. We formalize Uzawa's model using the same strategy as Goulder and Summers (1989) and McKibbin and Wilcoxen (1995). Adjustment costs increase with the square of the level of investment relative to the capital stock:

$$I_t^k = J_t^k \left(1 + \phi \frac{J_t^k}{K_t} \right).$$

This equation applies for sector-specific capital in Y, X_D, and X_F and in each period of the model. I_t measures forgone consumption due to investment (i.e. gross investment). Adjustments imply that only J_t^k (net investment) contributes to capital formation in the subsequent period. The difference between gross and net investment reflects the installation costs of capital formation. This formulation penalizes rapid expansion of the capital stock in the short run, but capital formation in the long run remains a constant-returns-to-scale activity as in the traditional Ramsey model. (Further details on our representation of the adjustment cost framework are provided in Appendix A.)

In our model, capital is sector specific following installation, and investment rates may fall to zero as a consequence of unanticipated changes in policy parameters.

Following a standard Solow growth model, investment in period t creates additional capital for production in the future, and the capital stock depreciates at a constant rate. This is represented by:

$$K_{t+1}^k = \lambda K_t^k + J_t^k,$$

which likewise applies for k = Y, X_D, and X_F.

2.4   Firms and production varieties

In sector X there is a one-to-one correspondence between firms and product varieties. The production of good X by firm f involves both fixed and variable costs. Variable costs include both capital and labour inputs. Fixed costs can have two components: (i) 'overheads', a recurring fixed capital cost that is incurred in every period that the firm operates, and (ii) 'setup costs', a one-time research and development (or blueprint) cost that must be incurred in order to produce a new product. For simplicity, we assume that blueprint costs are incurred solely by domestic firms whereas foreign firms license designs from abroad. We model the production of blueprints by domestic firms through the input of a single factor of production, labour. We assume in the present model that there is no international trade in blueprints. Hence firms may not license designs but must pay engineers to develop new products from scratch.

In the benchmark data set we find that most of the costs for foreign firms selling in the domestic market are associated with capital services and imported goods. In this setting the foreign firm's fixed costs of production may be interpreted as the cost of maintaining a distribution system within the country.

The model is deterministic and firms have perfect (point) expectations of future prices. Hence, a new firm will enter at time t if and only if there are positive net quasi-rents. This happens when the present value of markup revenue[4] over marginal costs into the future is equal to or greater than the present value of the fixed costs of operation, including fixed operating costs (for foreign and domestic firms) and the fixed costs of product development (for domestic firms). It is possible to interpret this decision using Tobin's q theory (see Baldwin et al. (1996)). The rate of investment in blueprints occurs to the point that the stock market value of the net income (i.e. the present value of net surplus) equals the replacement costs, namely the marginal cost of a blueprint, since R&D is perfectly competitive.

The Dixit–Stiglitz production function for good X is perfectly symmetrical with respect to domestic and foreign firms; i.e. we have firm-level product differentiation, with no brand or national preferences. Varieties of different vintages are equally preferred but differentiated. In this framework, all domestic firms that operate sell the same quantity of output and their varieties sell for the same markup-inclusive price. Likewise, all foreign firms that operate sell the same quantity at the same price. Domestic and foreign firms enter symmetrically in the final goods production function, so the derived demand for domestic and foreign intermediates is symmetrical; but they remain differentiated and their prices may therefore differ. Because foreign and domestic firms are treated differently regarding their cost structures, their prices usually differ.

We make a special assumption about the life-cycle of products and firms. This assumption applies for both domestic and foreign firms. Because we track markup revenue for both firm types, we are concerned primarily with how market shares for a particular vintage of a given firm type change over time. Let n_v equal the number of new firms introduced at time v. *We assume that the number of vintage-v firms that produce at later dates declines exponentially at a rate equal to the depreciation rate of physical capital.* Hence, we assume that at a time $t > v$, the number of vintage-v firms that remain in business is $n_v \lambda^{t-v}$.

Furthermore, we assume that any firm producing at time t produces the same quantity as all other firms, irrespective of vintage, but differing according to whether it is foreign or domestic. This implies that the share of total output produced by firms of vintage v is equal to the share of vintage-v firms in the total number of firms, i.e.:[5]

$$\theta_{vt} = \frac{n_v \lambda^{t-v}}{N_t} = \frac{n_v \lambda^{t-v}}{\sum_{\tau < t} n_\tau \lambda^{t-\tau}}.$$

These life-cycle assumptions impose a symmetrical structure on the equilibrium, which makes it possible to account for the share of markup revenue available in any period received by firms of vintage v.

The zero-profit condition for firms of vintage v is then:

$$[c_v^B f_B + \sum_{t>v} c_t^K f_K] = \sum_{t>v} \theta_{vt} M_t / n_v.$$

This expression accounts for markup revenue in all periods $t > v$, including the post-horizon period. This formulation extends the free-entry zero-profit model from a static to an intertemporal framework. Within this model, intertemporal lags and the time-path of future prices affect not only investment activity but the decisions by firms to enter markets and undertake product development. Optimization over the infinite horizon applies not only to consumers and competitive firms, but also to the managers of monopolistically competitive firms.[6]

Our model is one of a small open economy. In particular, we assume that the small open economy has only a negligible impact on the number of varieties available on world markets and on the cost of blueprints for foreign firms. In general, we observe that there are many more varieties of products available on world markets than are available in the small open economies. Accordingly, we assume that the decision facing foreign firms is how many of the products for which blueprints already exist can be profitably introduced into the small open economy; i.e. there is no blueprint cost for foreign firms associated with the introduction of a new product into the small open economy, but there are significant fixed costs associated with selling in the domestic market.

Analogous to the approach of Grossman and Helpman (1991), the number of varieties available on domestic markets reduces the cost of blueprints for domestic firms, according to the equation:

$$f_{\mathrm{B}} = \bar{f}_{\mathrm{B}} \left[2 - \left(\frac{N_{\mathrm{f}}}{\bar{N}_{\mathrm{f}}} \right)^{2} \right].$$

Thus, there is a spillover effect from foreign varieties such that an increase in the number of foreign varieties reduces the cost of a blueprint for domestic firms. We show that the spillover effect is fundamental. Without the spillover effect, the progressive reduction of the costs of blueprints for foreign firms leads to the progressive elimination of the domestic industry.

There is an asymmetric treatment of foreign firms for which we assume that blueprints are not required for entering the market; we assume that the economy is sufficiently small that the international supply of blueprints for foreign firms is essentially infinite. The entry decision for foreign firms hinges solely on the fixed costs of maintaining a marketing and distribution system in the country.

3   Benchmark data and calibration

For the purposes of exploring the implications of this theoretical model, we have implemented a stylized data set that bears some resemblance to the 1990 social accounts for Tunisia. We intend ultimately to develop a true empirical application of the model, but for the present paper we have restricted ourselves to a simple two-sector framework.

We construct a benchmark steady-state equilibrium before trade liberalization and then compare the results of the new equilibrium path of variables after trade liberalization with the corresponding values in the baseline model. Our model runs for thirty-one annual periods from 1990 to 2020. Owing to terminal effects associated with the infinite horizon approximation, we focus on the period 1990–2010, recognizing that results in the final five–ten years are to some extent dependent on our terminal conditions. (We investigate the magnitude of these effects in a sensitivity analysis presented at the end of the paper.)

We consider an economy that has only one distortion in the benchmark period, a 10 per cent tariff on imported intermediate goods.[7] The benchmark social accounting matrix is presented in Table 9.1, together with the values of all elasticities employed in the base case.

The data presented in Table 9.1 are in the form of a 'rectangular social accounting matrix', in which we have one row for every market and one column for each production sector and consumer. In the present model, there are four production sectors (Y, X_{D}, X_{F}, and I) and one consumer (column FD). This data table contains both positive and negative entries.

Table 9.1   Benchmark social accounting data and elasticities

Social accounting data (with some resemblance to Tunisia 1989)

	Macro output	Intermediate input		Investment	Final demand	
	Y	X_D	X_F	I	FD	
p_D	6.5			−2.0	−4.5	Domestic supply of Y
p_{FX}	2.5		−1.0	−1.0	−0.5	Foreign exchange
p_{XD}	−2.0	2.0				Domestic X (from firm D)
p_{XF}	−2.0		2.0			Imported X (from firm F)
p_L	−3.0	−1.0			4.0	Labour
p_K	−2.0	−1.0	−0.8		3.8	Capital
p_S				3.0	−3.0	Savings and investment
T_X			−0.2		0.2	Import tariff

Key elasticities

ESUB_X	Intra-firm elasticity of substitution in X	3.0
ESUB_T	Intertemporal elasticity of substitution	0.5
ETRN_Y	Elasticity of transformation in sector Y	2.0

Note: ESUB_X affects monopolistic competition and the gains-from-variety model. When this is a small number (closer to unity), we have much larger gains-from-variety effects.

Other assumptions

G	Rate of growth of the labour force	0.05
RDCOST	R&D cost share of benchmark labour inputs in X	0.20
GAMMA	Spillover transmission coefficient	2.00
LAMDA	One-year survival share for physical capital	0.93
PHI	Adjustment cost parameter	0.30

Sectors from the 1990 IO table included in sector X

31	produits sidérurgiques & métaux non ferreux & produits de fonderie
32	ouvrages en métaux
33	machines et équipements agricoles et industriels
34	automobiles & camions & cycles
35	matériels de transport divers et leur reparation
36	matériel électrique
37	matériel électronique
38	équipements ménagers
41	engrais
42	autres produits chimiques de base
43	produits de la parachimie
44	produits pharmaceutiques
45	articles en caoutchouc & pneumatiques

Table 9.1   (*cont*).

61	produits des industries du bois
62	papier & livres & journaux et disques
63	produits en matières plastiques
64	produits divers
65	minérais et minéraux
66	pétrole brut et produits petroliers & gaz
77	services de transport
78	services de poste et de télécommunication

A positive entry signifies a receipt (sale) in a particular market. A negative entry signifies an expenditure (purchase) in a particular market. Reading down a production column, we then observe a complete list of the transactions associated with that activity. For example, we can see that sector Y sells 6.5 in the domestic goods market (p_D) and 2.5 in the export market. The costs of production required to produce this output include 2 each of domestic and imported (foreign) X input, 3 of labour, and 2 of capital. The column sums for each of the production sectors are zero, indicating a balance between the costs of production and the value of output.

In static general equilibrium models, there is no need to distinguish between the benchmark return to capital and the value of the capital stock at market prices. In dynamic models, we must make such a distinction. The social accounting data in Table 9.1 reveal the gross return to capital ($\bar{V}_K$) and the value of investment costs ($\bar{I}$), but they do not report the value of the benchmark capital stock or the gross rate of return.

We solve a system of equations given base-year investment and capital earnings in order to infer the rate of time preference (the net interest rate) that is consistent with the base-year data being a steady-state equilibrium. The system of equations we solve corresponds to optimality conditions for investment in this environment.[8]

(1) Benchmark capital formation equals growth plus depreciation of the capital stock:

$$J = (\bar{\delta} + \bar{g})K.$$

(2) Investment inputs are related to capital formation through the cost-of-adjustment model:

$$\bar{I} = J\left(1 + \frac{\bar{\phi}}{2}\frac{J}{K}\right).$$

(3) The present value of new capital produced in the subsequent period is equal to the marginal cost in current prices:

$$p_K(1 - r) = 1 + \bar{\phi}\frac{J}{K},$$

in which r is the interest rate which is determined in the calibration.

(4) The value of one unit of capital in the base year is equal to the rental rate on capital services in the base year plus the premium associated with adjustment costs and the depreciated and discounted value of capital in the subsequent year:

$$p_K = r_K + \frac{\bar{\phi}}{2}\left(\frac{J}{K}\right)^2 + p_K(1 - \bar{\delta})(1 - r).$$

(5) The capital stock times the gross rate of return equals the base year return to capital as reported in the social accounting matrix:

$$Kr_K = \bar{V}_K.$$

Assuming base-year values:

$$\bar{\delta} = 0.07, \ \bar{g} = 0.05, \ \bar{I} = 3, \ \bar{V}_K = 3.8, \ \bar{\phi} = 0.3,$$

the solution to the system of equations characterizing the benchmark equilibrium implies an interest rate $r = 0.075$, a capital price $p_K = 1.12$, and gross return to capital $r_K = 0.16$. Once these values have been determined, we calibrate the utility discount factor to obtain a consistent balanced time-path for consumption by taking $\Delta = (1 - r)(1 + g)^{1/\sigma}$. Additional details regarding the benchmark calibration of the monopolistic firms are provided in Appendix B. (A complete set of equations for the model is provided in Appendix C.)

A subtle problem presents itself when calibrating this model to a balanced growth path. On this path, markup revenues grow with the overall size of the economy, implying that the number of firms increases proportionally. Increasing the number of firms in our monopolistic submodel in effect reduces the cost of X through increases in the number of varieties (one variety is produced per firm). With a Cobb–Douglas production function in the CRTS sector, a steady-state balanced growth path exists, but it is on a knife-edge of instability; i.e. the growth path is non-homogeneous for values of the elasticity of substitution between value-added and intermediates different from unity. In the present version of the model, we have employed a Leontief production function between intermediates and value-added, but have chosen to sidestep this problem through introduction of an appropriate 'fudge factor', which makes it possible to calibrate our model to a Solow balanced growth path. This factor is held constant through the simulations, so we have endogenous growth in counterfactual equilibria even though these growth effects are in essence purged from the benchmark steady-state model. In future work, we will report on the extent to which our results are altered when we begin from a non-homogeneous baseline or with a Cobb–Douglas production function.

4   Model results

We consider a thirty-year model horizon, with 2020 as the terminal year of the model. Initially there is only one distortion in the economy: a 10 per cent tariff on imports of good X, the pure intermediate good produced under IRTS and monopolistic competition. In order to establish a point of reference, we calibrate a model to a 'benchmark' steady-state equilibrium. In our counterfactual scenarios, we remove the 10 per cent tariff and compare the results in all scenarios with the benchmark steady-state equilibrium with the tariff in place. Thus, all key variables are reported as multiples of their values in the benchmark steady-state equilibrium.

For each scenario we present five figures that characterize the time-path of key variables for the thirty years of the model (relative to the steady state). The variables we report in the five figures are as follows: (a) output of the Y sector; domestic and foreign production of the IRTS sector, labelled X_D and X_F, respectively, where X_D is output of the representative firm times the number of firms, i.e. it excludes the variety impact of costs in the Y sector; and consumption; (b) investment, in the Y sector and in both domestic and foreign varieties of the X sector; (c) the number of domestic and foreign firms in the X sector; (d) future value prices for Y, X_D, and X_F, the exchange rate (labelled FX, where an increase is a real depreciation), and the wage rate, all deflated by the price of a unit of consumption in the same time-period, (e) the time-path of employment in sectors Y and X.

In all scenarios we present the Hicksian equivalent variation (EV). The EV is based on the intertemporal utility function defined over the thirty-year horizon. We present EV in percentage terms, where the denominator is the present value of consumption over the thirty-year horizon. Thus, we can compare our EV estimates in percentage terms with the EV of a static model as a percentage of consumption in one year.

4.1   Tariff removal: with spillovers

Figures 9.1a–e present the time-path of key variables in our base model. In this scenario, Hicksian equivalent variation (EV) increases by 7.2 per cent of the present value of consumption over the thirty-year horizon. Given that the initial distortion is only a 10 per cent tariff, this is a 50 per cent larger increase in welfare than results from a comparative static model. In fact, we show below that, even in a dynamic model with perfect competition and the absence of variety effects, the welfare gain is extremely small.

Moreover, per capita consumption progresses on an upward trend, advancing from 2–3 per cent above its steady-state level between 1990 and 1995, to more than 8 per cent above its steady-state level after 2005 (Figure 9.1a). This indicates that the growth rate is endogenously increased in this model and provides support for the empirical observation that countries that exercise protectionist policies consume much less in the long run.

What is driving these results is the following. The removal of the tariff on imported intermediates results in an increase in the tariff-ridden demand curve for imports, and an increase in the price that foreign firms receive for their products. This increases quasi-rents for foreign firms and temporarily creates a period of positive profits for foreign firms, which induces their entry. The increase in imports, however, results in a substitution effect that reduces the demand for and price of domestic varieties; this shuts down investment and firm creation for the domestic variety for a period of three–four years (Figures 9.1b and 9.1c).

The spillover effect of additional foreign firms on the costs of blueprints for domestic firms, however, results in a strong resurgence of domestic firms in the X sector after the first four years. After falling to 62 per cent of its benchmark level in 1994, the number of domestic varieties increases so that after 2009 it exceeds its benchmark steady-state level. An increase in the number of foreign varieties has two competing effects on investment in the domestic variety of X. On the one hand, as the number of foreign varieties increases, the demand for the domestic variety increases, so the quasi-rents available for domestic firms decrease – decreasing the likelihood of investment. On the other hand, the costs of domestic blueprints decrease with the number of varieties – increasing the likelihood of investment. In our model, the costs of blueprints decrease with the square of the number varieties; so, with our choice of parameters, a sufficient increase in foreign varieties results in the present value of the quasi-rents becoming sufficient to cover the costs of a blueprint plus the fixed costs of operating a firm.

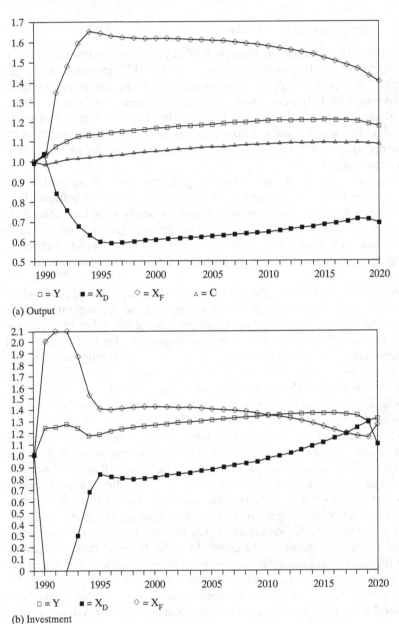

(a) Output

(b) Investment

Figure 9.1 (a) (b)

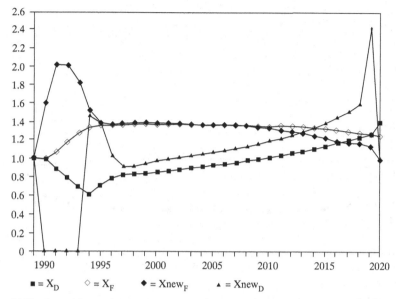

(c) Numbers of firms

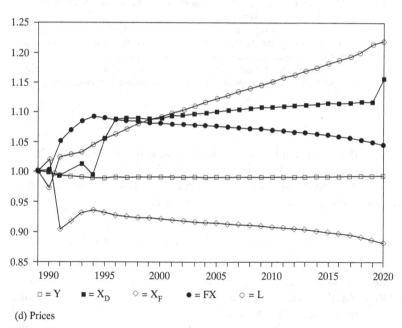

(d) Prices

Figure 9.1 (c) (d)

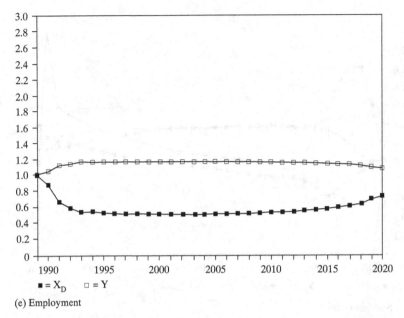

(e) Employment

Figure 9.1   Base model: long-lived firms; unanticipated tariff cuts in 1990; no capital flows; spillovers.

Note: quantities represent indices relative to the baseline steady-state equilibrium; prices represent future values relative to the price of a unit of domestic consumption. Key: Y = macro output; X = intermediate input, X_D = domestically produced, X_F = foreign imports; C = consumption; Xnew = new firms; L = labour wage; FX = foreign exchange.

Finally, there is a steady increase in the real wage over time (by 2020 it reaches 20 per cent above its steady-state level). The increase in the number of varieties of imported intermediates progressively decreases costs and increases the marginal productivity of labour.

4.2   Tariff removal: with spillovers and international capital mobility

In the next scenario, the results of which are presented in Figures 9.2a–f, we effect the same reduction in tariffs, but allow for international capital mobility. In the model without international capital flows, the home country must equate the value of exports and imports in each period. With international capital mobility, the present value of exports must equal the present value of imports over the horizon of the model. Trade deficits are permitted in any period if compensated in present-value terms by trade surpluses in other periods. Permitting trade deficits and surpluses for given periods allows the economy greater flexibility to optimize over time and increases welfare.[9] The increased imports that would be expected as a result of a tariff increase can be paid for out of future production rather than current consumption. As expected, we find that EV increases to 8.8 per cent. (The time-path of borrowing is presented in Figure 9.2f.)

Consistent with this interpretation, both output of foreign varieties and domestic consumption are larger in the early years with international capital mobility. That is, in response to the changed incentives, the economy is able to increase imports faster and smooth consumption over time owing to temporary trade deficits in the short run. At the same time, the shifts in resources (or adjustment costs) are much sharper in the short run with international capital mobility. In particular, either with or without international capital mobility, in the initial years the increase in the number of imported varieties in the X sector induces domestic resources to shift toward the Y sector. With capital mobility, however, the Y sector expands to 17 per cent larger than its benchmark steady-state value within four years, and domestic production of good X

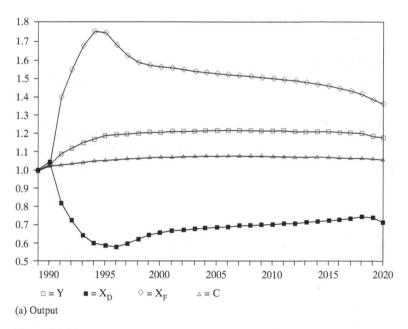

(a) Output

Figure 9.2 (a)

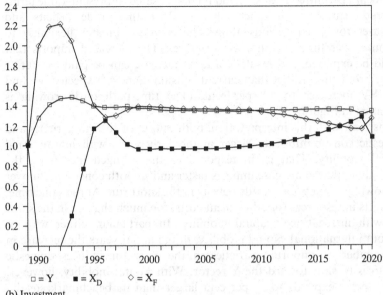

(b) Investment

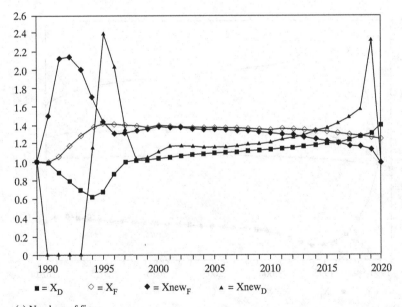

(c) Numbers of firms

Figure 9.2 (b) (c)

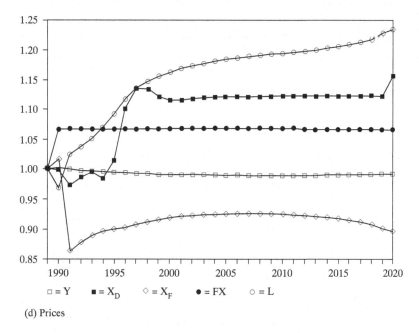

□ = Y   ■ = X_D   ◇ = X_F   ● = FX   ○ = L

(d) Prices

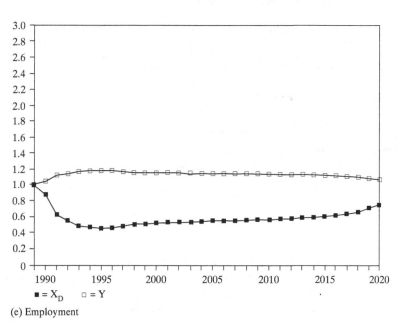

■ = X_D   □ = Y

(e) Employment

Figure 9.2 (d) (e)

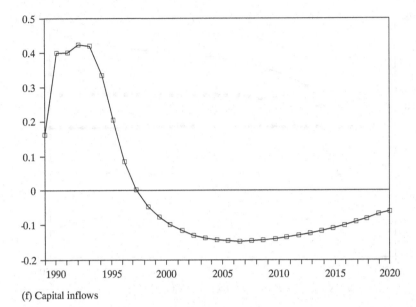

(f) Capital inflows

Figure 9.2   Capital flows: long-lived firms; unanticipated tariff cuts in 1990;
unrestricted capital flows; spillovers.
Note: quantities represent indices relative to the baseline steady-state
equilibrium; prices represent future values relative to the price of a
unit of domestic consumption; capital flows are measured in units of
future value foreign exchange. Key: Y macro output;
X = intermediate input, X_D = domestically produced, X_F = foreign;
C = consumption; Xnew = new firms; L = labour wage;
FX = foreign exchange.

declines to 60 per cent of its benchmark steady-state value; without
international capital mobility, output of the Y sector expands by only 13
per cent and domestic output of X declines to only 63 per cent of their
benchmark levels by 1994.

4.3   Tariff removal: without spillovers

In this scenario, the results of which are presented in Figures 9.3a–e, we
remove the tariff on X goods in 1990, without international capital
mobility. Crucially, we assume that there are no spillovers on the costs of
blueprints for domestic firms as a result of additional foreign firms. In
this scenario, the domestic industry producing X goes into progressive
decline, eventually producing at less than 10 per cent of its benchmark
steady-state value (see Figure 9.3a). Once the tariff on imported varieties

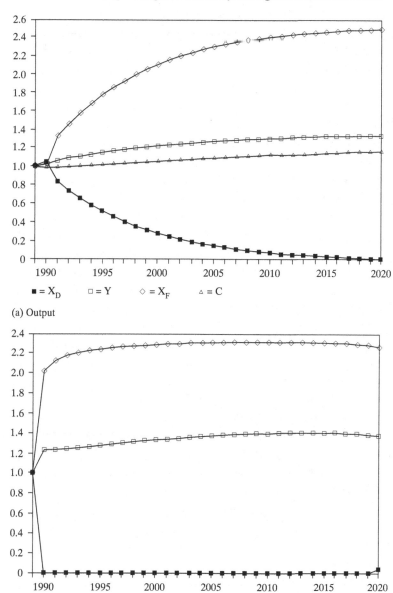

(a) Output

(b) Investment

Figure 9.3 (a) (b)

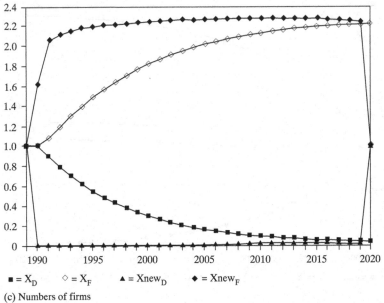

(c) Numbers of firms

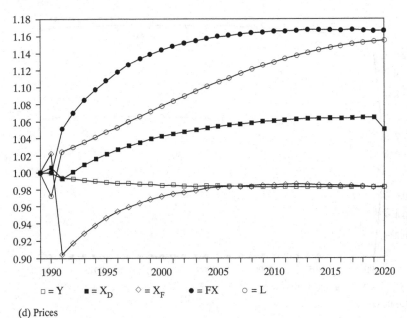

(d) Prices

Figure 9.3 (c) (d)

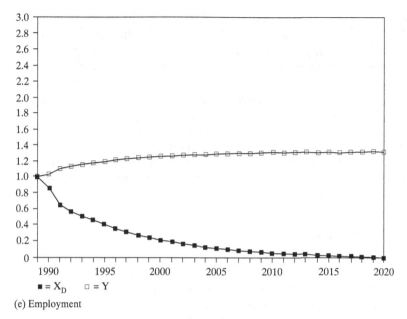

(e) Employment

Figure 9.3(e) **No spillovers: long-lived firms; unanticipated tariff cuts in 1990; no capital flows; no spillovers.**
Note: quantities represent indices relative to the baseline steady-state equilibrium; prices represent future values relative to the price of a unit of domestic consumption. Key: Y = macro output; X = intermediate input, X_D = domestically produced, X_F = foreign; C = consumption; Xnew = new firms; L = labour wage; FX = foreign exchange.

of the X good is removed, investment in the domestic variety of good X becomes unprofitable and remains unprofitable throughout the model horizon; thus investment in the domestic variety of good X is zero throughout the model horizon. As the quantity of the domestic industry diminishes, its relative price increases as the equilibrium moves progressively higher on the demand curve for domestic products.

The collapse of the domestic industry producing good X is principally attributable to the lack of a spillover effect of foreign entry on domestic firms' costs of blueprints. As explained above, the increase in foreign varieties has the impact of decreasing the demand for domestic varieties of X. Without the impact on the costs of blueprints, there is no offset to allow a comeback of the domestic industry. This process continues unabated, ending in the demise of the domestic X sector.

What is most interesting is that the welfare gain (EV) without spillovers is 7.6 per cent, comparable to the scenario with spillovers (7.2 per cent). That is, it may appear paradoxical that, if technology is such that the domestic industry has its costs reduced by foreign varieties, the economy does not gain more from the removal of the tariff on imported varieties. The reason is that there are more varieties introduced in the no-spillover case, and the cost of producing Y falls more than proportionally with an increase in varieties. With spillovers, once the profitability of investment is restored for the domestic industry producing good X, investment in new foreign varieties falls; and it falls by more than investment in the domestic industry increases when compared with the same years in the non-spillover case.[10]

4.4   Tariff removal: myopic firms with spillovers

In this scenario, the results of which are presented in Figures 9.4a–e, we remove the tariff in 1990, allowing spillovers but not international capital mobility. The key difference is that X-sector firms are formed and dissolved in every period. Entry decisions are made solely on the basis of current-period profitability. Entry by a domestic or foreign firm requires that quasi-rents in the subsequent period must be sufficient to cover all fixed costs.[11]

Output and investment (Figures 9.4a and 9.4b) show that there is a much more gradual adjustment in the model with myopic firms. For foreign firms, since they do not capitalize the future stream of improved profit opportunities engendered by the tariff reduction, in each of the early years their improved profit opportunities in the subsequent period must be sufficient to generate an increase in their investment and output. This results in a lower rate of expansion than with forward-looking firms.

For domestic firms producing X, the output and investment decline in the early years is similarly muted, since there is less of an expansion of their foreign competitors (see Figure 9.4c). On the other hand, the decline of the domestic industry producing X goes on for a much longer period before recovering, for two reasons. First, as discussed above, given a sufficiently large expansion of foreign firms, spillovers from foreign entry eventually induce an expansion of the domestic industry. But since foreign entry is muted, it takes longer to arrive at the critical value of foreign firms to induce entry. Second, since domestic firms are also myopic, analogous to foreign firms, investment will not be undertaken until relatively larger quasi-rents are available in the current period.

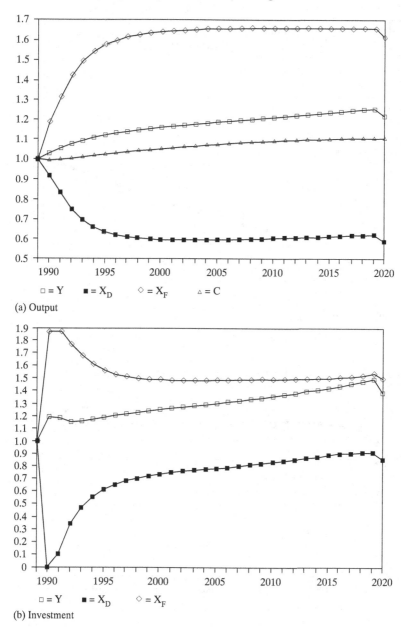

(a) Output

(b) Investment

Figure 9.4 (a) (b)

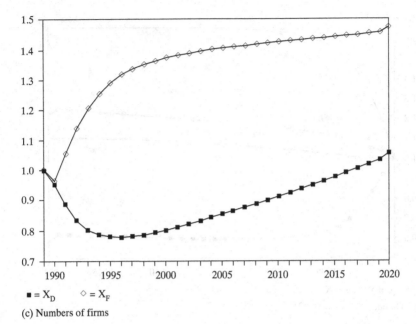

■ = X$_D$ ◇ = X$_F$

(c) Numbers of firms

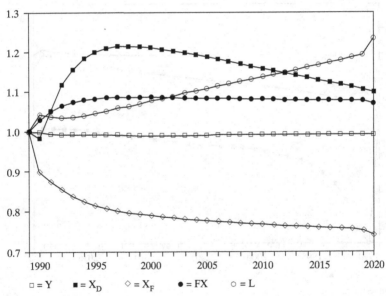

□ = Y   ■ = X$_D$ ◇ = X$_F$ ● = FX   ○ = L

(d) Prices

Figure 9.4 (c) (d)

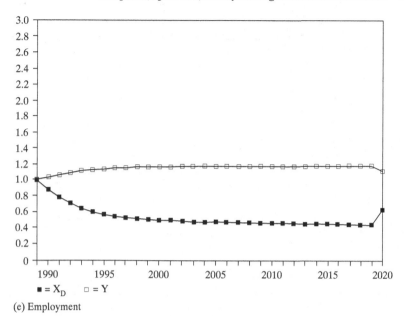

(e) Employment

Figure 9.4 **Myopic firms: firms reformed each year; unanticipated tariff cuts in 1990; no capital flows; spillovers.**
Note: quantities represent indices relative to the baseline steady-state equilibrium; prices represent future values relative to the price of a unit of domestic consumption. Key: Y = macro output; X = intermediate input, X_D = domestically produced; X_F = foreign; C = consumption; L = labour wage; FX = foreign exchange; this model does not distinguish new firms from total firms.

Although adjustment costs are lower with myopic firms, the less abrupt movement of resources leads to a marginally smaller gain in economic welfare: EV is 6.6 per cent of the present value of consumption. Similarly, there is a less significant expansion of the real wage.

4.5   Pre-announced tariff removal after five years, with spillovers

In discussions of the optimal sequencing of trade liberalization, it is sometimes argued that tariff reduction should be pre-announced. Proponents of this view contend that adjustment costs will be reduced as firms scale back gradually on investment in sectors that will be subject to increased competition.

In the scenario presented in Figures 9.5a–e, we consider a model in

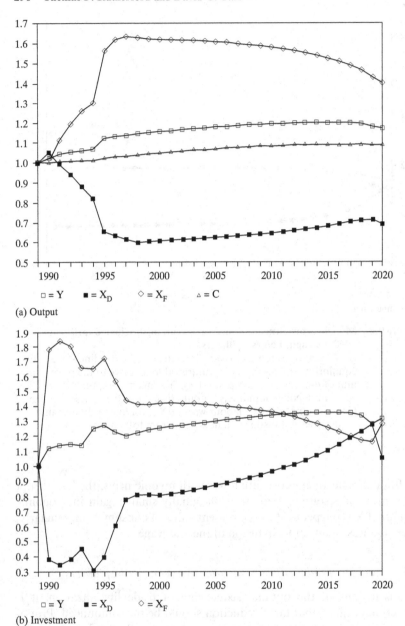

(a) Output

(b) Investment

Figure 9.5 (a) (b)

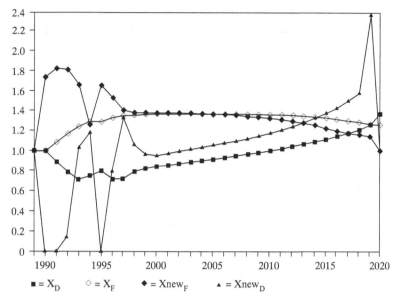

(c) Numbers of firms

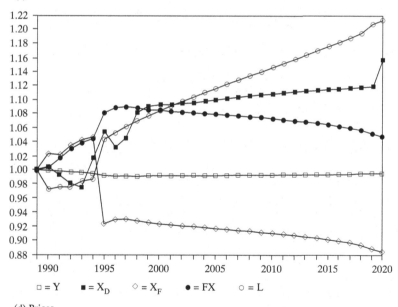

(d) Prices

Figure 9.5 (c) (d)

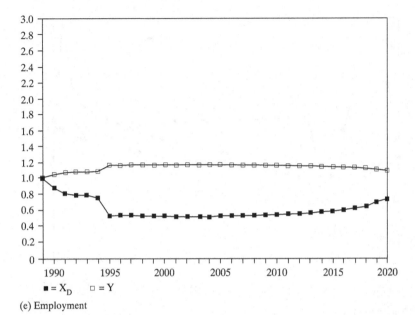

(e) Employment

Figure 9.5   Anticipated policy: long-lived firms; unanticipated tariff cuts in 1990; no capital flows; spillovers.

Note: quantities represent indices relative to the baseline steady-state equilibrium; prices represent future values relative to the price of a unit of domestic consumption. Key: Y = macro output; X = intermediate input, X_D = domestically produced, X_F = foreign; C = consumption; Xnew = new firms; L = labour wage; FX = foreign exchange.

which it is announced in 1990 that tariffs will be removed in 1995. There is no international capital mobility, but there are spillovers and firms are forward looking. As in all other models, there are three types of physical capital, all of which are sector specific following installation.

Foreign firms enter immediately in anticipation of the eventual removal of the tariff; and foreign entry serves to reduce the size of the domestic industry producing X. But the results presented in Figure 9.5 lead us to be sceptical regarding the benefits of delayed implementation as a means of forestalling adjustment costs. Comparing Figures 9.1 and 9.5, we see somewhat less adjustment in 1990 and 1991 with pre-announcement. On the other hand, with pre-announcement, there is a rather steep downward adjustment of the domestic industry in 1995, the year the tariff cut is actually implemented. The reason is that, for foreign firms, their incentive to invest jumps in 1995 compared with 1994, and the increase in the entry of foreign firms induces a sharp contraction in domestic firms and employment in X in 1995. The bottom line is that pre announcement appears to do little to reduce adjustment costs while delay is costly. The equivalent variation in income for this scenario is half a percentage point lower than in the reference case (6.6 versus 7.2 per cent).

It still may be possible to defend delayed implementation by adopting a different model, one in which the adjustment costs involve externalities. In our model, all adjustment costs are internalized by the firm in its investment decision (see Mussa (1984) for an elaboration).

4.6 Tariff removal: competitive model

In this scenario, the results of which are presented in Figures 9.6a–e, we assume that the X sector is perfectly competitive and employ the Armington assumption regarding the demand structure for imports and domestic versions of intermediates. For comparability with the IRTS model, we adopt an Armington substitution elasticity equal to 3, identical to the intra-firm elasticity in our base model. Although investors are forward looking, we do not have scale economies, product variety, or spillover effects in the competitive model.

The results are familiar. The relative price change in favour of imported intermediates induces production of imported intermediates to expand and domestic intermediates to contract (Figure 9.6a). Domestic resources shift into the production of the final good Y. In comparison with our basic scenario, resource movement is highly muted and output movement for each sector is approximately monotonic. For example, domestic production of intermediates converges to about 88 per cent of its benchmark steady-state level in roughly six years.

Adjustment costs in this model are minimal; however, the welfare change is also small, at 0.3 per cent with financial flows. The absence of product variety and dynamic effects and the consistent accounting for the costs of capital formation explain why the welfare effect is small.

4.7 Impact of the model horizon

In this scenario, the results of which are presented in Figures 9.7a–c, we examine the robustness of our results with respect to the model horizon. In these figures, we compare results from the base model (with a 2020 horizon) to an otherwise identical model with a 2015 horizon. Figure 9.7a plots output levels for the two models. We find that the results are quite robust for the first ten–fifteen years. After 2005–2010 the time-paths of the variables begin to diverge. It is clear that our formulation

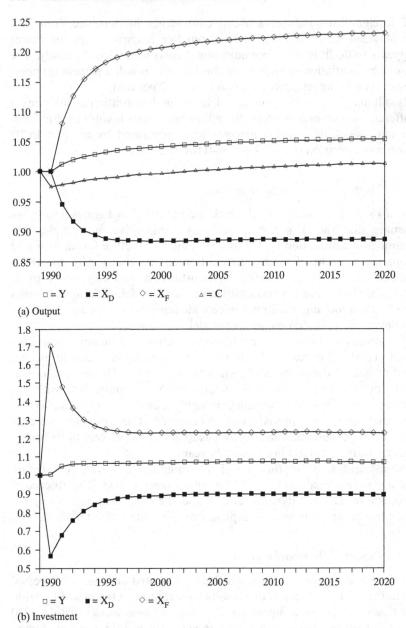

(a) Output

(b) Investment

Figure 9.6 (a) (b)

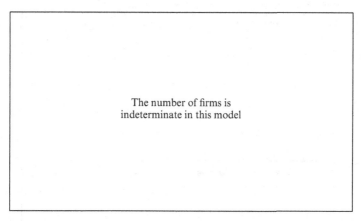

(c) Number of firms

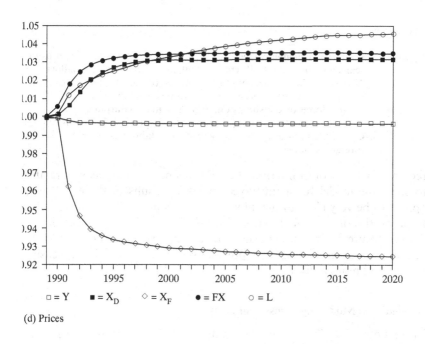

(d) Prices

Figure 9.6 (c) (d)

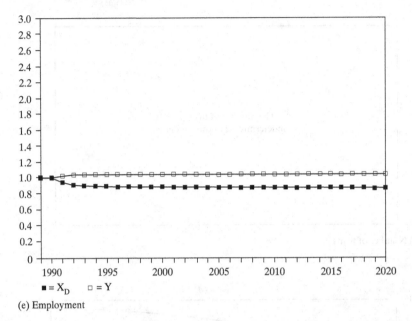

■ = X_D □ = Y

(e) Employment

Figure 9.6   Competitive model: competitive firms produce with constant returns to scale; unanticipated tariff cuts in 1990; no capital flows; no spillovers.
Note: quantities represent indices relative to the baseline steady-state equilibrium; prices represent future values relative to the price of a unit of domestic consumption. Key: Y = macro output; X = intermediate input, X_D = domestically produced, X_F = foreign; C = consumption; Xnew = new firms; L = labour wage; FX = foreign exchange.

requires further work on terminal conditions but, so long as we are able to solve the model for a thirty-year horizon, results in the early years appear to be very close to the infinite horizon values. This is attributable to properties of dynamic models with discounting, whereby years in the distant future have little impact on activity in the early years. It is promising that these properties prevail even in a model with increasing returns and monopolistic competition.

Appendix A: Modelling adjustment costs

These notes describe our implementation of the adjustment cost sub-model within the MPSGE framework. For notational simplicity, we ignore sectoral subscripts here. The same formulation applies for macro production, Y, domestic intermediate production, X_D, and imported intermediate production, X_F.

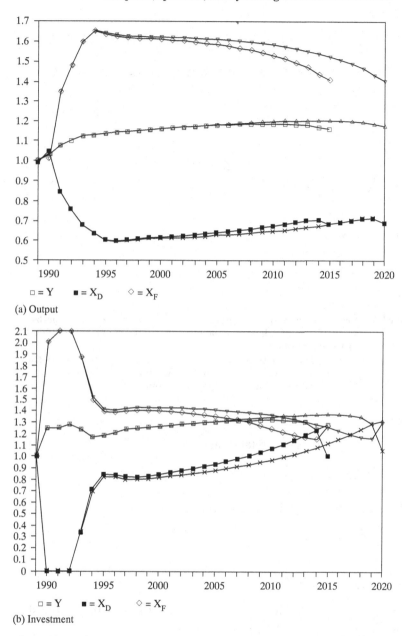

☐ = Y   ■ = X_D   ◇ = X_F

(a) Output

☐ = Y   ■ = X_D   ◇ = X_F

(b) Investment

Figure 9.7 (a) (b)

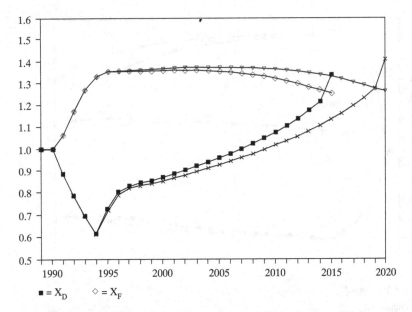

Figure 9.7   **Sensitivity analysis with respect to model horizon: equilibrium paths for 2015 and 2020 horizons; long-lived firms; unanticipated tariff cuts in 1990; no capital flows; no spillovers.**
Note: quantities represent indices relative to the baseline steady-state equilibrium. Key: Y = macro ouput; X = intermediate input; X_D = domestically produced; X_F = foreign.

Define:

J = number of units of capital formation, as in:

$$K_{t=1} = \lambda K_t + J_t$$

I = total cost of capital formation (investment), as in:

$$Y_t = C_t + I_t$$

ϕ = adjustment cost parameter
K = current capital stock.

We begin with the following equation, which describes the relationship between investment and capital accumulation:

$$I = J + \frac{\phi J^2}{2K} \equiv I_0 + I_A.$$

In this equation, I_0 is the constant marginal cost component of capital formation ($= J$), and I_A is the variable marginal cost of capital formation. I_A depends on the level of investment relative to the capital stock.

Inverting the equation for I_A, we can express units of capital formation (J) as a function of the two components of investment costs:

$$J = \min\left[I_0, \sqrt{\frac{2}{\phi}} \sqrt{K \, I_A} \right].$$

This is a nested Leontief–Cobb–Douglas production function. Within the Cobb–Douglas nest, we have equal budget shares for 'inputs' of the current capital stock and the level of variable investment costs.

It is important to recognize that, in dynamic models with adjustment costs, a unit of capital at the start of period t 'produces' three joint outputs:

1. capital services for current production (together with labour and other inputs),
2. future capital services through the provision of depreciated capital in the following period $t + 1$,
3. capital services for current investment in the form of reduced adjustment costs.

In order to distinguish between the value of a unit of capital, the rental value for capital in goods production, and the marginal value of the capital stock for reducing adjustment costs, we must have three separate prices in the model. These are defined as:

PK_t the present value price of a unit of capital provided at the start of period t;

RK_t the present value price of a unit of capital services for production in the current period;

PKA_t the shadow price representing the marginal value of reduced investment in the current period.

Introducing a production activity that converts capital at the start of period t into these three 'outputs', we have an exhaustion of product condition:

$$PK_t \geq RK_t + PKA_t + \lambda PK_{t+1}$$

and, defined in terms of these prices, the zero profit function for period t investment is given by:

$$P_t + \phi(\delta + g)\sqrt{P_t PKA_t} \geq PK_{t+1}.$$

Appendix B: Calibration of the IRTS submodel

One subtle aspect of our model with long-lived firms is the imposition of an intertemporal zero-profit condition on new firms and accounting for quasi-rents which accrue to firms that are already in existence at the start of the model. These notes describe how the intertemporal profit balance conditions apply along a steady-state path. The results presented here are used to specify the baseline steady-state growth path and to impose terminal conditions that are consistent with the return to a steady-state equilibrium in the post-terminal period. We begin with definitions:

δ = depreciation rate for firms
g = growth rate of the labour force
r = interest rate
$\bar{M}$ = benchmark (period 1) markup revenue
$\bar{F}_K$ = benchmark fixed cost of capital (recurrent)
$\bar{F}_B$ = benchmark fixed cost of product development (one-time)
N_1 = benchmark number of producing firms = 1 (normalized)
n_1 = benchmark number of new firms = $\delta + g$ (by steady-state assumption)

Firms experience exponential decay, so along the steady-state path we have:

$$N_{t+1} = (1 - \delta)N_t + n_t.$$

In the benchmark equilibrium, we have balanced growth:

$$N_{t+1} = (1 + g)N_t.$$

Product development costs per firm:

$$f_B = \frac{\bar{F}_B}{n_1} = \frac{\bar{F}_B}{\delta + g}.$$

Fixed costs of capital per firm may also be inferred from the benchmark, assuming steady-state growth at rate g, with depreciation of firms at rate δ:

$$\bar{F}_K = f_K \frac{\delta + g}{1 + g} \sum_{\tau=0}^{\infty} \left(\frac{1 - \delta}{1 + g}\right)^{\tau} = f_K.$$

The market share of vintage-v firms in period t is assumed proportional to the number of vintage-v firms in the total number of producing firms:

$$\theta_{vt} = \frac{n_v(1-\delta)^{t-v-1}}{N_t} = \frac{\delta+g}{1-\delta}\left(\frac{1-\delta}{1+g}\right)^{t-v}.$$

Discounting all values to period 1, we compare the value of markup revenue with the value of total fixed costs to determine the benchmark condition relating markup revenue to fixed costs. First, consider the present value of markup revenue for all vintage-v firms:

$$M_v = \bar{M}\sum_{t=v+1}^{\infty}(1+g)^{t-1}(1-r)^{t-1}\theta_{vt}$$

$$= (\delta+g)(1+g)^{v-1}(1-r)^v\frac{\bar{M}}{r+\delta-r\delta}.$$

The total fixed costs for vintage-v firms are given by:

$$C_v = n_v\left[f_B(1-r)^{v-1} + \sum_{t=v+1}^{\infty}f_K(1-\delta)^{t-v-1}(1-r)^{t-1}\right]$$

$$= (\delta+g)(1+g)^{v-1}(1-r)^v\left[\frac{f_B}{1-r} + \frac{f_K}{r+\delta-r\delta}\right].$$

Equating, we obtain the benchmark condition:

$$\frac{\bar{M}}{r+\delta-r\delta} = \frac{f_B}{1-r} + \frac{f_K}{r+\delta-r\delta}$$

or

$$\bar{M} = \left(\delta+\frac{r}{1-r}\right)f_B + f_K.$$

This says that, along a steady-state equilibrium path, markup revenues in each period equal current period fixed costs together with growth and interest costs for investments in product development.

Substituting for the benchmark values, we have:

$$\bar{M} = \left(\delta+\frac{r}{1-r}\right)(\delta+g)\bar{F}_B + \bar{F}_K.$$

Appendix C: Equilibrium conditions

Four classes of equations constitute the model's equilibrium conditions:
- Zero-profit conditions for constant-returns-to-scale production or demand activities. These are defined in terms of commodities prices, tax rates, and endogenous price–cost wedges.

- Market clearance conditions for all commodities including goods and primary factors.
- Income balance conditions for the domestic consumer.
- Free-entry zero-profit conditions for all vintages of monopolistic firms formed during the model horizon (excluding firms founded prior to the first period of the model).

Zero-profit conditions

Consumer welfare is 'produced' through consumption in every period over the horizon of the model. The price index for intertemporal utility is a CES aggregate of the consumption price aggregates with an intertemporal elasticity of substitution, σ_T:

$$- \Pi^W = P^W - \left(\sum_t \theta_t^C P C_t^{1-\sigma_T} \right)^{\frac{1}{1-\sigma_T}} \geq 0.$$

In this equation, θ_t^C is a preference parameter that reflects discounting and the demand for intertemporal consumption smoothing. These parameters are calibrated to the initial steady-state growth path and thereafter are held fixed.

The consumption aggregate within each period is a Cobb–Douglas aggregate of domestic and imported goods:

$$- \Pi_t^C = P C_t - P D_t^{\alpha_D} P M_t^{1-\alpha_D} \geq 0.$$

Sector Y produces goods for the domestic and export markets according to a constant elasticity of transformation (CET) technology. These are produced using inputs of labour, capital services, and X:

$$-\Pi_t^Y = \left(\beta_D P D_t^{1+\eta} + \beta_E P E_t^{1+\eta} \right)^{\frac{1}{1+\eta}} - \phi_v P L_t^{\alpha_L} R Y_t^{1-\alpha_L}$$
$$- \left(\sum_f \gamma_f [P X_{ft}(1+m)]^{1-\sigma_X} \right)^{\frac{1}{1-\sigma_X}} \geq 0.$$

The price indices for good X are multiplied by the monopoly markup, $m = 1/(\sigma_X - 1)$. The production of X by firm f potentially involves inputs of labour, capital services, and foreign exchange:

$$-\Pi_{ft}^X = - P X_{ft} \left(\frac{N_{ft}}{\overline{N}_{ft}} \right)^{\frac{1}{\sigma_v - 1}} + \phi_f^v P L_t^{\alpha_L} R X_{ft}^{1-\alpha_L}$$
$$+ \phi_f^M P M_t (1 + t_{ft}) \geq 0.$$

In this production function, the term $(N_{\mathrm{f}t}/\bar{N}_{\mathrm{f}t})^{1/(\sigma_X-1)}$ represents the variety-adjusted output coefficient, which is equal to unity along the steady-state growth path.

The unit fixed cost of a vintage-v firm is composed of the cost of creating blueprints and the cost of capital inputs over the model horizon:

$$\Pi_{\mathrm{f}v}^{\mathrm{NX}} = PF_{\mathrm{f}v} - \alpha_{\mathrm{B}} PL_v \Phi_{\mathrm{f}v}^{\mathrm{B}} - \alpha_K \sum_{t>v} \lambda_{vt} RX_{\mathrm{f}t} \geq 0.$$

In this expression, λ_{vt} is the survival share of vintage v in period t. The cost of blueprints *for domestic firms* is dependent on the term $\Phi_{\mathrm{f}t}^{\mathrm{B}}$, which equals unity along the steady-state growth path, but declines quadratically with the number of foreign firms in the market:

$$\Phi_{\mathrm{f}t}^{\mathrm{B}} = 2 - \left(\frac{N_{\mathrm{f}t}}{\bar{N}_{\mathrm{f}t}}\right)^2.$$

The present value of a unit of capital at the start of period t equals the value of capital services during the period, the depreciated value of capital remaining in the next period, plus a premium generated for capital-adjustment effects in the succeeding period. This condition applies for capital in sector Y:

$$-\Pi_t^{\mathrm{KY}} = PKY_t - RY_t - \lambda_{\mathrm{Y}} PK_{t+1}^{\mathrm{Y}} - PKA_t^{\mathrm{Y}} \geq 0$$

and for firm-f capital in sector X:

$$-\Pi_{\mathrm{f}t}^{\mathrm{KY}} = PKX_{\mathrm{f}t} - RX_{\mathrm{f}t} - \lambda_{\mathrm{X}} PK_{\mathrm{f},t+1}^{\mathrm{X}} - PKA_{\mathrm{f}t}^{\mathrm{X}} \geq 0.$$

The present-value price of a unit of capital at the start of period $t+1$ can rise no higher than the marginal cost of a unit of installed capital in period t, gross of adjustment cost. This equation applies for sector Y:

$$-\Pi_t^{\mathrm{IY}} = \beta PD_t^{1-\phi} (PKA_t^{\mathrm{Y}})^\phi + \alpha_{\mathrm{D}} PD_t + \alpha_{\mathrm{M}} PM_t - PK_{t+1}^{\mathrm{Y}} \geq 0$$

and for each of the firms f in sector X:

$$-\Pi_{\mathrm{f}t}^{\mathrm{IX}} = \beta_{\mathrm{f}} PD_t^{1-\phi} (PKA_{\mathrm{f}t}^{\mathrm{X}})^\phi + \alpha_{\mathrm{f}D} PD_t + \alpha_{\mathrm{f}M} PM_t - PK_{\mathrm{f},t+1}^{\mathrm{X}} \geq 0.$$

Market clearance conditions

The supply of the consumption aggregate within period t must be consistent with relative prices and aggregate utility:

$$C_t = W \frac{\partial \Pi^W}{\partial PC_t}.$$

The supply of aggregate output to the domestic market equals the use of domestic inputs for final consumption plus investment:

$$- Y_t \frac{\partial \Pi_t^Y}{\partial PD_t} \geq C_t \frac{\partial \Pi_t^C}{\partial PD_t} + IY_t \frac{\partial \Pi_t^{IY}}{\partial PD_t} + \sum_f IX_{ft} \frac{\partial \Pi_{ft}^{IX}}{\partial PD_t}.$$

The supply of X from firm f equals intermediate demand:

$$X_{ft} \left(\frac{N_{ft}}{\bar{N}_{ft}} \right)^{\frac{1}{\sigma_X - 1}} \geq Y_t \frac{\partial \Pi_t^Y}{\partial [PX_{ft}(1 + m)]}.$$

Labour supply is fixed and equal to labour demand:

$$\bar{L}_t = Y_t \frac{\partial \Pi_t^Y}{\partial PL_t} + \sum_f X_{ft} \frac{\partial \Pi_{ft}^X}{\partial PL_t} + \sum_f NX_{ft} \frac{\partial \Pi_{ft}^{NX}}{\partial PL_t}.$$

Capital services in period t are limited by capital supply:

$$KY_t = Y_t \frac{\partial \Pi_t^Y}{\partial RY_t}$$

and:

$$KX_{ft} = X_{ft} \frac{\partial \Pi_{ft}^X}{\partial RX_{ft}}.$$

Capital stocks at the start of period $t + 1$ equal the depreciated stock from period t plus investment:

$$KY_{t+1} = \lambda_Y KT_t + IY_t$$

and:

$$KX_{ft} = \lambda_X KX_{ft} + IX_{ft}.$$

Balance of payments equilibrium is expressed in terms of either period-by-period constraints or a single intertemporal constraint, depending on the capital flow assumption. In the model without capital flows, a balance of payments constraint appears in every period. Thus we have:

$$- Y_t \frac{\partial \Pi_t^Y}{\partial PE_t} = C_t \frac{\partial \Pi_t^C}{\partial PM_t} + IY_t \frac{\partial \Pi_t^{IY}}{\partial PM_t}$$

$$+ \sum_f IX_{ft} \frac{\partial \Pi_{ft}^{IX}}{\partial PM_t} + \sum_{ft} X_{ft} \frac{\partial \Pi_{ft}^X}{\partial PM_t}$$

In the model with free capital flows and a fixed international interest rate, we have:

$$-\sum_t (1 - r)^t Y_t \frac{\partial \Pi_t^Y}{\partial PE_t} = \sum_t (1 - r)^t \left[C_t \frac{\partial \Pi_t^C}{\partial PM_t} + IY_t \frac{\partial \Pi_t^{IY}}{\partial PM_t} \right.$$

$$\left. + \sum_f \left(IX_{ft} \frac{\partial \Pi_{ft}^{IX}}{\partial PM_t} + X_{ft} \frac{\partial \Pi_{ft}^X}{\partial PM_t} \right) \right].$$

Intertemporal income balance

The present value of consumption by the representative agent equals the cost of a unit of present-value welfare times the welfare index. In equilibrium, this equals the value of factor income, labour wage income for all periods of the model, and the value of entering (period 0) capital.

$$PW \ W = \sum_t PL_t \bar{L}_t + PK_0^Y \overline{KY}_0 + \sum_f PK_{f0}^X \overline{KX}_{f0}.$$

Free-entry zero-profit for vintage-v firms

$$\sum_{t>v} \theta_{fvt} \ m \ PX_{ft} \frac{\partial \Pi_t^Y}{\partial PX_{ft}(1 + m)} Y_t = NX_{fv} PF_{fv}.$$

Notes

The views expressed are those of the authors alone and should not be interpreted as the opinion of the World Bank. An earlier version of this paper was prepared for the CEPR conference 'Dynamic Issues in Applied Commercial Policy Analysis', 26–28 January 1996, Geneva. We are grateful to Jim Markusen for comments on an early version of this work.
  1. See, for example, de Melo and Tarr (1992), Harrison, Rutherford, and Tarr (1993, 1995), Morkre and Tarr (1995). While some estimates with increasing returns to scale models (such as Cox and Harris (1985)) have been larger (up to 10 per cent of GDP), these estimates have been more controversial, often based on regime switching (see Harrison et al. (1993) and Harrison, Rutherford, and Tarr (1995)). In our view, the results are less than convincing for a strong version of the paradigm.
  2. Our analysis can be viewed as an extension of Ethier (1982) and Markusen

(1989, 1991). Markusen investigated the implications of the substantial trade in imported intermediate inputs using static and two-period models. A related static analysis focusing on the market for auto parts in Mexico is Lopez et al. (1994).

3. The intertemporal elasticity of substitution $\sigma_T = 1/(1 - \rho)$. Note that we use the symbol ρ without a subscript in all the constant elasticity of substitution functions to simplify notation, even though these do not necessarily represent identical elasticities of substitution. (See Table 9.1 for the assumed values of elasticities in different sectors.)

4. This may be called 'operating surplus', 'operating profit', or 'Ricardian surplus' by different authors.

5. Note that the sum in the denominator extends to vintages ($\tau < 0$), which were introduced prior to the base year of the model.

6. A technical challenge in this framework is to approximate the infinite horizon results with a finite horizon model. In the current version of the model, we assume that the domestic consumer buys blueprints in the final period and pays a price consistent with the benchmark steady state. For the results in the text, the equivalent variation calculation for the consumer is adjusted to provide a credit for the purchased blueprints. Our calculations indicate that this procedure results in an underestimate of the welfare gains.

   In the alternative approach, we do not credit the equivalent variation calculation for the consumer for the purchased blueprints, but extend the terminal years out to 2030. We find that welfare as a percentage of total consumption continues to increase with the terminal year. This indicates that our finite-period approximation to the infinite horizon underestimates the welfare gain.

   We are aware that either of our approaches is inexact. We hope to improve upon these formulations in our next model revision, incorporating some of the ideas from Mercenier and Michel (1994).

7. This is not a precise representation of the current Tunisian economy, but we have chosen this approach in order to avoid confusing our initial analysis of this dynamic framework through complex second-best effects.

8. For clarity, we use a bar to indicate parameters and benchmark parameters that are specified exogenously. Symbols without a bar are inferred by solving this system of equations. It is possible to derive all of the values analytically by solving a single quadratic equation, but for transparency we pose the calibration problem as that of solving a system of non-linear equations.

9. Compare Neary and Ruane (1988), who show that the benefits of tariff removal should be larger with international capital mobility (FDI); there is greater elasticity of supply, which allows more resource movement and production efficiency gain from the removal of the tariff. See de Melo and Tarr (1992) for analogous numerical results in a comparative static model.

10. The real wage does not increase in this scenario because of an anomaly in the benchmark data set: foreign varieties are produced without labour. Thus, as production of foreign varieties increases (demanding domestic capital), production in the economy becomes much more capital intensive. As we convert to a more realistic data set, this anomaly will be removed.

11. We cannot distinguish recurring fixed costs from R&D fixed costs in this model. We calibrate this model to identical benchmark data, treating all fixed costs from the benchmark as a single vector.

References

Baldwin, R. E., R. Forslid, and J. I. Haaland (1996), 'Investment Creation and Diversion in Europe', *World Economy* 19(6): 635–59.

Cox, D. and R. Harris (1985), 'Trade Liberalization and Industrial Organization: Some Estimates for Canada', *Journal of Political Economy* 93: 115–45.

Ethier, W. J. (1982), 'National and International Returns to Scale in the Modern Theory of International Trade', *American Economic Review* 72: 389–405.

Goulder, L. H. and L. H. Summers (1989), 'Tax Policy, Asset Prices, and Growth: A General Equilibrium Analysis', *Journal of Public Economics* 38(3): 265–96.

Grossman, G. and E. Helpman (1991), *Innovation and Growth in the Global Economy*. Cambridge, Mass.: MIT Press.

Harrison, G. W., R. Jones, L. J. Kimbell, and R. Wigle (1993), 'How Robust Is Applied General Equilibrium Analysis?' *Journal of Policy Modeling* 15(1): 99–115.

Harrison, G. W., T. F. Rutherford, and D. G. Tarr (1993), 'Trade Reform in the Partially Liberalized Economy of Turkey', *World Bank Economic Review* 7(2): 191–217.

(1995), 'Quantifying the Uruguay Round'. In W. Martin and L. Alan Winters (eds.), *The Uruguay Round and the Developing Economies*, Discussion Paper No. 307. Washington, D.C.: World Bank, pp. 215–84.

Keller, W. (1995), 'Trade and the Transmission of Technology', Working Paper, Department of Economics, University of Wisconsin.

Lopez-de-Silanes, F., J. R. Markusen, and T. F. Rutherford (1994), 'Complementarity and Increasing Returns in Intermediate Inputs', *Journal of Development Economics* 45: 133–51.

McKibbin, W. J. and P. J. Wilcoxen (1995), 'The Global Costs of Policies to Reduce Greenhouse Gas Emissions', Final Report on US Environmental Protection Agency Cooperative Agreement CR818579–01–0. Washington, D.C.: Brookings Institution.

Markusen, J. R. (1989), 'Trade in Producer Services and Other Specialized Inputs', *American Economic Review* 79: 85–95.

(1991), 'First Mover Advantages, Blocked Entry and the Economics of Uneven Development'. In E. Helpman and A. Razin (eds.), *International Trade and Trade Policy*. Cambridge, Mass.: MIT Press.

Melo, J. de and D. Tarr (1992), *A General Equilibrium Analysis of US Foreign Trade Policy*. Cambridge, Mass.: MIT Press.

Mercenier, J. and P. Michel (1994), 'Discrete-Time Finite Horizon Approximation of Infinite Optimization Problems with Steady-State Invariance', *Econometrica* 62(3): 635–56.

Morkre, M. and D. G. Tarr (1995), 'Reforming Hungarian Agricultural Trade Policy: A Quantitative Evaluation', *Weltwirtschaftliches Archiv* 131(1): 106–31.

Mussa, M. (1984), 'The Adjustment Process and the Timing of Trade Liberalization', Working Paper Series. Cambridge, Mass.: NBER.

Neary, J. P. and F. Ruane (1988), 'International Capital Mobility, Shadow Prices, and the Cost of Protection', *International Economic Review* 29: 571–85.

Roberts, Mark, Theresa Sullivan, and James Tybout (1995), 'What Makes Exports Boom? Evidence from Plant-Level Data', World Bank, mimeo.

Romer, P. M. (1990), 'Endogenous Technological Change', *Journal of Political Economy* 98(5): 71–102.
  (1994), 'New Goods, Old Theory, and the Welfare Costs of Trade Restrictions', *Journal of Development Economics* 43: 5–38.
Sachs, J. D. and A. Warner (1995), 'Economic Reform and the Process of Global Integration', *Brookings Papers on Economic Activity* 1: 1–117.
Segerstrom, P. S., T. C. A. Anant, and E. Dinopoulos (1990), 'A Schumpeterian Model of the Product Life Cycle', *American Economic Review* 80: 1077–92.
Uzawa, H. (1969), 'Time Preference and the Penrose Effect in a Two Class Model of Economic Growth', *Journal of Political Economy* 77: 628–52.
World Bank (1987), *World Development Report*. New York: Oxford University Press for the World Bank.

Discussion

ULRICH KOHLI

It should not come as a surprise to anyone familiar with Tom Rutherford and David Tarr's earlier work that this is a very neat and carefully done paper. It is also very impressive and sophisticated: it contains a wealth of interesting features, ranging from capital accumulation to imperfect competition, from blueprint to spillover effects, from product diversity and increasing returns to scale to sector-specific capital, vintage and life-cycle effects, all this within an intertemporal optimization framework! This is truly a state-of-the-art CGE paper. Thanks to many of these features, Rutherford and Tarr (R&T) manage to get some rather large welfare gains from the removal of a fairly small tariff.

How credible these large effects are I do not know. Did the large welfare gains that Canada was entitled to expect (based on the first-generation CGE models) from the United States–Canada free trade agreement materialize? It might still be too early to tell. Admittedly, several of R&T's scenarios show an initial drop in domestic activity, not unlike what was observed in New Zealand, Chile, or Mexico following major reforms.

I am delighted to see imports modelled, at least in part, as an intermediate input. I have long argued (Kohli 1978, 1991) that this makes sense from an empirical viewpoint, since almost all imported goods must transit through the production sector before meeting final

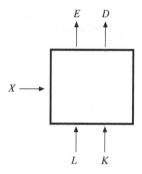

Figure 9D.1 The black box of technology.

demand: even so-called 'finished' imports must in most cases still go through a number of transformations – such as transportation, repackaging, marketing, insurance, storing, and retailing – before reaching their final destination, so that a substantial proportion of the final price tag is generally accounted for by domestic value-added. In fact, I am not sure why R&T even bother with direct imports of consumer goods: if all imports had to transit through the production sector, one might find that the welfare effects of liberalization are even larger.

One thing that I would like to emphasize is that the production structure, although fairly intricate and detailed, is also quite restrictive. Take the competitive industry. Rutherford and Tarr assume three inputs: labour (L), capital (K), and intermediate goods (X) of domestic and foreign origin. They also assume two outputs, domestic sales (D) and exports (E). They assume constant returns to scale and competitive behaviour. This is all very fine. All they really needed to assume on top of this is convexity and free disposals.

Think of the technology as a black box – it is depicted in Figure 9D.1, with its three inputs and two outputs. More formally, the technology could be described by a joint cost function (Hall 1973) defined as follows:

$$C(E, D, p_{\mathrm{L}}, p_{\mathrm{K}}, p_{\mathrm{X}}) \equiv \min_{L,K,X} \{p_{\mathrm{L}}L + p_{\mathrm{K}}K + p_{\mathrm{X}}X : (L, K, X, E, D) \in T\}, \quad (1)$$

where $p_i (i = L, K, X)$ is the price of input i, and T is the production possibilities set, which is assumed to be a convex cone. The joint cost function is linearly homogeneous, increasing and convex in output quantities, and it is linearly homogeneous, increasing and concave in input prices (Diewert 1974).

The substitution possibilities can be described by the substitution matrix, Σ, which is basically a normalization of the Hessian of $C(\cdot)$:

$$\Sigma = [\sigma_{ij}] = \left[\frac{CC_{ij}}{C_i C_j}\right], \tag{2}$$

where $C_i \equiv \partial C(\cdot)/\partial z_i, z_i \in \{E, D, p_L, p_K, p_X\}$, and so on. It is convenient to partition Σ and rewrite it as follows:

$$\Sigma = \begin{bmatrix} \Sigma_{qq} & \Sigma_{qp} \\ \Sigma_{pq} & \Sigma_{pp} \end{bmatrix}. \tag{3}$$

In our example, Σ is of dimensions 5×5. Σ_{qq} is of dimensions 2×2, and it contains the so-called inverse elasticities of transformation of the two outputs. Σ_{pp} is 3×3, and it contains the elasticities of substitution of the three inputs. Σ_{qp} (the transpose of Σ_{pq}) is of dimensions 2×3, and it contains the so-called inverse elasticities of intensity. The curvature conditions of $C(\cdot)$ imply that Σ_{qq} is positive semi-definite, and that Σ_{pp} is negative semi-definite. Other than that, Σ is fairly general (although the linear homogeneity properties of $C(\cdot)$ imply some additional restrictions), and it can easily be estimated by econometric techniques if price and quantity data on the five inputs and outputs are available (Kohli 1991).

Instead of adopting such a general specification, R&T make a number of additional – and fairly restrictive – assumptions. If we take an X-ray of the black box of technology, we get to see what takes place inside, i.e. how inputs are transformed into outputs according to R&T (Figure 9D.2). Thus, some labour (L) and capital (K) are combined into a domestic aggregate input (V); the technology is Cobb–Douglas (CD). This composite input is then combined with importables (X) to yield an intermediate good, called Y; the technology here is Leontief. Finally, this intermediate good is 'cracked' into two outputs, exports (E) and domestic sales (D); this technology is CET. These assumptions imply some rather severe restrictions on the form of the joint cost function and of Σ. The assumption that all inputs, on the one hand, and all outputs, on the other hand, can be aggregated implies that the technology is globally separable between inputs and outputs. It then follows that the joint cost function has the following multiplicative form (Hall 1973):

$$C(\cdot) = h(E, D)c(p_L, p_K, p_X). \tag{4}$$

$h(\cdot)$ can be interpreted as the 'upper-tier' transformation function, or input requirements function; it indicates the minimum amount of Y that

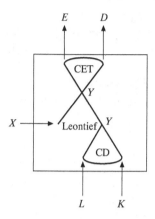

Figure 9D.2 An X-ray of the R&T black box of technology.

is necessary to produce a given amount of E and of D; $c(\cdot)$, on the other hand, can be interpreted as the 'lower-tier' cost function; it indicates the minimum cost of producing a given amount of Y:

$$c(p_L, p_K, p_X) \equiv \min_{L,K,X} \{p_L L + p_K K + p_X X : f(L, K, X) = Y\}, \quad (5)$$

where $f(\cdot)$ represents the 'lower-tier' production function. The assumption that $f(\cdot)$ is separable between imports, on the one hand, and labour and capital, on the other hand, implies furthermore that:

$$f(L, K, X) = \phi[V(L, K), X]. \quad (6)$$

Moreover, $\phi(\cdot)$ is Leontief:

$$\phi[V(L, K), X] = \min\left\{\frac{V(L, K)}{\bar{V}}, \frac{X}{\bar{X}}\right\}, \quad (7)$$

while $V(\cdot)$ is Cobb–Douglas:

$$V(L, K) = K^\alpha L^{1-\alpha}. \quad (8)$$

This implies that $c(\cdot)$ has the following additive form:

$$c(p_L, p_K, p_X) = \bar{V}\gamma(p_L, p_K) + \bar{X}p_X. \quad (9)$$

To sum up, the joint cost function can be written as:

$$C(\cdot) = h(D,E)\left[\bar{V}\gamma(p_L, p_K) + \bar{X}p_X\right], \tag{10}$$

where $h(\cdot)$ is CET and $\gamma(\cdot)$ is Cobb–Douglas. This clearly places some severe restrictions on the Hessian of $C(\cdot)$. In the R&T case, the substitution matrix Σ therefore has the following form:

$$\Sigma = \begin{bmatrix} \frac{1}{2}\frac{s_D}{s_E} & -\frac{1}{2} & 1 & 1 & 1 \\ & \frac{1}{2}\frac{s_E}{s_D} & 1 & 1 & 1 \\ & & -\frac{\alpha}{1-\alpha} & 1 & 0 \\ & & & -\frac{1-\alpha}{\alpha} & 0 \\ & & & & 0 \end{bmatrix}, \tag{11}$$

where s_D and s_E are the shares of domestic sales and exports in the value of output. Clearly, Σ is very structured, and contains many entries that are either zero or unity. These restrictions do have severe implications for the comparative statics – and the dynamics – of the model, and they may well not stand the test of the data.

I understand that these CGE models are kept as simple as possible to be trackable. To be honest, R&T's production structure is more general than most, and it is far from straightforward. Nevertheless, since the authors do not attempt to derive any analytical results, some additional flexibility, and less arbitrariness, would be a step in the right direction. Moreover, Tom Rutherford is uniquely qualified to undertake this type of generalization, because he has shown that by appropriately nesting CES – and, I presume, CET – functions one can reproduce just about any production structure, including – I am willing to bet – one consistent with joint production (see Perroni and Rutherford (1995)). I would therefore strongly recommend that, in future research, R&T try to model the production structure in a less restrictive way.

My second point is somewhat related to my first one, and it has to do with the modelling of investment. I certainly applaud the careful modelling of that process, and the distinction between the decisions to produce and install capital, the decision to own capital, and the decision to use capital. R&T consider that part of the output produced for the domestic economy can be used to increase the capital stock(s). However, owing to adjustment costs, the actual addition to the capital stock is generally less than the level of investment. The difference represents the resources used up in the installation of the investment goods. These installation costs increase with the amount of investment undertaken.

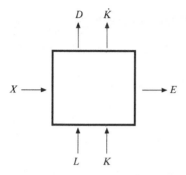

Figure 9D.3 Technology and investment.

Some economists might find this type of adjustment cost rather ad hoc. I do not necessarily share this view. I think it is quite legitimate to attempt to model installation activities. However, I would then argue that modelling installation in the way R&T did is rather restrictive. Why assume that the production and installation of capital goods are separable activities? It would be more general, and just as easy, to model it all at once. Thus, what I would suggest is that the competitive sector be modelled as a three-input, three-output production process, allowing for joint production, and without imposing global separability between inputs and outputs. The three outputs would be exports, consumer goods, and additions to the capital stock $(\dot{K})$. This approach would be somewhat similar to the one pioneered by Foley and Sidrauski (1970) a quarter of a century ago, although they did assume non-joint production. Note that, unlike Figure 9D.1, Figure 9D.3 also emphasizes that exports, like imports, are intermediate goods, or 'middle products', since they will presumably enter the foreign technology.

References

Diewert, W. Erwin (1974), 'Applications of Duality Theory'. In Michael D. Intriligator and D. A. Kendrick (eds.), *Frontiers of Quantitative Economics*, vol. II. Amsterdam: North-Holland.

Foley, Duncan K. and Miguel Sidrauski (1970), 'Portfolio Choice, Investment and Growth', *American Economic Review* 60: 44–63.

Hall, Robert E. (1973), 'The Specification of Technology with Several Kinds of Output', *Journal of Political Economy* 81: 878–92.

Kohli, Ulrich (1978), 'A Gross National Product Function and the Derived Demand for Imports and Supply of Exports', *Canadian Journal of Economics* 11: 167–82.

(1991), *Technology, Duality, and Foreign Trade: The GNP Function Approach to Modeling Imports and Exports*. London: Harvester Wheatsheaf.

Perroni, Carlo and Thomas F. Rutherford (1995), 'Regular Flexibility of Nested CES Functions', *European Economic Review* 39: 335–43.

10 Trade policy and North–South migration

JOSEPH F. FRANCOIS and DOUG NELSON

1 Introduction

Differential rates of population growth between North and South represent a phenomenon of first-rate importance, with implications for patterns of trade, migration, and the distribution of the gains from economic activity both within and between nations. After similar increases in population in the first half of the twentieth century, the second half of the century has been characterized by an extraordinarily rapid increase in Southern population relative to the North, with a continuation of that trend expected through the twenty-first century (see Table 10.1). The percentage increase in Northern population was 44 per cent from 1950 to 1990, and is projected to increase by 24 per cent from 1990 to 2100. At the same time, the Southern population increased by 143 per cent in the post-war period and is projected to increase by another 150 per cent over the twenty-first century. With land fixed, and under most reasonable estimates of physical and human capital creation, these data suggest a potentially rapid divergence in relative endowments between North and South. In an even moderately open world economy, relative endowment changes of this magnitude can reasonably be expected to play a substantial role in any explanations offered for change in wages, employment, and welfare.

The trend in differential population growth is given added significance by its perceived connection to the emergence over the past decade and a half of increasing inequality of earnings in the United States and increasing levels of unemployment in Europe. An exploding body of literature seeks to theoretically characterize and empirically evaluate the causes of increasing inequality in advanced industrial economies.[1] Although controversial among economists, it appears to be widely believed by the public in general and their political representatives in particular that the worsening economic conditions of poorer citizens

323

Table 10.1   Population: historical and projected (billions)

	1900	1950	1990	2025	2100
Developing countries	1.07	1.68	4.08	7.07	10.20
Developed countries	0.56	0.84	1.21	1.40	1.50
World	1.63	2.52	5.30	8.47	11.70

Source: Bongaarts (1995). These data are originally from Merrick (1989) and Bos et al. (1992).

are somehow (and in some degree) transmitted from abroad. The reason for this belief is clear enough: the declining labour market performance of poorer citizens is more or less contemporaneous with a deteriorating trade balance for labour-intensive industries and/or perceived surges in immigration. Both of these are easily connected conceptually to differential population growth: the deteriorating sectoral trade balance for labour-intensive industries via increasing comparative disadvantage in labour-intensive importables;[2] and the migration through straightforward arbitrage. Most recent research that has sought to evaluate the contributions of trade and migration to earnings inequality has tended to separate these two channels.[3] In this paper we focus directly on the connection between trade and migration and its implications for trade policy in the context of a stylized dynamic general equilibrium model.

Ongoing changes of the magnitude of those shown in Table 10.1 generate serious problems for the application of the standard qualitative models that are generally employed in the analysis of commercial policy and growth. On the one hand, these are clearly non-marginal changes, while, on the other, these differentials are not consistent with steady states. Deardorff (1990, 1994) has emphasized the importance of non-steady-state analysis for assessing the evolution of open economies with differential population growth rates. In the context of applied general equilibrium models, the application of significant underlying trends to baseline data to reflect such non-steady-state processes is called projection analysis. Recent work in this area includes Hertel et al. (1995) and Haaland and Norman (1996).

In this paper, we focus on migration trends and their interaction with trade and commercial policy.[4] The next section provides some background discussion of general theoretical issues, and is followed by more focused theoretical discussion of explicit theoretical linkages between trade policy and migration. The theoretical discussion is then supplemented by numerical analysis based on a stylized general equilibrium model that emphasizes the terms-of-trade effects of commercial policy. We finish with some suggestions for further research.

2   Background

The two primary direct channels through which the economic effects of differential rates of population growth can be transmitted internationally are trade in goods and factor flows.[5] Both channels have been widely studied in standard comparative static frameworks. The basic intuition of this literature can be drawn from a simple two-good × two-factor × two-country Heckscher–Ohlin–Samuelson (HOS) model. For obvious reasons we will call the two factors labour and capital, the countries North and South, and the goods 1 and 2. Good 1 will be assumed capital intensive relative to good 2 and North will be capital abundant relative to South. At initial prices, an increase in the Southern labour force will cause the Southern offer curve to rotate outward, producing a deterioration in the Southern terms of trade (i.e. a fall in the relative price of good 2). With free trade and identical technologies, and continuing to assume non-specialization, commodity-price equalization implies factor-price equalization, and thus labour-owning households in both countries experience a real deterioration in welfare via Stolper–Samuelson effects.[6] Of course, with factor-price equalization there is no incentive for migration, because international commodity mobility is a perfect substitute for international factor mobility.[7]

Now suppose that Northern labour is protected by a non-prohibitive tariff on imports of good 2. We know, from countless studies on the inter-industry incidence of protection, that labour is generally protected by both tariffs and non-tariff barriers in industrial countries. If the Northern government responds to increased Southern competitiveness through increased protection, say because the Northern government has a Corden-type conservative social welfare function, *and if this protection works as intended*, the Northern real wage will exceed the Southern real wage, inducing migration of Southern labour. If labour is costlessly mobile, and still assuming non-specialization in the post-migration equilibrium, migration will eliminate trade, completely undoing the effect of the tariff (Mundell 1957). That is, the downward pressure on the wage induced by the increase in the Southern labour endowment is transmitted to Northern labour, this time by migration.[8]

Surveys of the immigration–wages link include Borjas (1994) and Friedberg and Hunt (1995). Although this analysis very nicely links differential population growth to deteriorating returns to (unskilled) labour, and thus seems to rationalize political concerns about North–South trade, there are at least three broad classes of reason to treat such a conclusion/ rationalization with caution: uncertainty about the empirical magnitude of the effect; sensitivity of the static model to empirically plausible variations in the assumptions; and sensitivity to the specification of dynamics. We consider each briefly.

As with the trade–wage connection, attempts econometrically to evaluate the effect of migration on wages of unskilled native workers yield a wide range of estimates, ranging from essentially zero impact (e.g. Card 1991, Butcher and Card 1991, Altonji and Card 1991, Lalonde and Topel 1991) to something like 15–25 per cent of the differential between skilled and unskilled wages (Borjas et al. 1992). Virtually all of these attempts to quantify the effects of trade and migration on relative wages have been controversial, and this is true even in an environment with sizeable changes in both trade flows and migration flows. Although there are a large number of factors that might interfere with attempts empirically to evaluate the effect of trade and/or migration on wages, we isolate two for particular comment: technological change and worker heterogeneity. Substantial recent research on wage dispersion by labour economists now suggests that skill-biased technical change is a major, possibly *the* major, source of increasing wage inequality.[9] Most of the work that attempts to incorporate both trade and technological change simultaneously tends to find only a small role for trade. In a fully dynamic setting, however, the interpretation of this result is more difficult. If technological change responds to competitive pressure, foreign population growth may induce import-competing firms to seek technologies that economize on relatively expensive unskilled workers. Thus, whereas the proximate cause of increasing wage inequality would appear to be skill-biased technical change, the ultimate cause would be international competitive pressure caused by Southern population growth.

Worker heterogeneity is also a fundamental problem in empirical research on both trade and migration effects. The essential point about both migration and trade is that they are ways, direct and indirect, through which foreign factors of production compete with home factors of production. It seems utterly uncontroversial that, if we are actually examining home and foreign supplies of homogeneous factors between countries linked by trade, an increase in the foreign supply of a factor will put downward pressure on home suppliers of the same factor. That is, under standard HOS–Mundell assumptions, trade and migration work toward reproducing the integrated equilibrium. The difficulty, of course, is identifying factors that actually are perfect substitutes for one another. The case of migration is particularly clear. Attempts to evaluate the substitutability of migrants with respect to natives find only a very weak relationship. Furthermore, the strongest effects seem to be on other immigrants with the same properties (i.e. age, experience, education, country of origin). The essential point is that people offer complex, differentiated bundles of attributes in the labour market. Immigrants from different countries are only imperfect substitutes for one another and for home unskilled labour. The same problem applies just as well to evaluating the effect of trade on the wage of home workers. However, as Borjas et al. (1992) argue, these results of weak open economy linkages may reflect the focus on partial equilibrium models of local (i.e. urban) economies that are in fact linked by internal migration patterns that lead to underestimation. Thus, we follow Borjas et al. in taking a national and general equilibrium approach (see Borjas (1987, 1992, 1994)).

Another gross empirical fact that is inconsistent with the simplest versions of the standard conceptual model we have outlined is the magnitude of migration flows. That is, although the flows have been large, they have not been close to the magnitudes that the models would predict. Layard et al. (1992: 2) report that the average wage in Eastern Europe is about US$0.90 per hour whereas in Western Europe it is US$10.00 per hour. Similarly the average wage in Mexico remains well below the US average of US$13.00 per hour (even with the North American Free Trade Area, NAFTA). Differentials of this magnitude suggest massive arbitrage opportunities and, with relatively porous borders, imperfect detection of illegal migrants, and modest penalties, the costs of arbitrage would seem to be small relative to the potential gain. It seems that the only way to account for this is via some combination of informational costs and strong locational preference. In the numerical examples to follow we will simply assume, like others before us, that the international labour market adjusts to maintain a differential between wages in North and South.

Given uncertainty about the empirical magnitude of the open economy links as transmitters of differential demographic change in the standard HOS–Mundell model, it is useful to consider some plausible alternatives. Markusen (1983) presents a very useful analysis of precisely this sort. Markusen shows that, in a two-good × two-factor model with external economies in one sector and constant returns to scale in the other, if factors are mobile (so factor-price equalization (FPE) is an equilibrium condition), the technological conditions dictate the allocation of factors between countries. Specifically, it is shown that FPE requires each country to have more of the factor used intensively in the production of its export good. That is, factors move to create the basis for trade (i.e.

trade and factor mobility are complements). Although Markusen is interested in a different question, the implication of his model would seem to be that an increase in the endowment of Southern labour would induce migration from South to North to re-establish the relative endowment pattern necessary to generate FPE. In a closely related paper, Panagariya (1992) develops a two-good × three-factor model with external economies in one sector and constant returns in the other which generates patterns of migration similar to those considered by Markusen. Helpman and Razin (1983) and Quibria (1993) also consider migration in small-country models with national increasing returns to scale (IRS).

All of our comments to this point have focused on an essentially static model, but the empirical phenomenon with which we are concerned, a substantial and ongoing divergence in endowments driven by differential rates of population growth, is inherently dynamic and does not exhibit steady-state characteristics. This is not the place to review the enormous literature on the relationship between trade and growth, but most of it emphasizes small-country models or steady-state models in which both (all) countries grow at the same rate (see Smith (1977) and Findlay (1984)). The reason for assuming equal growth rates in long-run models is obvious – if countries are growing at different rates, then (at some point) one country will be large (so we can analyse it as a closed economy) and one country will be small (Khang 1971, Kemp 1970, Khang and Kemp 1973). In the meantime, however, we live in a world of dramatic ongoing demographic changes. Deardorff (1990) has emphasized that these phenomena call for non-steady-state general equilibrium analysis, which points to the usefulness of computational modelling in this regard.

3   Theoretical considerations

3.1   The basic framework

The preceding discussion suggests that, to examine commercial policy and migration linkages, we need to construct a model that incorporates differential rates of population growth in a large-country, general equilibrium environment. To this end, we assume two regions, designated Home and Foreign. The n-dimensional vector of quantities produced and consumed in each sector in each region is represented by Z. Preferences are assumed to be identical homothetic, defined over temporal consumption, and separable across time. These assumptions mean we can specify expenditure functions of the form:

$$e(P, q) = \min[PZ] \text{ for } q = q(Z) \tag{1}$$

$$e^*(P, q^*) = \min[PZ^*] \text{ for } q^* = q^*(Z^*) \tag{2}$$

where q represents a composite that enters into the temporal preference function, P represents prices, an asterisk denotes foreign-country values, and time subscripts are suppressed. These expenditure functions are taken to be differentiable and can be shown to be linearly homogeneous and concave in P. National revenue functions can also be specified in terms of P and productive factor endowments v.

$$R(P, v) = \max_Z[PZ|(Z, v) \text{ feasible}] \tag{3}$$

$$R^*(P, v) = \max_{Z^*}[PZ^*|(Z^*, v^*) \text{ feasible}] \tag{4}$$

The revenue functions are assumed to be differentiable and can be shown to be linearly homogeneous and convex in P and concave in v (Dixit and Norman 1980, Helpman and Krugman 1985). Assuming balanced trade and market clearing, and without intertemporal trade, we therefore also have:

$$e^*(P, q^*) = R^*(P, v^*). \tag{5}$$

Ignoring commercial policy for the moment, and assuming identical and homothetic preferences, we can combine (1) and (2), by defining $\varepsilon = (e + e^*)$ and $\Gamma = (q + q^*)$.

$$\varepsilon(P, \Gamma) = R(P, v) + R^*(P, v^*). \tag{6}$$

Continuously clearing goods markets also mean that

$$\frac{\partial \varepsilon}{\partial P} - \frac{\partial R}{\partial P} - \frac{\partial R^*}{\partial P} = 0. \tag{7}$$

Equations (7) represent n excess demand relations, as derived from the expenditure and revenue functions via the envelope theorem. Equations (6) and (7) define a system of $n + 1$ equations and n unknowns. Since, by Walras' law, one of these equations is redundant, we can take one of the goods as a numeraire and drop one of the market-clearing equations in (8). The rest of the system is determined by the solution values set by these n equations.

The theoretical framework developed so far is sufficient for net-trade or homogeneous goods models, such as the Heckscher–Ohlin or Ricardo–

Viner models. However, to reflect the characteristics of stylized models of two-way trade in differentiated intermediate or final products, additional structure is required. First, we assume identical homothetic cost functions for the increasing returns sectors. Combined with the assumption of free entry and average cost pricing under symmetric monopolistic competition, this means that the cost of inputs embodied in differentiated product production in sector j is equalized across producing regions. Second, Cobb–Douglas preferences for the composite sector products, designated Y, are assumed when two-way trade is discussed. Note that, in this case, we have fixed expenditure shares, with consumers behaving as if preferences were reflected through a pseudo-utility function defined in terms of inputs, where we now interpret the terms q and q^* as being Cobb–Douglas composites of homothetic factor input indexes Z, rather than as direct welfare measurements. Related to these assumptions, we also alter our interpretation of Z. The term Z still enters the above set of equations in the same way. However, it now indexes the national scale of production of differentiated products, by providing a measure of composite inputs. With Z as a measure of composite factor services allocated to production of differentiated products by sector, the revenue functions defined in equations (3) and (4) above are then defined over these indexes. With homogeneous goods sectors, this is identical to output itself, since Z will map linearly into output. By assumption, the cost functions for composite factor services Z are linearly homogeneous, and pricing of Z is at average cost, set equal to P. Differentiated products in sector j, as indexed by Z_j, are assumed to be combined, either by consumers or by producers, into a final composite sector product Y_j where the elements of world price vector, P_{Yj}, can be represented in reduced form as follows:

$$P_{Yj} = \beta_j (Z_j + Z_j^*)^{1-\eta_j} P_j = \beta_j \left(\frac{\partial R}{\partial P_j} + \frac{\partial R^*}{\partial P_j} \right)^{1-\eta_j} P_j = \beta_j \zeta^{1-\eta_j} P_j, \quad (8)$$

where β_j is a constant, η_j is industry specific, and $\eta_j > 1$. Note that P and P_Y are of an equal dimension, determined by the number of final goods. Equation (8) reflects, alternatively, reduced form pricing of the composite Y under models of monopolistic competition in Ethier-type models of trade in intermediates with constant elasticity of substitution (CES) final-stage production functions, and common specifications of monopolistic competition in final or intermediate product markets (i.e. the Ethier and Krugman models; see Francois (1996)). In the case of differentiated consumer goods, Y represents a composite goods index for the differentiated products sector that enters the utility function directly. In the case of both differentiated final goods and differentiated intermediate goods, two-way trade involves trade in differentiated products. In the present context, these flows are left implicit. The implications of this implicit two-way trade are reflected in the relationship between Z and P_Y in equation (8).

Analysis of welfare effects requires two more expenditure functions, one defined over P_Y and actual home country welfare (v), and one defined over P_Y and actual foreign country welfare (v^*).

$$E(P_Y, v) = R(P, v) \tag{9}$$
$$E^*(P_Y, v^*) = R^*(P, v^*) \tag{10}$$

The additional structure imposed by equation (8) still leaves us with a rather general specification. It covers homogeneous goods and net-trade models, as we can then simply assume that $\eta = 1$, so that equation (8) becomes a redundant identity. At the same time, equation (8) simply reflects average cost pricing under either specification. In cases of sectoral specialization (as may be expected when factor incomes diverge), the model collapses to one incorporating national scale economies.

We will focus on the implications of population growth in the foreign country. Formally, we specify the time-paths of the foreign country labour force as follows:

$$v_{l^*} = e^{\lambda t} \tag{11}$$
$$\dot{v}_{l^*} = \lambda e^{\lambda t} \tag{12}$$

where a dot denotes a rate of change with respect to time, i.e. $\dot{z} = dz/dt$. Taking the total derivatives of (7) and (8) and combining, we can derive the term:

$$\dot{P} = -\left[\frac{1}{S}\right]\left[\left(\frac{\partial\left(\frac{\partial\varepsilon}{\partial P}\right)}{\partial \Gamma}\right)\left(\frac{\partial\varepsilon}{\partial \Gamma}\right)^{-1}\left(\frac{\partial R^*}{\partial v_{l^*}}\right) - \left(\frac{\partial\left(\frac{\partial R^*}{\partial P}\right)}{\partial v_{l^*}}\right)\right]\dot{v}_{l^*}, \tag{13}$$

where S is the matrix of derivatives of the compensated global excess demands with respect to prices. It is negative definite. The first group of terms in brackets simply reflects uncompensated income effects on price, through demand, as a result of the evolution of changes in the foreign country's supply of labour. The second term reflects the direct output effect on price of the evolution of the foreign country's supply of labour. This effect is a function of the relevant Rybczynski derivatives.

With differentiated products and two-way trade, we also need to include the relationship between scale effects and the evolution of composite goods prices. From equation (8), we can relate changes in P_Y to changes in P by the following:

$$\frac{\dot{P}_Y}{P_Y} = \frac{\dot{P}}{P} + (1 - \eta)\frac{\dot{\varsigma}}{\varsigma}. \tag{14}$$

3.2   Welfare effects of population growth

We will examine both welfare- and wage-induced migration. Turning to welfare effects, from equations (9), (10), and (14) we can derive the following per capita equivalent variation terms:

$$\left(\frac{\partial E}{\partial v}\right)\left(\frac{\dot{v}}{\Pi}\right) = \left[\left(\frac{\partial R}{\partial P}\right)\dot{P} - \left(\frac{\partial E}{\partial P_Y}\right)P_Y\frac{\dot{P}}{P} - \left(\frac{\partial E}{\partial P_Y}\right)P_Y(1 - \eta)\frac{\dot{\varsigma}}{\varsigma}\right]\Pi^{-1} \tag{15}$$

$$\left(\frac{\partial E^*}{\partial v^*}\right)\left(\frac{\dot{v}^*}{\Pi^*}\right) = \left[\left(\frac{\partial R^*}{\partial P}\right)\dot{P} - \left(\frac{\partial E^*}{\partial P_Y}\right)P_Y\frac{\dot{P}}{p}\right]\Pi^{*-1}$$

$$- \left[\left(\frac{\partial E^*}{\partial P_Y}\right)P_Y(1 - \eta)\frac{\dot{\varsigma}}{\varsigma} + \left(\frac{\partial R^*}{\partial v^*}\right)\dot{v}^*\right]\Pi^{*-1} - \left(\frac{v^*}{\Pi^{*2}}\right)\dot{v}. \tag{16}$$

Here, we have defined the population base as Π, and have assumed that the change in population equals the change in the labour force.

In the home country equation, the welfare effects of population growth in the foreign region depend on three sets of effects, represented by the three sets of terms in brackets on the right side of equation (15). The first two terms, when combined, translate into terms-of-trade effects, which hinge on both income effects (the first term) and substitution effects (the second term). Essentially, if foreign population growth causes a secular decline in prices for goods that are more important for consumption than for income purposes (i.e. a positive terms-of-trade effect), then welfare effects will be positive. The third term in brackets reflects the potential effects of specialization/scale effects.

In the foreign country, the welfare effects are more complex. In addition to the types of effects found in equation (15), we also have both induced output effects (the fourth term in brackets) and the expansion of the consumption/population base, represented by the last term in brackets.

3.3　Wage effects of population growth

The effects on relative wage changes are similar to those driving welfare effects. For the home country, the impact is represented in equation (17).

$$
\begin{aligned}
\frac{\dot{\omega}_1 P_Y}{\omega_1 \dot{P}_Y} &= \left(\frac{\partial\left(\frac{\partial R}{\partial P}\right)}{\partial \nu_1}\right)\left[P\left(\frac{\partial R}{\partial \nu_1}\right)^{-1}\right]\left(\frac{\dot{P}}{\dot{P}_j + (1-\eta)(\dot{\zeta}/\zeta)P}\right) \\
&= \left(\frac{\partial\left(\frac{\partial R}{\partial P}\right)}{\partial \nu_1}\right)\left[P\left(\frac{\partial R}{\partial \nu_1}\right)^{-1}\right]\left(\frac{1}{1+(1-\eta)(\dot{\zeta}/\zeta)P/\dot{P}}\right)
\end{aligned}
\tag{17}
$$

We have changes in wages relative to prices being driven by Stolper–Samuelson effects (the first two terms), and by corresponding scale/variety effects (the last set of terms). Essentially, if labour force expansion in the foreign country forces a fall in the relative price of goods that are labour intensive in the home country, we expect home country wages to fall. This hinges on scale/variety effects, which may lead to a decline in consumer prices that outweighs the fall in wages relative to producer prices. The reader can verify that a similar set of conditions holds for the foreign country.

3.4　Migration effects

How do we add migration to this framework? Working with equations (15–17), we may want to specify economic incentives for migration in terms of changes in relative per capita welfare and/or changes in real relative wages. Consider migration based on general conditions of overall economic welfare. Formally, we may specify migration from the foreign to the home country, M_t, as follows:

$$
M_t = M_t\left(\frac{v}{\Pi_{t-1}}, \frac{v^*}{\Pi_{t-1^*}}\right).
\tag{18}
$$

With this lag mechanism, we then need to modify the labour force growth equations as follows:

$$
\dot{\nu}_{1^*} = \lambda e^{\lambda t} - M_t
\tag{19}
$$

$$
\nu_1 = M_t
\tag{20}
$$

A similar mechanism can be specified for wage migration.

Formally, introduction of (19) and (20) involves some modification of equations (15)–(16), though the basic mechanisms will remain the same. Qualitatively, we have a system where the implications of population growth for welfare and migration hinge on a mix of terms-of-trade effects (the classical growth effects of Bhagwati, etc.), variety scaling effects, the impact of an expanding consumption base, and the responsiveness of migration flows to changes in the arguments in equation (18). The expanding consumption base effect will depend on the type of model specified. For example, with limited land resources (i.e. specific factors), an expanding population base may more quickly lead to erosion of welfare both from declining marginal productivity within domestic agriculture and from worsening terms of trade for imported agricultural goods.

3.5   Commercial policy

Next, consider the implications of these migration mechanisms for commercial policy. The political arguments linking commercial policy to demographic trends can be quite complex. For example, in the case of NAFTA, Mexico was painted as placing wage pressure on labour in the United States both through trade and through migration. In the public debate, some members of the pro-NAFTA camp argued that migration effects tended to dominate, and that NAFTA would help to alleviate such migration-based wage pressure, albeit with the possibility of some offset from trade-based pressure (however, see Levy and van Wijnbergen (1994)). Similar concerns underlie the effort by the European Union (EU) to expand east into former communist-bloc countries, and its pursuit of agreements with certain developing Mediterranean economies.

In the framework developed here, trade intervention will interact with incentives to migrate through traditional terms-of-trade channels, through efficiency effects, and through associated scale/variety effects. In general terms, when production in the international scale economies (ISE) sector continues in more than one country, the national effects of trade protection involve both production efficiency and terms-of-trade effects. To illustrate these effects, consider a single country that taxes cross-border transactions in the Z sector. This requires the addition of the trade tax, t, directly to the revenue functions specified earlier. Such a tax has the potential, given prices, to correct for or worsen the non-tangency conditions that result from average cost pricing. In addition, prices themselves will depend, in reduced form, on the level of the trade tax, such that these rates also enter the expenditure and revenue functions indirectly through price effects:

$$e[P_Y(t),\ u] = R[P_Z(t),\ v, t],\tag{21}$$

where u denotes utility. Taking derivatives with t and rearranging, we have:

$$\frac{du}{dt} = \left(\frac{\partial e}{\partial u}\right)^{-1}\left[-\left(\frac{\partial e}{\partial P_Y}\right)\left(\frac{\partial P_Y}{\partial t}\right) + \left(\frac{\partial R}{\partial t}\right) + \left(\frac{\partial R}{\partial P_Z}\right)\left(\frac{\partial P_Z}{\partial t}\right)\right].\tag{22}$$

With reference to equations (21) and (22), the first term in square brackets represents the effect of a change in P_Y on welfare, through an increased cost of consumption. Efficiency and income-related terms-of-trade effects are represented by the last two terms. A trade tax will have the same qualitative effect as a production tax (a negative subsidy) on P_Y, and on efficiency, as represented by the second term in brackets. Protection reduces the extent of cross-border integration, forcing firms to use less efficient production methods biased toward the home Z sector and, under internationally increasing returns to scale (IIRS), weakening the base underlying external scale effects for home and foreign producers alike. Both the price and efficiency effects imply a reduction in national welfare. This is only offset if income (terms-of-trade) effects, as embodied in the last term, dominate the negative direct effects of the distortion.

Consider the impact of protection on the incentives for migration. From equation (22), if protection increases home country welfare through induced terms-of-trade effects, this would have the effect of increasing the relative wedge between the home and foreign country migration arguments in equation (18). The result is that, by boosting welfare *at the expense of trading partners*, one unintended consequence may be to induce more migration from those same trading partners. *Beggar-thy-neighbour implies invite-thy-neighbour* under this scenario. The addition of scale economies may magnify this incentive effect, since protection at home can force the effective production possibility set to shrink for the foreign country by reducing economies of specialization. The other side of this effect lurks behind the arguments for a liberal EU trade regime toward Eastern Europe and the Mediterranean countries. By mitigating adverse terms-of-trade effects, such an approach may alternatively moderate underlying migration incentives.

In a similar vein, protection aimed at propping up wages may also lead to increased incentives for migration. In particular, if such protection at home prevents the export of the abundant factor (i.e. labour) through goods from the foreign country, such labour may instead be exported directly through migration, again as reflected by a variation of equation (18). If we have a model with a non-traded labour-intensive sector, the negative wages effects of induced migration could conceivably outweigh the positive effects of protecting labour from trade-related pressure.

4   Numerical simulations

To illustrate some of the mechanisms discussed above, we next turn to a highly stylized two-region numerical model. Our objective is to illustrate the concepts discussed above, and to highlight additional factors not immediately obvious from the marginal calculus. The basic features of the model are described in the appendix to this chapter.[10]

We model migration through a variation of equation (18). We assume that, in each period, a share of the unskilled population of the South decides to migrate to the North, based on the gap between North and South per capita welfare (or wages) relative to the benchmark ratio of these values.

$$M_t = \mu_t \left[\Delta \ln\left(\frac{v}{\Pi_{t-1}}\right) - \Delta \ln\left(\frac{v^*}{\Pi_{t-1}^*}\right) \right] \Pi_t^*, \qquad (23)$$

where μ is the migration elasticity, reflecting the percentage of South population that decides to migrate for each percentage deviation in welfare (wages).

Our basic experiments are constructed as follows. We examine the impact of induced migration, starting from an initial assumption of zero migration. Migration is then induced through introduction of population growth (or, identically in this model, labour supply growth) in the South. This sets off a number of changes, including shifting production and wages and changes in per capita welfare. The levels of these variables are all solved for explicitly. These feed, through equation (23), into our migration mechanism, where we assume $\mu = .01$. Following this migration, we then solve for a new equilibrium. The result is a sequence of equilibria involving migration flows induced by the ongoing labour supply shocks in the South. The benchmark experiment involves wage or welfare migration, without any policy response from the North. The results are contrasted with a set of equilibria involving either an assumed tariff reduction or capital transfers by the North.

Figure 10.1 charts the basic pattern of induced migration with no policy response and with a tariff reduction. In our example, tariff reduction leads to an initial drop in the number of migrants over the full twenty-five-year period covered in the experiment. Similar patterns hold for capital transfers, and under specifications that include an endogenous capital stock.

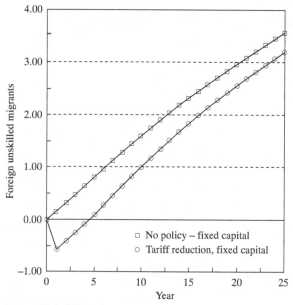

Figure 10.1 Migration.

The time trend for the price of unskilled and skilled labour is presented in Figures 10.2 and 10.3. A number of factors are illustrated. First, terms-of-trade effects dominate, in the medium run, when we incorporate endogenous capital stocks. Eventually, however, the underlying direct mechanism of migration comes to dominate, and real unskilled wages fall in the home country in the long run. With fixed capital stocks, terms-of-trade effects are less evident, and unskilled wage erosion is almost immediate. A second pattern illustrated in Figures 10.2 and 10.3 is that tariff reductions dominate increased tariffs as a strategy for propping up unskilled wages. This holds in both the fixed and endogenous capital specifications, and it does so because terms-of-trade gains from protection accelerate unskilled labour migration. By moderating these incentives through trade liberalization, the wage pressure of migration on home unskilled labour is moderated. Finally, skilled home labour does quite well under all scenarios. Not surprisingly, tariff reductions lead to a reduction in the increase in skilled wages. This is because they slow the inflow of unskilled labour and reduce the terms-of-trade gains, both of which act to drive up skilled wages.

The results of these numerical experiments illustrate an important point not immediately evident from marginal analysis. In particular, depending on the time-frame, different effects highlighted in the theory may

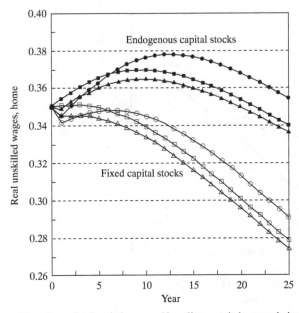

Figure 10.2 **Real wages for unskilled home labour.**

□ No policy – fixed capital   ■ No policy – capital accumulation
○ Tariff reduction, fixed capital ● Tariff reduction, capital accumulation
△ Capital transfer, fixed capital ▲ Capital transfer, capital accumulation

dominate for a given intervention. For such a policy, terms-of-trade effects may dominate over one time-frame, and the direct effects of migration on factor supply may dominate over a different time-frame. In addition, the endogeneity of capital is clearly important as well.

5   Summary

Tremendous differences in the rate of population growth between North and South have important implications for patterns of trade, migration, the distribution of income, and the distribution of the gains from trade. In this paper, we focus particularly on migration-related effects. Following an overview of the literature on trade and migration-related labour market linkages, we offer a theoretical discussion of explicit theoretical linkages between population growth, trade policy, and migration. The key channels we identify relate to direct factor market effects of population growth, terms-of-trade effects, and induced scale effects. Trade policy enters the analytical mix through its impact on the terms-of-

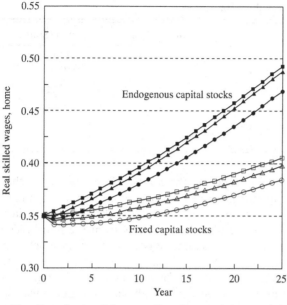

□ No policy – fixed capital   ■ No policy – capital accumulation
○ Tariff reduction, fixed capital   ● Tariff reduction, capital accumulation
△ Capital transfer, fixed capital   ▲ Capital transfer, capital accumulation

Figure 10.3 Real wages for skilled home labour.

trade, efficiency, and scale effects. We supplement the formal analysis with simple, numerical examples. The numerical analysis highlights issues not immediately evident in the theoretical analysis, including the dominance of different effects (such as terms-of-trade changes) over different time-horizons. This, in turn, points to the value of projection analysis based on computable general equilibrium for the study of the interaction of trade and migration policy.

Appendix: Migration and trade policy – numerical examples

Model description

The model includes two regions: the home region (a stylized North economy) and a foreign region (a stylized South economy). The benchmark data are summarized in Table 10A.1.

The GDP function in both regions is Cobb–Douglas, and is defined over a supply of skilled labour, unskilled labour, and capital. Preferences

Table 10A.1   Benchmark data for model

	Home (North)	Foreign (South)
GDP	130.34	27.15
Population	200.00	550.00
Per capita income	0.65	0.05
Unskilled wages	0.43	0.02
Labour force growth (%)	0.00	3.00
Savings rates (%)	5.00	15.00
Initial tariffs (%)	20.00	0.00

are also Cobb–Douglas with respect to the goods of both regions, so that trade takes place in Armington fashion. Preferences are identical, and are weighted toward the goods produced by the North. The benchmark data include a tariff imposed by the North on imports from the South. The basic migration mechanism is very simple. Based on divergence between real unskilled labour wages in the North and South, the share of the foreign (South) region's unskilled labour force that chooses to migrate is determined by a migration elasticity. The only factor that adjusts in model 1 is labour. In model 2, capital accumulates at a rate of 5 per cent of GDP in the North, and 15 per cent in the South. Here, the Cobb–Douglas utility composite is assumed to be a good that is used in consumption or investment.

Experiments

1. No policy – fixed capital
2. Tariff reduction, fixed capital
3. Capital transfer, fixed capital
4. No policy – capital accumulation
5. Tariff reduction, capital accumulation
6. Capital transfer, capital accumulation

Notes

This paper represents the opinions of the authors. It is not meant to represent, in any way, the opinions or official positions of any institution with which they may have ever been affiliated, or of staff of such institutions. It was presented at the CEPR conference on "Dynamic Issues in Applied Commercial Policy Analysis", which received support through a grant from the Ford Foundation. All remaining errors are our own.
1. See Francois (1996) for a theoretical overview. Levy and Murnane (1992) provide a very useful survey of the research related to the US case; also see

the February 1992 *Quarterly Journal of Economics* for a number of important empirical papers addressing the problem of increasing inequality in the USA A convenient source for the European case is Algoskoufis et al. (1995). The upshot of virtually all research on labour markets in industrial countries is that there has been a dramatic worsening of the distribution of benefits from participation in the labour market over the past fifteen or so years.

2. The key to this argument is the now well-established fact that import-competing industries use unskilled labour relatively intensively (e.g. Murphy and Welch 1991).

3. Borjas et al. (1992) is an important exception. Although Borjas et al. do explicitly consider the effects of both trade and migration, their focus is primarily on identifying labour-market effects at a fairly disaggregated level. Thus, trade and migration are treated as exogenous shocks to the labour market. Our work in this paper is interested in a different question, the interaction of trade and migration flows in general equilibrium. Borjas et al.'s finding that both trade and migration have had a significant effect on the labour market suggests that the attempt to examine the broader general equilibrium in which the labour market is embedded is a useful task.

4. The recent computational literature on migration has focused, for the most part, on USA–Mexico migration patterns. This includes Hill and Méndez (1984), Robinson et al. (1993), Levy and van Wijnbergen (1994), and Burfisher et al. (1994). Weyerbrock (1995) examines migration from the former Soviet Union and Eastern Europe to Western Europe, while Hamilton and Whalley (1984) have examined North–South migration.

5. We are well aware that indirect effects, such as those operating on the rates of growth of population, human capital, and physical capital, can easily dominate the direct effects in a well-specified dynamic model. Of at least equivalent significance are indirect effects that operate through the political system. However, as is well known, both of these sources of indirect effect are extremely sensitive to the microanalytical foundations of the relevant domain of choice. Thus, in this paper, we choose to focus on the direct transmission via migration and leave the indirect mechanisms unmodelled and implicitly fixed.

6. We are abstracting from perversities of the Metzler–Johnson sort. We should also note that aggregate Southern welfare could fall as a result of the increase in population. This is Bhagwati's (1958) immiserizing growth. As Dixit and Norman (1980: 135) show, such immiserization is linked directly to the Stolper–Samuelson effects.

7. Econometric estimates of the effect of trade on wages range from essentially zero (Lawrence and Slaughter 1993) to conclusions that trade is the main cause of declining wages of unskilled workers (Wood 1994, Batra 1993). To the extent that there is a median position, it is that the effect of trade is a small but significant – of the order of 10–15 per cent – cause of the increased wage inequality that has emerged in the past fifteen years. Recent surveys include Baldwin (1995) and Richardson (1995).

8. As a check on the reliability of the model as an intuition generator, it is useful to note that Southern labour growth is transmitted to the North *either* by trade *or* by migration, but not by both. This is just (once again) the fact that, in this model, trade and factor mobility are perfect substitutes. The fact that we observe sizeable flows of both suggests caution.

9. In addition to the useful discussion in Levy and Murnane (1992), see the widely cited papers by Davis and Haltiwanger (1991), Bound and Johnson (1992), Katz and Murphy (1992), and Berman et al. (1994).

10. Copies of the model (which is spreadsheet based) are available upon request from the authors.

References

Algoskoufis, G., C. Bean, G. Bertola, D. Cohen, J. Dolado, and G. Saint-Paul (1995), *Unemployment: Choices for Europe*. London: CEPR.

Altonji, J. and D. Card (1991), 'The Effects of Immigration on the Labor Market Outcomes of Less-skilled Natives'. In J. Abowd and R. Freeman (eds.), *Immigration, Trade and the Labor Market*. Chicago: University of Chicago Press/NBER, pp. 201–34.

Baldwin, R. (1995), 'The Effect of Trade and Foreign Direct Investment on Employment and Relative Wages', NBER Working Paper No. 5037.

Batra, R. (1993), *The Myth of Free Trade*. New York: Scribner's.

Berman, E., J. Bound, and Z. Grilliches (1994), 'Changes in the Demand for Skilled Labor within US Manufacturing: Evidence from the Annual Survey of Manufactures', *Quarterly Journal of Economics* 109(2): 367–97.

Bhagwati, J. N. (1958), 'Immiserizing Growth: A Geometric Note', *Review of Economic Studies* 12.

Bongaarts, J. (1995), 'Global and Regional Population Projections to 2025'. In N. Islam (ed.), *Population and Food in the Twenty-First Century*. Washington, D.C.: International Food Policy Research Institute, pp. 7–16.

Borjas, G. (1987), 'Self-Selection and the Earnings of Immigrants', *American Economic Review* 77: 531–53.

— (1992), 'National Origin and the Skills of Immigrants in the Postwar Period'. In G. Borjas and R. Freeman (eds.), *Immigration and the Work Force*. Chicago: University of Chicago Press/NBER, pp. 17–47.

— (1994), 'The Economics of Immigration', *Journal of Economic Literature* 32(4): 1667–717.

Borjas, G., R. Freeman, and L. Katz (1992), 'On the Labor Market Effects of Immigration and Trade'. In G. Borjas and L. Katz (eds.), *Immigration and the Workforce: Economic Consequences for the US and Source Areas*. Chicago: University of Chicago Press/NBER, pp. 213–44.

Bos, E. M. Vu, A. Levin, and R. Bulatao (1992), *World Population Projections, 1992–93 Edition*. Baltimore, Md.: Johns Hopkins University Press/World Bank.

Bound, J. and G. Johnson (1992), 'Changes in the Structure of Wages in the 1980's: An Evaluation of Alternative Explanations', *American Economic Review* 82(3): 371–92.

Burfisher, M., S. Robinson, and K. Thierfelder (1994), 'Wage Changes in a US–Mexico Free Trade Area: Migration versus Stolper–Samuelson Effects'. In J. Francois and C. Shiells (eds.), *Modeling Trade Policy: Applied General Equilibrium Models of North American Free Trade*. New York: Cambridge University Press, pp. 195–222.

Butcher, K. and D. Card (1991), 'Immigration and Wages: Evidence from the 1980s', *American Economic Review* 81(2): 292–96.

Card, D. (1991), 'The Impact of the Mariel Boatlift on the Miami Labor Market', *ILR Review* 43: 245–57.

Davis, S. and J. Haltiwanger (1991), 'Wage Dispersion between and within U.S. Manufacturing Plants', *Brookings Papers on Economic Analysis*, micro.

Deardorff, A. (1990), 'Trade and Capital Mobility in a World of Diverging Populations'. In D. G. Johnson and R. Lee (eds.), *Population Growth and Economic Development: Issues and Evidence*. Madison: University of Wisconsin Press, pp. 561–88.

(1994), 'Growth and International Investment with Diverging Populations', *Oxford Economic Papers* 46: 477–91.

Dixit, A. and V. Norman (1980), *Theory of International Trade*. Cambridge: Nisbet/Cambridge University Press.

Findlay, R. (1984), 'Growth and Development in Trade Models'. In R. W. Jones and P. B. Kenen (eds.), *Handbook of International Economics – volume I*. Amsterdam: Elsevier.

Francois, J. (1996), 'Labour Force Growth, Trade, and Wages', *Economic Journal* 107(339).

Friedberg, R. and J. Hunt (1995), 'The Impact of Immigrants on Host Country Wages, Employment and Growth', *Journal of Economic Perspectives* 9: 23–44.

Haaland, J. and V. Norman (1996), 'Scenarios as Tools to Assess the Effects of Trade Policy', Norwegian School of Business Administration, May.

Hamilton, B. and J. Whalley (1984), 'Efficiency and Distributional Implications of Global Restrictions on Labour Mobility: Calculations and Policy Implications', *Journal of Development Economics* 14: 61–76.

Helpman, E. and P. Krugman (1985), *Market Structure and Foreign Trade*. Cambridge, Mass.: MIT Press.

Helpman, E. and A. Razin (1983), 'Increasing Returns, Monopolistic Competition, and Factor Movements: A Welfare Analysis', *Journal of International Economics* 16.

Hertel, T., W. Martin, K. Yanagashima, and B. Dimaranan (1995), 'Liberalizing Manufactures Trade in a Changing World Economy'. In W. Martin and L. Alan Winters (eds.), *The Uruguay Round and the Developing Economies*. World Bank Discussion Paper No. 307, Washington, D.C.: World Bank.

Hill, J. and J. Méndez (1984), 'The Effect of Commercial Policy on International Migration Flows: The Case of the US and Mexico', *Journal of International Economics* 17(1/2): 41–53.

Katz, L. and K. Murphy (1992), 'Changes in Relative Wages, 1963–1987: Supply and Demand Factors', *Quarterly Journal of Economics* 107(1): 35–78.

Kemp, M. (1970), 'International Trade between Countries with Different Natural Rates of Growth', *Economic Record* 46: 467–81.

Khang, C. (1971), 'Equilibrium Growth in the International Economy: The Case of Unequal Natural Rates of Growth', *International Economic Review* 12(2): 239–49.

Khang, C. and M. Kemp (1973), 'International Trade and Investment between Countries with Different Natural Rates of Growth', *Metroeconomica* 25(3): 214–28.

Lalonde, R. and R. Topel (1991), 'Labor Market Adjustments to Increased Migration'. In J. Abowd and R. Freeman (eds.), *Immigration, Trade and the Labor Market*. Chicago: University of Chicago Press/NBER, pp. 167–99.

Lawrence, R. and M. Slaughter (1993), 'Trade and US Wages: Giant Sucking

Sound or Small Hiccup?' *Brookings Papers on Economic Analysis* 1993(2): 161–210.

Layard, R., O. Blanchard, R. Dornbusch, and P. Krugman (1992), *East–West Migration: The Alternatives.* Cambridge, Mass.: MIT Press.

Levy, F. and R. Murnane (1992), 'US Earnings Levels and Earnings Inequality: A Review of Recent Trends and Proposed Explanations', *Journal of Economic Literature* 30(3): 1333–81.

Levy, S. and S. van Wijnbergen (1994), 'Labor Markets, Migration and Welfare: Agriculture in the North-American Free Trade Agreement', *Journal of Development Economics* 43: 263–78.

Markusen, J. (1983), 'Factor Movements and Commodity Trade as Complements', *Journal of International Economics* 14: 341–56.

Merrick, T. (1989), 'World Population in Transition', *Population Bulletin* 41(2): 10–22.

Mundell, R. A. (1957), 'International Trade and Factor Mobility', American Economic Review 47(2): 321–35.

Murphy, K. and F. Welch (1991), 'The Role of International Trade in Wage Differentials'. In M. Kosters (ed.), *Workers and Their Wages: Changing Patterns in the US.* Washington, D.C.: AEI, pp. 39–69.

Panagariya, A. (1992), 'Factor Mobility, Trade and Welfare – A North–South Analysis with Economies of Scale', *Journal of Development Economics* 39: 229–45.

Quibria, M. (1993), 'International Migration, Increasing Returns and Real Wages', *Canadian Journal of Economics* 26(2): 456–68.

Richardson, J. D. (1995), 'Income Inequality and Trade: How to Think, What to Conclude', *Journal of Economic Perspectives* 9(3): 33–55.

Robinson, S., M. Burfisher, R. Hinojosa-Ojeda, and K. Thierfelder (1993), 'Agricultural Policies and Migration in a US Mexico Free Trade Area', *Journal of Policy Modeling* 15(5/6): 673–701.

Smith, M. A. M. (1977), 'Capital Accumulation in the Open Two-Sector Economy', *Economic Journal* 87, November: 273–282.

Weyerbrock, S. (1995), 'Can the European Community Absorb More Immigrants? A General Equilibrium Analysis of the Labor Market and Macroeconomic Effects of East–West Migration in Europe', *Journal of Policy Modeling* 17(2): 85–120.

Wood, A. (1994), *North–South Trade, Employment and Inequality: Changing Fortunes in a Skill-Driven World.* New York: Oxford University Press.

11 Long-term modelling of trade and environmental linkages

JOHN BEGHIN, DAVID ROLAND-HOLST, and DOMINIQUE VAN DER MENSBRUGGHE

1 Introduction

Trade and environment linkages are coming under increasing scrutiny and a considerable literature is emerging on the subject.[1] Some papers have looked formally at coordination of policies toward the environment and trade in a polluted open economy. These include Markusen (1975), Baumol and Oates (1988), Krutilla (1991), and Choi and Johnson (1992). With the exception of Copeland (1994), however, they emphasize optimal interventions and abstract from the more practical issues of designing second-best and piecemeal reforms. Copeland investigated piecemeal trade and environmental policy reforms in a small, open, production-polluted, and distorted economy and identified sufficient conditions for welfare enhancement. This approach initiated an important new line of thinking in the literature on second-best trade reform, following Hatta,[2] because it addressed the problem of coordination of trade and environment policies. It also identified situations in which a tariff can be used to abate pollution without decreasing welfare.

Building on these results, we account for pollution in consumption as well as production activities and let firms use two approaches to pollution abatement in production. Toxic effluents arising from final consumption are substantial, e.g. non-electrical energy, chemicals, and post-consumption waste materials. Consumption-induced pollution critically undermines tariffs as second-best instruments for environmental policy. Further, the presence of consumption-based pollution externalities complicates the welfare effects of trade liberalization and can defeat the intentions of narrower, production-oriented policies. On the production side, firms in polluting sectors can change output (effluent level) or technology (effluent intensity) in response to the policies considered.

Next, we consider alternative price-oriented instruments, including tariffs, consumption and output taxes, and effluent taxes. Effluent taxes

may be impractical for developing economies because of costly monitoring. Output and consumption taxes may provide a more realistic
approach to unregulated pollution. Each instrument provides distinct
incentives for firms to use one or both abatement strategies. We devote
substantial attention to the decomposition of these incentive effects on
substitution in consumption, shifting output composition, and 'choice of
technique' (altering effluent rates).[3]

Identifying and elucidating these effects will clarify two issues in the
trade and environment debate. The first is whether trade liberalization
induces developing economies to specialize in pollution-intensive activities, particularly in exports. Lack of policy coordination or poor
instrument choice may explain output and consumption bias towards
pollution-intensive goods as well as high effluent rates. The second issue
relates to a sobering stylized fact: although toxic intensity per unit of
wealth eventually decreases in high-income economies, toxic intensity *per
unit of industrial output* increases with growth and remains high in these
economies (Hettige et al. 1992).

We first consider policy reforms (optimum and gradual) aimed at
decreasing pollution in the presence of fixed distortions, showing in
particular that two welfare effects arise for all reforms. First, the level of
pollution is affected. Following the intuition of the targeting principle, the
closest instrument, the effluent tax, does the best job in terms of pollution
abatement. Production and consumption taxes are the next best, followed
distantly by tariffs as the worst of the environmental policy options
considered. Second, each instrument has an indirect effect on allocative
efficiency. For example, lower pollution can mean reduced economic
opportunities in developing economies (Lee and Roland-Holst 1997).

Next, we combine a piecemeal trade liberalization scenario with pollution reforms starting from a trade-distorted economy in which pollution
previously has been unregulated. For these joint reforms, we identify a
similar dichotomy of direct effects on welfare. These two indirect effects
tend to be symmetric. We identify sufficient conditions for welfare-
improving reforms for these coordinated policies.

These theoretical results provide a universe of discourse for evaluating
policies, but they also make it clear that quantitative judgements will be
required more often than qualitative ones. Apart from confirming the
basic targeting principle, most of the outcomes differ by degree, and thus
empirical work in this area will be essential to support effective policy
design and implementation. To illustrate the scope and magnitude of the
forces at work here, we complement our theoretical discussion with
simulation results from a dynamic computable general equilibrium
(CGE) model of Indonesia.

2 The basic model

Following Hatta (1977), Dixit and Norman (1980), and Copeland (1994), we use a dual treatment of a perfectly competitive and open economy. Pollution is produced by consumers and producers at different rates and all pollution produced accumulates into a public bad. This in turn enters the utility function and the expenditure function of the representative consumer, expressing its disutility and environmental damage, respectively.[4] The derivative of the expenditure function with respect to pollution is the increase in expenditure necessary to keep utility constant, given an increase in pollution.

Given the assumption of a perfectly competitive economy, production decisions are modelled by a revenue or GDP function:

$$R(P + \tau - \beta, \varepsilon, \nu) = \max_{(x,y)} \{ (P + \tau - \beta)'x - \varepsilon\gamma'x \mid (x, \gamma)$$
$$\text{feasible given inputs } \nu \}, \tag{1}$$

where P is the vector of exogenous world prices, τ is the vector of trade taxes, ε represents the tax on effluents, γ is the vector of per unit effluent rates of output x of n commodities, and β is a vector of production taxes/subsidies. The function R exhibits the desired properties, i.e. it is homogeneous of degree one in prices and taxes,[5] the usual envelope theorem results such as $R_p = x$; $R_\varepsilon = -\gamma'x$, hold, R_{pp} is the Hessian of price responses of the output vector x, $R_{\varepsilon\varepsilon}$ is minus the response of production pollution to the effluent tax, $R_{\varepsilon p}$ is minus the cross-price response of production pollution to output prices, $R_{\varepsilon p} = R'_{p\varepsilon}$ and is the response of output to the effluent tax. For expository purposes, our attention is limited to a single pollutant type, but this framework extends without difficulty to a vector of k pollution types (γ becomes a $k \times n$ matrix and ε is a $k \times 1$ vector of taxes).

The matrix $R_{\varepsilon\varepsilon}$ is positive by convexity of R in prices and taxes. Moreover, $R_{\varepsilon\varepsilon}$ can be decomposed into three effects, i.e. $R_{\varepsilon\varepsilon} = \gamma'R_{pp}\gamma + \gamma'(\partial\gamma/\partial P)x - x'(\partial\gamma/\partial\varepsilon)$.[6] The first of these is the output price response, holding effluent rates γ constant, and is positive because R is positive semi-definite. The second effect is that of prices on effluent rates, difficult to sign for individual γ_i and dependent on the effluent 'production technology', but one can argue that this is positive as well (i.e. $\gamma'(\partial\gamma/\partial P)x$ is positive). The last is the effect of the effluent tax on the effluent rate, which is negative but preceded by a negative sign.

The economy has a representative consumer with expenditure function:

$$E(P + \tau + \eta, \varepsilon, T, U_0) = \min_{(c,\alpha)} \{ [(P + \tau + \eta)'c + \varepsilon\alpha'c] \mid U \geq U_0 \}, \tag{2}$$

where c represents the n-good consumption vector, η is a vector of consumption taxes on the same goods, ε is the per unit effluent tax, and α denotes the vector of effluent per unit of consumption of c. As noted, pollution is a scalar and is the sum of different effluent emissions in consumption and production activities, but all refer to the same effluent type. Variable T is the public bad (or the variable constrained by a non-economic target). It is defined as $T = \alpha'c + \gamma'x$, the sum of consumption and production externalities. The scalar U represents utility with a reference level U_0. The usual optimality conditions for E include $E_p = c$ and $E_\varepsilon = \alpha'c$. Here E_{pp} is the Hessian of price responses of the consumption vector c; $E_{\varepsilon p}$ denotes the cross-price response of consumption pollution to consumption prices; $E_{\varepsilon p} = E'_{p\varepsilon}$ is the response of consumption to the effluent tax; and $E_{\varepsilon\varepsilon}$ is the response of consumption pollution to the effluent tax.

Analogously, $E_{\varepsilon\varepsilon}$ can be decomposed into three effects:[7]

$$E_{\varepsilon\varepsilon} = \alpha' E_{pp}\alpha + \alpha'(\partial\alpha/\partial P)c + c'(\partial\alpha/\partial\varepsilon). \tag{3}$$

It is assumed for the rest of the paper that the consumer cannot alter the pollution coefficient as is possible in production. Stylized facts suggest that most of technology-induced abatement is achieved in production and not in final consumption.[8] Hence, the identity reduces to $E_{\varepsilon\varepsilon} = \alpha' E_{pp}\alpha$, which is negative. Another derivative, E_T, represents the marginal damage of total pollution on utility or the necessary increase in expenditure to maintain U constant. It is positive. The final derivative of interest is the inverse of the marginal utility of income, E_U, which is positive as well. Derivatives E_U and E_T have derivatives with respect to the consumption price vector and pollution taxes (E_{pU}, $E_{\varepsilon U}$, E_{pT}, and E_{pT}).

Equilibrium for this economy is described as follows:

$$E = R + \tau'(E_p - R_p) + \eta'E_p + \beta'R_p + \varepsilon(\alpha'E_p + \gamma'R_p), \tag{4}$$

with

$$T \equiv E_\varepsilon - R_\varepsilon = \alpha'E_p + \gamma'R_p \tag{5}$$

and

$$M = E_p - R_p. \tag{6}$$

Foreign and domestic specific commodities exhibit the same effluent rate. To develop some intuition about how imports, pollution, and welfare interact, we temporarily set consumption and production taxes, η and β, equal to zero and focus on effluent taxes and tariffs. Differentiating (4) for changes in imports, welfare, and pollution yields:

$$E_U dU = \tau' dM + (\varepsilon - E_T) dT. \tag{7}$$

There are two sources of distortions and welfare effects. Non-zero tariffs and non-optimal effluent taxes (ε not equal to E_T) are distortions which in turn have an impact on imports, M, and pollution, T. Changes in welfare, pollution, and trade are endogenously determined by policy changes. Totally differentiating (5) yields:

$$dT = (E_{\varepsilon\varepsilon} - R_{\varepsilon\varepsilon})d\varepsilon + (E_{\varepsilon p} - R_{\varepsilon p})d\tau + E_{\varepsilon T}dT + \varepsilon_{\varepsilon U}dU. \tag{8}$$

Hence, abatement of pollution (positive or negative) has four components. First, the effluent tax induces pollution abatement in consumption and production; second, there are the cross-price responses of pollution to tariff changes ($\partial M/\partial \varepsilon = \partial T/\partial \tau$); third, a feedback effect of pollution on itself arises because of changes in the marginal damage of pollution; and, last, a real income effect induced by changes in welfare occurs (Grossman and Krueger's scale effect). Copeland's model was recursive because changes in production pollution, dT, did not depend on T or U and could be solved independently for changes in policies ($d\tau$ and $d\varepsilon$). Further, the abatement induced by the effluent tax can be decomposed into four sources (substitution in consumption and in production, and changes in emission intensities in production; see the decomposition of $R_{\varepsilon\varepsilon}$ above). Equation (6) also shows that tariffs are ineffective to target pollution because they have opposite effects on consumption-induced and production-based pollution. One is subsidized while the other is taxed. These offsetting effects can be decoupled by using production and consumption taxes instead of tariffs.

Similarly to pollution, T, imports, M, can also be differentiated for changes in policy instruments, welfare, and pollution. Differentiating (6) in this way yields:

$$dM = (E_{p\varepsilon} - R_{p\varepsilon})d\varepsilon + (E_{pp} - R_{pp})d\tau + E_{pT}dT + \varepsilon_{pU}dU. \tag{9}$$

3   Policy interventions for trade and pollution reform

In this section, we contrast piecemeal and coordinated approaches to trade and pollution reform.[9] Subsection 3.1 sets forth three types of second-best intervention, followed by discussion of policies that design and implement trade and pollution taxes in concert.

3.1   Second-best policies

Equations (7) to (9) can be solved for exogenous changes in policy instruments. Taking the available instruments one at a time, we first vary only effluent taxes, assessing their effects on domestic pollution and trade. Then we evaluate production and consumption taxes as next-best abatement instruments. Finally, tariffs alone are evaluated in the same context.

3.1.1   Effluent taxes

Consider changes in ε, holding tariffs constant and assuming $\eta = \beta = 0$, i.e.

$$AdU = \{\tau'(E_{p\varepsilon} - R_{p\varepsilon}) + [\varepsilon - (P'E_{pT})/(1 - E_{\varepsilon T})](E_{\varepsilon\varepsilon} - R_{\varepsilon\varepsilon})\}d\varepsilon \quad (10)$$

with

$$A = E_U - \tau'E_{pU} - \varepsilon'E_{\varepsilon U} + [(E_T - \tau'E_{pT} - \varepsilon'E_{\varepsilon T})E_{\varepsilon U}/(1 - E_{\varepsilon T})] > 0 \ (11)$$

for stability.[10] The scalar A represents the general equilibrium inverse of the marginal utility of income, or a general equilibrium dE/dU, inclusive of feedback via pollution and trade distortions. The term $(P'E_{pT})$ is the general equilibrium marginal damage of pollution since $P'E_{pT} = E_T - \tau'E_{pT} - \varepsilon'E_{\varepsilon T} > 0$.[11]

Assuming a well-informed policy maker, the optimal effluent policy can be determined by setting (10) equal to zero. The optimum effluent tax is then:

$$\varepsilon = -\tau[E_{p\varepsilon} - R_{p\varepsilon}][E_{\varepsilon\varepsilon} - R_{\varepsilon\varepsilon}]^{-1} + \frac{P'E_{pT}}{1 - E_{\varepsilon T}}$$

$$= -\tau[E_{p\varepsilon} - R_{p\varepsilon}][E_{\varepsilon\varepsilon} - R_{\varepsilon\varepsilon}]^{-1} + D = \varepsilon^*. \quad (12)$$

This optimum policy equates the effluent tax to the general equilibrium marginal damage, D, of pollution minus the feedback effect of the tax on welfare via trade.

Any pollution policy reform introducing effluent taxes, such that $d\varepsilon = k\varepsilon^*$, will be welfare improving as well because $(E_{\varepsilon\varepsilon} - R_{\varepsilon\varepsilon})$ is negative in this case and would be negative semi-definite if pollution were represented by a vector.

With the interpretation of a non-economic target on maximum pollution, the instrument providing the maximum abatement response, with the least induced distortions elsewhere in the economy, is the best one for a given pollution target. In actual policy-making, and in the absence of reliable estimates of marginal pollution damage, pollution targets are the only tractable procedure and the targeting principle is further supported on practical grounds.

3.1.2   Production and consumption taxes

Now consider reform via production and consumption taxes, β and η, assuming effluent taxes are not available and no distortions exist other than tariffs. Clearly, when both consumption and production pollute and at different rates (α and γ not equal), using two separate policy instruments allows one to decouple consumption and production pollution. Tariffs are incapable of doing so, and this reveals a major advantage of production and consumption taxes.

The comparative-statics corresponding to this scenario are:

$$BdU = \left\{ (\tau + \eta)' E_{pp} - DE_{\varepsilon p} \right\} d\eta + \left\{ (\tau - \beta)' R_{pp} - DR_{\varepsilon p} \right\} d\beta \quad (13)$$

with

$$B = P' E_{pU} + DE_{\varepsilon U} > 0 \quad (14)$$

for stability. Optimal consumption and production taxes are found by setting $dU/d\beta = dU/d\eta = 0$ in (13), which yields two sets of equations that are solved for the optimum tax vectors. They are given by $\eta = -\tau' + D\alpha$ and $\beta = \tau' - DR_{\varepsilon p}R_{pp}^{-1}$, respectively.[12] Note that the optimum consumption tax vector mimics the effluent tax, because it is related to the marginal damage of pollution, but directly offsets the presence of tariffs. The production taxes are less effective for abatement, because, other things being equal, they 'overshoot' the optimum effluent tax, i.e. $\beta = \tau' + D[\gamma + x'(\partial\gamma/\partial P)R_{pp}^{-1}]$. Note that the correction for the existence of tariff distortions is one-to-one.

Any pollution reform undertaken with consumption and production taxes proportional to these optimal levels would be welfare enhancing because E_{pp} is negative semi-definite and R_{pp} is positive semi-definite.

3.1.3   Tariffs

The last pollution reform uses tariff changes to reduce pollution. The comparative-statics of tariff reforms, $d\tau$, are:

$$AdU = \left\{ [\tau'(E_{pp} - R_{pp})] + [(\varepsilon - D)(E_{\varepsilon p} - R_{\varepsilon p})] \right\} d\tau \tag{15}$$

with

$$A = E_U - \tau' E_{pU} + [(E_T - \tau' E_{pT})E_{\varepsilon U}/(1 - E_{\varepsilon T})] > 0 \tag{16}$$

for stability. The first policy issue is the optimal tariff. By setting (15) equal to zero, we obtain the optimum tariff vector $\tau = D(E_{\varepsilon p} - R_{\varepsilon p})(E_{pp} - R_{pp})^{-1}$, which may be positive or negative. The vector of optimum tariffs is different from zero, reflecting the public pollution externality, and is related to the marginal damage of pollution, representing a compromise between pollution abatement in production and consumption and efficiency losses induced by the trade effects of the tariffs. In addition, if the vector of price responses of pollution, $(\partial T/\partial P)$, has both positive and negative elements, it is not clear that tariffs can successfully move total pollution to an optimum or targeted level. This ambiguity and the information required to compute the optimum tariff are prime motivations for more empirical work on trade and environmental linkages. The Lee and Roland-Holst (1997) investigation suggests in the case of Indonesia that pollution abatement with tariffs is virtually impossible and induces large trade effects.

Finally, trade reform achieved by proportional tariff cuts $(d\tau = -k\tau)$ has a positive effect on imports and an ambiguous effect on pollution. This latter indirect effect is symmetrical to the indirect effect of the effluent tax on trade. Here we have two special cases as well, exactly symmetrical to those of the effluent tax reform and based on the sign of the tariff vector and the substitutability or complementarity of imports and pollution. For example, if τ is positive and imports and pollution are substitutes, then a proportional decrease in tariffs is welfare improving.

3.2   Coordinated policies

This section considers two types of reforms simultaneously: trade liberalization and pollution targeting – first with effluent taxes, then with product taxes. The optimum policy mix for the two sets of instruments is derived and piecemeal changes are also considered.

3.2.1   Tariffs and effluent taxes

The comparative-statics of joint tariff reduction with introduction of effluent taxes are:

$$AdU = \{\tau'(E_{p\varepsilon} - R_{p\varepsilon}) + [(\varepsilon - D)(E_{\varepsilon\varepsilon} - R_{\varepsilon\varepsilon})]\}d\varepsilon + \{\tau'(E_{pp} - R_{pp})$$
$$+ [(\varepsilon - D)(E_{\varepsilon p} - R_{\varepsilon p})]\}d\tau \tag{17}$$

with

$$A = E_U - \tau'E_{pU} - \varepsilon'E_{\varepsilon U} + [(E_t - \tau'E_{pT} - \varepsilon'E_{\varepsilon T})E_{\varepsilon U}/(1 - E_{\varepsilon t})] > 0 \tag{18}$$

and assuming that $\varepsilon = 0$ prior to the reform.

If the two policy instruments are freely implementable, then their optimum levels are obtained by setting $dU/d\tau = 0$ and $dU/d\varepsilon = 0$. This yields $\tau = 0$, and $\varepsilon = D$, assuming that the matrix $[(E_{pp} - R_{pp}) - (E_{p\varepsilon} - R_{p\varepsilon})(E_{\varepsilon T})^{-1}(E_{\varepsilon p} - R_{\varepsilon p})]$ is of full rank. Hence, the optimum policy mix is the standard result – free trade and an effluent tax equal to the general equilibrium marginal damage of pollution.

Now assume that $d\tau = -k\tau$ and $d\varepsilon = kD$, which correspond to proportional tariff reductions and an effluent tax proportional to and towards the general equilibrium marginal damage of pollution. The direct effect of the trade reform on utility is $-k\tau'(E_{pp} - R_{pp})\tau$, which is non-negative because the Hessian of import demand price responses is negative semi-definite. The direct effect of effluent taxes on pollution abatement is $[(-kD)^2(E_{\varepsilon\varepsilon} - R_{\varepsilon\varepsilon})]$, which is also non-negative.

The corresponding indirect effects are $k\tau'(E_{p\varepsilon} - R_{p\varepsilon})D$ and they are symmetrical because they show the impact of tariffs on pollution or the effect of the effluent tax on imports, $(E_{\varepsilon p} - R_{\varepsilon p} = \partial T/\partial \tau = \partial M/\partial \varepsilon)$. However, by convexity of $(R - E)$ in prices and taxes, the quadratic form corresponding to this joint reform is positive and, although we do not know the sign of the indirect symmetrical effects or the magnitude of any of the effects, their sum must be positive. Empirical analysis is still essential to assess these magnitudes and the direction of the cross-effects or underlying externalities.

3.2.2 Tariffs, production, and consumption taxes
The second scenario for joint reform is tariff reduction accompanied by the introduction of taxes on consumption and production. Optimum tariff and production and consumption tax vectors are found by setting $dU/d\tau = 0$, $dU/d\beta = 0$, and $dU/d\eta = 0$. The optimal tariff would be zero, since it is redundant with the consumption and production taxes which are $\eta = DE_{\varepsilon p}E_{pp}^{-1}$ and $\beta = -DR_{\varepsilon p}R_{pp}^{-1}$. Except for the tariff correction, they are equal to the optimum taxes described in the section on pollution policy reform.

Next, consider proportional changes of all policies, i.e $d\tau = -k\tau$,

$d\eta = kD\alpha$, and $d\beta = Kd\gamma$. According to the individual effects of each policy (obtained in the previous section), the tariff reform includes a positive utility effect and an ambiguous indirect pollution impact. Similarly, the production and consumption taxes bring positive environmental impacts but ambiguous indirect effects on imports. Unfortunately, the two indirect effects are cumulative but not symmetrical as in the previous case, and convexity of R and $(-E)$ can be used to sign partial effects but not the total welfare effect. If one abstracts from the effects of the policies on effluent rates ($\partial\gamma/\partial\tau$ and $\partial\gamma/\partial\beta$), the welfare effect of joint reform via substitution in consumption (E_{pp}) and production (R_{pp}) is positive. Further, if the reform's effect via effluent rates is positive, then the joint reform certainly enhances welfare. The latter effect is $(-d\tau + d\beta)'(\partial\gamma/\partial P)xD$, and sufficient conditions are $(d\beta - d\tau) > 0$ and production is pollution intensive (γ increases with output expansion).

The evidence gathered in Lee and Roland-Holst (1997) shows that welfare improvements are bigger when both policy instruments are used simultaneously, with tariffs set optimally to zero. Pollution taxes for a given pollution target have a larger detrimental effect on welfare than combining trade and pollution reform to achieve the same target. The welfare gains from lower tariffs offset some of the welfare loss on imports induced by the pollution taxes.

4   An application to Indonesia

4.1   Introduction

In this section, we apply the theoretical principles laid out above to the economy of Indonesia, using a dynamic CGE model to evaluate the empirical significance of the distortions and adjustments induced by these policies. The passage from theory to its application is not straightforward, and the empirical model used to elucidate the arguments above deviates somewhat from theoretical purity. A succinct description of the empirical model is provided in an appendix.

The single most important difference between the theoretical and empirical models is the treatment of time. The theoretical model is static, whereas the empirical model is recursive dynamic. The stock of factors is not exogenous when computing the static equilibrium within or between time-periods, but depends upon endogenous investment behaviour. All the policy scenarios simulated below start in 1995, and the results are all reported with respect to baseline trends predicted for the same terminal period, 2010.

A second difference involves the objective function. Rather than postulating an economy-wide utility function, in the present experiments we report only a few salient aggregate variables, including real GDP, consumption, and total measured pollution levels. This finesses the rigorous measurement of utility effects set forth in the analytics of the previous section, but the sign and relative magnitudes of the results reported here support unambiguous conclusions about principles for targeting economic instruments.

Model results also depend on closure rules. In all of the simulations, it is assumed that the net government real fiscal balance is fixed and that the balance of trade (in dollar terms) is likewise exogenous. Investment is savings driven. To the extent public and foreign savings are fixed, changes in nominal investment will mostly be driven by changes in household saving, and real investment will also be influenced by the investment price index. Owing to the specification of the model, the investment price index will be influenced by the emission tax and tariffs as well as by endogenous changes in goods prices, but no direct taxes are imposed on investment.

4.2   Description of the simulations

Prior to undertaking any policy simulations, a reference simulation was run to calibrate the efficiency of the capital factor against baseline projected GDP trends.[13] The reference simulation is also used to calibrate the pollution abatement function, using the reference level of pollution as the reference point. In all subsequent simulations, the parameters of the logistic function and the capital efficiency factors are exogenous. In the reference run, tariffs are held fixed at their base-year levels, and the existing production tax (which is small) is phased out in the first period of the simulation. Hence, the only distortions in the model by 1995 are the tariffs.[14]

Four basic simulations are used to illustrate the relative efficacy of alternative economic instruments. The objective here is to abate a selected pollutant, SO_2, by 0.5 per cent per year against baseline emission trends, resulting in a 10 per cent reduction by the year 2010. Even in this relatively moderate abatement scenario, the efficiency differences between the policies are very apparent. In the first simulation, a direct emission tax is used, in the second, a tax on production. Both these tax instruments are oriented toward the supply side, where the pollution originates, but still differ markedly in their economy-wide incidence.

Departing from specificity completely, the next two scenarios evaluate demand-side pollution 'penalties' – consumption and import taxes,

Table 11.1   Aggregate simulation results (% change with respect to baseline, 2010)

	Experiment			
	1 Emission tax	2 Production tax	3 Consumption tax	4 Import tax
Real GDP	−0.5	−0.9	−0.9	−5.2
SO$_2$	10.0	10.0	10.0	10.0
Total pollution	−11.8	−13.8	−13.4	−19.4
Real consumption	−1.1	−1.3	−2.1	−13.0

respectively – as a means of reducing the SO$_2$ intensity of output. As the theoretical results indicate, these can be quite inefficient at achieving abatement, and at the same time induce many undesirable indirect effects. In the case of import tariffs, there were so many indirect effects that it proved infeasible to compute the required tariffs endogenously. Instead, an across-the-board tariff of 100 per cent was implemented as an example, yielding SO$_2$ abatement of 10.7 per cent.

4.3   Simulation results

Aggregate results for the four different types of economic instruments are given in Table 11.1, and these strongly support the analytical results of the previous section in terms of targeting or specificity. The most specific instrument, a direct emission tax, achieves the intended abatement with the lowest real cost in terms of forgone GDP and aggregate consumption. More indirect instruments, such as producer or consumer taxes, are clearly second-best, with nearly twice the real GDP cost and, in the latter case, about double the real consumption cost. The import tax is, as one might expect, by far the least efficient, reducing real GDP over 5 per cent and consumption by 13 per cent to achieve the desired SO$_2$ abatement. This supports a fairly strong argument against import policy as an environmental policy instrument. Ironically, import taxes achieve the highest reduction in aggregate pollution, via general economic contraction, because they are not specific enough.

The detailed structural adjustments to these policies help clarify the differences in incidence between first- and second-best policies. When emissions are taxed directly (experiment 1) real sectoral output is reduced in the most pollution-intensive activities (Table 11.2), and resources shift to expand less pollution-intensive sectors. The big losers under such a

Table 11.2   Sectoral real output (% change with respect to baseline, 2010)

Sector	Experiment			
	1 Emission tax	2 Production tax	3 Consumption tax	4 Import tax
Accommodation	3.1	−6.6	−6.8	7.5
Advanced manufacturing	−19.5	−20.1	−20.2	44.3
Air, water transport	−0.4	−4.3	−4.8	1.9
Financial services	1.0	−0.8	−1.1	1.1
Fishing	1.1	−0.3	−0.9	−7.7
Food crops	1.8	−0.6	−1.2	0.2
Forestry	−1.9	−4.6	−4.5	−14.1
Livestock	0.8	−5.1	−5.8	−5.8
Metal, oil, coal	6.3	16.6	17.0	−35.4
Non-food crops	−2.1	−6.6	−6.5	−6.3
Other mining	−4.9	−8.5	−7.7	−7.9
Other services	−3.6	−3.7	−4.1	−5.1
Primary manufacturing	−17.3	−22.3	−19.9	−22.9
Processed food	1.8	−4.6	−5.4	−3.9
Public administration	2.3	6.0	5.8	14.3
Real business services	0.2	−0.1	−0.7	−1.3
Restaurants	0.7	−6.0	−6.9	−8.3
Road, rail transport	−0.8	−1.6	−2.0	−0.8
Textiles and apparel	6.4	−34.6	−35.3	−14.4
Trade	0.0	−0.2	−0.2	11.2
Utilities	−4.6	−18.1	−19.5	−13.9
Wood products	−1.9	−4.7	−4.5	−15.2

policy regime in Indonesia would be Primary and Advanced Manufacturing, both of which are significant direct and indirect SO_2 emitters, and they shrink significantly, whereas sectors such as Accommodation, Processed Food, Textiles and Apparel, and extractive mining (mainly for export) expand. These kinds of adjustment are not only logical but desirable consequences of a policy intended to reduce the pollution intensity of domestic production.

When the tax is more indirect, structural adjustments can depart from both logic and original intentions. In the case of both consumption and production taxes to reduce SO_2 emissions, the more indirect nature of the instrument shifts the tax burden to a wider set of economic activities, propagating inefficiency and price distortions that undermine domestic purchasing power and real consumption. Apart from greater efficiency costs, the sector-specific effects are difficult to generalize, depending as they do on the combined supply and demand responses to the new price wedges. Suffice to say that this approach is not only less efficient but significantly less transparent to policy makers and other observers, with the attendant political risks of such uncertainty.

The least efficient and the most obtuse policy, in terms of linkage between objectives and ultimate effects, is certainly the import tariff as a means of reducing SO_2 pollution. A number of perverse and unintended linkages are brought into play here, including import substitution with pollution-intensive domestic output, unintended contraction of many sectors because of intermediate import price inflation, and collapse of export sectors in response to real exchange rate appreciation. In any case, the only way the economy can really achieve abatement with such an indirect set of instruments is via a general contraction of domestic activity. Because SO_2 is a relatively stubborn pollutant, at least against such indirect instruments, total pollution under this scenario drops by almost double the 10 per cent target for SO_2. This will probably give little consolation in the context of a 5 per cent drop in real GDP and 13 per cent lower real aggregate consumption, however.

The results in Table 11.3 provide detailed effluent changes for each experiment, and many interesting indirect linkages are revealed. For example, in the case where SO_2 is taxed directly (experiment 1), all other pollutants are abated in varying degrees. Some, including BIOAIR, BIOSOL, CO, VOC, and TSS, experience emissions reductions that exceed the intended percentage for the target pollutant. This fact has significant implications for policy, because it means that a small subset of instruments might be used to achieve much broader environmental objectives. Dessus et al. (1994) argue, for example, that this can be exploited by countries with limited monitoring infrastructure and administrative capacity to manage a more limited set of economic instruments.

5   Conclusions

This paper explored second-best policy issues related to trade and the environment. We derived sufficient conditions for welfare improvement with piecemeal trade and environmental policy reforms in a small, polluted economy. Pollution, a public bad, originates in both consumption and production, the latter being decomposed into composition and technique effects. Moving distortions proportionally towards their optimal level increases welfare monotonically. Proportional reductions in tariffs and gradual increases in effluent taxation also increase welfare. The existence of consumption-based pollution undermines the use of

Table 11.3   Detailed emissions (% change with respect to baseline, 2010)

Pollutant	Experiment			
	1 Emission tax	2 Production tax	3 Consumption tax	4 Import tax
TOXAIR	−6.9	−10.2	−9.7	−15.8
TOXWAT	−6.3	−9.9	−9.4	−15.5
TOXSOL	−7.0	−10.6	−10.0	−17.7
BIOAIR	−14.8	−16.4	−16.2	−20.1
BIOWAT	−3.4	−4.7	−4.5	−12.6
BIOSOL	−17.2	−18.0	−17.8	−22.5
SO_2	−10.0	−10.0	−10.0	−10.7
NO_2	−9.1	−9.2	−9.2	−9.5
CO	−13.9	−14.0	−14.0	−17.5
VOC	−10.1	−12.8	−12.5	−14.8
PART	−8.9	−9.1	−9.1	−10.4
BOD	−6.0	−10.0	−9.3	−17.9
TSS	−19.7	−19.6	−19.5	−25.0
All emissions	−11.8	−13.8	−13.4	−19.4

tariffs as a second-best abatement instrument because tariffs tax and subsidize pollution simultaneously.

The analysis emphasized the specific effects of tariffs, effluent taxes, and production and consumption taxes on market allocation and pollution through substitution in consumption, changes in output composition, and choice of technique. Effluent taxes have the most direct effect on toxic intensity, with limited indirect effects on imports and thereby utility in consumption. This result supports the case for economic instruments, against 'command and control' measures, to achieve reductions in pollution intensity. Indeed, over-reliance on the latter policies may explain why OECD countries have experienced stubbornly high levels of pollution intensity in production. More frequent recourse to effluent taxes or their quantitative equivalent, marketable permits, might do much to get these economies on flatter pollution growth trajectories and to minimize collateral disutility effects in consumption.

Trade policy reforms increase feasible consumption but have indirect effects on pollution that are ambiguous. This calls into question any presumption that outward orientation induces specialization in pollution-intensive activities. We actually established two special cases in which trade liberalization decreases pollution and pollution intensities, based on substitution relationships between pollution and imports. Evidence obtained separately for the Mexican economy suggests that greater outward orientation can actually induce specialization in less pollution-intensive production activities (Beghin et al. 1995).

Coordination of pollution and trade policies is important because the direct beneficial effects of the reform will always be larger than the indirect ones. When policies are set or changed in proportion to their optimal levels, aggregate welfare also improves. Reducing tariffs and setting effluent taxes proportionally to optimal levels increase welfare as well and, requiring less information, emerge as a robust policy recommendation. In practice, estimating magnitudes of the individual effects of these coordinated trade and environmental policies is an empirical task.

This paper strengthens the conceptual foundations for the extensive empirical work that is ultimately required to support coherent policies towards trade and the environment. Although some general conclusions have been drawn, it is clear that linkages between economic efficiency and environmental values are complex, and policies to promote and reconcile the two must be designed and implemented with care. As emphasized in Lee and Roland-Holst (1997) and Beghin et al. (1995), more detailed sectoral modelling and estimation are essential to such an enterprise. Future work should include sector-specific programme evaluation in a general equilibrium framework, especially in sectors where the trade/environment nexus is prominent (e.g. agriculture, energy). Without detailed empirical support of this kind, it is questionable whether policy makers relying on intuition and rules-of-thumb alone will achieve sustainable welfare improvements or anything close to optimality.

Appendix: A summary overview of the Indonesian model

This appendix provides a brief summary of the Indonesian applied general equilibrium model.[15] For the purposes of this paper, the Indonesian Social Accounting Matrix (SAM) was collapsed along certain dimensions. The model incorporates all twenty-two sectors of the original (1990) SAM. The labour and household accounts were collapsed into single accounts.

Production

All sectors are assumed to operate under constant returns to scale and cost optimization. Production technology is modelled by a nesting of constant elasticity of substitution (CES) functions. See Figure 11A.1 for a schematic diagram of the nesting.

In each period, the supply of *primary* factors – capital, land, and labour

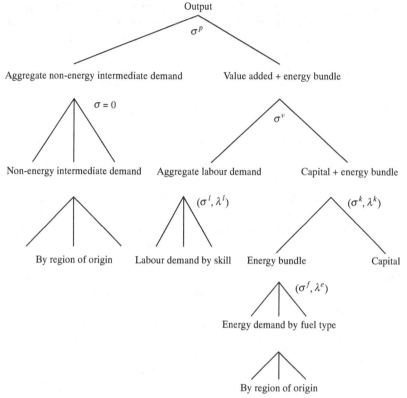

Figure 11A.1   Production nesting

Notes:

1. Each nest represents a different CES bundle, where the different substitution elasticities are represented by the σ variables. The elasticity may take the value 0. Owing to the putty/semi-putty specification, the nesting is replicated for each type of capital, i.e. *old and new*. The values of the substitution elasticity will generally differ depending on the capital vintage, with typically lower elasticities for *old* capital. Three bundles have an additional parameter representing technological change. The capital productivity parameter can vary across sectors and vintage. The labour productivity parameter can vary across sectors and labour type. The energy productivity parameter can vary across sectors and by type of fuel.
2. Intermediate demand, both energy and non-energy, is further decomposed by region of origin according to the Armington specification. However, the Armington function is specified at the border and is not industry specific.
3. The decomposition of the intermediate demand bundle, the labour bundle, and the energy bundle will be specific to the level of aggregation of the model. The diagram represents the decomposition only schematically and is not meant to imply that there are only three components in the CES aggregation. In the case of Indonesia, there is a single labour aggregate, and therefore the labour nest is redundant.

– is usually predetermined.[16] The model includes adjustment rigidities. An important feature is the distinction between old and new capital goods. In addition, capital is assumed to be partially mobile, reflecting differences in the marketability of capital goods across sectors.[17]

Once the optimal combination of inputs is determined, sectoral output prices are calculated assuming competitive supply (zero-profit) conditions in all markets.

Consumption and closure rule

All income generated by economic activity is assumed to be distributed to consumers. Each representative consumer allocates his/her disposable income optimally among the different commodities and saving. The consumption/saving decision is completely static: saving is treated as a 'good' and its amount is determined simultaneously with the demand for the other commodities, the price of saving being set arbitrarily equal to the average price of consumer goods.[18]

The government collects income taxes and indirect taxes on intermediate inputs, outputs, and consumer expenditures. The default closure of the model assumes that the government deficit/saving is exogenously specified.[19] The indirect tax schedule will shift to accommodate any changes in the balance between government revenues and government expenditures.

The current account surplus (deficit) is fixed in nominal terms. The counterpart of this imbalance is a net outflow (inflow) of capital, which is subtracted from (added to) the domestic flow of saving. In each period, the model equates gross investment to net saving (equal to the sum of saving by households, the net budget position of the government, and foreign capital inflows). This particular closure rule implies that investment is driven by saving.

Foreign trade

Goods are assumed to be differentiated by region of origin. In other words, goods classified in the same sector are different according to whether they are produced domestically or imported. This assumption is frequently known as the Armington assumption. The degree of substitutability as well as the import penetration shares are allowed to vary across commodities. The model assumes a single Armington agent. This strong assumption implies that the propensity to import and the degree of substitutability between domestic and imported goods are uniform across economic agents. This assumption reduces tremendously the dimensionality of the model. In many cases this assumption is imposed by the data. A symmetrical assumption is made on the export side where domestic producers are assumed to differentiate the domestic market and the export market. This is modelled using a constant elasticity of transformation (CET) function.

Dynamic features and calibration

The current version of the model has a simple recursive dynamic structure because agents are assumed to be myopic and to base their decisions on static expectations about prices and quantities. Dynamics in the model originate in three sources: (i) accumulation of productive capital and labour growth; (ii) shifts in production technology; and (iii) the putty/semi-putty specification of technology.

Capital accumulation

In the aggregate, the basic capital accumulation function equates the current capital stock to the depreciated stock inherited from the previous period plus gross investment. However, at the sectoral level, the specific accumulation functions may differ because the demand for (old and new) capital can be less than the depreciated stock of old capital. In this case, the sector contracts over time by releasing old capital goods. Consequently, in each period, the new capital vintage available to expanding industries is equal to the sum of disinvested capital in contracting industries plus total saving generated by the economy, consistent with the closure rule of the model.

The putty/semi-putty specification

The substitution possibilities among production factors are assumed to be higher with the new than the old capital vintages – technology has a putty/semi-putty specification. Hence, when a shock to relative prices occurs (e.g. the imposition of an emissions tax), the demands for production factors adjust gradually to the long-run optimum because the substitution effects are delayed over time. The adjustment path depends on the values of the short-run elasticities of substitution and the replacement rate of capital. Because the latter determines the pace at which new vintages are installed, the larger is the volume of new investment, the greater is the possibility to achieve the long-run total amount of substitution among production factors.

Dynamic calibration

The model is calibrated on exogenous growth rates of population, labour force, and GDP. In the so-called business-as-usual (BaU) scenario, the dynamics are calibrated in each region by imposing the assumption of a balanced growth path. This implies that the ratio between labour and capital (in efficiency units) is held constant over time.[20] When alternative scenarios around the baseline are simulated, the technical efficiency parameter is held constant, and the growth of capital is endogenously determined by the saving/investment relation.

Notes

The views expressed here are those of the authors and should not be attributed to their affiliated institutions.

1. Several recent survey papers using different taxonomies examine 'trade and environment' linkages (e.g. Cropper and Oates 1992, Dean 1992, and Beghin, Roland-Holst, and van der Mensbrugghe 1994).
2. See Vousden (1990: Ch. 9) for a survey of many of these second-best results.
3. Grossman and Krueger (1991) suggested this categorization of pollution effects. Copeland and Taylor (1994) model trade and environment linkages following that decomposition. Their definition of composition refers to the range of goods produced within a continuum. Our definition refers to different output 'baskets' of a fixed number of commodities.
4. Alternatively, pollution can enter the expenditure function of the economy even if it is not valued directly but is constrained from above by a non-economic target.
5. One of the goods can be chosen as a numeraire to impose homogeneity. R satisfies other properties (convex in prices and effluent taxes, increasing in prices, decreasing in effluent taxes, and the feasible technology set underlying R is convex). We refer readers to Hatta (1977) and Dixit and Norman (1980) for more details on revenue and expenditure functions.
6. This decomposition comes from $R_{\varepsilon\varepsilon} = \partial(-\gamma R_{p})/\partial\varepsilon = -x'(\partial\gamma/\partial\varepsilon) - \gamma' R_{p\varepsilon} = -x'(\partial\gamma/\partial\varepsilon) + \gamma' R_{pp}\gamma + \gamma'(\partial\gamma/\partial P)x$.
7. This is obtained by noting that $E_{\varepsilon\varepsilon} = \partial(\alpha' E_{p})/\partial\varepsilon = \alpha'\partial c/\partial\varepsilon + c'\partial\alpha/\partial\varepsilon = \alpha'\partial(\alpha'c)/\partial P + c'\partial\alpha/\partial\varepsilon = \alpha' E_{pp}\alpha + \alpha'(\partial\alpha/\partial P)c + c'(\partial\alpha/\partial\varepsilon)$.
8. Modelling and implementing endogenous effluent rates in consumption may be more difficult than in production. In production we have or can develop good data on intermediate consumption (inputs), and on effluent linked to these inputs (Dessus et al. 1994). Substitution between value-added (labour and capital) and these intermediate inputs allows for lower effluent rates per unit of output. This approach has no obvious counterpart in consumption. This implementation problem motivates our simplifying assumption.
9. The results in this section draw heavily on work reported in Beghin, Roland-Holst, and van der Mensbrugghe (1997).
10. A can be rearranged as follows: $A = E_{U} - \tau' E_{pU} - \varepsilon' E_{\varepsilon U} + [(E_{T} - \tau' E_{pT} - \varepsilon' E_{\varepsilon T})E_{\varepsilon U}/(1 - E_{\varepsilon T})] = E_{U} - \tau' E_{pU} - [\varepsilon - (P' E_{pT})/(1 - E_{\varepsilon T})] E_{\varepsilon U}$.
11. By homogeneity we know that $(P + \alpha'\varepsilon + \tau)' E_{p} = E$. Taking the derivative of this identity with respect to T and U yields the following identities: $(P + \varepsilon\alpha + \tau)' E_{pT} = E_{T}$ and $(P + \varepsilon\alpha + \tau)' E_{pU} = E_{U}$,   or

$(P + \tau)' E_{pT} + \alpha' E_{\varepsilon T} = E_T$ and $(P + \tau)' E_{pU} + \alpha' E_{\varepsilon U} = E_U$, which lead to the definition of A.

12. We assume that E_{pp} and R_{pp} are full rank.
13. The other productivity factors are assumed to be known and exogenous: labour and energy.
14. Hypothetical lump-sum taxation is imposed on the single representative household to maintain the government's fiscal balance.
15. See Beghin et al. (1996) for a complete model description.
16. Capital supply is to some extent influenced by the current period's level of investment.
17. For simplicity, it is assumed that old capital goods supplied in second-hand markets and new capital goods are homogeneous. This formulation makes it possible to introduce downward rigidities in the adjustment of capital without increasing excessively the number of equilibrium prices to be determined by the model.
18. The demand system is a version of the Extended Linear Expenditure System (ELES), which was first developed by Lluch (1973). The formulation of the ELES in this model is based on atemporal maximization (see Howe 1975). In this formulation, the marginal propensity to save out of supernumerary income is constant and independent of the rate of reproduction of capital.
19. In the reference simulation, the real government fiscal balance converges (linearly) towards 0 by the final period of the simulation.
20. This involves computing in each period a measure of Harrod-neutral technical progress in the capital–labour bundle as a residual. This is a standard calibration procedure in dynamic CGE modelling (see Ballard et al. 1985).

References

Ballard, C. L., D. Fullerton, J. B. Shoven, and J. Whalley (1985), *A General Equilibrium Model for Tax Policy Evaluation.* Chicago: University of Chicago Press.

Baumol, W. J. and W. E. Oates (1988), *The Theory of Environmental Policy.* Cambridge: Cambridge University Press.

Beghin, J., D. Roland-Holst, and D. van der Mensbrugghe (1994), 'North–South Dimensions of the Trade and Environment Nexus', *OECD Economic Studies* 23: 167–92.

— (1995), 'Trade Liberalization and the Environment in the Pacific Basin: Coordinated Approaches to Mexican Trade and Environment Policy', *American Journal of Agricultural Economics* 77: 778–85.

— (1997), 'Trade and Pollution Linkages: Piecemeal Reform and Optimal Intervention', *Canadian Journal of Economics* 30(2): 442–55.

Beghin, J., S. Dessus, D. Roland-Holst, and D. van der Mensbrugghe (1996), *General Equilibrium Modeling of Trade and the Environment*, OECD Development Centre Technical Papers No. 119. Paris: OECD.

Choi, E. K. and S. R. Johnson (1992), 'Regulation of Externalities in an Open Economy', *Ecological Economics* 5: 251–65.

Copeland, B. R. (1994), 'International Trade and the Environment: Policy Reform in a Polluted Small Open Economy', *Journal of Environmental Economics and Management* 26: 44–65.

Copeland, B. R. and M. S. Taylor (1994), 'North–South Trade and the Environment', *Quarterly Journal of Economics* 109: 755–87.

Cropper, M. L. and W. E. Oates (1992), 'Environmental Economics: A Survey', *Journal of Economic Literature* 30: 675–740.

Dean, J. M. (1992), 'Trade and the Environment: A Survey of the Literature', World Bank Working Paper WPS 966, Washington, D.C., August.

Dessus, S., D. Roland-Holst, and D. van der Mensbrugghe (1994), *Input-based Estimates for Environmental Assessment in Developing Countries*, OECD Development Centre Technical Papers No. 101. Paris: OECD, August.

Dixit, A. K. and V. Norman (1980), *Theory of International Trade*. Cambridge: Cambridge University Press.

Grossman, G. M. and A. B. Krueger (1991), 'Environmental Impact of a North American Free Trade Agreement', NBER Working Paper No. 3914, November.

Hatta, T. (1977), 'A Theory of Piecemeal Policy Recommendations', *Review of Economic Studies* 44: 1–21.

Hettige, H., R. E. B. Lucas, and D. Wheeler (1992), 'The Toxic Intensity of Industrial Production: Global Patterns, Trends, and Trade Policy', *American Economic Review. Papers and Proceedings* 82: 478–81.

Howe, H. (1975), 'Development of the Extended Linear Expenditure System from Simple Savings Assumptions', *European Economic Review* 6: 305–10.

Krutilla, K. (1991), 'Environmental Regulation in an Open Economy', *Journal of Environmental Economics and Management* 20: 127–42.

Lee, H. and D. Roland-Holst (1997), 'The Environment and Welfare Implications of Trade and Tax Policy', *Journal of Development Economics* 52(1): 65–82.

Lluch, C. (1973), 'The Extended Linear Expenditure System', *European Economic Review* 4: 21–32.

Markusen, J. R. (1975), 'International Externalities and Optimal Tax Structures', *Journal of International Economics* 5: 15–29.

Vousden, N. (1990), *The Economics of Trade Protection*. Cambridge: Cambridge University Press.

12   Labour markets and dynamic comparative advantage

DAVID ROLAND-HOLST

1   Introduction

Although international migration has received more public attention because of its complex political implications, domestic migration is often of greater historical significance, both numerically and economically.[1] While in some countries like the United States, the first type is a necessary condition for the second, the latter still deserves attention in its own right. Patterns of domestic migration have dramatically influenced both internal economic structure and trade orientation in many nations. This has often followed a two-stage process, where migration into the hinterland to develop the primary resource base is succeeded by migration to the cities seeking opportunity in the modern sector. Such demographic trends can influence and be influenced by shifting trade orientation; i.e. changes in the composition of human resources have important implications for dynamic comparative advantage, and terms-of-trade changes can exert significant pressure on domestic labour markets.

The magnitudes of this kind of population adjustment can truly be impressive. In the nineteenth century, Latin America was about 15 per cent urban, and the figure now is 90 per cent. Indonesia expects its total population to grow modestly, from 180 million in 1990 to about 240 million by 2040, but at the same time the urban population is projected to grow from 24 per cent to 65 per cent. China's population, while still predominantly rural, is experiencing strong migratory pressures. According to official estimates, some 100 million Chinese are currently classified as migrants, while officials at the Chinese Academy of Social Sciences estimate (conservatively) a labour surplus in agriculture of about 250 million. These figures imply the existence of a volatile labour force exceeding the population of the European Union.[2] As most of these individuals shift their labour from rural to urban areas and from

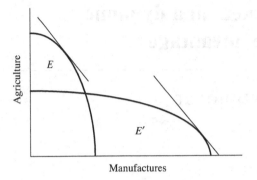

Figure 12.1 Resource shifts in response to terms of trade.

traditional to more modern modes of production, China's production possibilities and trade opportunities will shift accordingly.[3]

The present paper has two objectives. First, a formal approach to incorporating migration in an explicit dynamic economic model is developed. This is followed in section 3 by an empirical application of the approach to the Chinese economy. Section 4 closes with conclusions and some remarks on extensions of this work.

2 The basic model

Imagine an envelope function $E(x,y) = 0$, characterizing maximal output combinations for. fixed endowment composition. In response to the classic situation where prices are more favourable to the modern sector with the opening of an economy, one might expect to see resource shifts (e.g. migration) that deform E into E' (see Figure 12.1). This is the process that underlies regional and occupational migration (i.e. from unskilled to skilled, informal to formal, etc.) in many developing countries, although it is often accompanied by market failures and other institutional problems.

A hybrid overlapping-generations model will be used to capture such linkages between migration, economic growth, and trade.[4] Although it can be implemented in more elaborate contexts, for the present discussion consider a two-sector model of a small open economy. What emerges from this simple framework is an economy with endowments that are sector specific in the short run but fungible in the longer run. Because relative prices influence factor prices, labour will migrate, shifting the economy's comparative advantage dynamically in response to externally determined price signals.[5]

Formally, assume that the two goods, called manufactures (x) and agriculture (y), are made with C^2, linearly homogeneous technologies utilizing capital (K) and sector-specific urban (U) and rural (R) labour, which take the forms:

$$x = F(U, K) \tag{1}$$
$$y = G(R, K) \tag{2}$$

Assume further that manufactures are the numeraire good, so the economy-wide relative price,

$$p = \frac{p_y}{p_x}, \tag{3}$$

denotes the agricultural terms of trade. In any given period t, with endowments K_t, U_t, and R_t, factor rewards are given by:

$$w_t = F_U(U_t, K_{xt}) \tag{4}$$
$$v_t = p_t G(R_t, K_{yt}) - r_t(K_t - K_{xt}) \tag{5}$$
$$r_t = F_K(U_t, K_{xt}) \tag{6}$$
$$r_t = p_t G_K(R_t, K_t - K_{xt}) \tag{7}$$
$$K_i = K_{xt} + K_{yt} \tag{8}$$

yielding within-period equilibria for all the above, given commodity price p_t.

Capital is mobile between sectors within each period. The labour types are defined in an implicitly regional way (rural and urban), but, with a broader definition of migration, could be distinguished more functionally (informal–formal, unskilled–skilled, etc.).[6] Within periods, the two types of labour are fixed in total supply and specific to the two production sectors of the present discussion. Between periods, labour mobility between the two groups is described by a C^2 concave transformation surface $G(U, R) = 0$. This function implicitly maximizes employment of each type, given relative wages and other end-of-period equilibrium conditions.[7]

To represent intertemporal economic linkages within this framework, the basic structure outlined in equations (1)–(8) is expanded to include a variant of the standard overlapping-generations model. The representative agent lives for two periods, working, consuming, and saving in the first, and consuming from savings in the second. Assume that total population remains constant throughout the analysis and that an individual works in one location (rural or urban) in the first period of life.

However, prior to entering the workforce, progeny are allowed to take a decision to migrate, after which they work at the destination during the first period of their life.

Assuming that the numeraire good is also the capital good, consumption is given by:

$$c_t = \bar{w}_t - s_t = \bar{w}_t - k_{t+1} \tag{9}$$
$$c_{t+1} = (1 + r_{t+1})k_{t+1} \tag{10}$$

where

$$\bar{w}_t = w_t U_t + v_t R_t \tag{11}$$

denotes the average wage and

$$s_t = s(w_t, v_t, r_{t+1}, p_t, p_{t+1}) \tag{12}$$

is the representative savings function. On a period-by-period basis, this model satisfies the factor market conditions

$$K_{t+1} = (U_t + R_t)k_{t+1} = (U_t + R_t)s(w_t, v_t, r_{t+1}, p_t, p_{t+1}) \tag{13}$$

and

$$U_{t+1} = M(z_t), \tag{14}$$

where $z_t = w_t/v_t$ and $M()$ denotes the reduced-form, end-of-period migration function.

From this information, within-period variational equations for factor prices can be derived, given exogenous and between-period changes in prices (p), capital stock (K_t), and, e.g., the urban labour force (U_t), i.e.

$$\hat{w}_t = [-\alpha_{Kx}\beta_y\gamma_y\hat{p}_t + \alpha_{Kx}\alpha_R(\hat{K}_t - \beta_x\hat{U}_t)]\Delta \tag{15}$$
$$\hat{v}_t = [(\beta_x\gamma_x + \alpha_U\beta_y\gamma_y)\hat{p}_t + \alpha_U\alpha_{Ky}(\hat{K}_t + \beta_x\hat{U}_t)]\Delta \tag{16}$$
$$\hat{r}_t = [\alpha_U\beta_y\gamma_y\hat{p}_t - \alpha_U\alpha_R(\hat{K}_t - \beta_x\hat{U}_t)]\Delta \tag{17}$$

where

$$\alpha_U = F_U \frac{U_t}{x_t}$$

$$\alpha_{Kx} = F_K \frac{K_{xt}}{x_t} = 1 - \alpha_U$$

$$\alpha_R = G_R \frac{R_t}{y_t}$$

$$\alpha_{Ky} = G_K \frac{K_{yt}}{y_t} = 1 - \alpha_R$$

$$\beta_i = \frac{K_{it}}{K_t}$$

$$\gamma_1 = \frac{F_U F_K}{F_{UK}}$$

$$\gamma_2 = \frac{G_U G_K}{G_{UK}}$$

$$\Delta = (\alpha_R \beta_1 \gamma_1 + \alpha_U \beta_2 \gamma_2)^{-1}$$

Expressions (15)–(17) reflect the expected links between factor markets and commodity prices. An exogenous rise in the agricultural terms of trade (p) leads to a rise in rural wages and rental rates and a fall in urban wages. Rental rates vary inversely with the capital stock, and wages of both groups vary in different positive proportions. A reallocation of labour from rural to urban areas raises rural and lowers urban wages.

To embed this in the dynamic framework, consider now the following steady-state conditions:

$$\bar{K} + (U + R)s(\bar{K}, \bar{p}) = (U + R)s[w(\bar{K}, \bar{p}), v(\bar{K}, \bar{p}), r(\bar{K}, \bar{p}), \bar{p}, \bar{p}] \tag{18}$$

$$\bar{z} = \frac{w(\bar{K}, \bar{p})}{v(\bar{K}, \bar{p})}. \tag{19}$$

Assuming sufficient conditions for existence of the steady state, we then have additional variational equations of the form:[8]

$$\hat{K} = (\hat{U} + \hat{R})s + \sigma_w \hat{w} + \sigma_v \hat{v} + \sigma_r \hat{r} + \sigma_p \hat{p} \tag{20}$$

$$\hat{z} = \hat{w} - \hat{v} \tag{21}$$

$$\hat{U} = \mu_z \hat{z}, \tag{22}$$

where $\sigma_a = s_a a / s$ and $\mu_a = M_a a / U$ are the appropriate savings and migration elasticities, respectively. For a complete set of comparative static results, the seven expressions (14)–(17) and (20)–(22) can be solved for changes in the terms of trade and other exogenous factors. Unfortunately, however, these solutions have little to offer in terms of general qualitative results. Consider for example the two reduced-form expressions for relative wage and capital stock changes:

$$\hat{z} = -[1 - \Delta(\alpha_U - \alpha_R)\beta_1\mu_z]^{-1}\Delta[(\beta_1\gamma_1 + \beta_2\gamma_2)\hat{p}_t - (\alpha_U - \alpha_R)\hat{K}_t] \qquad (23)$$

$$\hat{K} = (1 - \Delta E_3)^{-1}\Delta[(\beta_1\gamma_1\sigma_v + \beta_2\gamma_2 E_1 + E_2)\hat{p}_t - \beta_1 E_3\mu_z\hat{z}] \qquad (24)$$

where

$$E_1 = \alpha_U\sigma_r + \alpha_U\sigma_v - \alpha_{K1}\sigma_w$$
$$E_2 = \Delta^{-1}\sigma_p$$
$$E_3 = \alpha_{K1}\alpha_R\sigma_w + \alpha_U\alpha_{K2}\sigma_v - \alpha_U\alpha_R\sigma_r.$$

It is evident from these expressions that, although some direct effects might be interpreted in this two-sector framework, factor market links here and in higher dimensional cases can better be elucidated by empirical means. For this reason, we devote the next section to an empirical application of the above framework.

3   An application to China

This section presents simulation results obtained with a calibrated general equilibrium (CGE) model of China, specified with endogenous rural–urban migration of the type set forth above. This particular CGE model has been extensively documented elsewhere and will not be discussed in detail here.[9] Suffice to say for the present that the model is based on a detailed 1987 social accounting matrix for China and is calibrated dynamically over the intervals 1987, 1990, 1995, 2000, 2005, and 2010. Although the full form of the model details sixty-four sectors and ten different household types, an aggregate, four-sector, two-household version is used for this exercise.

To simulate the intertemporal process of migration discussed in section 2, a simple CET function is used to specify a 'transformation' of rural into urban labour (or vice versa). As can be seen in the following reduced-form expressions, this function relies on two parameters: an elasticity and a calibrated intercept relating the base employment and wage ratios.

$$\frac{U}{R} = \alpha\left(\frac{w}{v}\right)^\gamma. \qquad (25)$$

The elasticity represents sensitivity of the rural and urban labour forces to changes in the wage ratio, and adjustments represent migration. The intercept, on the other hand, represents a reference level of 'tolerance' for rural–urban wage differentials. In the case of China, nominal average wages are conservatively estimated at over four to one in favour of urban workers.

By analogy to the two parameters of this simple migration function, the experiments reported here take two approaches to the forces inducing internal migration. In the first instance, we examine cases where nominal wages change in favour of urban workers in response to an exogenous shift in terms of trade. Secondly, we examine a change in the tolerance of rural workers for existing wage differentials. Put another way, migrants generally respond not to the ratio of market wages but to the ratio of risk-adjusted (or search-cost-adjusted) expected income. In this context, rising risk in the agricultural sector (e.g. drought, rising labour productivity, and concomitantly rising labour surpluses) or falling risk of unemployment in the urban sector make migration more attractive even at constant market wage ratios. Our results indicate that these two types of migration, the one induced by rising market wage ratios, the other by rising expectations with respect to existing differentials, have very different economic consequences.

A set of seven simulations is reported in Table 12.1. The first two represent external shocks of about the same magnitude, one expanding demand for Chinese manufacturing exports ten-fold against the baseline trend over the period 1987–2010, the second specifying a 30 per cent appreciation of manufacturing export prices over the same period. In the case of no rural–urban migration, economy-wide real GDP is unchanged and urban households benefit while rural ones lose as a result of other resource (mainly capital) diversion to manufacturing. When migration is permitted, using a long-run elasticity over the five-year intervals period of 10, international adjustments are comparable but domestic ones are quite different. Migration does occur, with about 3 per cent more urban workers in the terminal period under both trade scenarios. Although positive, the migration is still smaller than might be expected, but this is due in part to the effectiveness with which it stifles (by over 75 per cent) the rise in urban wages and partially offsets the fall in rural wages. The offset in equivalent variation (EV) incomes is even greater, and is only slightly larger than the gain in real GDP. This latter effect arises from reallocating labour from lower- to higher-wage (read productivity) activities.[10]

It is perhaps surprising that these strong trade effects do not induce more migration and output expansion, but the current specification of the model biases such results downwards. In particular, the magnitude of population and output shifts is probably underestimated by the use of a full employment base case in agriculture. As mentioned in the introduction, official sources estimate that China has a few hundred million

Table 12.1 Selected aggregate results (% change with respect to trend values in the terminal year)

	Experiment						
	1	2	3	4	5	6	7
Real GDP	0.0	0.0	0.7	0.7	5.3	5.9	5.9
Urban EV income	9.6	9.9	1.1	1.2	−45.4	−43.4	−43.3
Rural EV income	−2.5	−2.6	−1.2	−1.3	10.4	9.5	9.5
Urban wage	23.5	24.2	5.0	5.2	−74.9	−73.2	−73.2
Rural wage	4.7	4.9	4.6	4.7	17.4	24.8	25.0
Urban employment	0.0	0.0	3.0	3.1	22.9	25.6	25.7
Rural employment	0.0	0.0	−0.7	−0.7	−5.4	−6.1	−6.1
Agricultural terms of trade	−6.7	−6.9	−4.9	−5.1	19.1	16.4	16.3
International terms of trade	20.4	21.1	20.4	21.0	−0.2	20.2	20.9
Total exports	14.1	14.5	14.5	14.9	2.4	16.6	17.0
Total imports	36.1	37.3	36.5	37.7	2.2	38.7	39.9

Experiment 1: Ten-fold expansion of manufacturing export demand. No migration.
Experiment 2: 30 per cent appreciation of manufacturing export prices. No migration.
Experiment 3: Experiment 1 with migration against existing wage differential.
Experiment 4: Experiment 2 with migration against existing wage differential.
Experiment 5: Migration in response to changing relative wage expectations.
Experiment 6: Experiment 5 with export demand growth as in Experiment 1.
Experiment 7: Experiment 5 with export demand growth as in Experiment 2.

workers in agriculture who could take up other activities and even residences without significant reductions in rural output. We are also not modelling differential productivity for new urban labour force entrants, a well-established trend in expanding Asian economies. These factors all imply higher levels of migration and manufacturing growth, and smaller contractionary effects on agriculture.

Experiment 5 takes a different approach to the migration question, examining the effect of lowering the 'tolerance' wage differential or, from a different perspective, a change in the ratio of expected or risk-adjusted wages. In this experiment, the migration function is re-calibrated to impose a unitary rural–urban wage differential. This extreme but illustrative case occasions a 74.9 per cent drop in urban wages and a 17.4 per cent rise in their rural counterpart. To achieve this, 5.4 per cent less of the rural population is needed, while the urban workforce swells 22.9 per cent. This type of migration, basically impelled from the supply side

Table 12.2 Sectoral adjustments (% change)

Sector	Experiment						
	1	2	3	4	5	6	7
Exports							
Agriculture	−20.4	−20.9	−22.9	−23.5	−37.2	−52.3	−52.7
Energy	−41.5	−42.3	−43.2	−44.1	−5.9	−45.6	−46.4
Manufacturing	34.2	35.1	34.6	35.5	2.3	37.5	38.4
Services	−35.5	−36.2	−29.3	−30.0	64.6	12.2	11.0
Output							
Agriculture	−0.2	−0.2	−1.1	−1.1	−5.6	−6.5	−6.5
Energy	−7.8	−8.0	−8.3	−8.4	−2.2	−9.7	−9.8
Manufacturing	0.1	0.1	0.5	0.4	1.9	2.1	2.0
Services	1.1	1.2	3.2	3.3	9.4	11.5	11.6
Labour demand							
Agriculture	0.0	0.0	−0.7	−0.7	−5.4	−6.1	−6.1
Energy	−8.2	−8.4	−6.7	−6.9	15.9	8.4	8.3
Manufacturing	−0.4	−0.4	2.0	2.0	20.0	21.8	21.9
Services	0.8	0.8	4.4	4.5	25.4	29.4	29.5

without a corresponding expansion of labour requirements, has an effect more analogous to the African or Latin American urban experiences than to Asian ones.[11] Real GDP rises significantly, again because of a Katz–Summers labour reallocation effect, but urban real incomes are severely hit and incomes of the remaining rural population actually rise. This illustrates an important difference between expectations and changes in economic fundamentals.

In experiments 6 and 7, expectations-driven migration is coupled with each of the external trade shocks. Although the resulting impacts are generally better than additive, the benefits of improved trading opportunities cannot significantly offset the negative effects of the larger migratory shifts.

Table 12.2 presents more detailed sectoral results of the seven experiments. Most of these adjustments are intuitive, particularly those in agriculture. The difference between demand- and supply-driven migration is even more striking on a sectoral basis, however. Because of the greater urban labour supply shifts in experiments 5–7, all urban sectors expand employment, even when their output may be shrinking. This is particularly evident in the low-wage service sector. Despite this dramatic job growth, however, urban price-adjusted incomes have plummeted.

4   Conclusions and extensions

In many economies, domestic migration has been one of the primary forces animating economic modernization. In other contexts, it has intensified both urban and rural poverty and led to chronic social and economic problems. Whether it leads to long-term benefits or hardship, however, it has been and will remain a powerful force to be reckoned with by policy makers. This is particularly true in populous Asia, where the main adjustments in the rural–urban balance have yet to run their course. A better understanding of the preconditions for beneficial migration and the warning signs of detrimental trends may help avert unpleasant experiences that have already occurred in some parts of Africa and Latin America.

This paper sets out a theoretical framework for analysing migration in the context of a dynamic trade model. Using a hierarchical approach to market adjustment, a between-period migration function was embedded between the within-period equilibria in an overlapping-generations model of a small, open economy. This specification is simple enough to elucidate the main forces at work, but it also reveals that this process is in significant respects still too complex to admit general interpretation. It was apparent from the analytics that, even in a simple two-sector, three-factor model, important inferences about linkages and policy effects could be made only by recourse to empirical analysis.

This conclusion led to the second part of the paper, applying the migration specification in a dynamic CGE model of China. Although this exercise was intended to give only general indications about how to implement such a model, two important insights arose from the empirical results. First, the impetus for migration can arise from the demand or the supply side of labour markets, and this can have dramatically different implications for its economic consequences. As one might reasonably expect, demand-driven migration is more likely to be beneficial, particularly to those at the destination (including the migrants).

The second conclusion from this simple example regards the importance of embedding migration in a more complete specification of labour markets generally. Although it is instructive to incorporate a transfer process of the type presented here, its practical implications cannot be clearly understood without consideration of structural features in labour markets at both the origin and destination. The most important of these include labour surplus conditions, which would influence both the output effects of departures and the employment prospects of arrivals. Historically, market imperfections at both ends have undermined the potential of an economy to shift comparative advantage by reallocating its labour force geographically and functionally. Indeed, market and institutional failures, notoriously difficult for economists to model, are probably the main reason the economic promise of migration has so often gone unfulfilled.

Notes

Special thanks are due to Dominique van der Mensbrugghe and Joe Francois for helpful discussion. The opinions expressed here are those of the author and should not be ascribed to the OECD.

1. For example, whereas Burfisher et al. (1994) have examined cross-border migration issues related to the North American Free Trade Area (NAFTA), Levy and van Wijnbergen (1994) have argued that the most important migration results of the NAFTA are likely to be realized within Mexico.
2. Personal communication.
3. The Chinese government already recognizes that this trend may lead to exploding demand for urban infrastructure in the form of residential housing and a wide array of public goods. If they are to avoid the fate of urban Latin America, the implied fiscal commitments are prodigious.
4. See e.g. Samuelson (1958).
5. See Lee and Roland-Holst (1994) for an extensive empirical example of this process.
6. See Maechler and Roland-Holst (1997) for a broader discussion of these specifications.
7. Here we are placing a hierarchy on market adjustments, assuming migration takes longer than commodity market clearing, for example. This assumption is much like gestation of capital in standard discrete time growth models, but it has non-trivial implications for the way equilibria are determined. For more discussion of hierarchical market specifications, see Roland-Holst (1995).
8. See Eaton (1987) for discussion of these conditions.
9. See Dessus et al. (1998) for complete model documentation.
10. This essentially reiterates the logic of Katz and Summers (1989) concerning the productivity implications of sectoral wage differentials.
11. Compare, e.g., results in Collado et al. (1995).

References

Burfisher, M. E., S. Robinson, and K. E. Thierfelder (1994), 'Wage Changes in a U.S.–Mexico Free Trade Area: Migration versus Stolper–Samuelson Effects'. In J. F. Francois and C. R. Shiells (eds.), *Modeling Trade Policy: Applied General Equilibrium Models of North American Free Trade*. New York: Cambridge University Press.

Collado, J. C., D. W. Roland-Holst, and D. van der Mensbrugghe (1995), 'Latin American Employment Prospects in a More Liberal Trading Environment'. In D. Turnham, C. Foy, and G. Larrain (eds.), *Social Tensions, Job Generation, and Economic Policy in Latin America*. Paris: OECD Development Centre; Washington, D.C.: Inter-American Development Bank.

Dessus, S., D. W. Roland-Holst, and D. van der Mensbrugghe (1998), 'A

Dynamic General Equilibrium Model of China', Working Paper, Department of Economics, Mills College.

Eaton, J. (1987), 'A Dynamic Specific-factors Model of International Trade', *Review of Economic Studies* 54: 325–38.

Katz, Lawrence F. and Laurence H. Summers (1989), 'Can Interindustry Wage Differentials Justify Strategic Trade Policy?' In Robert C. Feenstra (ed.), *Trade Policies for International Competitiveness*. Chicago: NBER, pp. 85–124.

Lee, H. and D. W. Roland-Holst (1994), 'Shifting Comparative Advantage and the Employment Effects of US–Japan Trade', *The World Economy* 17(3): 323–45.

Levy, S. and S. van Wijnbergen (1994), 'Agriculture in a Mexico–U.S. Free Trade Agreement: A General Equilibrium Analysis'. In J. F. Francois and C. R. Shiells (eds.), *Modeling Trade Policy: Applied General Equilibrium Models of North American Free Trade*. New York: Cambridge University Press.

Maechler, A. M. and D. W. Roland-Holst (1997), 'Labor Market Structure and Conduct'. In J. F. Francois and K. A. Reinert (eds.), *Applied Methods for Trade Policy Analysis*. New York: Cambridge University Press.

Roland-Holst, D. W. (1995), 'Hierarchical Trade and the Persistence of Disequilibrium', Working Paper, Department of Economics, Mills College, December.

Samuelson, P. A. (1958), 'An Exact Consumption Loan Model of Interest with or without the Social Contrivance of Money', *Journal of Political Economy* 66: 467–82.

Index